TURNING POINTS IN THE HISTORY OF
AMERICAN EVANGELICALISM

Turning Points in the History of American Evangelicalism

Edited by

Heath W. Carter *&* Laura Rominger Porter

WILLIAM B. EERDMANS PUBLISHING COMPANY
GRAND RAPIDS, MICHIGAN

Wm. B. Eerdmans Publishing Co.
2140 Oak Industrial Drive N.E., Grand Rapids, Michigan 49505
www.eerdmans.com

23 22 21 20 19 18 17   1 2 3 4 5 6 7

ISBN 978-0-8028-7152-7

Library of Congress Cataloging-in-Publication Data

Names: Carter, Heath W., editor.
Title: Turning points in the history of American evangelicalism / edited by Heath W.
    Carter & Laura Rominger Porter.
Description: Grand Rapids : Eerdmans Publishing Co., 2017. | Includes bibliographical
    references and index.
Identifiers: LCCN 2016049555 | ISBN 9780802871527 (pbk. : alk. paper)
Subjects: LCSH: Evangelicalism—United States.
Classification: LCC BR1642.U5 T87 2017 | DDC 277.3/082—dc23
    LC record available at https://lccn.loc.gov/2016049555

For Mark Noll

Contents

Foreword   ix
Nathan O. Hatch

Introduction   xiv
Heath W. Carter and Laura Rominger Porter

1. What Made the Great Awakening Great?   1
   Harry S. Stout

2. The Evangelical Encounter with the Enlightenment   19
   Catherine A. Brekus

3. Disestablishment as American Sisyphus   44
   Jon Butler

4. Antebellum Reform   65
   Richard Carwardine

5. The Rise of the Domestic Ideal in the United States and Canada   84
   Marguerite Van Die

6. The Civil War and the Making of Conservative American Evangelicalism   107
   Luke E. Harlow

CONTENTS

7. The Rise of Fundamentalism   133
  George M. Marsden

8. Urban Pentecostalism: Chicago, 1906–1912   154
  Edith L. Blumhofer

9. The Great Migration   180
  Dennis C. Dickerson

10. The Global Turn in American Evangelicalism   203
  Mark Hutchinson

11. Billy Graham's 1949 Los Angeles Revival   226
  Grant Wacker

12. Lausanne '74 and American Evangelicalism's Latin Turn   247
  Darren Dochuk

Afterword   282
  Martin E. Marty

Contributors   287

Index   290

Foreword

Nathan O. Hatch

It is a privilege, indeed, to write the foreword for a book of essays dedicated to Mark Noll, who has been a treasured friend and colleague over the last forty years. Mark and I graduated together in the Wheaton College class of 1968. We did not know each other well as undergraduates, but I did have great admiration for his abilities—as a versatile starting forward on the Wheaton basketball team.

By different routes both of us ended up studying early American history and wrote dissertations on the relationship of religion and politics in the age of the American Revolution. Both of us ended up teaching in the Midwest, he at our alma mater, Wheaton College, and I ninety miles to the east at Notre Dame, a place, interestingly, where the Nolls took up residence the year after the Hatches moved to Wake Forest in 2005.

Mark found his vocation after college—through a liberating engagement with history. At Wheaton he had principally studied literature and philosophy and, upon graduation, pursued studies in comparative literature, English and German, at the University of Iowa. During that time he also began to read deeply in the writings of Luther, Calvin, and other Reformers. The result was nothing less than a personal awakening and a reorientation of his intellectual interests, more in the direction of history and historical theology.

In the Reformers, Noll found a captivating new vision of the Christian faith, one that was intellectually rich and powerful, one that captured his heart and imagination. "The riches of classical Protestantism opened a new and exceedingly compelling vision of existence," Noll has written about himself. "Intellectually, theologically, existentially, I was rescued by the Reformation."

Mark's calling as a historian and Christian intellectual has led to enormously fruitful work in at least five areas: (1) as a distinguished historian of religious experience in North America—and, in recent years, of Christianity as a worldwide, cross-cultural phenomenon; (2) as an interpreter of the American evangelical experience, for scholars and for a broader public, including the church; (3) as a Christian intellectual and firm advocate for American evangelicals to take up the challenge of serious intellectual engagement; (4) as an institution-builder in developing efforts such as The Institute for the Study of American Evangelicals at Wheaton College, the journal *Books and Culture*, and the launching and editing of Eerdmans's Library of Religious Biography; and (5) as a consequential builder of networks, through engagement with graduate students and younger scholars around the world, through consistent participation in conferences and colloquia, and through careful reading and critiquing of papers and books.

Mark is a historian of enormous erudition, range, and impact. He has written or edited more than forty books and does so with prose that is clear, interesting, and readable—capable of explaining complexity in understandable terms. His magnum opus, *America's God: From Jonathan Edwards to Abraham Lincoln*, is a magisterial synthesis of the cultural context of American theology from the 1730s to the 1860s. This work, which emphasizes the characteristically American shape of religious ideas in this land, manifests a lifetime of immersion in every conceivable primary source and an active engagement with every important interpreter of the period.

For most historians, this work, and all the research and writing leading up to it, could constitute the major project of a lifetime. Yet, at the same time, Mark Noll has continued to mine other historical veins. He has studied deeply and written cogently on the relationship of religion and science, on the intellectual and religious significance of race and the Civil War, on the importance of hymnody in religious life, on Canadian religious history, on the relationship of Protestants and Catholics, and, most recently, on the dimensions of global Christianity. He is also engaged in writing a two-volume history of the role of the Bible in American public life. The range of his interests and expertise is remarkable and has never stopped expanding.

His standing in the historical academy is indicated by his election in 2005 to the American Academy of Arts and Sciences. A year later, at the White House, President George W. Bush presented him the National Humanities Medal.

At the heart of Mark's work has been a passion to understand the characteristic shape and orientation of evangelical Christianity in America. He has always been forthright in owning that tradition, even being so bold as to make that plain when accepting the National Humanities Medal: "I am a historian who happens to be an evangelical Christian." At the same time, he treats his own tradition with a remarkably even hand, putting it into the perspective of the broader sweep of Christianity—historically and globally.

He has not been afraid to criticize its distinct and parochial elements; its approach to science, politics, and biblical hermeneutics; and its overall lack of engagement with culture. But he has never done this with anger or dismissal—as is often the case with those who grow up in an orthodox tradition and then define themselves in dismissive reaction. Mark's rare gift has been to identify thoroughly his own heritage, however flawed, and to interpret it in comparative context. He describes his book *The Scandal of the Evangelical Mind* as "an epistle from a wounded lover." Mark Noll found history to be life-giving initially because it opened powerful and renewing strains of the Christian tradition that he had not known. Likewise, his study of American evangelicals was freeing for him—and a whole generation of students and younger scholars—because it helped to explain the characteristic shape and dynamic of that tradition. By becoming conscious of certain influences, one did not have to accept them as self-evident but could discriminate and compare them to the broader reaches of Christianity.

Mark's third great contribution has been as a versatile Christian intellectual and a firm advocate of Christian intellectual life. In his own work, he has brought a remarkably broad range of intellectual perspectives to the understanding and justification of Christian learning. He is conversant with contemporary analytic philosophy, with literary theory and hermeneutics, with theology, with the history and philosophy of science and political theory, and with the field of missiology. His book *The Scandal of the Evangelical Mind* laments the inability of the evangelical tradition to mount serious intellectual activity. And his book *Jesus Christ and the Life of the Mind* points a way forward, offering compelling Christological justification for serious learning and guidelines for thinking and acting in specific disciplines. These books, like so much of Mark's writing, are rare examples of work that is academically serious and thoroughly accessible to an educated lay public.

In all of this, Mark has been a responsible citizen of two worlds—as a critical historian at home in the secular academy and as a person of faith. In negotiating these different identities and languages, he has clearly pointed the way for many younger scholars.

Mark Noll is most at home as a scholar, studying, writing, engaging ideas. But he has also been willing to work toward the building of programs and institutions. He cofounded The Institute for the Study of American Evangelicals at Wheaton College and, over the last thirty years, guided many of its conferences and publications. The network of scholars associated with that institute, many of whom are represented in this volume, have done much to reshape the ways in which scholars understand evangelicals in American culture.

Mark was also instrumental in launching the Library of Religious Biography series that the William B. Eerdmans Publishing Company began in 1991 with the publication of Harry Stout's marvelous biography of George Whitefield, *The Divine Dramatist*. Mark Noll's recruitment of authors and steady editorial hand since that time have led to almost thirty serious but accessible biographies published, including George Marsden on Jonathan Edwards, Marvin O'Connell on Blaise Pascal, Edwin Gaustad on Thomas Jefferson, Nancy Koester on Harriet Beecher Stowe, Robert Bruce Mullen on Horace Bushnell, Edith Blumhofer on Aimee Semple McPherson, Alan Guelzo on Abraham Lincoln, Charles Hamrick-Stowe on Charles Finney, David Bebbington on William Gladstone, and more. This series illustrates, again, Mark Noll's abiding convictions that history and biography have great contemporary relevance and that serious historians can, and should, make their work accessible to a broader public.

Mark Noll was also a principal architect of the journal *Books and Culture: A Christian Review* and has served with Philip Yancey for the last twenty years as co-chair of its editorial board. Mark's own essays and reviews have regularly graced the pages of this bimonthly review, which seeks to bring Christian perspectives to bear on the broader worlds of nature, society, politics, and the arts. He has also enlisted a broad range of diverse contributors to write for this journal, which, like Mark Noll himself, begins with Christian assumptions but seeks "common ground with like-minded souls from other communities of faith."

Perhaps Mark's greatest gift to the profession has been his tireless investment in the work of colleagues. This begins with his remarkable mentoring of students at Notre Dame, at Wheaton, and at other places he has visited: Harvard, Chicago, and Regent College in Vancouver. I have heard him admit that his typical Saturday is taken up with writing letters of recommendation for students and former students.

More than anyone I know, he also gives himself to reading and critiquing the work of other scholars, particularly young and emerging faculty and those from other cultures—British and Irish, Canadian, Australian, and African. Mark has read and offered detailed comment on hundreds and hundreds of manuscripts for his colleagues. This steady work, often unknown and unheralded, has been a great gift to individual scholars and to the common enterprise of historical writing.

My greatest debt to Mark, and his wife Maggie, is being able to learn from how they live. They have gone about their calling in winsome and compelling ways, sustaining commitments and friendships, investing deeply in church communities, and reaching out to others in quiet but effective ways. There is no pretense or posturing. In academe, persons of great talent often carry the baggage of giant egos with which their colleagues have to contend. In Mark's case, I have never known anyone who accomplished so much but wanted so little attention drawn to himself. He has always reckoned his achievements as good gifts.

Mark's talent and his demeanor have meant that he has been at the center of many intellectual networks. And in this engagement, many friendships have been forged. In fostering real intellectual community, like-minded friends, Mark Noll has advanced the quality of historical work and made that work a delight for many.

Introduction

Heath W. Carter and Laura Rominger Porter

Just over forty years ago, in the autumn of 1976, George Gallup Jr. proclaimed "The Year of the Evangelical." The designation seemed fitting
enough. Both of the major candidates for president of the United States—
the incumbent, Gerald Ford, and his challenger, Jimmy Carter—identified as "born again"; and fully 34 percent of their fellow Americans did
too, according to a Gallup poll soon touted by both *Time* and *Newsweek*.[1]
For those who had not been keeping a close eye on shifts in the religious
landscape, such mainstream media coverage served notice that the nation had entered a period of profound evangelical influence. This "Age of
Evangelicalism" dawned with the election of Richard Nixon and persists
to the present day. Throughout these decades pundits have often stressed
evangelicalism's impressive political clout, and for good reason: evangelical voters played decisive roles in any number of key elections, including
most recently that of President Donald J. Trump. But evangelicalism's
cachet was evident in countless other realms as well. As historian Steven P. Miller writes, "There were Marabel Morgan's marriage seminars,
Hal Lindsey's prophecy guides, Tammy Faye Bakker's eyelashes, and
Thomas Kinkade's oil paintings."[2] One could add endlessly to the list.
In more recent years, Rick Warren's bestselling book *The Purpose-Driven
Life*, Carrie Underwood's Grammy Award-winning single, "Jesus, Take

---

1. "Counting Souls," *Time*, October 4, 1976; and Kenneth L. Woodward, "Born
Again!" *Newsweek*, October 25, 1976.
2. Steven P. Miller, *The Age of Evangelicalism: America's Born-Again Years* (New York:
Oxford University Press, 2014), 5.

the Wheel," and Joel Osteen's toothy smile have all served as signs of evangelical ascendancy.

Yet what were the origins of this cultural juggernaut? Back in 1976, had an especially enterprising and inquisitive reader of the aforementioned *Time* or *Newsweek* articles sought answers to this question, she would have been hard pressed to find them. To be sure, she could have picked up a copy of Sydney Ahlstrom's mammoth *A Religious History of the American People* (1972), and there she would have found scattered references to the evangelical tradition; and had she the time and interest, she could have waded also into a number of much more specialized studies.[3] But the going would have been tough. On the eve of the 1976 election, few doubted evangelicalism's importance for the present moment. Yet its history remained largely to be written.

Little could our imagined reader have known that she was standing at a pivotal turning point in the historiography of American evangelicalism. Consider what transpired immediately in the wake of the "Year of the Evangelical." In the spring of 1977 and again in the spring of 1978, a group of mostly younger historians convened at Trinity College in Deerfield, Illinois, to discuss "evangelical perspectives" on the American Revolution. These gatherings sparked ideas and connections that led eventually to the 1982 founding of the Institute for the Study of American Evangelicals (ISAE) at Wheaton College in the western suburbs of Chicago.[4] Scholars in the ISAE's larger orbit would go on to lead nothing short of a historiographical revolution. In their work they located evangelicalism at the very center of American religious history. They contended that the roots of the faith most post–World War II Americans associated with Billy Graham extended all the way back to colonial revivals led by the likes of George Whitefield, Jonathan Edwards, and Sarah Osborn. The evangelical tradition was in fact older than the United States itself; and no other faith had so powerfully shaped the nation's course, from the American Revolution

3. Sydney E. Ahlstrom, *A Religious History of the American People* (New Haven: Yale University Press, 1972). For examples of the latter, see Timothy Smith, *Revivalism and Social Reform: American Protestantism on the Eve of the Civil War* (New York: Harper & Row, 1957); Ernest R. Sandeen, *The Roots of Fundamentalism: British and American Millenarianism, 1800-1930* (Chicago: University of Chicago Press, 1970); and George Marsden, *The Evangelical Mind and the New School Presbyterian Experience: A Case Study of Thought and Theology in Nineteenth-Century America* (New Haven: Yale University Press, 1970).

4. For a helpful chronology of the ISAE's development see http://www.wheaton.edu/ISAE/About/Chronology-of-Projects.

through the sectional crisis and all the way up to the rise of the Religious Right. By the early 1990s Yale's Jon Butler had pinpointed this "evangelical paradigm" as "the single most powerful explanatory device adopted by academic historians to account for the distinctive features of American society, culture, and identity."[5] A historiographical revolution, indeed.[6]

This momentous scholarly intervention was, from the very beginning, a deeply collaborative venture involving many of the contributors to this volume and many more besides. Yet arguably no single individual loomed so large in the process as Mark A. Noll. Noll received his PhD from Vanderbilt University in 1975, just one year before "the Year of the Evangelical," and in the decades since has written or edited more than fifty books, making him one of the most prolific historians of American Christianity. His wide-ranging body of work includes landmark scholarly studies such as *America's God: From Jonathan Edwards to Abraham Lincoln* (2002), *The Civil War as a Theological Crisis* (2006), and most recently *In the Beginning Was the Word: The Bible in American Life, 1492–1783* (2015); in recognition of such scholarly contributions, Noll was awarded the National Humanities Medal in 2006. A year earlier he received a very different kind of recognition, being named one of *Time* magazine's "25 Most Influential Evangelicals in America," an honor that reflected the fact that his influence has extended well beyond the academy.[7] Through books such as *The Scandal of the Evangelical Mind* (1994), *Turning Points: Decisive Moments in the History of Christianity* (1997), and *From Every Tribe and Nation: A Historian's Discovery of the Global Christian Story* (2014), he became one of the most noted interpreters of the Christian past for the wider public.

This volume is dedicated to Noll and seeks to both honor and build upon his contributions by exploring a number of key turning points in the history of American evangelicalism. The very notion of an evangelical tradition is not without its problems, of course. In recent decades, even as some scholars have elaborated evangelicalism's history, others have questioned whether the term "evangelical" has a consistent historical referent.[8]

5. Quoted in Harry S. Stout and Robert M. Taylor Jr., "Studies of Religion in American Society: The State of the Art," in *New Directions in American Religious History*, ed. Harry S. Stout and D. G. Hart (New York: Oxford University Press, 1997), 19.

6. For a recent account of this historiography's development, see Miller, *Age of Evangelicalism*, 100–102.

7. http://content.time.com/time/specials/packages/completelist/0,29569,1993235,00.html.

8. See, for example, D. G. Hart, *Deconstructing Evangelicalism: Conservative Protestantism in the Age of Billy Graham* (Grand Rapids: Baker Academic, 2005).

To be clear, this volume does not presume to identify a single, unified, comprehensive American "evangelicalism" that transcended historical contexts. As Noll's own work and several of the essays here make clear, few historians would confine evangelical Protestantism to a specific region or institution, even as many emphasize the fragmenting effects of race, class, and gender—to say nothing of theology. This volume therefore represents a variety of historical approaches to a term that, when employed carefully and thoughtfully, points to a set of family resemblances that spring from a shared genealogy. We contend that the "evangelical" label, whatever its shortcomings, continues to illuminate more than it obscures within the wider history of American Protestantism.[9]

While this volume embraces a generous definition of evangelicalism, it certainly does not pretend to be a comprehensive treatment of the same. The "turning points" explored here represent significant transitional moments of American religious history, each with a distinct "before" and "after." Yet we might just as easily have emphasized the religious changes wrought by consumer culture, mass media technologies, suburbanization, or immigration. The virtue of the "turning point" theme is that it is also a starting point for engaging larger questions about the historical evolution of the evangelical tradition, the relationship between evangelical Protestantism and American history, and indeed the very nature of historical causation and interpretation—questions that we hope will stimulate further conversations in classrooms, in church basements, and around many a kitchen table.

In these essays alone we see that turning points take different shapes and sizes, from the intricacies of a particular revival in Grant Wacker's chapter to the more theorized notion of a "global turn" in Mark Hutchinson's; we see in Jon Butler's essay that the First Amendment was no endpoint to debates over church and state but the beginning of a centuries-long contest, and in Marguerite Van Die's how histories of religious practice complicate narratives of sudden historical change. Finally, these "turning points" illuminate how some historical forces and events—the Enlightenment, the Civil War, and the Great Migration—altered evangelicalism from without,

9. The standard definition of "evangelicalism" is David Bebbington's, which combines the four characteristics of "biblicism, conversionism, crucicentrism, and activism." David W. Bebbington, *Evangelicalism in Modern Britain: A History from the 1730s to the 1980s* (London: Unwin Hyman, 1989), 3. Mark Noll's approach to the broader "evangelical family" or "kin network" is enumerated in *The Rise of Evangelicalism: The Age of Edwards, Whitefield and the Wesleys* (Downers Grove, IL: InterVarsity, 2003), 18-19.

while other kinds of changes were initiated and consciously shaped by evangelicals themselves, as seen in the rise of moral reform movements, Pentecostalism, and fundamentalism. These "turning points" do not comprise a complete history of American evangelicalism. But together they invite us to contemplate the role of people, ideas, structures, and events in that history, as well as the pace and degree of change over time.

Finally, it bears saying that the stories collected here do not have a singular arc. The history of evangelicalism is one neither of continual progress nor of steady decline, and its moral legacies for American life have been decidedly mixed. Even when evangelicals sought to advance religious causes, they seldom found consensus on moral questions, and many endorsed acts considered sinful by evangelicals today: slaveholding, callous expansionism, race war, and racial segregation, to name a few. Like all humans, they have never been fully conscious of how their own cultures and interests shaded their deepest religious intuitions. And yet, even seeing through a glass darkly, American evangelicals have also made vital contributions to various struggles for a more just society. Such moral ambiguities should come as no surprise to evangelicals themselves. One hallmark of their tradition has been a robust appreciation for both the gravity of sin and the abundance of grace. Readers may reasonably disagree over how to weigh their relative importance in evangelicalism's past. But the conviction that grace will, in the end, triumph over sin is as old as Christianity itself; and this belief has remained at the very center of evangelical belief and practice down through the centuries, even as both the tradition and the world around it have been transformed in the manifold ways documented in this book. In 1719 noted hymn writer Isaac Watts penned these lyrics:

> My crimes are great, but not surpass
> The power and glory of Thy grace:
> Great God, Thy nature hath no bound,
> So let Thy pardoning love be found.[10]

While contemporary believers might choose different words, there can be no doubt that a kindred longing for redemption persists even today. As much as the stories in these pages revolve around change, this venerable hope, woven deeply into the fabric of American evangelicalism, endures.

---

10. Isaac Watts, "Show Pity, Lord, O Lord, Forgive," available at http://www.hymn time.com/tch/htm/s/h/o/showpity.htm.

CHAPTER 1

What Made the Great Awakening Great?

Harry S. Stout

What made the Great Awakening great? It is a question that first pressed upon me after reading my colleague Jon Butler's brilliant and provocative article "Enthusiasm Described and Decried: The Great Awakening as Interpretive Fiction."[1] In that article, Butler argued that nothing novel or revolutionary occurred around 1740 making for a "Great Awakening." Rather, the "Great Awakening" was a pseudo-event invented by historians. While much of what Butler argued is plausible, I propose that something "great" did indeed happen around 1740, and the chief protagonists were George Whitefield and Jonathan Edwards. In making the case for a truly great awakening in the middle of the eighteenth century, I do not intend to follow the path of earlier church historians whose explanations focused on theology and church history. Left unexplored in these earlier filiopietistic accounts is the question of religious innovations on the level of rhetoric and communications embodied by Whitefield. Also left out for the most part is the question of overlaps between the Great Awakening and the "New Learning" associated with the Enlightenment, where Edwards is the chief exemplar. In their own ways, each of these luminaries contributed something unique and revolutionary to their inherited faith.

First the Great Awakening as a revolution in rhetoric and communications: on August 14, 1739, the famed itinerant George Whitefield embarked on a preaching tour of colonial America after enjoying a superstar's success in his native England. Soon Americans would get their

---

1. Jon Butler, "Enthusiasm Described and Decried: The Great Awakening as Interpretive Fiction," *Journal of American History* 69, no. 2 (September 1982): 305-25.

first exposure to the open-air preacher, and their churches would never be the same. Audiences numbering in the thousands appeared seemingly out of nowhere to hear the "Grand Itinerant" preach the gospel in new and exciting ways. With Whitefield's preaching tour, a new pulpit rhetoric emerged that would redefine preaching and lead to the rise of a novel form of Protestantism we identify today with "evangelicalism." Historian Perry Miller described this new rhetoric as "the rhetoric of sensation."[2] While the content of Whitefield's sermons remained traditionally Calvinist, he revolutionized the "rhetoric" or delivery of his sermons and redefined the social context in which public address took place. In the process, he "awakened" a new religious enthusiasm within the traditional church's rank and file and inaugurated a new model of social organization and public address—a model that could be applied to a broad range of social, political, and religious contexts.

The first arena, however, in which a revolutionary rhetoric of sensation appeared in America was religion. In time it would spread to politics and inform an egalitarian ideology that challenged traditional assumptions of hierarchy and social deference in the American Revolution. But for that ideology to take root there had to appear new forms of communication that could model a new social order. At some point prior to the popular reception of a revolutionary ideology, a new rhetoric was needed in which familiar terms could be used to mean something different—and this change in the *form* as distinguished from the *content* marks the moment of a profound cultural transformation. Any revolution in worldview requires a new rhetoric. The most conspicuous and revolutionary product of the Great Awakening was not to be found in doctrine, in the creation of new ecclesiastical or academic institutions, or competing theological schools of pro-revival "New Lights" and anti-revival "Old Lights." Evangelicalism's enduring legacy was a new mode of persuasion that could redefine the norms of social order. Doctrinal differences between New Lights and Old Lights were, in historian Alan Heimert's words, "of less ultimate significance than the remarkable differences between their oratorical strategies and rhetorical practices."[3]

Heimert's recognition of the revolutionary potentialities of the reviv-

---

2. Perry Miller, "The Rhetoric of Sensation," in Perry Miller, *Errand into the Wilderness* (Cambridge, MA: Harvard University Press, 1956), 167-84.

3. Alan Heimert, *Religion and the American Mind: From the Great Awakening to the Revolution* (Cambridge, MA: Harvard University Press, 1966), 18.

als suggests a closer look at evangelical oratory, particularly in relation to the forms of public worship that prevailed before the revivals. Despite differences in style and substance between Puritans and Anglicans, all seventeenth-century churchmen agreed with Boston clergyman Samuel Willard that God did "ordain Orders of Superiority and Inferiority among men."[4] This hierarchical worldview presupposed a society of face-to-face personal relationships in which people identified themselves with reference to those around them as superiors, inferiors, or equals. Superiors demanded that their inferiors defer to them and govern their actions according to their rank in the community. Forms of attire, patterns of speech, or where one was "seated" in the meetinghouse were among the more conspicuous indications of a pervasive social stratification that separated the leaders from "ordinary people." As social superiors, college-educated ministers assumed their congregants would be properly subordinate. Any acting out of "place" would be met with severe punishment.

Before Whitefield's transatlantic itineraries, all churches were designed to sustain a deferential perception of proper social organization. In this traditional social ethic, itinerancy was inconceivable because, in the Puritan minister Increase Mather's words, "to say that a Wandering Levite who has no flock is a pastor, is as good sense as to say, that he that has no children is a Father."[5] What made a pastor was not simply the preaching of the Word but also a direct, authoritarian identification with a specific flock. To ignore the personal and deferential relationship of a minister with his congregation would be to threaten the organic, hierarchical principles upon which both family and social order rested. In terms of communications, this meant that speaker and audience were steadily reminded of their personal place in the community; in no context were they strangers to one another, for no public gatherings took place

4. In Perry Miller and Thomas H. Johnson, eds., *The Puritans* (New York: American Book Company, 1938), 251. For a discussion of the inherited social ethic that the revivals challenged see especially William G. McLoughlin, *Isaac Backus and the American Pietistic Tradition* (Boston: Little, Brown, 1967), 1-22; Rhys Isaac, "Religion and Authority: Problems of the Anglican Establishment in Virginia in the Era of the Great Awakening and the Parson's Cause," *William and Mary Quarterly* 30 (1973): 3-36; and Isaac, "Evangelical Revolt: The Nature of the Baptists' Challenge to the Traditional Order in Virginia, 1765 to 1775," *William and Mary Quarterly* 31 (1974): 3345-68.

5. Quoted in Cedric B. Cowing, *The Great Awakening and the American Revolution: Colonial Thought in the Eighteenth Century* (Chicago: Rand McNally, 1971), 23.

outside of traditional associations based upon personal acquaintance and social rank.

As Whitefield and a growing band of homegrown imitators began holding forth in new settings, established, college-educated ministers realized that something dramatically different was appearing in the revivalists' preaching performances. The problem raised by the revivals was not their message of the New Birth. Indeed, it was the familiar message of regeneration that lulled leaders into an early acceptance and even endorsement of the revivals. The problem, it soon became clear, was the revolutionary setting in which the good news was proclaimed. The secret of Whitefield's success and that of other evangelists was not simply a booming voice or a charismatic presence. It was a new style: a rhetoric of persuasion that was strange to the American ear. The revivalists sought to transcend both the hyper-rational manner of "polite" Liberal preaching and the "plain style" of orthodox Puritan preaching in order to speak directly to the people at large.[6] Their technique of mass address to a voluntary audience of strangers forced a dialogue between speaker and hearer that disregarded social position and local setting.

To attract ordinary people to leave their homes and neighborhoods and travel to gather with strangers and hear a stranger speak required a new rhetoric. This is precisely what Whitefield offered. Whitefield was no theoretician and evidenced no close reading of Lockean "sensationalism." But he intuitively understood the rhetoric of sensation and practiced it on an international stage of Anglo-American revivals that were, in fact, sensational. Taking his rhetorical cues from the theater rather than the university lectern, Whitefield shaped his sermon rhetoric to create an emotional catharsis that would precipitate a New Birth or, what was the same, a new sense of the heart. Before Whitefield, everybody knew the difference between preaching and acting. With Whitefield's preaching, the distinction blurred between church and theater. More than any of his peers or predecessors, he turned his back on the academy and traditional homiletical manuals and adopted the assumptions and poses of the actor. Passion would be the key to his preaching, and his body would be enlisted in raising passions in his audience to embrace traditional Prot-

---

6. I discuss these contrasting styles of seventeenth-century preaching in *The New England Soul: Preaching and Religious Culture in Colonial New England* (New York: Oxford University Press, 1986), 32-49.

estant truths. He would literally embody a fundamental turning point in defining what constituted acceptable preaching.

Whitefield was not content simply to talk about the New Birth; he had to sell it with all the dramatic artifice of a huckster. Any churchgoer could understand the theological status of a new creation, but to see a preacher travailing in labor as the new birth took place was to encounter an unprecedented and shocking demonstration. Whitefield not only asserted that the new creation was more than mere metaphor; he enacted and embodied it.

One favorite sermon of Whitefield's that illustrates his theatrical delivery centered on "Abraham Offering His Son." In this sermon Whitefield created a series of dramatic scenes. The first scene opened with the "good old man walking with his dear child . . . now and then looking upon him, loving him, and then turning aside to weep." At this point in the sermon Whitefield himself may well have wept and momentarily halted the discourse, allowing the pathos to sink in. Then followed a second scene at the altar where Abraham was barely prevented from taking his beloved son's life in a profound moment of faith and obedience. By now the audience would be locked into Whitefield's performance, and they would see with Abraham's eyes what Whitefield wanted them to see: "Fancy that you saw the aged parent standing by weeping. Methinks I see the tears trickle down the patriarch Abraham's cheeks . . . adieu, my Isaac, my only Son, whom I love as my own soul; adieu, adieu." In the third and climactic scene, Whitefield bridged the gap separating Abraham from Christ through the passions:

> Did you weep just now when I bid you fancy that you saw the altar? Look up by faith, behold the blessed Jesus, our all-glorious Immanuel, not bound, but nailed on an accursed tree: see how he hangs crowned with thorns, and had in derision of all that are round about him: see how the thorns pierce him, and how the blood in purple streams trickles down his sacred temples! Hark! And now where are all your tears? Shall I refrain your voice from weeping? No, rather let me exhort you to look to him whom you have pierced, and mourn, as a woman mourneth for her first born.[7]

Whitefield's demonstrative preaching rendered him one of the best-known persons in Anglo-America, perhaps second only to King George

---

7. Quoted in Harry S. Stout, *The Divine Dramatist: George Whitefield and the Rise of Modern Evangelicalism* (Grand Rapids: Eerdmans, 1991), 93-94.

III. He was, to borrow a modern phrase, a celebrity. Before Whitefield, no one had fully tested the ability of public opinion to build a movement that was intercolonial and even international in scope. No one before Whitefield had sufficient popularity to found an international movement. In a circular logic that would in time come to define modern America, appeals to public opinion required public access, and public access depended on popularity. As the first intercolonial religious celebrity, Whitefield paved the way for extra-institutional movements that would reverse traditional order and travel from the bottom up. This turning point was fundamental to what made the Great Awakening great.

Whitefield's transatlantic revivals involving tens of thousands of rapt listeners taught him the invaluable lesson that churches with visions of national hegemony, such as the Anglicans or Puritans, could be a thing of the past: they could be made old history—the history of a traditional, localistic, and coercive culture. His revivals therefore marked a transition not just in his rhetoric of sensation, but also in his new conception of evangelical association based on individual choices that transcended ecclesiastical institutions. His revivals were, in short, interdenominational and market-responsive. A new history would be transdenominational and experience centered. In this emergent, enlightened world, existing churches would not be supplanted so much as sidestepped in the interest of creating larger, translocal associations grounded in sensational revivals. These associations would be purely voluntary and would allow people to remain in their favorite denomination even as they bound themselves to larger networks with international significance. Like other market-related products, the new forms would succeed or fail in direct relation to their ability to attract religious consumers.

Whitefield's market-driven vision was profound not in its theological depth but in its very popularity. His revivals were not really a church, nor were they connected to local communities and congregations. He received no financial support from his national church or the state and instead depended on voluntary offerings. The appearance of Whitefield's audiences as religious congregations defied the traditional sense of the term. The audiences changed with every meeting, evidencing no permanent structure or leadership aside from Whitefield's own charismatic ministry. In reality, Whitefield's audience and loyal supporters represented what we would call powerful new "parachurches"—voluntary religious associations based on a marketplace organization and destined to characterize pan-Protestant "evangelical" organizations in the nineteenth, twentieth, and twenty-first centuries. These parachurches represented a force entirely new and one that defined the future for much of modern American Protestantism.

In an ironic process that Whitefield could not have foreseen and probably did not recognize, his revivals became, in effect, an institution. He brought new meaning to the term "revival" and, in so doing, eventually achieved an unanticipated social respectability among religious elites.

Although Whitefield was no theologian, his new rhetoric of sensation was profoundly theological. He avoided denominational creeds and denominations in his revivals, but at the same time presented a new theological perspective contained less in his own Calvinist convictions than in the radical new significance ascribed to religious experience and spiritual legitimacy. In answer to the question of what makes for membership in the true church of Christ, Whitefield implicitly set forth an alternative model that fit with the modern circumstances of his transatlantic revivals.

In the evangelical parachurch that Whitefield created (and Jonathan Edwards would defend), individual experience became the ultimate arbiter of authentic religious faith. Experience—or, in Locke's terms, "sensation"—came to be the legitimating mark of religion over and against family, communal covenants, traditional memberships, baptisms, or sacraments. As sensation represented the only avenue for natural knowledge in Lockean epistemology, so the supernatural experience of the "New Birth" became the sole authentic means to spiritual knowledge in the evangelical revivals. Both were of a piece with the eighteenth-century enlightened world in which they emerged. But in an ironic juxtaposition that neither could perceive, the appeal to inner experience veered dangerously close to the seventeenth-century heresy of antinomianism. We might think of this as Anne Hutchinson's revenge.

The evangelical parachurch was not a school for communal nurture and theological indoctrination so much as it was a context for individual experience in which the conversion experience engulfed all else. Calvinist and Arminian revivalists might argue about the means of the New Birth and the respective role of human will and supernatural grace in regeneration, but the experience itself ruled supreme. If there was no new denomination with a capital letter reflecting its establishment, the New Birth itself assumed capital letters as the institutional and theological embodiment of a new religious movement.

Experience. It all came back, in every revival, to this. Seventeenth-century dissenters had spoken often of regeneration, but always in the context of local congregations, corporate covenants, and weekly education in the sermon. When pressed, they had denied that those who were ignorant of the theological terms on which true conversion rested could experience it. This meant that the teaching, authoritarian function of the church had always received primary emphasis. In a subtle but profound way, Whitefield reversed this emphasis. Instead of theological indoctrination being the foundation of spiritual experience, individual experience became the ground for a shared theology of revival. As long as the foundation was individual experience and the sensation of grace, whatever—or whoever—created it received theological legitimacy at once. Whitefield's stated theological preference was Calvinist and predestinarian. But other revivalists could, and did, build quite different theological frameworks that enjoyed the same experiential legitimation. In the end the revivals were simply not about theology but about experience. Calvinists, Moravians, Methodists, Whitefield—and their evangelical heirs—would all discover legitimation in the experiences they produced. All would ask the same question: Would God bless a counterfeit movement with true saving grace? The answer would always be no. By their experiential fruits they would be known.

The full implications of Whitefield's radical redefinition of revival were never clear to him. But they were to Jonathan Edwards, who stands as the greatest theoretician ever to justify the Great Awakening. In his own way, Edwards's reimagining of traditional Christian theology was as revolutionary as Whitefield's rhetorical reimagining. Edwards came of intellectual age as the Enlightenment luminaries John Locke and Isaac Newton inaugurated the British Enlightenment. Edwards read Locke with avidity and applied himself to employing Locke's epistemology against Enlightenment naturalism and in support of Whitefield's revivals as "a work of God." While Whitefield popularized the delivery of the gospel, Edwards revolutionized the language of faith and its relation to reason and emotions.

To understand how Edwards expropriated Locke, I begin with John Locke's separation of words and meaning in his seminal *Essay concerning Human Understanding*. Here Locke famously denied the existence of innate ideas, which led him, in turn, to assert that language is "arbitrary." Rather, Locke asserted, "all Ideas come from sensation or reflection."[8] In other words, all knowledge comes directly or indirectly from experience.

---

8. John Locke, *An Essay concerning Human Understanding* (New York: New American Library, 1964), 89.

There is no innate "common sense," as the Scottish philosophers asserted, nor is there an innate "moral sense" as Thomas Jefferson claimed.

As products of sensory perception and the reflection of the mind on its own operations, all ideas can be further subdivided into two categories. First are "simple ideas" where the understanding is passive in receiving incoming data: "These simple ideas, when offered to the mind, the understanding can no more refuse to have nor alter when they are imprinted nor blot them out and make new ones itself, than a mirror can refuse, alter, or obliterate the images or ideas which the objects set before it do therein produce."[9] Besides simple ideas, Locke claimed, there are "complex ideas" where the understanding is active and abstract thought proceeds: "When the understanding is once stored with these simple ideas, it has the power to repeat, compare, and unite them, even to an almost infinite variety, and so can make at pleasure new complex ideas."[10] In Perry Miller's apt characterization: "Simple ideas are the hard pellets of sensation, the irreducible atoms of impression, out of which complex ideas are built."[11] Complex ideas of solidity, number, space, time, power, identity, and moral relations arise from sensation and reflection. They combine much like atoms to configure discrete sensory data into reconfigured patterns. Take solidity, for example. The key to solidity was said to be "resistance": "This resistance, whereby it keeps other bodies out of the space which it possesses, is so great, that no force, how great soever can surmount it."[12] Edwards would appropriate Locke's language of resistance, solidity, sensation, and experience to frame his own epistemology, but in radically different ways that suited his Calvinistic purposes.

Edwards was especially influenced by Locke's account of language as rooted in individual experience rather than innate ideas. By separating words from things, Locke was able to refashion the very concept of language in relation to sensation so that simple ideas can be given a name only by those who have first had the sensation. As Locke put it, no word alone can impart a simple idea, and therefore such ideas are not capable of any definition; all the words in the world, made use of to explain or define any of their names, will never be able to produce in us the idea

9. Locke, *Essay concerning Human Understanding*, 98.
10. Locke, *Essay concerning Human Understanding*, 99.
11. Miller, "Rhetoric of Sensation," 181.
12. Locke, *Essay concerning Human Understanding*, 104.

it stands for. No definition of light or redness is more fitted or able to produce either of those ideas in us, than the sound "light" or "red" by itself. He who has never tasted pineapple cannot get from any number of words "the true idea of the relish of that celebrated and delicious fruit."[13] A young Jonathan Edwards would make this same argument with the same analogy, substituting "honey" for "pine apple," and he would apply Locke's concept to the supernatural language of regeneration.

Despite a similar vocabulary, there was much to distinguish between Locke and Enlightenment evangelicalism. Like Newton, Locke was a materialist or "corpuscularian" who accounted for physical objects based on mechanical philosophy and corpuscular hypothesis. And, like Newton, he was also an atomist holding to indivisible or atomic particles as the basic building blocks of nature. For Locke, atomic particles have properties including extension and solidity. This was an Enlightenment evangelicals did not endorse because it supported deism and skepticism. But who would respond to this mechanistic world on a theoretical level? None other than Jonathan Edwards—a very young Jonathan Edwards.

Edwards first encountered Locke as a young student at Yale College, perhaps as young as fourteen. He was immediately smitten, or, as he would later say, awakened, with more pleasure "than the most greedy miser finds, when gathering up handfuls of silver and gold, from some newly discovered treasure." Locke's *Essay concerning Human Understanding* shocked him out of his Aristotelian world and the Aristotelian world of his father into a radically new and empirical worldview. But even as Edwards absorbed Locke's meaning and vocabulary, he turned it toward a defense of his inherited Calvinistic faith. Edwards was freed, by the very arbitrariness of the language Locke proclaimed, to attach very different meanings to this vocabulary. When Locke asserted that "since sounds are voluntary and indifferent signs of any ideas, a man may use what words he pleases to signify his own ideas to himself," he was inadvertently setting out a concept that could hoist him on his own petard. In this sense Locke and Edwards shared similarities, but they would ultimately come to be defined more by their differences than by their similarities. Taking Locke's idea of language seriously, Edwards was freed to adopt a Lockean vocabulary and attach to it arbitrary meanings of an entirely different order, an order grounded in a transcendent, utterly active God undergirding sensation, solidity, experience, resistance, and gravity. In

13. Locke, *Essay concerning Human Understanding*, 369.

the end, Edwards would retain Calvin's sovereign God with a vengeance that even Calvin could not have imagined and build with "great" effect on the foundation of "awakening" that Whitefield had laid.

Edwards's enlightened God was so sovereign in this new Newtonian universe that he ultimately upheld and maintained every single atom in every planet to the furthest reaches of the cosmos. Thus, for example, in his meditation "Of Being," Edwards reasoned: "all that we mean or can be meant by solidity is resistance—resistance to touch, the resistance of some parts of space. This is all the knowledge we get of solidity by our senses, and, I am sure, all that we can get any other way."[14] So far, so good; but then he proceeds to turn Locke around by asking,

> What then is become of the universe? Certainly, it exists nowhere but in the divine mind . . . from hence we may see the gross mistake of those who think material things the more substantial beings, and spirits more like a shadow; whereas spirits only are properly substance. . . . If we would get a right notion of what is spiritual, we must think of thought or inclination or delight. How large is that thing in the mind which they call thought? Is love square or round? Is the surface of hatred rough or smooth? Is joy an inch, or a foot in diameter? These are spiritual things. And why should we then form such a ridiculous idea of spirits, as to think them so long, so thick, or so wide; or to think there is necessity of their being square or round or some other certain figure?[15]

Edwards's great inversion worked out as a young man in his *Notes on the Mind* proceeded something like this. From "atoms" Edwards absorbed Locke's notion of that which served as the basic building blocks of nature. But then, in an abrupt reversal, Edwards denied that atoms were material "particles" and reasoned that ultimately atoms were ideas.

For Edwards, as for us, the whole question was altered as soon as he realized that the atom is a concept. It was useful in physics, not because it had spatial dimensions, but because it played only the one role, though an essential one, of providing a point on which resistance would be concentrated. Obviously, no imaginable physical power can break up

14. Jonathan Edwards, "Of Being," in *The Works of Jonathan Edwards*, vol. 6: *Scientific and Philosophical Writings*, ed. Wallace Anderson (New Haven: Yale University Press, 1980), 205.

15. *A Jonathan Edwards Reader*, ed. John E. Smith, Harry S. Stout, and Kenneth Minkema (New Haven: Yale University Press, 1995), 12, 28.

solidity. In Edwards's terms, "It must needs be an infinite power which keeps the parts of atoms together; or, which with us is the same, which keeps two bodies touching by surfaces in being; for it must be infinite power, or bigger than any finite, which resists all finite power, how big soever, as we have proved these bodies to be."[16]

Concepts where? Concepts, or ideas, in the mind of God. From Newton, Edwards concluded that the essence of atoms was their indivisibility; they cannot be made any smaller. This resistance to division must be, in turn, the essence of solidity. So solidity did not have to do most basically with taking up a certain amount of space ("extension" the Cartesians called it), but was rather essentially a power, the power of what he called "resistance." Resistance, in turn, arose ultimately from God. For Edwards the true substance of all bodies and particles "is the infinitely exact, and precise, and perfectly stable Idea, in God's mind, together with his stable Will, that the same shall gradually be communicated to us, and to other minds, according to certain fixed and exact established methods and laws."[17] In Miller's words, "an atom is not a thing but a way of speaking about a locus of attraction and repulsion. Edwards was divining the great line of the future."[18]

On one level, Edwards's abstract reasoning seems miles distant from Whitefield's dramatic rendering of the New Birth. But on closer examination they were of a piece. Both grounded their worldviews around a sovereign, saving God presented in a new key. The most profound relationship, for Edwards as for Whitefield, was the relationship of humanity to its Creator. Because of the entrance of sin into the world, that relationship was mortally wounded and humans were predisposed to hate God and love themselves. That was the essence of original sin. The only escape from this impasse was a divine intervention called "supernatural grace." And the primary means of communicating and instilling this grace was revival.

As with anything in Edwards, physics had an ultimately theological relevance that pointed to a sovereign, all-controlling God. Creation, for the young Edwards, was not something once in the past, but constantly ongoing: "the universe is created out of nothing every moment, and if it were not for our imaginations, which hinder us, we might see that won-

16. Smith, Stout, and Minkema, eds., *Jonathan Edwards Reader*, 91.
17. Smith, Stout, and Minkema, eds., *Jonathan Edwards Reader*, 92.
18. Perry Miller, *Jonathan Edwards* (New York: W. Sloane Associates, 1949), 96.

derful work performed continually." Without ongoing divine emanation enlivening every atom, the universe would collapse like a punctured balloon. Something as seemingly mechanical as gravity was, for Edwards, an emanation of divine empowerment. In George Marsden's words: "Gravity . . . was not something for which one should expect to find a mechanical cause; it was an inherent quality of solidity. It was a power closely related to the power of resistance, and these two powers determined the harmonious relations of bodies to each other."[19] Everything created existed in relationship to something else. In Edwards's relational ontology there was not a solitary atom anytime, anywhere.

The Great Awakening marked the triumph of sensation over ratiocination. To understand supernatural grace, Edwards did not resort to the language of theology and logic but to aesthetics and, again drawing on Locke for his own purposes, what he termed a "new sense of the heart." In his classic 1734 sermon "A Divine and Supernatural Light" (much more the essential Edwards than his better known sermon "Sinners in the Hands of an Angry God"), Edwards employed a sensory visual vocabulary to describe the essence of regeneration as a "divine light," an evangelical enlightenment. At its essence, the divine light was a new sense of the heart. Drawing on a vocabulary grounded in aesthetics and Locke, rather than medieval logic, Edwards described the new sense of the heart, not as a set of theological propositions dutifully memorized and endorsed, but as a new perception of beauty:

> This spiritual light primarily consists in . . . a real sense and apprehension of the divine excellency of things revealed in the Word of God. A spiritual and saving conviction of the truth and reality of these things, arises from such a sight of their divine excellency and glory; so that this conviction of their truth is an effect and natural consequence of this sight of their divine glory. There is therefore in this spiritual light a true sense of the divine and superlative excellency of the things of religion; a real sense of the excellency of God, and Jesus Christ, and of the work of redemption. . . . There is a divine and superlative glory in these things; an excellency that is of a vastly higher kind, and more sublime nature, than in other things; a glory greatly distinguishing them from

19. George M. Marsden, *Jonathan Edwards: A Life* (New Haven: Yale University Press, 2003), 74.

all that is earthly and temporal. He that is spiritually enlightened truly apprehends and sees it, or has a sense of it. He don't [*sic*] merely rationally believe that God is glorious, but he has a sense of the gloriousness of God in his heart. There is not only a rational belief that God is holy, and that holiness is a good thing; but there is a sense of the loveliness of God's holiness. There is not only a speculatively judging that God is gracious, but a sense how amiable God is upon that account; or a sense of the beauty of this divine attribute.[20]

If you were counting, you will have noticed that Edwards repeated the word "sense" ten times in this paragraph. By understanding grace aesthetically as a "new sense of the heart," rather than logically, Edwards represented regeneration or the "new birth" in ways to be visually pictured rather than logically deduced. By shifting the ground to aesthetics, Edwards participated directly in the Enlightenment project in ways that would usher in a new spirit of romanticism.

In addition to speaking of regeneration as a new sense of the heart, Edwards revolutionized the traditional "faculty psychology" that had governed theology by giving primacy to reason and the understanding over the heart and the affections. Edwards reversed the priority, giving primacy to the affections and, in the process, again turned Locke on his head. As summarized by Miller: "Edwards's great discovery, his dramatic refashioning of the theory of sensational rhetoric, was his assertion that an idea in the mind is not only a form of perception but is also a determination of love and hate. . . . For Edwards, in short, an idea became not merely a concept but an emotion."[21] This would lead to a radical definition of grace as "a new simple idea" supernaturally implanted.

In so framing his argument in the context of love and hate, or in Locke's terms "delight or uneasiness," Edwards, more than any other eighteenth-century theologian, would anticipate Freud.[22] In his *Treatise on the Religious Affections*, Edwards collapsed the distinctions of the faculty of the will and the affections, asserting that "the will, and affections of the soul, are not two faculties; the affections are not essentially distinct from the will, nor do they differ from the mere actings of

---

20. Smith, Stout, and Minkema, eds., *Jonathan Edwards Reader*, 111.
21. Miller, "The Rhetoric of Sensation," 179.
22. Locke, *Essay concerning Human Understanding*, 108.

the will and inclination of the soul."[23] In his new ordering of the senses, Edwards again borrowed from the Enlightenment to say that humans do not act in response to rational calculations but in response to their emotional predispositions of love or hatred. There was no possibility of a "perfect indifference" to anything. The difference between Edwards and Locke was Edwards's emphasis on overweening supernatural grace. For the affections to be redirected toward their proper spiritual objects, God had to intervene.

Edwards's Enlightenment brand of evangelicalism would enjoy a wide influence in nineteenth-century America. One remarkable example is the Newport, Rhode Island, female evangelist and home-preacher Sarah Osborn. In her remarkable new biography of Osborn, Catherine Brekus points out that, alongside a powerful traditional piety in Osborn, she evidenced distinctive patterns of enlightened thought. In Brekus's words:

> Evangelicals borrowed this language of sensation from the same Enlightenment thinkers whom they suspected of Arminianism and deism. . . . If the mind should be described as "White Paper, void of all characters, without any Ideas," John Locke asked, then "How comes it to be furnished?" His answer was simple: "from Experience." Echoing this language, evangelicals insisted that Christianity was based on the palpable experience of being born again.[24]

Alongside the experience-driven New Birth, eighteenth-century evangelicals absorbed the individualism that accompanied spiritual appeals to personal experience. In Brekus's words: "In earlier periods of history it had seemed almost inevitable that children would grow up to follow in their parents' footsteps. . . . But because of religious toleration, technological innovation, social and geographical mobility, and the expansion of political and economic choices, personal identity no longer seemed as fixed in the eighteenth century, and individuals gained a new sense of self-determination." Sarah Osborn's case illustrates how historical change issued from the bottom up as well as from the top down through ministers such as Jonathan Edwards or George Whitefield. Like

23. Smith, Stout, and Minkema, eds., *Jonathan Edwards Reader*, 142.
24. Catherine A. Brekus, *Sarah Osborn's World: The Rise of Evangelical Christianity in Early America* (New Haven: Yale University Press, 2013), 100.

many of her contemporaries, Osborn was looking for a new kind of Christianity, and in enlightened evangelicalism she found what she was looking for. This new kind of Christianity gave people like Osborn a sense of empirical proof that they had been regenerated and, with that sense, a new empowerment. This was especially true for women as it gave them a powerful new vocabulary to justify their religious authority (in Osborn's case to justify her preaching to "mixed" audiences of males and females, whites and blacks). By combining the Christian language of sin and divine regeneration with a new Enlightenment vocabulary of benevolence and empiricism, Sarah Osborn crafted a narrative that was both uniquely her own and "distinctly evangelical."[25]

Besides Osborn, enslaved people and their advocates discovered their own voices in Edwards's evangelical world. Scholars have recently identified extraordinary abolitionist sentiments coming from the heirs of Edwards. In contrast to earlier historians of abolitionism who tended to associate it with Unitarians and skeptics, the "New Divinity" advocates were actually in the forefront of antislavery thought and activity.[26] Although Edwards himself owned at least three slaves in a colony that had the largest number of slaves in New England, his intellectual heirs would depart adamantly from accepting slavery.

Edwards's own son, Jonathan Jr., was a staunch "immediate" abolitionist. Building on his father's *Treatise on True Virtue*, Edwardseans applied his definition of love as "disinterested benevolence to being in general" (Edwards's term for God) to argue that slavery could not coexist with such love. The American Revolution compelled the New Divinity theologians to explore anew the meaning of virtue and its importance to society. Applying the concept of true virtue to the social covenant, Edwards Jr. stated that a benevolent goodwill toward being in general was the essence of a harmonious society. But because of sin, republicanism was exposed to strife. Only a commitment to the good of all on the part of the citizenry and government could save society. "All" included slaves. In keeping with the Edwardsean emphasis on immediate repentance, the younger Edwards believed that the only way a society could correct its fault was wholly and immediately to repent of it. Otherwise, true virtue could not be exercised. The institution of slavery was an ob-

25. Brekus, *Sarah Osborn's World*, 102.

26. See Harry S. Stout and Kenneth Minkema, "The Edwardsean Tradition and the Anti-Slavery Debate, 1740-1865," *Journal of American History* 92 (June 2005): 1-28.

struction because it hindered both master and slave from acting benevolently. Ultimately, national regeneration and reform were blocked by the perpetuation of slavery.

Besides Edwards Jr., New Divinity abolitionist clergy included Samuel Hopkins, Joseph Bellamy, Levi Hart, and the African American Edwardsean Lemuel Haynes. In his recent biography of Haynes, John Saillant demonstrates how the New Divinity conditioned Haynes's republicanism and abolitionism. When whites denied blacks their rights as human beings and Christians, they were not Christian. To quote Saillant: "Benevolence and benevolent affections were real, Haynes argued, only when men and women loved humankind impartially and disinterestedly."[27] In true Edwardsean fashion Haynes asserted in his first sermon: "Only God effected regeneration since the exercises of an unregenerate individual were motivated not by disinterested love, but by selfishness."

In his Pulitzer Prize–winning book, *What Hath God Wrought*, American historian Daniel Walker Howe points out how

> The young American republic enjoyed a Protestant Enlightenment that bestowed an enthusiastic religious endorsement upon scientific knowledge, popular education, humanitarianism, and democracy. The most widespread form of Christian millennialism added faith in progress to this list. The spread of literacy, discoveries in science and technology, even a rising standard of living, could all be interpreted— and were—as evidences of the approach of Christ's Second Coming and the messianic age foretold by the prophets, near at hand.[28]

In his work on "civil millennialism" in the American Revolution, Nathan Hatch demonstrates how Christian millennialism and the Enlightenment ideal of progress became so intertwined that it was virtually impossible to separate them.[29] For their part, Enlightenment theorists resistant to traditional ideas of biblical inspiration and inerrancy crafted a secular version of Christian salvation, substituting natural law for biblical reve-

27. John Saillant, *Black Puritan, Black Republican: The Life and Thought of Lemuel Haynes, 1753-1833* (New York: Oxford University Press, 2003), 69.

28. Daniel Walker Howe, *What Hath God Wrought: The Transformation of America, 1815-1848* (New York: Oxford University Press, 2007), 469.

29. Nathan O. Hatch, "The Origins of Civil Millennialism in America: New England Clergymen, War with France, and the Revolution," *William and Mary Quarterly* 31 (1974): 407-30.

lation, the love of humanity for the love of God, and human perfectibility for divine redemption, rendering them, as Carl Becker has noted, virtually a religion of their own.[30]

In sum, the intersections and overlaps of Whitefield's revivals and Edwardsean enlightened evangelicalism appeared virtually everywhere. The "simple idea" of individual experience, whether written on the "white paper" of the infant mind or ignited by a divine and supernatural light—this impulse embodied the sense and spirit of revolution that would invigorate complex new ideas of government, theology, freedom, and the New Birth. And it was precisely this impulse that made the Great Awakening great.

30. Carl L. Becker, *The Heavenly City of the Eighteenth-Century Philosophers*, 2nd ed. (New Haven: Yale University Press, 2003).

CHAPTER 2

The Evangelical Encounter with the Enlightenment

Catherine A. Brekus

In 1743, Sarah Osborn, a schoolteacher in Newport, Rhode Island, decided to write a memoir. Inspired by the emotional revivals that historians have called the Great Awakening, she wanted to share the dramatic story of her conversion, the religious crisis that had changed the meaning of her life. Looking back, she remembered longing for God's grace because of her feelings of hopelessness and worthlessness, but fearing that she was too sinful to be saved. She felt as if there were an immense gulf separating her from God. She was depraved; he was perfect. She was empty; he was full. She was helpless; he was all-powerful and free. And yet just at the moment when she felt most broken in spirit, he had healed her. "It is not possible for me to make any one sensible what joy I was instantly filled with," she testified, "except those who experimentally know what it is." She had been born again, "restored as it were from the grave."[1]

Lost but now found, doubtful but now sure, dead but now reborn—this was not only Sarah Osborn's story but the story of thousands of other Americans in the eighteenth century. At the same time that Osborn was writing her memoir, a young man in Delaware named Samuel Davies

---

1. Sarah Osborn, Memoir, Beinecke Rare Book and Manuscript Library, Yale University, New Haven, Connecticut. For more on Osborn, see Samuel Hopkins, *Memoirs of the Life of Mrs. Sarah Osborn* (Worcester, MA: Leonard Worcester, 1799); Samuel Hopkins, ed., *Familiar Letters, Written by Mrs. Sarah Osborn and Miss Susanna Anthony, Late of Newport, Rhode Island* (Newport: Newport Mercury, 1807); and Catherine A. Brekus, *Sarah Osborn's World: The Rise of Evangelical Christianity in Early America* (New Haven: Yale University Press, 2013).

experienced his own religious crisis, suddenly realizing the depth of his sinfulness and his complete reliance on God's grace. He was "vile," he confessed, and filled with corruption. After being born again, he decided to devote his life to Christ, eventually becoming a minister in Virginia and an outspoken defender of religious freedom.[2]

And sometime during the mid-1760s, a slave named Newport Gardner began learning how to read the Bible, moved by its description of a loving Jesus who offered healing and redemption. He had been kidnapped from Africa around the age of fourteen and sold into slavery in Newport, Rhode Island, but somehow, probably by attending Sarah Osborn's meetings, he became convinced that his life had a deeper religious purpose. Certain that he had been redeemed by Jesus Christ, he resolved to spend the rest of his life sharing the gospel with other Africans.[3]

A goodwife, a minister, and a slave—Sarah Osborn, Samuel Davies, and Newport Gardner—seemed to share little in common, but each rejoiced to have been born again, and each was part of a new religious movement that began to coalesce in the eighteenth century, a movement that we now describe as evangelical Christianity. Today evangelicalism has become such a familiar part of the American religious landscape that it seems virtually timeless, as if it has always existed. But, like Christianity itself, evangelicalism has a history, and when it emerged in the mid-eighteenth century it represented a distinctive turning point in the history of religion.[4] The word "evangelical" was not new, and its roots stretch back to the Greek word *evangelion*, meaning "gospel."[5] The sixteenth-century Protestant Reformers used the word "evangelical" as an adjective to emphasize their reliance on the Bible alone. Yet during the eighteenth century the word became increasingly identified with the pop-

2. John Ferguson, *Memoir of the Life and Character of Rev. Samuel Hopkins* (Boston: Leonard W. Kimball, 1830), 50. See also George William Pilcher, *Samuel Davies: Apostle of Dissent in Colonial Virginia* (Knoxville: University of Tennessee Press, 1971).

3. Newport Gardner's African name was Occramar Marycoo. See Edward E. Andrews, "The Crossings of Occramar Marycoo, or Newport Gardner," in *Atlantic Biographies: Individuals and Peoples in the Atlantic World*, ed. Jeffrey A. Fortin and Mark Meuwese (Boston: Brill, 2014), 101-24. See also George Champlin Mason, *Reminiscences of Newport* (Newport: Charles E. Hammett, Jr., 1884), 154-59.

4. Mark Noll highlights the turning point represented by the conversion of John and Charles Wesley in 1738. See Mark A. Noll, *Turning Points: Decisive Moments in the History of Christianity*, 3rd ed. (Grand Rapids: Baker Academic, 2012), 215-38.

5. D. Bruce Hindmarsh, *The Evangelical Conversion Narrative: Spiritual Autobiography in Early Modern England* (New York: Oxford University Press, 2005), 13.

ular preachers of the Great Awakening, including the celebrated George Whitefield, and by the early nineteenth century it had become a noun. In his *Letters from England*, Robert Southey explained, "The countess of Huntingdon was a great patroness of Whitefield, and his preachers were usually called by her name,—which they have now dropt for the better title of Evangelicals."[6]

The stories of Sarah Osborn, Samuel Davies, and Newport Gardner can help us to understand how and why the evangelical movement emerged in the eighteenth-century transatlantic world. On one hand, the movement was not entirely new, and it had deep affinities with sixteenth- and seventeenth-century Puritanism. No historical turning point is ever completely divorced from what came before it, and in many ways evangelical Christians revitalized an older Puritan tradition.[7] Yet, on the other hand, the nascent evangelical movement looked forward as well as backward, and it drew many of its ideas from the intellectual movement known as the Enlightenment. Evangelicals rejected the skeptical and rationalist strains of the Enlightenment, but they absorbed its focus on personal experience as the foundation of knowledge, its elevation of the individual as the most important source of religious authority, and its humanitarian sympathies. In the words of Bruce Hindmarsh, evangelical Christianity should be understood as a "vector of the Enlightenment."[8]

How should we define the Enlightenment? Borrowing the title of Thomas Paine's controversial book, many historians have argued that the eighteenth century should be understood as "the Age of Reason," a new historical era in which leading intellectuals enshrined rationality and free enquiry as the ultimate values.[9] In recent years, however, many scholars have emphasized that the Enlightenment should be understood in broader terms as a popular as well as elite movement: it changed the way that ordinary people thought about the meaning of their lives. For example, Norman Fiering has argued that most eighteenth-century Amer-

6. Robert Southey, *Letters from England*, vol. 2 (London: Longman, Hurst, Rees, Orme and Brown, 1814), 359.

7. On this theme, see Mark A. Noll, *A History of Christianity in the United States and Canada* (Grand Rapids: Eerdmans, 1992), 104-5.

8. Bruce Hindmarsh, "Reshaping Individualism: The Private Christian, Eighteenth-Century Religion, and the Enlightenment," in *The Rise of the Laity in Evangelical Protestantism*, ed. Deryck Lovegrove (New York: Routledge, 2002), 77.

9. *The Age of Reason* was published in the United States in two parts in 1794 and 1795. The full texts are available online: http://www.ushistory.org/paine/reason/.

icans assumed that humans beings were instinctively compassionate—a startling reversal of the Puritan past that suggests the growing acceptance of humanitarian ideas.[10]

Besides emphasizing the Enlightenment's wide-ranging influence, historians have also argued that it should not be reduced to a single-minded quest for rationality. As Roy Porter has explained, enlightened thinkers were less focused on "*a priori* reason" as the key to knowledge than on "experience and experiment." Instead of making judgments based on clerical authority or inherited tradition, they insisted on the value of "first-hand experience." In his *Essay concerning Human Understanding*, John Locke wrote, "All our knowledge is founded [on] *Experience*." If the mind should be described as "White Paper, void of all Characters, without any Ideas," he asked, then "How comes it to be furnished?" His answer was simple: "from Experience." The Enlightenment was not only an "Age of Reason" but also an "Age of Experience," and Enlightenment thinkers insisted that knowledge must be based on empirical proof rather than clerical authority or inherited tradition.[11]

Since historians have often portrayed the Enlightenment as aggressively secular in its outlook, it may seem surprising to argue that some of its ideas came to fruition in the evangelical movement. According to Peter Gay, the French philosophers of the Enlightenment wanted to destroy the church, or in Voltaire's famous words, "*ecrasez l'infame*" (crush the infamous). Rejecting the "mythical thinking" of Christianity in favor of "critical thinking" based on reason, the "little flock of *philosophes*" often quarreled over how to understand human nature and society, but they remained unified by "their tension with Christianity, and their pursuit of modernity."[12]

As Gay and other historians have demonstrated, there is good reason to describe much of enlightened thought as hostile to religion. Many

10. See Norman Fiering, "Irresistible Compassion: An Aspect of Eighteenth-Century Sympathy and Humanitarianism," *Journal of the History of Ideas* 37 (April-June 1976): 195-218.

11. Roy Porter, *The Enlightenment*, 2nd ed. (Basingstoke, New York: Palgrave, 2001), 2, 15; John Locke, *An Essay concerning Human Understanding* (1690; repr. London: Awnsham and J. Churchill, 1706), 1:51.

12. Peter Gay, *The Enlightenment: An Interpretation*, vol. 1 (New York: Knopf, 1966), 3, 423, 8. On the "secularization of European thought," see Porter, *The Enlightenment*, 66. See also Jonathan Irvine Israel, *Radical Enlightenment: Philosophy and the Making of Modernity, 1650-1750* (New York: Oxford University Press, 2001).

eighteenth-century intellectuals condemned the "priestcraft" of Christianity and portrayed the church as an enemy to human progress. "All national institutions of churches—whether Jewish, Christian, or Turkish—appear to me no other than human inventions set up to terrify and enslave mankind and monopolize power and profit," wrote Thomas Paine in 1794.[13]

Yet the portrait of a rigorously rational Enlightenment doing battle with religious "superstition" is overdrawn. The Enlightenment was a diverse movement, and there was no single relationship between enlightened thought and Christianity. Some historians, for example, have speculated that the Enlightenment may have grown out of the Protestant Reformation: for example, John Locke was raised in a Puritan family, and he may have been shaped by Reformed thought despite rejecting it later.[14] Historians have also suggested that the Enlightenment contributed to the growth of more liberal, optimistic forms of Protestantism such as Latitudinarianism, Deism, and, in New England, "Catholick" Congregationalism.[15] In addition, American historians have shown that Protestant thinkers eventually assimilated aspects of enlightened thought in order to buttress their faith against skepticism. As Henry May argued in his 1976 survey, *The Enlightenment in America*, nineteenth-century Protestants defended their faith by appealing to Francis Hutcheson's common

13. Thomas Paine, *Common Sense*, reprinted in *The Portable Enlightenment Reader*, ed. Isaac Kramnick (New York: Penguin Books, 1995), 175.

14. On the relationship between Calvinism and the Enlightenment, see Helena Rosenblatt, "Calvinism," in *Encyclopedia of the Enlightenment*, ed. Alan Charles Kors (New York: Oxford University Press, 2003).

15. "Latitudinarians" were British Anglicans who prized tolerance and rationality. See John Gascoigne, "Latitudinarianism," in *Encyclopedia of the Enlightenment*, ed. Kors. Deists were skeptics who rejected traditional Christian doctrine, including the divinity of Christ, but who still believed in a God who created a mechanistic universe. See Kerry S. Walters, *The American Deists: Voices of Reason and Dissent in the Early Republic* (Lawrence: University Press of Kansas, 1992); Kerry S. Walters, *Rational Infidels: The American Deists* (Durango, CO: Longwood Academic, 1992); Peter Byrne, *Natural Religion and the Nature of Religion: The Legacy of Deism* (London, New York: Routledge, 1989). "Catholicks" were New England Congregationalists who incorporated enlightened ideas about the "rational order of the universe, and human capability to detect that order" in the early eighteenth century. See John Corrigan, *The Prism of Piety: Catholick Congregational Clergy at the Beginning of the Enlightenment* (New York: Oxford University Press, 1991), vii. See also Hugh Trevor-Roper, "The Religious Origins of the Enlightenment," in *Religion, the Reformation, and Social Change, and Other Essays* (London: MacMillan, 1967), 1-42.

sense tradition and claiming that all humans have an innate moral sense given by God.[16]

While all of these studies have found crucial links between enlightened thought and Protestantism, David Bebbington's analysis of eighteenth-century, transatlantic evangelicalism offers the most intriguing analysis of the Enlightenment's profound influence on religion. According to Bebbington, the roots of modern evangelicalism can be traced back to the eighteenth century, when the older faith of the Puritans was replaced by a new kind of confident, optimistic Protestantism. Rejecting stereotypes of eighteenth-century evangelicals as reactionary, Bebbington has made the provocative claim that "the Evangelical version of Protestantism was created by the Enlightenment." Unlike earlier Protestants, evangelicals tended to be more optimistic, pragmatic, and humanitarian; and, most important, they expressed much greater assurance about their salvation. Influenced by John Locke's emphasis on the authority of personal experience, they insisted that converts could "feel" and "know" whether they had been saved. Rather than arguing that the Enlightenment was constructed against Protestantism, Bebbington has insisted that it also took place *within* Protestantism. What made evangelicals unique—what separated them from the seventeenth-century Puritans—was their embrace of the Enlightenment language of assurance, certainty, experience, and proof.[17]

Influenced by this argument, historians have found surprising traces of Enlightenment thought throughout the transatlantic evangelical movement. Mark Noll has argued that British, American, and Scottish evangelicals, like Locke, believed that "the self's personal experience was foundational for obtaining reliable knowledge," and both Frederick Dyer and David Hempton have noticed close parallels between Enlightenment ideas and Methodist religious practice. As Hempton explains, "The characteristic features of Methodist spirituality—its tendency to morbid introspection, its ruthless self-examination, and its compulsion to share and tell—are all products of its Lockean emphasis on sensible

16. Henry Farnham May, *The Enlightenment in America* (New York: Oxford University Press, 1976). See also Mark A. Noll, "The Rise and Long Life of the Protestant Enlightenment in America," in *Knowledge and Belief in America: Enlightenment Traditions and Modern Religious Thought*, ed. William M. Shea and Peter A. Huff (Cambridge: Cambridge University Press, 1995), 88-124.

17. See D. W. Bebbington, *Evangelicalism in Modern Britain: A History from the 1730s to the 1980s* (Boston: Unwin Hyman, 1989), 1-74; May, *Enlightenment in America*, 42-65.

experience." Even though John Wesley, the founder of the Methodist movement, was often accused of religious "enthusiasm," his defense of religious toleration and his opposition to slavery were influenced by his encounter with Enlightenment ideas. According to Bruce Hindmarsh, Protestants absorbed not only the Enlightenment's empiricist strands but its individualistic ones as well.[18] By the early nineteenth century, as Mark Noll has argued, evangelicals had accepted the common sense philosophy of the Enlightenment as their own.[19]

The stories of Sarah Osborn (1714-1796) and Samuel Davies (1723-1761) reveal the complicated relationship between the Enlightenment and evangelical Christianity. A generation older than Newport Gardner, both Osborn and Davies were profoundly influenced by the revivals of the Great Awakening, and both helped to construct a new religious movement that emphasized the joy of being born again, a personal relationship with God, and the call to spread the gospel around the globe.

Born in 1714 in England, Sarah Osborn was a mother, a wife, and a schoolteacher who moved to the colonies as a child, eventually settling in Newport, Rhode Island. She is remembered today only because she left an extraordinary record of her experiences in thousands of pages of letters, diaries, and a memoir, more than 2000 pages of which still survive. These manuscripts tell the story of a remarkable woman who suffered many tragedies during her life, including a suicidal crisis in adolescence, the loss of her first husband at sea, the death of her only child, and chronic bouts of illness. Though it is impossible to diagnose her across the span of almost three centuries, her symptoms suggest that she may have suffered from either multiple sclerosis or rheumatoid arthritis.

Yet, despite these tribulations, Osborn never lost her faith in God's goodness, and she was so charismatic that many people in Newport sought her spiritual counsel. During the winter of 1766-67, she emerged as the leader of a remarkable religious revival that brought hundreds of people—including large numbers of slaves—to her house each week. Al-

18. See Mark A. Noll, *The Rise of Evangelicalism: The Age of Edwards, Whitefield and the Wesleys* (Leicester: Inter-Varsity, 2004), 140; David Hempton, *Methodism: Empire of the Spirit* (New Haven: Yale University Press, 2005), 52, 41; Frederick A. Dreyer, *The Genesis of Methodism* (Bethlehem, PA: Lehigh University Press, 1999); Hindmarsh, "Reshaping Individualism," 67-84; Hindmarsh, *Evangelical Conversion Narrative*.

19. Mark A. Noll, *America's God: From Jonathan Edwards to Abraham Lincoln* (New York: Oxford University Press, 2002), 93-113.

though she remained poor, strangers from as far away as Canada and the West Indies sent money to help defray her expenses. By the time of her death in 1796, she had become virtually a Protestant saint.[20]

There is no evidence that Osborn ever met Samuel Davies, but they had mutual friends—including her uncle, the influential Reverend John Guyse of England—and it is likely that they knew of each other.[21] Born in 1723 in Delaware, Davies experienced conversion at the age of fifteen, and although he was too poor to attend college, he trained for the Presbyterian ministry with Samuel Blair, a well-known revivalist. In 1747 he made the courageous decision to become a dissenting preacher in Virginia, where he faced stiff opposition from the Church of England, the legally established church. Like Osborn, he was afflicted with a chronic illness—in his case, tuberculosis—and he suffered many private losses. His first wife died in childbirth after only a year of marriage, along with their newborn son, and he lost another child after his second marriage. But Davies became one of the best-known evangelicals of his time, a forceful preacher who reportedly made his listeners tremble and cry out in fear or joy. The great orator Patrick Henry grew up hearing Davies preach, and some have speculated that Henry imitated his fiery style.[22] According to a story told many times after his death, Davies preached in front of King George II during a trip to England to raise money for Princeton, and when he noticed the king speaking to someone in the middle of his sermon, he looked toward him and proclaimed, "When the lion roars, the beasts of the forest all tremble; and when King Jesus speaks, the princes of the earth should keep silence."[23] Despite his reputation for ferocity in the pulpit, Davies also published heartfelt poems and hymns about his deep love for God. In 1752 he published *Miscellaneous Poems, Chiefly on Divine Subjects*, which included a poem on John 21:17, "Lord, thou knowest all things; thou knowest that I love thee":

20. On Osborn's life, see Brekus, *Sarah Osborn's World*.

21. Davies mentions Guyse in his journal. See William Pilcher, ed., *The Reverend Samuel Davies Abroad: The Diary of a Journey to England and Scotland, 1753-55* (Urbana: University of Illinois Press, 1967), 61, 74; Brekus, *Sarah Osborn's World*, 35.

22. John A. Ragosta, *Wellspring of Liberty: How Virginia's Religious Dissenters Helped Win the American Revolution and Secured Religious Liberty* (New York: Oxford University Press, 2010), 50.

23. Albert Barnes, *Sermons on Important Subjects, by the Reverend Samuel Davies* (New York: Robert Carter, 1851), 1:xxx.

O! if Thy Love does not my heart inflame,
Why do I thus delight in Jesus' Name?
His Name is Music to my ravish'd Ears,
Sweeter than that which charms the heav'nly Spheres:
A cheering Cordial to my fainting Breast;
My Hope, my Joy, my Peace, my Heav'n, my Rest.[24]

Preaching to large numbers of slaves as well as whites, Davies tried to convince them that a loving God offered them redemption. In 1759 he became the president of Princeton, a post that he held for only two years before dying of his illness at the age of thirty-eight.

Neither Osborn nor Davies would have recognized that they were influenced by Enlightenment ideas; nor would they have seen themselves as pioneers of a new religious movement. Since the word "Enlightenment" was not coined until Immanuel Kant's famous essay in 1784, "What Is Enlightenment?," they did not have a name for the intellectual developments that were transforming their world. Yet they were profoundly troubled by what they perceived as a growing faith in human goodness and individual freedom, and they imagined themselves as defenders of a Reformed tradition that seemed to be under attack. As Samuel Davies explained, he feared that religion had declined, and he wanted to increase "experimental religion" or "vital piety."[25]

Based on booksellers' catalogs and the records of both private and circulating libraries, we know that few educated Americans were attracted to French Enlightenment thinkers such as Voltaire, who tended to be particularly radical and anticlerical, but they were profoundly influenced by British thinkers such as John Locke, Francis Hutcheson, John Tillotson, and Anthony Ashley Cooper, the third earl of Shaftesbury.[26] Even though these men were moderates who never condemned Christianity as "priestcraft" or discarded the authority of biblical revelation, they undermined older assumptions about the self and God in quieter,

24. Samuel Davies, *Miscellaneous Poems, Chiefly on Divine Subjects* (Williamsburg: William Hunter, 1751), 4.

25. Samuel Davies, *Memoir of the Rev. Samuel Davies: Formerly President of the College of New Jersey* (Boston: Massachusetts Sabbath School Society, 1832), 113.

26. David Lundberg and Henry May, "The Enlightened Reader in America," *American Quarterly* 28, no. 2 (1976): 262–93. On the multiplicity of Enlightenments in different national contexts, see Roy Porter and Mikuláš Teich, eds., *The Enlightenment in National Context* (New York: Cambridge University Press, 1981).

more subtle ways. Shaftesbury, for example, argued that all humans have an innate moral sense that inclines them to ethical behavior, an idea that threatened the doctrine of original sin.[27] In both England and America, the Enlightenment gradually led to the emergence of a new, liberal form of Protestantism that emphasized tolerance, reason, free will, and God's benevolence.[28] In 1757, for example, the Reverend Samuel Webster published a tract condemning the belief in original sin as cruel because it logically led to the conclusion that infants as well as adults could be damned. He found it difficult to reconcile a belief in infant damnation with "the *goodness, holiness* or *justice* of God."[29]

Alarmed by the spread of enlightened ideas about God and human nature, both Sarah Osborn and Samuel Davies tried to set themselves apart from liberals who emphasized human goodness. Defending the doctrine of original sin, Davies insisted that "every Person born into this World . . . deserves God's Wrath and Damnation."[30] In a sermon delivered to children in 1758, *Little Children Invited to Jesus Christ*, he portrayed them as inherently corrupt rather than as innocent. "Young as you are, you have been guilty of sins beyond number," he warned. "You have spoken many bad words: you have been peevish, sullen, angry, obstinate, disobedient to Parents, wild, thoughtless, and too full of play. And which is worse than all, you have bad hearts." Unless they repented, they would suffer eternal damnation. "The great God is justly angry with you every day," he threatened. "The Lions of Hell are going about seeking to devour you."[31]

Judgments about style are hard to quantify, but Davies seems to have expressed his beliefs in more extreme language than earlier generations of Protestants, perhaps because of his fear that the Reformed tradition

27. On Shaftesbury, see Michael B. Gill, *The British Moralists on Human Nature and the Birth of Secular Ethics* (New York: Cambridge University Press, 2006), 27-134. Roy Porter argues that the "Enlightenment in Britain took place within, rather than against, Protestantism." Porter, *The Creation of the Modern World: The Untold Story of the British Enlightenment* (New York: Norton, 2000), 99.

28. Roland N. Stromberg, *Religious Liberalism in Eighteenth-Century England* (London: Oxford University Press, 1954).

29. Samuel Webster, *A Winter Evening's Conversation upon the Doctrine of Original Sin* (New Haven: James Parker, 1757), 5.

30. Samuel Davies, *The Impartial Trial, Impartially Tried, and Convicted of Partiality* (Williamsburg: W. Parks, 1748), 5.

31. Samuel Davies, *Little Children Invited to Jesus Christ: A Sermon, Preached in Hanover County, Virginia, May 8, 1758* (Northampton, MA: William Butler, 1798), 8-9.

was under attack. In a memoir that Osborn wrote in 1743, she constructed an image of herself that stood in stark contrast to the enlightened, optimistic view of selfhood that had begun to gain ascendancy in the eighteenth-century transatlantic world. At a time when many Enlightenment thinkers argued that humans were born with an innate tendency toward virtue, she chose to emphasize the depth of her sinfulness even in her childhood. In her opening pages, she described herself as "the most ignorant and vile of all creatures, whose deep rooted enmity against thee and thy laws broke out into action as soon as I was capable of any." She criticized herself as "a monster in sin" and a "liar" whose "base ingratitude," "angry ungrateful temper," and dreadful "corruptions" had made her entirely unworthy of God's love. She also condemned herself as "guilty," "peevish," "wretched," "filthy and polluted," "churlish," and "worthless."[32]

Besides resisting enlightened ideas about human goodness, Osborn and Davies also rejected the assumption that the purpose of God's creation was individual happiness. Many Enlightenment thinkers criticized Christians (especially Calvinists) for portraying God as a cruel and vindictive judge, and they claimed that God never deliberately inflicted either physical or psychological pain. Using one of the key words of the eighteenth century, they insisted that God was benevolent, and his ultimate purpose was human fulfillment.[33] In contrast, evangelicals argued that God was the best of beings, the epitome of perfection, and it would be illogical for him to prefer anything inferior to himself as his ultimate end. Since God had created the world to glorify himself, not to foster human happiness, they did not see the existence of sin, suffering, and even hell as problems that needed to be explained, but rather as demonstrations of God's power and glory. Even though both Davies and Osborn experienced many afflictions in their lives—including chronic illness, poverty, and war—they insisted that their sufferings had been ordained by God. In a sermon that Davies preached in 1756 in response to a drought, a military defeat, and a Native American massacre, he insisted that these disasters were God's will. Quoting from the prophet Amos, he asked, "Is there evil in a city . . . and the Lord hath not done it?" Warning

32. Osborn, Memoir, 1–3, Beinecke Library; Osborn, Diary #14 (July 8, 1753–March 1, 1754), Newport Historical Society, entries for the following dates in 1753: July 9, September 8, September 19, and October 30.

33. Norman Sykes, "The Theology of Divine Benevolence," *Historical Magazine of the Protestant Episcopal Church* 16 (1947): 278–91.

the people of Virginia to repent, he urged them to "submit to calamities as from his Rod."[34] Similarly, Sarah Osborn wrote in her diary, "It is good for me that I have been afflicted." She imagined God as a loving but strict father who stood above his disobedient children with a rod in his hand, chastising them for their own good. "O, strike in what way . . . thou Pleasest," she wrote to him during an illness. "I'll adore and Kiss the Hand, the dear Hand, that smites. . . . O purge and purify me though in a furnace of affliction." When she reflected on the meaning of her life, she emphasized that true happiness required obeying God's sovereign will, even if it involved suffering. "Happiness . . . is not to be found in all the world," she testified. "None but God alone can fill and satisfy."[35]

Osborn and Davies also insisted on the reality of hell. Influenced by Enlightenment ideas, a small number of liberal-leaning Protestants, including the Reverend Charles Chauncy, began to question the existence of hell, troubled by the idea that a loving God could sentence sinners to eternal punishment.[36] Responding to these doubts, Davies quoted from Psalm 7:11, "Is not God angry with the wicked every day?" Warning his listeners not to be deluded by false promises of heaven, he asked, "Does not his wrath abide upon unbelievers? Shall not the wicked be turned into hell?" Osborn believed that Satan wanted to destroy her and other Christian believers, and she imagined him as an enraged lion or a bull lying in wait to attack her. "Put his hook in his nose," she pleaded with God, "and turn him back by the way he came."[37] Fearful of the devil's power, she prayed that God would protect her from harm.

Given their belief in the reality of evil, it is not surprising that evangelicals also resisted the Enlightenment's affirmation of everyday life. Many Enlightenment thinkers insisted that the meaning of life could be

34. Samuel Davies, *Virginia's Danger and Remedy: Two Discourses, Occasioned by the Severe Drought in Sundry Parts of the Country; and the Defeat of General Braddock* (Williamsburg: William Hunter, 1756), 14.

35. Sarah Osborn, Diary, March 28, 1754, Connecticut Historical Society; Sarah Osborn, Diary, April 2, 1757, Newport Historical Society.

36. Charles Chauncy, *The Mystery Hid from Ages and Generations, Made Manifest by the Gospel Revelation; or, The Salvation of All Men* (London: Charles Dilly, 1784). On controversies over the existence of hell, see Norman Fiering, "Hell and the Humanitarians," chapter 5 of his *Jonathan Edwards's Moral Thought and Its British Context* (Chapel Hill: University of North Carolina Press, 1981), 201-60; Philip C. Almond, *Heaven and Hell in Enlightenment England* (New York: Cambridge University Press, 1994).

37. Davies, *Impartial Trial*, 45; Sarah Osborn, Diary, March 17, 1767, Newport Historical Society. She was quoting from the Bible: 2 Kings 19:28; Isaiah 37:29.

found here on earth, not in a distant heaven, and they celebrated the pleasures of marriage, family, and meaningful work as good in themselves.[38] In contrast, Davies and Osborn were ambivalent about how much they should value ordinary life. Despite affirming the essential goodness of creation, they insisted that they must be willing to sacrifice the pleasures of the world for God. In a sermon titled "Indifference to Life Urged from Its Shortness and Vanity," Davies preached, "How trifling are all the concerns of time—to those of immortality! What is it to us who are to live forever—whether we now live happy or miserable for an hour? Whether we have wives, or whether we have none; whether we rejoice, or whether we weep."[39] Even when Sarah Osborn's only son died in 1744 at the age of eleven, she tried to place God's glory over her own happiness. Despite her sorrow, she affirmed her acceptance of God's will. "I adored him as a sovereign God," she wrote, "and blessed his name, for he had given, and it was he who had taken."[40]

On the surface, the Enlightenment, with its emphasis on reason, and evangelicalism, with its heart-centered piety, seem to have stood in stark opposition to each other. Evangelicals resisted Enlightenment ideas in multiple ways: they disavowed images of human goodness; they denied that the purpose of life was human happiness; they rejected the affirmation of everyday life; and they defended the real existence of hell. They deliberately tried to set themselves apart from the new, modern world that was beginning to emerge in the eighteenth century, a world that valued freedom, choice, and the pursuit of happiness.

Yet even though evangelicals were theologically conservative, they could not ignore the intellectual challenges to their faith, and as they tried to adapt to a changing world they unconsciously absorbed many Enlightenment ideas as their own. Influenced by the long Christian interest in religious experience, they were especially attracted to John Locke's emphasis on firsthand experience as the basis of knowledge. True religion, according to Samuel Davies, was "experimental": it could be validated by concrete, measurable experience.[41]

With Christian roots stretching back to Bernard of Clairvaux and the

38. Charles Taylor, *Sources of the Self: The Making of the Modern Identity* (Cambridge, MA: Harvard University Press, 1989), 211-33.

39. Barnes, *Sermons on Important Subjects*, 1:427.

40. Hopkins, *Memoirs of the Life of Mrs. Sarah Osborn*, 68.

41. Samuel Davies, *The State of Religion among the Protestant Dissenters in Virginia; in a Letter to the Rev. Mr. Joseph Bellamy* (Boston: S. Kneeland, 1751), 25.

Protestant Reformers, this emphasis on personal religious experience was not new, and seventeenth-century Puritans had often scrutinized their lives for visible proof of God's grace. But evangelicals spoke the language of experience with a fervor that few other Christians could match.[42] Evangelicals claimed that an intellectual, rational understanding of doctrine was less valuable than a personal experience of the Holy Spirit. According to Sarah Osborn, her faith was based not on abstract reason but on the palpable experience of being born again. "*How do I know this God is mine; and that I myself am not deceived?*" she asked. "By the Evidences of a *work of grace* wrought in my Soul."[43] Unlike earlier generations of Puritans, who had been hesitant to appear too confident about their salvation (lest they be guilty of pride), evangelicals claimed that they could empirically feel and know whether they had been spiritually reborn. When Osborn wrote about her conversion, she explained that most people would not be able to understand her sense of joy "except those who experimentally know what it is."[44] After struggling with painful religious doubts in her youth, even considering suicide, she seems to have been deeply attracted to the idea that she could be virtually certain of her salvation. In a particularly poignant diary entry that she wrote at a time when she had little money or food, she comforted herself that God had *proven* that he would never abandon her. Addressing him directly, she wrote: "My own experience has ever Proved to me, that thou art the God that has fed me all my Life Long—the God that didst never Leave me upon the mount of difficulty, but always appeared and wrought deliverance." On the cover of one of her diaries, she wrote, "blessed be God for the experiences of God's mercy, truth, and faithfulness recorded in this book."[45]

Evangelicals did not trust personal experience in the abstract, and in

42. See Bernard McGinn, "The Language of Inner Experience in Christian Mysticism," *Spiritus: A Journal of Christian Spirituality* 1, no. 1 (2001): 156-71; Susan Elizabeth Schreiner, *Are You Alone Wise? The Search for Certainty in the Early Modern Era* (New York: Oxford University Press, 2011), 209-60.

43. Sarah Osborn, *The Nature, Certainty and Evidence of True Christianity* (Boston: S. Kneeland, 1755), 3. On seventeenth- and eighteenth-century attitudes toward experience, see Martin Jay, *Songs of Experience: Modern American and European Variations on a Universal Theme* (Berkeley: University of California Press, 2005), 9-78.

44. Sarah Osborn, Memoir, Beinecke Library.

45. Sarah Osborn, Diary, July 29, 1753, Newport Historical Society. See the cover of Sarah Osborn, Diary 21 (May 9, 1757-November 6, 1757), Beinecke Library.

fact they assumed that most people viewed the world with eyes clouded by sin. But they insisted that Christians gained new powers of perception during conversion. As Osborn explained in her memoir, she had been overwhelmed by a new "sense" of God's "excellence, glory and truth" that was as real as the sense of seeing, tasting, or touching.[46] Critics of the evangelical movement complained that this sort of language was offensive, and Osborn was accused of being "puffed up with spiritual pride" and "holier than thou." According to Samuel Davies, many evangelicals were attacked for "a bold talking of experiences." Yet despite this opposition, he continued to defend the idea that "Vital religion is a sensible thing."[47]

Though only the most educated evangelicals realized it, they borrowed the image of a "new sense" from Enlightenment thinkers such as the third earl of Shaftesbury and Francis Hutcheson, who argued that all humans have an innate "moral sense" that helps them to distinguish good from evil. Although evangelicals rejected this positive view of human nature, they agreed that all knowledge comes from sense perception, and they appropriated the Enlightenment language of sensation as their own. According to Samuel Davies, sinners were required to have a "deep sense" of their "undone, helpless condition" in order to be saved. In a sermon entitled *The Method of Salvation through Jesus Christ*, he explained, "you must be sensible at heart that this is your condition in particular, before you can believe in him as your Savior."[48] By insisting that religion must be heartfelt, "experimental," and "sensible," evangelicals tried to give their beliefs an empirical foundation.

This emphasis on experience and sensation was deeply empowering for the ordinary men and women who were drawn to the evangelical movement. Although most eighteenth-century evangelicals valued learning, they claimed that religious authority must be based first and foremost on a personal experience of God's grace. According to Davies, for example, ministers had no right to preach unless they had experienced conversion. "Is not an unconverted Minister a monstrous incongruous Absurdity?" he asked. "How absurd, to employ One that suffers his own soul to perish, to save others from Perdition! How incongruous,

46. Sarah Osborn, Diary, July 8, 1753, Newport Historical Society.
47. Davies, *Impartial Trial*, 43, 13.
48. Samuel Davies, *The Method of Salvation through Jesus Christ*, 2nd ed. (Providence: J. Carter, 1793), 19.

that a Subject of the Prince of Hell should be an Ambassador to the King of Zion! That wolves should be placed to watch the sheep! That men unacquainted with spiritual exercises, should be made spiritual guides! These are incoherent, ridiculous inconsistencies."[49] By the same token, an ordinary person who had been "born again"—even a simple farmer or a goodwife—could serve as a model for other Christians to emulate. After Sarah Osborn wrote a letter of spiritual advice to a female friend, a minister asked for permission to publish it as a tract, convinced that it would inspire others to seek a closer relationship to God. In 1755 Osborn's letter appeared in print with a title that sounded curiously "enlightened": *The Nature, Certainty and Evidence of True Christianity*. In her tract, Osborn explained that whenever she wrestled with doubts, she searched for evidence of God's providence in her life. "Having treasured up the Experiences of many Years," she wrote, "I repair to them in a dark and cloudy Day." "Religion is no imaginary Thing," she testified, "but a substantial Reality."[50]

Besides being influenced by the Enlightenment language of sensible experience, evangelicals also absorbed its individualism—one of the most enduring legacies of the eighteenth century. In earlier periods of history it had seemed almost inevitable that children would grow up to follow in their parents' footsteps: a farmer's son would usually become a farmer, and a goodwife's daughter would live in the same neighborhood as her mother. But because of religious toleration, technological innovation, social and geographical mobility, and the expansion of political and economic choices, personal identity no longer seemed as fixed in the eighteenth century, and individuals gained a new sense of self-determination. Enlightenment philosophers defended the right of the sovereign individual to choose his own government, to pursue his own economic interests in the marketplace, and to worship according to the dictates of his own conscience. As this masculine language suggests, Enlightenment thinkers imagined the individual as a white man, but their ideas eventually proved too powerful to control. By the end of the eighteenth century, many disenfranchised groups—including white women, African Americans, and Native Americans—insisted that they, too, possessed rights as individuals.

Evangelicals were ambivalent about the individualism that was

49. Davies, *Impartial Trial*, 29.
50. Osborn, *Nature, Certainty and Evidence*, 3, 8, 10.

enshrined by the Enlightenment, but in response to the challenges of their time they crafted a new form of Protestantism that was based more on the converted individual than the covenanted community.[51] Earlier generations of Puritans had emphasized the morality of the entire commonwealth, imagining New England in collective terms as the people of God, the "new Israel." In contrast, even though evangelicals agreed that *both* personal and communal transformation were important, they put their emphasis more on the individual, arguing that one could not be a Christian without a personal experience of grace. As a minister explained, "True religion is an inward thing, a thing of the heart."[52] Sarah Osborn's *Nature, Certainty and Evidence of True Christianity* overflowed with the words "I" and "me." "I'll tell you truly what GOD has done for my Soul," she declared at the beginning of her letter. "GOD the FATHER *manifested* himself to me." "God made with me an *everlasting Covenant.*"[53]

Because of their focus on an individual relationship to God, evangelicals followed Enlightenment thinkers in defending freedom of conscience, insisting that the state did not have the right to prescribe what an individual should believe or how he or she should worship. In Virginia, Samuel Davies agreed to abide by the principles of the 1689 Toleration Act by paying taxes to the established Anglican Church, but he chafed against the government's efforts to control him. "I cannot grant that civil rulers have authority to preside in and determine controversies about matters of faith and affairs that peculiarly concern the church," he declared. In an angry letter, he protested that the state had no right to claim a power that "belongs ultimately to God speaking in his World"; nor could it coerce "the inviolable right of private judgment." Not even the king had the right to elevate himself over God by acting as the ultimate judge of religious truth. "'Tis much controverted in the Christian World, whether a sinner be justified in the sight of God, by faith alone, without his own good works and personal righteousness," Davies explained. "Now I can't allow that the King's majesty is supreme judge in this case, and that his

51. Hindmarsh, "Reshaping Individualism," 74; Harry S. Stout, *The Divine Dramatist: George Whitefield and the Rise of Modern Evangelicalism* (Grand Rapids: Eerdmans, 1991), 205; Jerald C. Brauer, "Conversion: From Puritanism to Revivalism," *Journal of Religion* 58, no. 3 (July 1978): 241.

52. Josiah Smith, *A Sermon, on the Character, Preaching &c. of the Rev. Mr. Whitefield* (1740), in *The Great Awakening: Documents Illustrating the Crisis and Its Consequences*, ed. Alan Heimert and Perry Miller (Indianapolis: Bobbs-Merrill, 1967), 65.

53. Osborn, *Nature, Certainty and Evidence*, 3, 5-6.

majesty has the chief authority to determine it."[54] His defense of individual religious freedom became a hallmark of the evangelical movement.

Finally, the nascent evangelical movement was also influenced by the stream of Enlightenment thought known as humanitarianism. Humanitarians were a loose coalition of thinkers who were involved in many different causes—including prison reform, antislavery, and poor relief—but they were linked together by their faith that humans were essentially good and were called to alleviate suffering and create a better world.[55] On one hand, evangelicals refused to see human happiness as the greatest good, and they defended doctrines that humanitarians found abhorrent, especially eternal punishment. Yet, on the other hand, evangelicals were fervent about creating a kinder, more compassionate world, and ultimately they forged an understanding of "benevolence" that was uniquely their own. Although Sarah Osborn and Samuel Davies believed that they were called to give charity to the poor, minister to the sick, and visit the imprisoned, they thought there was no greater act of charity than saving sinners from damnation. Evangelicals became renowned for their missionary work, placing more emphasis on evangelism than virtually any other group of Christians before them.

Both Osborn and Davies extended their fervent evangelism to include slaves. Davies lived in Virginia, where slaves comprised 44 percent of the population in 1750, and Osborn lived in Newport, one of the largest slave-trading ports in America.[56] Like most evangelicals at the time, Osborn and Davies seem to have been accustomed to seeing slaves bought and sold at auction, and they assumed that blacks were inferior to whites. Yet they also affirmed the spiritual equality of all souls before God, and they encouraged slaves to seek salvation. Besides inviting slaves to his meetings, Davies taught them to read the Bible, and by 1755 he reported

54. "Letters of Patrick Henry, Sr., Samuel Davies, James Maury, Edwin Conway and George Trask," *William and Mary Quarterly* 1, no. 4 (1921): 269.

55. On humanitarianism, see Norman Fiering, "Irresistible Compassion: An Aspect of Eighteenth-Century Sympathy and Humanitarianism," *Journal of the History of Ideas* 37, no. 2 (1976): 195-218; Daniel Wickberg, "Humanitarianism," in *Encyclopedia of American and Cultural History*, ed. Mary Kupiec Cayton and Peter W. Williams (New York: Scribner's, 2001), 2:689-97; Karen Haltunnen, "Humanitarianism and the Pornography of Pain in Anglo-American Culture," *American Historical Review* 100, no. 2 (April 1995): 303-34; Ava Chamberlain, "The Theology of Cruelty: A New Look at the Rise of Arminianism in Eighteenth-Century New England," *Harvard Theological Review* 85, no. 3 (1992): 335-56.

56. Peter Kolchin, *American Slavery, 1619-1877* (New York: Hill and Wang, 1993), 11.

that he had baptized one hundred of them, with as many as three hundred crowding into his church every Sunday. "Their masters generally neglect" them, he complained to a friend, "as though immortality were not a privilege common to them as with their masters."[57] After Sarah Osborn invited a small number of slaves to come to her house on Sunday evenings to read the Bible in the early 1760s, her meetings became so large that her house could barely hold the crowds. More than one hundred slaves attended her meetings each week, meaning that about one-tenth of Newport's black population passed through her doors each Sunday. Inspired by the stories of the dramatic conversions taking place at Osborn's house, whites as well as blacks began clamoring for the opportunity to pray with her, and during the height of the revival in 1766 and 1767 as many as 525 people attended her meetings each week. "We were so thronged that there was scarcely room to stir hand or foot," she wrote in a letter.[58] Whether addressing whites or blacks, her message was always the same: a loving, compassionate Jesus had offered up his own life to save them.

Unlike Davies, who never seems to have questioned the morality of slavery, Osborn eventually decided that it had to be immediately abolished. Perhaps she was influenced by the tragic stories that she heard during her Sunday night prayer meetings, or perhaps she was influenced by her pastor, the Reverend Samuel Hopkins, who became an antislavery activist soon after arriving in Newport in 1770. Whatever the catalyst, Osborn combined the Christian belief that "God hath made of one blood, all nations" (Acts 17:26) with a humanitarian ethos of sympathy and compassion. By the end of her life she had resolved that slavery was a "horrid sin."[59]

One of the slaves who seems to have attended Osborn's meetings was Occramar Marycoo (1746-1826), later known as Newport Gardner,

57. Davies, *Memoir of the Rev. Samuel Davies*, 25.

58. Sarah Osborn, Diary, April 7, 1767, Newport Historical Society. On the revival, see also Mary Beth Norton, "'My Resting Reaping Times': Sarah Osborn's Defense of Her 'Unfeminine' Activities," *Signs* 2, no. 2 (1976): 515-29; and Brekus, *Sarah Osborn's World*, 248-88.

59. Hopkins, *Memoirs of the Life of Mrs. Sarah Osborn*, 278. On Hopkins and antislavery, see Jonathan D. Sassi, "'This Whole Country Have Their Hands Full of Blood This Day': Transcription and Introduction of an Antislavery Sermon Manuscript Attributed to the Reverend Samuel Hopkins," *Proceedings of the American Antiquarian Society* 112, no. 1 (2004): 29-92.

who had been kidnapped from Africa at the age of fourteen. We know little about Marycoo's journey in chains across the Atlantic, but after being torn away from his family and forced into the hold of a slave ship, he must have been frightened, angry, and filled with despair. Conditions on slave ships were brutal. Captains wanted to keep as much of their human cargo alive as possible, but assuming that large numbers would die, they pressed as many as possible into cramped, unsanitary quarters below the deck. The enslaved spent weeks shackled together, suffocated by the stench of vomit, urine, and excrement. When Marycoo arrived in Newport, he was auctioned off to Caleb Gardner, a wealthy merchant, who stripped him of his name. Although he continued to call himself Occramar Marycoo in the presence of other Africans, his master and other whites called him Newport Gardner. Eventually he chose to accept the name as his own.

Despite his sufferings, Gardner was determined to survive. He was an intelligent man who quickly mastered the English language, and somehow in his few moments of leisure he also taught himself how to read and write. A gifted singer, he also became a well-known composer. Today he is remembered as a pioneering black musician who composed several popular songs, including *Crooked Shanks*, which was published in 1803 in *A Number of Original Airs, Duettos and Trios*.[60]

Gardner also distinguished himself as one of the leaders of Newport's black Christian community. Since Sarah Osborn never mentioned him by name, we cannot be certain that he attended the revival at her house, but there are several pieces of evidence pointing in that direction. First, even though Gardner's master belonged to the Second Church, he joined Osborn's church, the First Church, and became a close associate of her pastor, the Reverend Samuel Hopkins. His children were baptized at the First Church, and he served as its sexton.[61] Second, Gardner mentioned Osborn (as well as her close friends Susanna Anthony and Samuel Hopkins) in a letter that he wrote in 1826, soon before emigrating to Africa. Even though she had been dead for thirty years, he testified, "Miss Susannah Anthony, Mrs. Osborn, and D. D. Hopkins have procure[d] me good & cheerfull friends in Boston, both ministers and members of

---

60. Ferguson, *Memoir of the Life and Character of Rev. Samuel Hopkins*, 90. The composer of *Crooked Shanks* was listed only as "Gardner," but historians have speculated that this was Newport Gardner. See Eileen Southern, *The Music of Black Americans* (New York: Norton, 1997), 69-70; Andrews, "Crossings of Occramar Marycoo," 108.

61. Edwards, "Crossings of Occramar Marycoo," 107, 117.

churches."[62] The fact that Gardner mentioned Osborn so many years after her death (and immediately before embarking on his mission to Africa) suggests that she held an important place in his memory.

Gardner's conversion to evangelical Christianity seems to have given him both comfort and a sense of religious purpose. On one hand, the evangelical emphasis on original sin may have heightened his sense of shame, adding to the degradation he may have already felt at being enslaved. Yet, on the other hand, evangelicals also gave him a powerful vocabulary to criticize white slaveholders and to make sense of his suffering. When evangelicals described the world as a fallen, broken place in which humans selfishly pursued their own interests, Gardner knew exactly what they meant. And when they insisted that a sovereign God was in control of every moment of his existence, he dared to hope that his life meant more than his enslavement. In a letter that he wrote to a niece after the death of his wife and grandson, he expressed his faith that God knew what was best for him. "Thou merciful Jesus, thou compassionate savior," he testified, "I dare not to find fault with thy dealing with me, or dare to dispute thy will."[63]

Although Gardner was poor, uneducated, and a slave, he shared the evangelical faith that Christianity was "experimental," and he claimed that his personal experience of divine grace had transformed him into one of God's chosen. Even though the evangelical movement began as a defense of Christian orthodoxy, it always had a potentially radical edge, and Gardner became convinced that God had called him to become a spiritual leader of his people, perhaps even as a missionary to Africa. In 1791 he won Newport's lottery, an event that he saw as providential, and he used the money to help buy his freedom as well as the freedom of his wife and several of his children.[64] By working as a singing teacher, a

62. Letter from Occramar Marycoo (Newport Gardner) to Samuel Vinson, January 2, 1826, Vault A, Box 106, Folder 13, Newport Historical Society.

63. Letter from Newport Gardner to Sarah Burk, October 16, 1821, Newport Historical Society.

64. There are conflicting reports of how Gardner gained his freedom. In a letter to Levi Hart dated April 27, 1791, Samuel Hopkins claimed that Gardner won the lottery, which was not enough money to buy himself, his wife, and his children. After he prayed and fasted for a day, Caleb Gardner summoned him to announce that he and his family would be free, "adding some conditions which could be easily complied with." See Samuel Hopkins to Levi Hart, April 27, 1791, reprinted in *Works of Samuel Hopkins*, ed. Edwards Amasa Park (Boston: Doctrinal Tract and Book Society, 1854), 1:155. But in a letter to Levi Hart dated June 10, 1791, Hopkins claimed that Caleb Gardner agreed to

blacksmith, and a shoe shiner, he was able to buy his own house, and he helped to found the Free African Union Society in 1784, an organization that was dedicated to black uplift.[65] In 1808 he opened a free school for African children, and in 1824 he helped to organize the Colored Union Church, Newport's first black church.[66]

At the age of eighty, soon after his wife's death, Gardner felt a strong call to return to Africa, where he hoped to preach the gospel and to prepare a refuge for former slaves. Frustrated by the discrimination that blacks faced in America, he wanted them to have their own nation. Before his departure, the Park Street Church of Boston ordained him and Salmar Nubia, another former slave who had probably attended Osborn's meetings, to be the deacons of the church that they hoped to found in Liberia.[67] As part of the celebration, the Reverend Sereno Dwight (a grandson of the famous revivalist Jonathan Edwards) preached a sermon on Psalm 68:31: "Ethiopia shall stretch forth her hands to God."[68]

In January of 1826 Gardner boarded a ship to Liberia with thirty-five other Africans, including one of his sons, reversing the brutal journey he

free Newport Gardner only if he lived with him another two years and paid him three dollars per month. Samuel Hopkins to Levi Hart, June 10, 1791, reprinted in *Works of Samuel Hopkins*, ed. Park, 1:136. There are also conflicting reports of the number of Gardner's children. Akeia A. F. Benard lists four; see "The Free African American Cultural Landscape: Newport, R.I., 1774-1826" (PhD diss., University of Connecticut, 2008), 197. In contrast, Edward E. Andrews suggests that he had a dozen or more; see "Crossings of Occramar Marycoo," 102.

65. On Gardner's house, see Richard C. Youngken, *African Americans in Newport: An Introduction to the Heritage of African Americans in Newport, Rhode Island, 1700-1945* (Providence: Rhode Island Historical Preservation and Heritage Commission and Black Heritage Society, 1995), 49. On the Free African Union Society, see William Henry Robinson, ed., *The Proceedings of the Free African Union Society and the African Benevolent Society, Newport, Rhode Island, 1780-1824* (Providence: Urban League of Rhode Island, 1976).

66. On Gardner's school, see the ad in the *Newport Mercury*, March 26, 1808: "The African Benevolent Society of Newport announces that they have opened a school, kept by Newport Gardner 8 School Street, the object of which is the free instruction of all the coloured people in this town, who are inclined to attend. As the plan of this School is approved by many judicious persons, it is hoped that white people as well as coloured will encourage the attendance of the Africans under their care who need instruction."

67. On Salmar Nubia, see *Memoir of the Life and Character of Samuel Hopkins*, ed. Park, 135-36, 154-56.

68. *Boston Recorder and Telegraph*, December 30, 1825; Andrews, "Crossings of Occramar Marycoo," 120.

had made sixty-six years earlier. "I go to set an example to the youth of my race," he testified. "I go to encourage the young. They can never be elevated here. I have tried for sixty years—it is vain."[69] Sadly, both he and his son died of a fever within two weeks of their arrival.[70]

Before leaving for Liberia, Gardner published one of his songs, "Promise Anthem," which he had composed for the service at the Park Street Church. Quoting from the book of Jeremiah and the Gospels of Matthew and Mark, he affirmed two of his strongest convictions as an evangelical Christian: God was in control of everything that happened in the world, even things that appeared evil; and genuine faith was more important than distinctions of race, sex, or social status.

In the first part of the song, based on Jeremiah 30, he remembered that the Israelites had been enslaved in Egypt, and yet a loving God had promised to lead them to freedom:

The word that came to Jeremiah from the Lord, saying:
Write thou all the words which I have spoken unto thee in a book.
For lo! The days come, saith the Lord, that I will bring again the cap-
tivity of my people Israel and Judah, saith the Lord;
And I will cause them to return to the land that I gave to their fathers,
and they shall possess it.
Therefore, fear thou not, O my servant Jacob, saith the Lord; neither
be dismayed, O Israel.
For lo! I will save thee from afar, and thy seed from their captivity,
And Jacob shall return and be in rest and quiet, and none shall make
him afraid. Amen.

69. Mason, *Reminiscences of Newport*, 159. Historians disagree over the number of Africans who traveled to Liberia with Occramar Marycoo. Benard states that there were twenty-nine emigrants. See "Free African American Cultural Landscape," 197. Ralph Luker claims there were thirty-six total. See "Under Our Own Vine and Fig Tree': From African Unionism to Black Denominationalism in Newport, Rhode Island, 1760–1876," *Slavery and Abolition* 12, no. 2 (1991): 24, I have used Luker's figure because it accords with contemporary newspaper accounts. According to the *Newport Mercury*, January 14, 1826: "36 colored people sailed from Boston on Wednesday last, accompanied by Rev. Mr. Sessions, agent of the Colonization Society and Rev. Mr. Holton."

70. *The Rhode Island Republican* of June 15, 1826, printed a letter from one of Newport's black emigrants to Liberia. The letter reported that several emigrants had died within two weeks of arrival, including Newport Gardner and Ahama Gardner. They were stricken with "the fever common to the climate."

Like many other slaves, Gardner was drawn to the story of the captive Israelites because it spoke to his own experience. Africans, too, had been torn from their land and taken captive, and they longed for a Moses to set them free. The words of Jeremiah gave them hope that someday they would reach the promised land, a place where they could live without fear.

In the second part of the song, Gardner remembered the story of the woman of Canaan who had begged Jesus to save her child. (This was one of Sarah Osborn's favorite biblical stories as well.)[71] At first Jesus had refused, saying, "it is not meet to take the children's bread and cast it to the dogs," but he relented when the woman pleaded, "Truth, Lord, yet the dogs eat the crumbs that fall from the master's table" (Matt. 15:26-27; Mark 7:27-28). Not only did Jesus praise her for having such great faith, but he healed her child:

> Hear the words of the Lord, O ye African race; hear the words of promise.
> But it is not meet to take the children's bread and cast it to the dogs.
> Truth, Lord, yet the dogs eat the crumbs that fall from the master's table.
> O, African, trust in the Lord. Amen.
> Hallelujah. Praise the Lord. Praise ye the Lord. Hallelujah. Amen.[72]

Comparing Africans to the Canaanite woman, Gardner rejoiced that Jesus would redeem even the lowliest and most humble if they cried out for salvation. All souls were equal before God.

If we could travel back in time to ask Newport Gardner about the origins of the evangelical movement and the reasons for its popularity, he almost certainly would not mention its resistance to Enlightenment ideas about innate human goodness, the value of everyday life, and the pursuit of happiness. Nor would he mention the many ways in which the nascent evangelical movement drew on an Enlightenment language of experience, individualism, religious tolerance, and humanitarianism. Without the benefit of historical distance, he would not have recognized

71. See Osborn, Memoir, Beinecke Library; Hopkins, *Memoirs of the Life of Mrs. Sarah Osborn*, 67.
72. The text of this hymn is reprinted in Ferguson, *Memoir of the Life and Character of Rev. Samuel Hopkins*, 186; and *Boston Recorder and Telegraph*, December 30, 1825.

that evangelical Christianity grew and flourished in conversation with Enlightenment ideas.

Yet Gardner, like Sarah Osborn and Samuel Davies, would probably tell us something just as important. He had become a part of the evangelical movement because it answered his deepest questions about the meaning of human life and the nature of God, and, most of all, because it offered him hope. He was certain that his "experimental" faith would lead him to redemption. The evangelical movement has endured for more than three centuries because of its simple yet powerful message of hope and transformation. As Gardner expressed it in his "Promise Anthem," to be born again was to transcend fear, to trust in the future, and to believe in a promised land.

CHAPTER 3

Disestablishment as American Sisyphus

Jon Butler

In December 2014 the *New York Times* published a short Civil War essay by Joseph S. Moore entitled "Lincoln, God, and the Constitution." Moore told a largely forgotten story about Abraham Lincoln's several meetings with Scottish "Covenanters," an American Presbyterian group that "believed the Constitution contained two crippling moral flaws: its protection of slavery, and its failure to acknowledge God's authority." Covenanter clergy demanded both and visited Lincoln several times. No one knows if the conversations helped move Lincoln toward emancipation, but they might momentarily have moved him toward recognizing God in the Constitution. Navy Secretary Gideon Welles recorded in his diary for December 3, 1864, that Lincoln, "having been urged by certain religionists," proposed "an Amendment to the Constitution recognizing the Deity" in his proposed state of the union address. But since it "met with no favorable response from any one member of the Cabinet," Welles wrote that Lincoln "expressed his own doubts in regard to it," and the proposition disappeared, all but unnoticed.[1]

Lincoln's aborted 1864 proposal and the *New York Times* account in 2014 illustrate disestablishment's persistent intensity as the most transformative, yet ultimately Sisyphean, event in the history of religion in the United States. No other turning point has proven so consequential

---

1. Joseph S. Moore, "Lincoln, God, and the Constitution," *New York Times*, December 4, 2014; *Diary of Gideon Welles, Secretary of the Navy under Lincoln and Johnson*, 3 vols. (New York: Houghton Mifflin, 1911), 2:190.

for so many aspects of American religion, and no other development has generated such long-lasting tussles about its meaning.

The now-classic view of disestablishment is straightforward and important. The freedom that disestablishment provided stimulated enormous religious creativity in America, especially in the nineteenth century, a freedom whose impact on Protestants Mark Noll especially has elucidated through much of his career.[2] But disestablishment also roiled nineteenth- and twentieth-century American culture and politics and does so now well into the twenty-first century, a tumult caught in the bitterly argued opinions handed down in the 2014 US Supreme Court case, *Burwell v. Hobby Lobby*.

Little wonder that American parents have long cautioned adolescents when visiting relatives, "Don't bring up religion and politics." Disestablishment raised anxieties about religion and society in America as much as it eased them. Almost ironically and certainly without intention, disestablishment brought on two centuries of Sisyphean struggle about its meaning and extent, disestablishment's boulder pushed up and down our national hill with no end in sight. In this American parallel to the Greek myth of Sisyphus, no solution agreeable to everyone ever appears, and every advance by one side only produces anger on the other, all the more because everyone stands on principle.

Peculiarly, the religious toleration that stands so close to disestablishment emerged erratically and not always on principle. Seventeenth-century Dutch authorities "connived" to allow Lutherans, Catholics, and Jews to live and worship in the Netherlands but restricted some liberties and privileged Dutch Reformed Protestants. England's 1689 Act of Toleration permitted dissenting Protestants to worship, but only if they upheld the Trinity, rejected transubstantiation, registered their churches, and did not worship in homes. The Act rejected toleration for Catholics and did not mention Jews, and a Jewish Naturalization Act passed in 1753 was repealed in 1754. In England's mainland American colonies, the 1649 Maryland Act concerning Religion, the 1657 Flushing Remonstrance, and William Penn's promise of religious toleration in his new Pennsylvania colony in the 1680s signaled greater religious toleration in America than in England. Yet formal discrimination still limited the freedom of Catholics and Jews especially, and for a decade after 1760 previously indiffer-

---

2. This is most obvious in Noll's *America's God: From Jonathan Edwards to Abraham Lincoln* (New York: Oxford University Press, 2002), which is discussed below.

ent Virginia authorities harassed Baptists with whippings and jailing to protect the colony's Church of England establishment.[3]

Many histories, old and new, infer that disestablishment emerged from the colonies' "de facto" religious toleration. By the 1770s Britain's mainland colonies housed an amazing number of religious groups—the Church of England, Baptists, Congregationalists, Presbyterians, Quakers, French Protestants, Sephardic and Ashkenazi Jews, Dutch Reformed, German Lutherans, German Reformed, Seventh Day Baptists, Moravians, Mennonites, plus seemingly exotic Swedenborgians and the home-grown Rogerenes of eastern Connecticut and Rhode Island. They quietly enhanced public willingness to allow a wide variety of religious worship, practices, and opinions in the colonies, at least among its European immigrants. Certainly, no European nation encompassed the religious diversity of the new United States.[4]

But two powerful exceptions demonstrated the limits of the colonies' toleration: Native Americans and enslaved Africans. Colonists "tolerated" Native American religious practices largely because suppressing them could bring Native American attacks. Only a few, such as Thomas Jefferson, found them curious enough to warrant study, and missionaries who did, such as David Brainerd in New Jersey and Moravians in western Massachusetts, tracked them to aid Christian conversion. Slaveholders freely suppressed traditional African religious practices, castigated African "paganism" in word and deed, and feared both traditional African ceremonies and independent African Christian worship because their resulting group cohesion could foster revolt.[5]

3. The literature on disestablishment and the history of religious toleration and freedom is enormous. Books to begin exploring each of these topics might include *Calvinism and Religious Toleration in the Dutch Golden Age: From "Case" to "Model,"* ed. R. Po-Chia Hsia and Henk Van Nierop (New York: Cambridge University Press, 2002); Steven C. A. Pincus, *1688: The First Modern Revolution* (New Haven: Yale University Press, 2009); William R. Hutchison, *Religious Pluralism in America: The Contentious History of a Founding Ideal* (New Haven: Yale University Press, 2003); Rhys Isaac, *The Transformation of Virginia, 1740-1790* (Chapel Hill: University of North Carolina Press, 1982).

4. Jon Butler, "Church Formation in Colonial America: Era of Expansion, 1680-1770," in *Mapping America's Past: A Historical Atlas*, ed. Mark C. Carnes and John A. Garraty (New York: Henry Holt, 1996), 46-47; Hannah Adams and Thomas Prentiss, *An Alphabetical Compendium of the Various Sects which Have Appeared in the World from the Beginning of the Christian Era to the Present Day* (Boston: B. Edes & Sons, 1784).

5. Thomas Jefferson, "Notes on the State of Virginia," in *Thomas Jefferson Writings*, ed. Merrill D. Peterson (New York: Library of America, 1984), Query 11, 218-32; Ra-

Still, the colonies' spiritual and ritual cacophony brought European settlers and political leaders face-to-face with the breadth and ubiquity of human religious practice. Thus, it is remarkable how a concern for "religion" broadly rather than a narrower Christian toleration emerged as victorious revolutionaries turned to governance and the realities of the new nation's uneven religious landscape. Both Virginia's 1786 Statute for Religious Freedom, based on Thomas Jefferson's 1777 proposal, and the sixteen words that opened the First Amendment to the Federal Constitution ratified by 1791 focused on the term "religion," not on churches, Christianity, institutions, or groups. Similarly, the opening words of the First Amendment—"Congress shall make no law respecting an establishment of religion, or prohibiting the free exercise thereof"—employ the term "religion," as though the new Americans knew its broad meaning. Moreover, neither the First Amendment nor even the 727-word Virginia Statute defines "religion." However, the Statute does employ words and phrases that inferred the subject broadly, such as "Almighty God," "sinful," "pastor," "righteousness," "principles," "judgment," "worship," "opinions," "belief," and, of course, "religion" and "religious," which appear five times in the Statute, including its title. Taken together or singly, the words infer an eighteenth-century sense of the divine, of forces beyond nature, and, therefore, a basis—some believed *the* basis—for right and wrong and ethical and moral behavior in society as well as individuals.[6]

Perhaps some had read Hannah Adams's 1784 *Alphabetical Compendium of the Various Sects which Have Appeared in the World from the Beginning of the Christian Era to the Present Day*. Assembled by an otherwise unknown New England woman, it was the first American book to describe the seemingly endless varieties of religion in the world and the new United States. Adams hardly was original. She cribbed many entries from European books

---

chel M. Wheeler, *To Live upon Hope: Mohicans and Missionaries in the Eighteenth-Century Northeast* (Ithaca: Cornell University Press, 2008); Richard W. Pointer, "'Poor Indians' and the 'Poor in Spirit': The Indian Impact on David Brainerd," *New England Quarterly* 67, no. 3 (1984): 403-26; Jon Butler, *Awash in a Sea of Faith: Christianizing the American People* (Cambridge, MA: Harvard University Press, 1990), 129-63.

6. The text of Virginia's Act for Religious Freedom is available many places. Jefferson's original bill, from which about seventy words were deleted during the legislative discussion, is found in an annotated version on the National Archives website: "A Bill for Establishing Religious Freedom" (June 18, 1779), http://founders.archives.gov/documents/Jefferson/01-02-02-0132-0004-0082.

about religions across the globe, scorned most, and defended Christianity. Significantly, however, she substituted the word "Religions" for the more pejorative "Sects" in the titles of new 1791 and 1801 editions, and despite Adams's editorializing, the books gave American readers an unprecedented education in the breadth of religion as a phenomenon, elements of which already were dramatically visible in the new nation.[7]

Not surprisingly then, amid a world and nation overflowing with religions, disestablishment did far more than merely end varied forms of government support for the Church of England in New York and the southern colonies and for Congregational churches in Massachusetts and Connecticut. Disestablishment's far more important consequence scarcely could have been more significant. It opened the whole notion of "religion" broadly to public speculation without government oversight. Americans have run with it, and away from it, ever since.

The easy part occurred after one major contest. Before disestablishing the Church of England, the Virginia Burgesses first considered Patrick Henry's bill to create a multiple establishment that would tax citizens to support "teachers of the Christian religion," meaning many Protestant groups, including the Church of England, but not Catholics. George Washington initially seemed favorable, like many others. But Washington backtracked when opposition led by Baptists became so pronounced that he feared that the whole debate would "rankle and convulse the state." The Burgesses tabled Henry's bill and, led by Madison, adopted Jefferson's Statute on Religious Freedom, which forbade government coercion and tax support for any religion, arguing that "truth is great, and will prevail if left to herself." Congressional discussion of what became the First Amendment proved simpler, although that conclusion is somewhat deceptive because the congressional records are incomplete and sometimes inaccurate, and the state ratification debates produced no legislative records and no significant public discussion. Outside Virginia, then, the revolutionary abandonment of government-sanctioned Christianity remains remarkable yet mysterious.[8]

7. James Turner, *Religion Enters the Academy: The Origins of the Scholarly Study of Religion in America* (Athens: University of Georgia Press, 2011), 24-31, Adams quotation on 27; Thomas A. Tweed, "An American Pioneer in the Study of Religion: Hannah Adams (1755-1831) and Her 'Dictionary of All Religions,'" *Journal of the American Academy of Religion* 60, no. 3 (Autumn 1992): 437-64.

8. Leonard W. Levy, *The Establishment Clause: Religion and the First Amendment* (New York: Macmillan, 1986), 257-59.

David Sehat argues that the First Amendment's wording was so "totally unclear" that it created "a symbolic moment of little import." An opposite view seems more persuasive. The First Amendment said what it meant and meant what it said. Congress could not legislate "an establishment of religion," a broad prohibition, not merely prevented from "establishing any Religious Sect or Society," wording the Senate had rejected. Nor could Congress prohibit the "free exercise thereof," meaning the free exercise of religion broadly, not merely the free exercise of Christianity.[9]

Inadequate wording cannot account for the subsequent controversies over the meaning of disestablishment and the First Amendment. Adopting a lengthier statement as in the Virginia Statute scarcely would have prevented debate about its meaning. The multiple books of the Hebrew Bible and New Testament have never prevented debate about their meaning, no more than the Book of Mormon, with all its new words, turned traditional Protestants away from denominational squabbling, as Joseph Smith had hoped.[10]

Rather, the debate over disestablishment stemmed directly from a radicalism far beyond the mere question of government and churches. Through the First Amendment, a brash new nation turned religion questions previously shepherded by central governments over to the public without stipulations and without even defining religion. This had never occurred in the West since Roman authorities began discouraging and then banning other religions after Constantine's recognition of Christianity in the fourth century. Most European nations still maintain Christian church establishments even if they now tolerate a wide range of religions, although Scientology has a precarious status in Germany and France bans the burqa, the Muslim full-body covering for women.

The First Amendment applied only to the new federal government and could not require the end of formally established churches in the states. But six of the nine states with colonial establishments ended theirs by 1786, with Connecticut, New Hampshire, and Massachusetts

9. David Sehat, *The Myth of American Religious Freedom* (New York: Oxford University Press, 2011), 48–49; quotation from US Senate debate, September 3, 1789, in John Wilson and Donald Drakeman, *Church and State in American History*, 2nd ed. (Boston: Beacon, 1987), 77.

10. Joseph Smith's hopes and expectations for the Book of Mormon are discussed at many places in Richard L. Bushman, *Joseph Smith: Rough Stone Rolling* (New York: Alfred A. Knopf, 2005).

holding out until 1818, 1819, and 1833 respectively, and none of them replicated the Virginia debate about possible tax support for multiple Christian groups. The far deeper and ultimately more divisive question involved the broader meaning of disestablishment embodied in the First Amendment. What should be meant by forbidding "an establishment of religion" and by protecting religion's "free exercise"? These deceptively simple phrases brought division and argument first in the nineteenth century, then perhaps surprisingly and at least as deeply and bitterly in the twentieth and twenty-first centuries, demonstrating the visceral force with which something as seemingly uncontroversial as religious disestablishment became and remains a turning point in America history.

The debate emerged not long into the nineteenth century. David Sehat's *Myth of Religious Freedom* explores the numerous ways in which the states restricted religious freedom throughout the nineteenth century. They legislated Protestant standards on blasphemy and prosecuted free thinkers, patterns perfected in the 1920 Prohibition Amendment banning the manufacture and sale of "intoxicating liquors" in the United States. Federal legal cases exploded from the 1940s forward, most obviously in *West Virginia State Board of Education v. Barnette* (1943), which exempted Jehovah's Witness children from saluting the flag in schools, then in *Engel v. Vitale* (1962) and *Abington School District v. Schempp* (1963), which banned public school prayer and Bible reading. In 1990 the legal scholar and sometime federal judge Michael McConnell argued that overemphasis on the separation of church and state violated any reasonable reading of the free exercise clause. In 2002 Philip Hamburger argued that the First Amendment had been a stalking horse for anti-Catholic legislation and public bigotry. In 2005 Winnifred Sullivan argued that the very nature and sprawl of the subject made the concept of religious freedom impossible in any setting.[11]

The debates are not without their depth and ironies. Jefferson's famous phrase in his Danbury Baptist Association letter of 1802, "building a wall of separation between Church & State," actually narrowed the meaning and, certainly, the words of the First Amendment, which refer-

---

11. Michael W. McConnell, "The Origins and Historical Understanding of Free Exercise of Religion," *Harvard Law Review* 103 (1990): 1409-1517; Philip Hamburger, *Separation of Church and State* (Cambridge, MA: Harvard University Press, 2002); Winnifred Fallers Sullivan, *The Impossibility of Religious Freedom* (Princeton: Princeton University Press, 2005); David Sehat, *The Myth of American Religious Freedom* (New York: Oxford University Press, 2011).

enced religion, not "church." Hamburger's account of the anti-Catholic First Amendment bypasses broad philosophical support for disestablishment far outside nineteenth-century American anti-Catholic prejudice. Sehat's historical argument about the myth of American religious freedom turns historical hypocrisies into political generalizations that miss the power of the mere notion of religious freedom to shape American history broadly and individual lives personally. Sullivan's emphasis on the impossibility of religious freedom and the frequent futility of the First Amendment takes root in a perfectionism that would doom the practical application of almost any broad concept, starting with the idea of freedom itself.

Not surprisingly, the contemporary turmoil around disestablishment and "free exercise" stands at the heart of two modern issues: faith healing and clerical sex abuse. Although at least 170 children died after parents followed a faith-healing regimen between 1975 and 1995, religious parents prosecuted for neglect have been punished far less severely than neglectful parents who did not offer religious defenses of their behavior. In 2011 Oregon passed a law eliminating faith healing as a defense for homicide and established mandatory sentencing guidelines for child deaths. But most states have been cautious in limiting that right. New York City health officials have struggled with some Orthodox rabbis over health risks in circumcisions performed by mohels who suck blood from the infant's wound. City health officials have proposed requiring parental consent forms acknowledging health risks in such circumcisions because they can cause and have caused herpes. But rabbis have argued strenuously that the forms would intrude on "freedom of religion and speech." Lawyers defending several Catholic archdioceses have argued that criminal charges against priests accused of sex abuse intrude on the Church's religious freedom, succeeding in a Missouri case with arguments that inquiries about priests' behavior ventured improperly into religious doctrine and, therefore, violated the First Amendment's free exercise clause.[12]

12. Rebecca Williams, "Faith Healing Exceptions versus *Parens Patriae*: Something's Gotta Give," *First Amendment Law Review* 10 (Spring 2012): 692-730; Ashley Luthern, "High Court Upholds Convictions of 2 Who Let Daughter Die as They Prayed," *Milwaukee Journal Sentinel*, July 3, 2013; Shawn Francis Peters, *When Prayer Fails: Faith Healing, Children, and the Law* (New York: Oxford University Press, 2008); Harper S. Seldin, "Circumcision, Child Fatalities, and Constitutional Free Exercise in New York," *Journal of Law and Social Deviance* 6 (2013): 99-153; Sharon Otterman, "Consent Rule

It could be argued that more recent struggles to protect religious freedom have been waged to delay or disrupt secularization. The 2010 sociological and historical study by Robert Putnam and David Campbell, *American Grace: How Religion Unites and Divides Us*, offered real evidence that "nones"—people of no religious inclinations—were rising faster than all other groups measured in American religious surveys. Of course, the reputed rise of nonbelievers has been noted, feared, and denounced by American Protestant leaders especially from Increase and Cotton Mather to Billy Graham. But substantial historical evidence demonstrates that adult engagement with organized religion moved past the 50 percent mark only after World War II, shifting recently through declines in mainstream Christianity and contradictory rises among evangelicals and young Americans without religious inclinations. Finding a clear link between Americans' surprisingly uneven religious attachments and the nation's struggles with disestablishment comes close to the definition of a fool's errand. Still, if the new republic's religious complexity precluded considering a national church establishment in the 1780s, America's explosive religious creativity in the next two American centuries only raised the stakes on disestablishment.[13]

Few books have documented disestablishment's pre–Civil War explosiveness more grandly than Noll's *America's God*, and especially its implications for Protestant evangelicalism. Noll treats Jonathan Edwards as American Protestantism's premiere intellectual for all centuries. But Noll also luxuriates in thousands of Protestant clergy, laymen, and laywomen, mostly white, some black, who devoted their lifetimes to bringing the new nation to Christ in the wake of disestablishment. As the federal government and the states moved away from formal religious ties, the nation's Protestant groups scrambled to make their place. The

---

May Proceed for a Circumcision Ritual," *New York Times*, January 20, 2013. I wish to acknowledge the gracious assistance of Mary Anderlik Majumder of Baylor University with the literature on legal cases involving faith healing.

13. Robert D. Putnam and David E. Campbell, *American Grace: How Religion Divides and Unites Us* (New York: Simon & Schuster, 2010), 91-133; Wilson N. Brissett, "Puritans and Revolution: Remembering the Origin; Religion and Social Critique in Early New England," in *Prophesies of Godlessness: Predictions of America's Imminent Secularization, from the Puritans to the Present Day*, ed. Charles Mathewes and Christopher McKnight Nichols (New York: Oxford University Press, 2008), 21-34; Roger Finke and Rodney Stark, *The Churching of America, 1776-1990: Winners and Losers in Our Religious Economy* (New Brunswick, NJ: Rutgers University Press, 1992).

old Church of England renamed itself the Episcopal Church. Britain's Tory-supporting Methodists returned with a gospel of free will and salvation for all who accepted Christ. Presbyterians and Baptists used their denominations to organize new congregations in a quickly growing nation. But Methodists emerged as the nation's most vibrant spiritual organizers, becoming the largest American denomination by 1830. Moreover, Noll stresses the Americanization of Europe's religious groups operating in the new United States. They began speaking in distinctive New World voices that appealed to New World peoples of incredible variety and interest, including freed and enslaved Africans for whom the gospel meant more than spiritual liberation.[14]

Disestablishment also spurred religions far beyond traditional Protestant bounds. I have argued elsewhere that early-nineteenth-century America became a "spiritual hothouse" seen nowhere else. Immigration only raised its temperature. German Jews accustomed to tight ghettos and political and cultural repression and Irish and German Catholics accustomed to a politically powerful church in markedly different European nations dramatically spread themselves out among the American populace. Americans, unguided by government, imbibed dreams, ecstatic visions, revelations, and fortune-telling to foster new groups, such as Shakers, Mesmerists, Swedenborgians, Mormons, Adventists, and Spiritualists, among others. Protestant women began preaching, some becoming famous, and not only white women such as Jemima Wilkinson, Salome Lincoln, and Harriett Livermore, but black women such as Jarena Lee, Maria Stewart, and Sojourner Truth. Prophets appeared in New York City and upstate New York—Robert Mathews, the Prophet Matthias, and Joseph Smith. Protestants also divided. Followers of Barton Stone and Thomas and Alexander Campbell stressed restoration of ancient Christianity in a movement known variously as the Stone Movement, the Campbellite Movement, and the Disciples of Christ. Dissident Methodists objected to the denomination's hierarchical episcopal structure and formed the Methodist Protestant Church in 1828 to effect congregational governance. Mormons divided after Joseph Smith's assassination in 1844. Most followed Brigham Young to Utah while others divided into several different groups in Illinois and Missouri. "American" Bibles flooded the nation, ranging from newly annotated King James versions to new or at least "corrected" transla-

14. Noll, *America's God*, 177, 227-364.

tions, some, like Joseph Smith's "Inspired Version," prepared from new revelations.[15]

Perhaps inevitably, the early national and antebellum explosion of religious activity and success furthered disestablishment's Sisyphean struggles. Protestants simply found it difficult to let government proceed without acknowledging—establishing—Protestant Christianity's presence and power in laws and governmental institutions. Some constituent Protestant parts of this impulse emerge in Noll's *America's God*. Many patriots linked Revolutionary republicanism directly to Christianity. Thomas Payne littered *Common Sense* with biblical citations and anti-monarchical biblical stories despite his personal doubts about Christianity. The Pennsylvania Presbyterian Robert Smith linked the "cause of America" to the "cause of Christ," and clergy popularized Christianity to create a moral foundation for the republic. Not all historians would agree with Noll that "by the early nineteenth century, [Protestant] evangelicalism was the unofficially established religion in a nation that had forsworn religious establishments." But Protestant evangelicals clearly aspired to establishment, informal if necessary.[16]

It is here that historian David Sehat has found the origins of "the myth of American religious freedom." Public officials, most of them church members, could not help but chip away at disestablishment. Sehat describes how the 1790 Pennsylvania constitution no longer referenced Christianity in oaths for office holders but required that they "acknowledge 'the being of a God and a future state of rewards and punishments.'" Delaware's 1792 constitution did not require church attendance but insisted that public worship "of the Author of the universe" remained a duty because it "promoted the 'piety and morality, on which the prosperity of communities depends.'" More than chipping occurred. "Moral reform" became American Protestantism's principal public cause in the early republic and antebellum eras, ranging from temperance and education to women's rights and abolition. Blasphemy could be prosecuted

15. Butler, *Awash in a Sea of Faith*, 225-56, 269; Jay P. Dolan, *The American Catholic Experience: A History from Colonial Times to the Present* (Garden City, NY: Doubleday, 1985), 101-57; Jonathan D. Sarna, *American Judaism: A History* (New Haven: Yale University Press, 2004), 31-134; Catherine A. Brekus, *Strangers and Pilgrims: Female Preaching in America, 1740-1845* (Chapel Hill: University of North Carolina Press, 1998); Paul Gutjahr, *An American Bible: A History of the Good Book in the United States, 1777-1880* (Stanford: Stanford University Press, 1999).

16. Noll, *America's God*, 83, 206-7, quotation on 208.

in New York even without a blasphemy statute. As James Kent, the state's chief justice, put it, religion provided "the best sanctions of moral and social obligation," Americans being "a Christian people." The US Supreme Court's devastating 1857 *Dred Scott* decision held that enslaved Africans were simple property outside the "family of nations," an argument common in Christian pro-slavery literature.[17]

The rise of German and Irish Catholic immigration further strained Protestant commitments to disestablishment. The New York City Common Council cited the principle of separating church and state when it refused funds for Catholic schools in 1840 even as it continued to fund the Public School Society whose schools required reading the King James Bible. Protestant Know-Nothings of the 1850s denied that the First Amendment meant unfettered Catholic worship and sought to restrict Catholic immigration and the property rights of Catholic bishops. The "Blain Amendment" offered in 1875 by the presidential candidate James G. Blain would have required that both state and federal public funds "never be under the control of any religious sect," the amendment widely viewed as an instrument to prevent the Catholic Church from ever receiving public funds for any purpose.[18]

President Grant's euphemistically named 1869 "Peace Policy" pushed the boulder of disestablishment farther down the hill for Native Americans already segregated to newly created reservations. The Peace Policy outlawed traditional Native American religious practices and assigned seventy-three reservations to the exclusive spiritual care of twelve different Protestant groups, plus Catholics. Churches actually objected even before the plan had been implemented, not to suppressing traditional Native American practices, but to removing missionaries who had previously ministered on reservations that now had been assigned to other groups. Thus, Oregon's Catholic clergy protested in 1874, without irony, that Native Americans had a "right to choose whatever Christian belief they wish, without interference from the Government," and in 1881 the Board of Indian Commissioners allowed missions that predated the Peace Policy to remain on reservations assigned to other groups. But the ban on traditional Native American religious practices drove them underground through 1934, when John Collier, the new Commissioner of

17. Sehat, *Myth of American Religious Freedom*, 54, 60–61, 84.
18. Hamburger, *Separation of Church and State*, 218–19, 221–25; Sehat, *Myth of American Religious Freedom*, 162–65, quotation from Blain Amendment, 163.

Indian Affairs, opened reservations to all religions, including the Native Americans' own traditional religions.[19]

Missionaries might accept Christian pluralism for themselves, but they were aghast that Collier's disestablishment meant freedom for Native American religions. An article in the liberal *Christian Century*, "Does Uncle Sam Foster Paganism," by one former missionary to the Native Americans complained that Collier now allowed "medicine men and shamans," not the "sacred books" and "formal theology" of true religion, meaning Christianity. Collier demurred. Grant's Peace Plan had been adopted with "no sophisticated debate concerning religious liberty or other constitutional rights," and Native Americans had never been "allowed the protection of the Constitution."[20]

The missionaries' upset illustrated disestablishment's Sisyphean struggle. Disestablishment offered all religious groups opportunities to create their own foundations for success apart from government, especially traditionally strong Protestants, and Protestants everywhere worked assiduously to perfect voluntary institutional structures for effective proselytizing in a dynamic nineteenth-century nation. They succeeded. Protestant membership, congregations, and interdenominational organizations expanded before the Civil War and after, and did so across every region. Catholics prospered as well, even if church authorities found religion without state support uncomfortably outside Catholic tradition. Jews found in American disestablishment an unprecedented haven from diasporic tribulations and European discrimination.

But the dramatic post-1880 increase in Catholic and Jewish immigration, plus the Protestant sense of power deriving from their own nineteenth-century success, turned Protestants toward new, not so elusive, forms of Protestant establishment. Protestant reformers such as Josiah Strong sought to push disestablishment back down the hill, using social, cultural, and political reform "to preserve republican institutions" they associated with Protestantism and to stanch the religious and cultural erosion destroying traditional Protestant America. They strove to destroy "machine" politics that thrived on immigrant recruitment, and they dras-

19. Sehat does not discuss Grant's Peace Policy; Francis P. Prucha, *American Indian Policy in Crisis: Christian Reformers and the Indian, 1865-1900* (Norman: University of Oklahoma Press, 1976), 30-71, quotation on 58.

20. Quotations from Benjamin J. Butler, "U.S. Government Suppression of Native American Religion, 1869-1934," University of Minnesota senior essay, December 1997, in possession of the author.

tically restricted southern and eastern European immigration through the 1924 Immigration Act, whose quotas remained in place until 1965. Arkansas, Florida, and Georgia passed state convent inspection laws in 1915, revived from the 1840s and 1850s, aimed at freeing nuns who might be held against their will. Discrimination against Jews in housing, employment, education, and travel increased substantially. In the name of "professionalization," New York's 1916 Strong Commission took pointed aim at Catholic orphanages staffed by nuns lacking formal social-work training, whose large-scale institutions violated the newer professional social work preference for smaller-scale "cottage model" child welfare.[21]

In contrast, mid-to-late-twentieth-century US Supreme Court cases ushered in the now seemingly classic expansion of disestablishment. Before 1940 the Court seldom dealt with religion cases, the most notable exception being the 1878 *Reynolds v. United States* decision outlawing Mormon polygamy. But two cases, *Minersville School District v. Gobitis* (1940) and *West Virginia State Board of Education v. Barnette* (1943), illustrated the continuing struggle over disestablishment. In *Gobitis* the Court held that school requirements to recite the pledge of allegiance and salute the American flag did not warrant religious exceptions because the regulations were general, promoted patriotism, and were aimed at promoting "national unity," which was "the basis of national security." Remarkably, three years later the Court reversed itself in *Barnette*, exempting Jehovah's Witness children from school flag salute ceremonies. As Robert Jackson wrote, "If there is any fixed star in our constitutional constellation, it is that no official, high or petty, can prescribe what shall be orthodox in politics, nationalism, religion, or other matters of opinion or force citizens to confess by word or act their faith therein." Ominously, however, even *Gobitis*, which upheld the flag salute ceremonies, produced over three hundred instances of mobs, beatings, and assaults of Jehovah's Witnesses as well as a castration, demonstrating that many

21. Josiah Strong, *Our Country*, ed. Jurgen Herbst (Cambridge, MA: Belknap Press of Harvard University Press, 1963), esp. 171–86, quotation on 183; Maureen Fitzgerald, *Habits of Compassion: Irish Catholic Nuns and the Origins of New York's Welfare System, 1830-1920* (Urbana: University of Illinois Press, 2006), 25–26, 214–23; "Convent Inspection in Arkansas," *Sacred Heart Review*, 1915, 3; Charles P. Sweeney, "Bigotry in the South," *Nation*, November 24, 1920, 585–86; William J. Phalen, *American Evangelical Protestantism and the European Immigrants, 1800-1924* (Jefferson, NC: McFarland, 2011), 154–92; Leonard Dinnerstein, *Antisemitism in America* (New York: Oxford University Press, 1994), 58–104.

Americans, including mainstream Protestants, were not enamored by a broad interpretation of the free exercise clause that guaranteed First Amendment rights to small Christian minorities.[22]

Robert Jackson's stars scarcely remained fixed. Strongly contradictory developments in the 1950s moved disestablishment's rock up as well as down its strenuously contested hill. On one hand, the Supreme Court moved the rock up the hill in its momentous *Engel v. Vitale* (1962) and *Abington School District v. Schempp* (1963) decisions banning prayer and Bible reading in public schools. Both Protestant and Catholic leaders attacked the decisions as secularism run amok, with virulent rhetoric that very nearly matched the physical violence that met *Gobitis*; their common attack has sometimes blurred their differences. *Engel v. Vitale* took up the establishment clause's "religion" wording most directly, arguing that the invocation of "Almighty God" in the non-denominational New York state "Regent's Prayer," which the plaintiffs had contested, constituted an establishment of religion broadly and rejected claims that the establishment clause meant only to prohibit choosing one church over another (a view William Rehnquist nonetheless put forward in a dissent to *Wallace v. Jaffree* twenty-three years later). Thomas Clark's majority opinion and William Brennan's unusually long seventy-three-page concurrence in *Abington School District v. Schempp* argued that religion's simple importance in America, rather than allowing or demanding Bible reading, instead demanded that the religious text of any one religion could not be required reading for public school students when the Constitution not only prohibited establishing religion but guaranteed freedom of worship to all.[23]

Protestant and Catholic groups defending Christianity, on the other hand, pushed disestablishment's rock back down the hill by emphasizing "God" and religion generally, although few of the same groups had supported Jehovah's Witnesses a decade earlier. Vermont's Senator Ralph Flanders proposed a Constitutional amendment in 1954 recognizing "the authority and law of Jesus Christ, Savior and Ruler of nations." But it never came to a vote, a fate that also awaited several "religious freedom

22. Sarah Barringer Gordon, *The Spirit of the Law: Religious Voices and the Constitution in Modern America* (Cambridge, MA: Harvard University Press, 2010), 24–33, 43–47, quotation from *Gobitis* on 32; *West Virginia State Board of Education v. Barnett*, 638, 642; Gregory L. Peterson et al., "Recollections on West Virginia State Board of Education v. Barnette," *St. John's Law Review* 81, no. 4 (2007): 755–96.

23. Gordon, *Spirit of the Law*, 84–92.

amendments" guaranteeing the right to pray on public property and to read the Bible in schools proposed in the wake of *Engel v. Vitale* and *Schempp*.[24]

Far more successful were broader efforts to establish the sovereignty of "God" over nation and people in the 1950s and 1960s through government-sponsored public ritual, such as the Pledge of Allegiance. Backers deftly avoided referring to Jesus, as Flanders had mistakenly done, but they clearly meant to assert the sovereignty of a Christian God, not any other. Leadership came primarily from lay figures, both men and women, and especially evangelicals. Newly elected President Dwight D. Eisenhower served as one surprising source, surprising because of Eisenhower's previous religious nonchalance. He startled many at a news conference at New York's Waldorf Astoria Hotel when he observed, "Our government has no sense unless it is founded in a deeply felt religious faith, and I don't care what it is," and he became a church member for the first time after moving into the White House. He quickly lent support to a movement to add the words "under God" to the Pledge of Allegiance, itself a late-nineteenth-century creation. When he signed the bill accomplishing this fact on Flag Day, June 14, 1954, he touted the achievement in linking God to the nation, at least for children: "From this day forward, the millions of our school children will proclaim daily in every city and town, every village and rural school house, the dedication of our nation and our people to the Almighty." This success with the Pledge had been prefaced by an earlier campaign to introduce a postage stamp emblazoned with the motto "In God We Trust," which had first been placed on currency in 1864, and in April 1954 Eisenhower introduced the stamp personally, something no president had ever done, not even the avid stamp collector Franklin D. Roosevelt.[25]

As Kevin Kruse stresses in *One Nation under God: How Corporate America Invented Christian America*, the 1950s and 1960s witnessed an extraordinary effort led by evangelical Christian business and corporate

24. "Amendment Loses in Church Council," *New York Times*, June 5, 1959; David E. Rosenbaum, "Anderson's Shift from Orthodox Conservatism: 'I Have Matured,'" *New York Times*, April 28, 1980; Katharine Q. Seelye, "Republicans in Congress Renew Push for Vote on School Prayer Amendment," *New York Times*, July 16, 1996; Eric Schmitt, "Church Leaders Split on Plan for School Prayer," *New York Times*, July 24, 1996; Seelye, "Lawmaker Proposes New Prayer Amendment," *New York Times*, March 25, 1997.

25. Kevin M. Kruse, *One Nation under God: How Corporate America Invented Christian America* (New York: Basic Books, 2015), 95–125, Eisenhower quotation on 110.

leaders to stamp a Christian identity on the nation. They represented updated versions of nineteenth-century lay Christian denominational and interdenominational efforts spawned by disestablishment. "Spiritual mobilization" linking a vague Christianity to "freedom" and anti-Communism won massive support in business and corporate communities. Congress approved a "National Day of Prayer" to be proclaimed by the president on any day except a Sunday. Billy Graham's revivals employed new techniques in organization, advertising, and public relations and shifted from hard-edged, quasi-fundamentalist rhetoric to a more broadly Protestant "conversion" language strongly linked to national identity and purpose. The first "National Prayer Breakfast" to promote "Government under God" was organized in 1953 by hotelier Conrad Hilton. Hilton commissioned a picture of a kneeling "Uncle Sam" representing a prayerful nation, and Eisenhower quickly hung it in the White House Oval Office. Groups ranging from "Project Prayer" to the "Mothers Crusade to Establish Prayers in the Public Schools" lobbied for legislation to reverse the US Supreme Court's decision in *Engel v. Vitale*. The American Advertising Council's campaign for "Religion in American Life" promoted both church and synagogue attendance. It ignored the many other religions in modern America, from traditional Native American religions to Hinduism, Buddhism, Confucianism, and Islam, but prefaced the conservative evangelical Protestants' embrace of the term "Judeo-Christian" after about 1990 as they united with theologically and politically conservative Catholics and Jews to oppose abortion.[26]

The continuing union of religion and politics in struggles about national purpose and identity pushed the Sisyphean struggle over disestablishment into the twenty-first century. In *Lynch v. Donnelly* (1984), the Court decided that the city government of Pawtucket, Rhode Island, could display at Christmas a crèche portraying the birth of Jesus. Chief Justice Warren Burger wrote that there was no evidence that "the inclusion of the creche is a purposeful or surreptitious effort to express some kind of subtle governmental advocacy of a particular religious message." The crèche was a "passive symbol," Burger wrote, an assertion he made three times in his opinion. William Brennan noted the irony of the ma-

26. Kruse, *One Nation under God*, 11–64, 203–37; Robert Wuthnow, *The Restructuring of American Religion: Society and Faith since World War II* (Princeton: Princeton University Press, 1988), 54–99; Daniel K. Williams, *God's Own Party: The Making of the Christian Right* (New York: Oxford University Press, 2010), 105–32.

jority's view in his dissent. Christians themselves, if not the Chief Justice, viewed the crèche as "a mystical re-creation of an event that lies at the heart of the Christian faith"; in viewing the crèche as a mere "passive symbol" the Court merely bowed to "the sectarian preferences of the majority at the expense of the minority." Two 2005 cases involving Ten Commandment displays on government property, *Van Orden v. Perry*, a Texas case, and *McCreary County v. ACLU of Kentucky*, brought seemingly contradictory decisions. The Court approved a forty-year-old granite Ten Commandment display at the Texas state capitol because the Commandments had "undeniable historical meaning" long recognized in many public buildings; only the dissent by John Paul Stevens mentioned the fact that the Hollywood producer Cecil B. DeMille funded the display to promote his 1956 movie, *The Ten Commandments*. But the Court rejected a Ten Commandments display in a Kentucky courthouse because local officials had planned the display so specifically to support Christianity.[27]

Two 2014 US Supreme Court decisions dramatically illustrate the anger that attended the intense pushing and shoving around the boulder of disestablishment. *Town of Greece v. Galloway* hinged on the appropriateness of offering prayers to open monthly town meetings. Anthony Kennedy's majority opinion argued that the prayers were permissible because the practice "comports with our tradition," meaning the prayer practices of Congress and state legislatures, "and does not coerce participation by nonadherents." By all accounts, the prayers were overwhelmingly Christian, non-Christians rarely being asked to speak. Kennedy's opinion stressing the "permissible ceremonial purpose" of the prayers bore an intriguing parallel to Warren Burger's argument in *Lynch v. Donnelly* that the crèche was a "passive symbol." In contrast, Elena Kagan's dissent noted that the prayers were directed to everyone attending open town meetings, not just public officials as in the case of Congress and state legislatures, and that the prayers were sometimes assertively Christian, with little effort to make them inclusive.[28]

The tensions generated in *Town of Greece v. Galloway* produced four separate opinions even in the five-member majority. Justices specified

27. *Lynch v. Donnelly*, 104 S. Ct 1355; Linda Greenhouse, "High Court Rules Cities May Put Up Nativity Displays," *New York Times*, March 6, 1984; *Van Orden v. Perry*, 545 U.S. 677; *McCreary County v. ACLU of Kentucky*, 545 U.S. 844; Greenhouse, "Justices Allow a Commandments Display, Bar Others," *New York Times*, June 27, 2005; Kruse, *One Nation under God*, 145-48.

28. *Town of Greece v. Galloway*, 572.

which parts of an opinion they were joining and which they weren't, and testiness emerged among all the justices. Kagan pointedly noted how Alito "falters in attempting to excuse the Town Board's constant sectarianism," and Alito belittled the dissenters' points as "really quite niggling." *Christianity Today* columnists split on the case, suggesting divisions among evangelicals about engaging government in prayerful moments. Steve Thorngate, writing in the liberal *Christian Century*, specifically noted the religious split among the justices, the majority opinions all by Catholics, two of the three dissenters being Jewish.[29]

Burwell v. Hobby Lobby Stores exposed an enormous gulf in twenty-first-century understandings of disestablishment. The majority opinion by Samuel Alito gave "closely held corporations" protection under the 1993 Religious Freedom Restoration Act (RFRA). It exempted Hobby Lobby Stores, owned by a Protestant evangelical family, and Conestoga Wood Specialties, owned by a Mennonite family, from providing insurance for certain kinds of birth control methods under the Affordable Care Act, by transferring the families' religious objections to the corporations, a position favored by Protestant evangelicals and the American Catholic hierarchy. The decision raised significant concerns about gender and religious tension on the Court. Three of the four justices opposing the decision were Jewish and women, and, as in *Town of Greece v. Galloway*, all five justices supporting it were Catholic and men, divisions that have brought much public speculation but no comment from the justices.[30]

A cheeky observer (Nikolai Gogol were he still alive) might wonder if the Supreme Court's five male Catholic justices had not accomplished a miracle even beyond cloning—which the Catholic Church and conservative Protestant evangelicals oppose—having turned business corporations into soulful beings eligible for the protections of the Religious Freedom Restoration Act. Ruth Bader Ginsburg did not make that claim in her edgy dissent, though she came close enough. She called *Hobby Lobby*

29. *Town of Greece v. Galloway*, 572. Ted Olson, "Why We Pray Before Public Meetings (and Let Pagans Do, Too)," *Christian Century*, May 5, 2014; Carl E. Esbeck, "Why I'm Not Cheering Today's Supreme Court Prayer Decision," *Christian Century*, May 5, 2014; Steve Thorngate, "On 'Tolerating' and Perhaps Appreciating a Ceremonial Prayer," *Christian Century*, May 13, 2014.

30. Samuel G. Freedman, "Among Justices, Considering a Divide Not of Gender or Politics, but of Beliefs," *New York Times*, July 11, 2014; Adam Liptak, "Supreme Court Rejects Contraceptives Mandate for Some Corporations; Justices Rule in Favor of Hobby Lobby," *New York Times*, June 30, 2014.

"a decision of startling breadth." Through it, "commercial enterprises including corporations, along with partnerships and sole proprietorships, can opt out of any law (saving only tax laws) they judge incompatible with their sincerely held religious beliefs." She also wrote that the decision was particularly devastating for women and that its exemptions open the gate to objections to insurance covering "blood transfusions (Jehovah's Witnesses), antidepressants (Scientologists); and medications derived from pigs, including anesthesia, intravenous fluids, and pills coated with gelatin (certain Muslims, Jews, and Hindus)."[31]

Alito's majority opinion discussed the case entirely on the basis of the RFRA statute and ignored the disestablishment and First Amendment issues that the plaintiffs themselves had raised. In contrast, Ginsburg went directly to the First Amendment. She criticized the majority for actions "approving some religious claims while deeming others unworthy of accommodation," which "could be 'perceived as favoring one religion over another,' the very risk the Establishment clause was designed to preclude." Alito took pains to deny Ginsburg's charges about the potential implications of the decision. He argued that the decision was "very specific" and would not allow corporations to avoid a wide variety of laws on religious grounds, but he described no principle on which such claims could be denied.

These most recent Supreme Court cases witnessed new strategies in pushing and shoving around the boulder of disestablishment. While the Court's 1960s decisions emphasized the First Amendment's establishment clause in eliminating public school prayers, the Court has more recently employed the free exercise clause to support majoritarian religious practices in government meetings and business employee benefits. Anthony Kennedy brushed aside residents' objections to the Christian prayers that opened town meetings in Greece, New York, writing that their "offense, however, does not equate to coercion." Similarly, in *Burwell v. Hobby Lobby Stores* Samuel Alito opined that government "can readily arrange for other methods of providing contraceptives, without cost sharing, to employees" to protect the religious consciousness newly granted to legal corporations.

Standing somewhere near disestablishment's hill in the 2010s, it is

---

31. The reference is to Nikolai Gogol's 1842 novel, *Dead Souls*; *Burwell v. Hobby Lobby*, 573 US (2014); Liptak, "Supreme Court Rejects Contraceptives Mandate for Some Corporations."

doubtful that America's struggles over disestablishment will take even a momentary rest. Irregularly yet persistently, disestablishment's Sisyphean struggles have gained strength across American history, eliciting ferocious, bitter argument among the religious, nonreligious, and indifferent and at every level of American politics and jurisprudence. Few turning points have ever been so consequential.

CHAPTER 4

Antebellum Reform

Richard Carwardine

During the closing days of 1830 a resident of Troy, New York, wrote in much excitement to his cousin. "God is in this city in very deed," he exulted. Under the "great power" of the preachers, "Christians seem to be on their faces, impenitent sinners are alarmed. Conversions occur daily." An upstate manufacturing and commercial center, Troy and its ten thousand inhabitants were in the midst of a series of protracted revival meetings whose boundless prospects thrilled this particular observer. "If the church[es] keep at their posts and watch and pray, a wonderful story will be told about this city." By contrast, he confessed to deep anxieties over the state of his own soul. "I am more than 5000 degrees behind the spirit of the time here. I feel absolutely like a lump of ice. . . . I fear I have no heart—such stupidity—such selfishness—such phlegm." He distilled his fears into two intimately related questions: "Do I really make God's glory the chief concern? Is *benevolence* the ruling passion?"[1]

The correspondent was a young man, Theodore Clark; his confidant was Theodore Dwight Weld—an evangelical convert of the era's most celebrated Presbyterian revivalist, Charles Grandison Finney—who would shortly secure national fame as an antislavery evangelist. Clark's words revealed his sense that the world stood on the verge of a new dispensation, a common conviction throughout this religiously "burned-over" terrain of western New York—and, indeed, in regions well beyond. Clark's

---

1. Gilbert H. Barnes and Dwight L. Dumond, eds., *Letters of Theodore Dwight Weld, Angelina Grimke Weld, and Sarah Grimke, 1822-1844* (Washington, DC: American Historical Association, 1934), 1:38.

concern for the supremacy of "benevolence" was an expression of an advancing theology of disinterested—that is, selfless—philanthropy. Weld himself gave memorable expression to this humanitarian sentiment when, two years later, he dedicated his life to the "*immediate universal*" abolition of slavery, saying that "as long as I am a moral agent I am fully prepared to *act out* my belief in that thus saith the Lord—'*Faith without WORKS is dead.*'"[2]

Clark's letter was in essence a tribute to the burgeoning power of evangelicalism that, during the early and middle decades of the nineteenth century, was electrified by the pulses of revivals collectively described by historians as the Second Great Awakening. The disestablishment of the churches during the early republic and the consequent growth of a voluntary system that empowered evangelizing organizations gave special opportunity to those Christian denominations most nimble in reaching out to a growing and mobile population: notably Methodists, Baptists, and Presbyterians. Had these churches been exclusively focused on personal conversion and private inner transformation, and had their converts simply espoused a private religion of personal devotion, there would have been no edifice of benevolence and philanthropy. But the evangelical surge shaped among its converts a millennialist cast of mind and a perfectionist critique of the society, key elements in the hunger for doing good.

The reform impulse that resulted from the growth of Protestant numbers and the expansion of evangelical power during this period marked a turning point in the narrative of American evangelicalism. This chapter in that narrative falls into three sections. First, it notes the chief features of that initially unifying impulse. Next, it explains how the millennialist imperative that underpinned reform was open to conflicting interpretations, which in turn increased bad feeling, poisoned relationships, and eventually provoked institutional schism. Finally, it shows how evangelicals, North and South, mobilized politically to defend their "purified" churches and their reform agendas. Evangelicals' reforming vision and pursuit of righteousness, once seen as a force for national cohesion, now took on a sectional form that would shake the country to its foundations.

During the era of the great evangelical surge, the well-established Wesleyan doctrine of perfectionism—"entire sanctification"—reached an audience beyond its Methodist core thanks to its theological reengineer-

2. Barnes and Dumond, eds., *Letters*, 1:99.

ing by Finney and other "modern" Calvinists. While it alienated many by its seeming dalliance with the idea that some people could reach a state of absolute sinless perfection before death, it attracted many others by its emphasis on the sinner's continued growth in grace after conversion, as well as its encouragement of human efforts to reform and improve society and its moral well-being. A similar hope in the possibilities of human achievement informed the prevailing evangelical understanding of the millennium. Only a small minority of Christian believers took the despairing "premillennialist" view that no material progress could be achieved before Christ's second coming inaugurated his thousand-year reign; descended theologically from the highest of high Calvinist doctrine, these "antimission" elements eschewed both evangelism and organized moral improvement. Most evangelicals, however, subscribed instead to a positive, profoundly nationalist, understanding of progress on earth that enjoined active missionary effort to bring about worldwide conversion before the millennial reign of the Savior. Actively spreading the gospel message—not preposterously decoding the books of Daniel and Revelation to establish the date of Christ's return—would inaugurate the kingdom of God.

This optimistic "postmillennialism" reflected the broader spirit of the age. The setting within which churches worked during the early and middle decades of the nineteenth century encouraged their faith in progress and their active social engagement. The era saw the consolidation of national independence in the aftermath of the Napoleonic wars; the rapid growth of population, which increased by a third each decade, from five to thirty million between 1800 and 1860; and a thriving market economy, linking commercial agriculture to a burgeoning urban and manufacturing sector, with pulses of boom and bust. With few exceptions, Americans believed in the destiny of their young republic to shape the world for the better, at home and abroad.

As they tallied their responsibilities for the infant United States, the leaders of religious institutions sometimes deployed an alarmist language that stressed the challenge of maintaining a Christian moral order and evangelizing the new nation—particularly its teeming cities and unchurched western settlements—without the benefit of formal state support. In Europe, church and state had been conjoined since Emperor Constantine had converted to Christianity; the American experiment in separating the two thus marked a radical new departure in the history of the church, one that required voluntary organizational force to impose moral discipline, fight irreligion and social degeneracy, and ensure that the Protestant vision and purposes of the pre-independence colonies would endure.

Just as commonly, however, the public rhetoric and private conversations of enterprising evangelicals had as much to do with liberation as coercion, with freeing citizens' human potential for self-improvement and moral self-realization in a republic of self-disciplined citizens. Many shared this positively liberating vision, but few were as consistently enterprising as Lyman Beecher, who during the first three decades of the century as minister of Presbyterian and Congregationalist churches—successively in New York, Connecticut, and Massachusetts—offered a telling example of pastoral care, revivalist preaching, theological modernization, and imaginative institution building. Convinced that God's hand had fashioned the United States for a radical new departure in human history—hitherto "the history of human nature in ruins"—Beecher saw the prospect of national and republican glory through the work of bringing "liberty and equality to all the dwellings of men." The present generation, he believed, would see the inauguration of "the last dispensation of heaven for the relief of this miserable world," secured by the voluntary efforts of churches beneficially emancipated from the dominion of government.[3] The agencies for this moral revolution, in whose founding and operation Beecher himself played a conspicuous part, were the ambitious national benevolent societies that sprang into existence immediately after the war of 1812. Recognizing that individual congregations were, as the historian Charles Foster has noted, "too weak, divided, conservative, and lacking in imagination" to achieve what was needed on their own, Beecher and like-minded entrepreneurs fashioned several dynamic, bureaucratically complex, and interconnected agencies. Together these formed an "evangelical united front" that comprised a dozen or so interdenominational organizations devoted to a mixture of moral uplift and social welfare. They included the American Bible Society, the American Tract Society, the American Board of Foreign Missions, the American Education Society, the American Sunday-School Union, and the American Temperance Society.

These agencies offered life-changing opportunities to the pious

---

3. Lyman Beecher, *The Memory of Our Fathers: A Sermon* . . . (Boston: T. R. Marvin, 1828), 5, 7.

young men and women they inspired to serve.[4] The activists' "immediatist" temper, shaped by evangelical conversion and (in the case of
many of the men) ministerial training, disdained the gradualism of the
Enlightenment; they championed individual moral transformation as
the remedy for a toxic cluster of social ills that included drunkenness,
prostitution, gambling, Sabbath-breaking, dueling, flogging, and other
expressions of human waste, cruelty, violence, and war. Such was their
success in publishing and distributing propaganda, prosecuting missions,
sustaining Christian education, and promoting temperance and other reforms that by the 1830s their hopes of world conquest for Christ seemed
to many Americans no longer a visionary dream but a practical proposition. Beecher himself celebrated the cascades of religious revival as evidence of God's blessing on the new voluntary arrangements. "The course
which is now adopted by christians of all denominations to support and
extend at home and abroad religious and moral influence; would seem
to indicate the purpose of God to render this nation, extensively, the al-
moners of his mercy to this world."[5]

Cross-denominational support for the benevolent empire was at its
most energetic and durable wherever and whenever evangelicals thought
they saw the rising power of the Catholic Church. The waves of Irish and
German immigration during the 1840s and 1850s gave special urgency
to Protestants' perception of a Catholic threat. Their concern extended
beyond anxieties over Catholics' creed, liturgy, and ceremonial to alarm
over the challenge Rome posed to American republicanism. Catholicism, they insisted, corroded the high standards of personal behavior
that citizenship demanded in a moral republic, not least because licentious priests condoned the drunkenness, theft, and sexual immorality
that were badges of the Sabbath-breaking, reveling, whisky-swilling, and
beer-drinking Irish and German immigrant laborers. Unlettered Catholics, controlled by priests and corrupt politicians, perverted the democratic ballot by bloc voting. Papists also threatened the Protestant spirit
of free inquiry by seeking state support for their parochial schools.

Those evangelical leaders who regarded "popery" as the single
greatest threat to the Christian republic exploited a mixture of ideological, political, ethnic, and class antagonisms in seeking to fashion a co-

4. Charles I. Foster, *An Errand of Mercy: The Evangelical United Front, 1790-1837*
(Chapel Hill: University of North Carolina Press, 1960), 131-32, 202-3, 214, 239-44.
5. Beecher, *Memory of Our Fathers*, 17.

hesive Protestant response. A number of new organizations sprang up to secure Protestant unity against the pope and to rebut Catholics' sneers about Protestants' fractiousness and sectarianism. Most influential was the Protestant Reformation Society, founded in 1836, and its successors, the American Protestant Society, which by 1849 was publishing over two million pages of tract material a year, and the American and Foreign Christian Union, whose agents found allies in all Protestant denominations. With some justification a Protestant journal declared in 1843 that anti-Catholicism "becomes the very center of Christian unity."[6]

That unity, however, designed though it was to supercharge the evangelical impulse for moral and social reform, proved largely unsustainable. By the late 1830s the evangelical united front had collapsed. On one reading, this was a result of the movement's own success: the revitalizing of Protestant religion in general had actually strengthened the competitive—even combative—ambitions of individual denominations, now enjoying greater numbers and prestige than at the turn of the century. But this alone did not explain why the good temper of the benevolent societies in their early years yielded later to disputation, schism, and bitterness. For this we must look in part to their relatively narrow sectarian and regional base. Organized mainly in the Northeast, the societies' leadership was drawn very largely from the ranks of the Congregationalist, Presbyterian, and Dutch Reformed churches. Methodists and Baptists—churches with a booming membership but mostly lacking social cachet—played a role in the united front, but class antagonisms did little to help these denominations look warmly on the "Presbygationalists" whose call to arms seemed presumptuously to ignore Methodist and Baptist achievements in the West.

Yet more threatening to the churches' unity in the pursuit of reform was an issue that would shake them to their foundations: the future place of slavery in the United States. Widely recognized by most northern evangelicals as a social evil, and described as such by some white southerners, too, the "peculiar institution" was, even so, rarely treated as a matter of personal sin. The hundreds of thousands of African American slave members of Baptist and Methodist churches, most of whose individual voices the historian can only guess at, quite probably did hold a damning view of slave-owners: few were likely to have quarreled with Frederick

6. Ray Allen Billington, *The Protestant Crusade, 1800-1860: A Study of the Origins of American Nativism* (New York: Macmillan, 1938), 185.

Douglass's judgment that some masters' "pretensions to piety" were a thin disguise for their cruelty and personal depravity.[7] But among most white critics of slavery, North and South, who put their faith in schemes of gradual, step-by-step reform, there was great reluctance to question the moral character of individual slave-owners. When in 1833 Theodore Weld declared that his Christian work as an abolitionist organizer, writer, and speaker was "the cause of *changeless eternal right* . . . of humanity and justice and righteousness," he set a prescription for religious purity and follow-up action on which, at the time, only a radical minority of fellow evangelicals could agree.[8] Like other spiritually reborn men and women of this subset, who preached the duty of all men and women immediately to separate themselves from sin, Weld had a romantic vision of a redeemed society where black and white would live in justice and Christian harmony.

Thus, when that radical minority—many of them, like Weld, converts of the revivals of the 1820s and 1830s—made heroic efforts to organize and campaign for the immediate abolition of slavery, they attracted the fire of the more conservative majority. Mainstream evangelicals took alarm at the launching of a national organization in 1833—the American Anti-Slavery Society (AASS)—that demanded not only the immediate start of a process of unconditional and uncompensated freedom for all slaves, but also their integration into American society as equal members. The presence within that movement of William Lloyd Garrison and his "Christian anarchist" followers only added to the mainstream's perception of the AASS as a "whole tribe of lunaticks."[9] Garrison's notorious critique of human government, as well as his assaults on the Scriptures, the conventional Sabbath, and the orthodox ministry, actually alarmed conventional evangelicals within the AASS as much as he did their more conservative coreligionists. But this did not save abolitionist evangelicals from conservatives' rebuke for deeming slavery a sin in all circumstances and demanding the end of all church fellowship with slaveholders, regardless of context. "I do not believe that all slaveholders are sinners," one leading free-state Methodist explained: "I know that some of them are pious men, so far as human judgment can go, and I would not harm

7. *Narrative of the Life of Frederick Douglass, Written by Himself* (Boston: The Anti-Slavery Office, 1849), 53–56.
8. Barnes and Dumond, eds., *Letters*, 1:99–101.
9. Cyrus L. Blanchard to Jonathan Blanchard, May 17, 1841, Blanchard Papers, Wheaton College.

them, even in my thoughts, for the world. I pity them."[10] Abolitionists' denunciation of Christian slaveholders would set brother and sister against sister and brother, threaten convulsions in the church, tighten the bonds of slavery by alienating masters from the work of evangelicals among their slaves, and derail progress toward the millennium.

What, above all, angered mainstream evangelicals in the free states was that the radical abolitionists' doctrine and methods of agitation brought the reformers' goal of human emancipation into disrepute. That slavery was cruel and unjust was a widely held view among northern churchgoers. Even those who considered the institution sanctioned by Scripture spoke out to censure several of its features as practiced south of the Mason-Dixon Line: the separation of slave families, the prohibition of legal marriage, the sanction of sexual assault, and the restrictions on reading and religious instruction. Northern evangelicals generally fused Enlightenment philosophy and a reading of the Bible to declare slavery a "dark spot upon our national character," one that violated the slave's natural rights and the equity of God's law.[11] But for these critics the remedy lay not in violent and sudden emancipation imposed on the South from outside. Rather, it lay in the voluntary freeing of slaves by slave masters through the benevolent work of the American Colonization Society. Settling freed men and women in West Africa would offer them the chance of self-government and self-improvement denied to them in the United States. Civilized Liberia would become a millennial beacon for the rest of the African continent. Most of these reformers, while well intentioned, were also anxious about the expanding population of free blacks in the United States, although black advocates of reform were largely skeptical of the colonization "solution."

The fault line within northern evangelicalism between these two approaches to millennial progress—the reforming gradualism of the colonizationists and the immediatist radicalism of those who damned the emigration schemes as a delusional bromide—was revealed in microcosm at Cincinnati's newly established Lane Theological Seminary, where Lyman Beecher had been appointed its first president and professor of theology in 1832. The student leader there was the eloquent Theodore

10. John McClintock to Stephen Olin, December 31, 1846, McClintock Papers, Drew University.

11. Benjamin Labaree, *A Sermon on the Death of General Harrison* . . . (Middlebury, VT: E. Maxham, 1841), 20; *The African Repository and Colonial Journal* 15 (October 1839): 303.

Weld, whose charismatic advocacy of immediate abolitionism during a series of "Lane Debates" in 1834 won over the majority of his fellow students from their support for gradual measures. Their radical stance, when combined with the seminary's religious, educational, and other welfare work with the local African American community, led Lane's trustees to yield to white Cincinnatians' outrage at the social mingling of the races and to order the students to disband their antislavery society. President Beecher himself was a convinced supporter of the American Colonization Society. Fearing the divisive implications of abolitionist agitation for national unity and God's millennial mission for the United States, and also concerned for the prosperity of a seminary that he judged essential to the religious well-being of the West, he sought a compromise. Unwilling to yield, Weld led a walkout of the majority of the students. Most of these "Lane Rebels" provided the nucleus for a new collegiate foundation at Oberlin, under revivalist and abolitionist auspices. Weld devoted himself to lecturing on abolition, facing down hostile mobs, and organizing the AASS's forces in the West. Beecher, however, remained committed to his alternative prescription for millennial glory and never gave up his support for colonization.

Divisive though it was within the North, the issue of the proper Christian relationship to slavery had even more powerful ramifications nationally, both for the churches and for their missionary societies. Early in the century, evangelicals North and South had widely understood that the institution was a necessary evil that would gradually die out and was—as a Charleston Presbyterian put it—"at least injudicious as far as the happiness of the master was concerned."[12] But the doubling, and then tripling, of the slave population and a booming economy in staples, particularly cotton, encouraged a sea change in southern attitudes. By mid-century white evangelicals in the slave states had come publicly to present something of a proslavery consensus around the view that the peculiar institution was neither transient nor evil, but a positive good. In the construction of a usable *defense* of slavery, evangelical piety fused with southern ideas of honor to produce a more "manly" reforming evangelicalism than was current in the North. It fused, too, with a form of republicanism more deferential and class stratified than that which prevailed in the North.

12. Ernest Trice Thompson, *Presbyterians in the South* (Richmond: John Knox, 1963-73), 1:535.

Southerners knew exactly what they were doing in choosing to march to the new tune of proslavery millennialism. The Baptist Iveson L. Brookes recalled how as a student at Chapel Hill from 1816 to 1819 he spoke out against slavery as "a moral wrong to the African race, ... justified only upon the ground of necessity," but how he later, by the late 1840s, became convinced that it was "God's Institution." Slavery sustained republican peace and safety by uniting labor and capital, cultivating "the mutual good feeling" of master and servant, and preventing the strife inherent in a free labor system. In Brookes's view the non-slaveholding states, "ignorantly fighting against God & the Bible," contained the elements of their own destruction, since the ballot box was open to the control of agrarians and anarchists: "None other than a monarchical and military despotism can ultimately control the populace, and secure the rights of the property-holders, where slavery is not the basis of society." In contrast, southern slaves were "the most contented and happy people on earth," while whites enjoyed "equality of social and political intercourse" unparalleled in the civilized world.[13]

In this intellectual refashioning and evolution there was no single watershed moment. But one way or another, by 1850 southern churches had come to champion slavery as a Christianizing agent that would continue to improve as the millennium approached. The South's deepening economic stake in slavery and cotton, the threat of slave revolts, and a concern for social cohesion: all encouraged this reappraisal. But an important catalyst, too, was the abolitionists' campaign against the South. "I do believe," John Adger mused (unconvincingly, it has to be said), "that if these mad fanatics had let us alone, in twenty years we should have made Virginia a free State. As it is, their unauthorized attempts to strike off the fetters of our slaves have but riveted them on the faster."[14] To prevent abolitionists from "infecting the consciences of weak minded good Christian people of the South," southern churchmen deployed Scripture to show that slavery was not a sin before God.[15] Old Testament society

13. Iveson L. Brookes to W. Heath, March 20, 1849, Iveson L. Brookes Papers #3249, Southern Historical Collection, Wilson Library, University of North Carolina at Chapel Hill; Iveson L. Brookes, *A Defence of the South* ... (Hamburg, SC: Republican Office, 1850), 45–47.

14. Thompson, *Presbyterians in the South*, 1:535.

15. Orville Vernon Burton, *In My Father's House Are Many Mansions: Family and Community in Edgefield, South Carolina* (Chapel Hill: University of North Carolina Press, 1985), 27.

was founded on it. God had sanctioned "negro slavery, or the bondage of the Canaanitish descendants of Ham."[16] Slaveholding was equally recognized under the new dispensation. Christ and his apostles, living and working where it existed under Roman law, fixed the duties of masters and slaves as precisely as they did those of parents and children, rulers and subjects. Those who argued that the Golden Rule ("All things whatsoever ye would that men should do unto you, do ye even so to them") demanded the freeing of slaves misunderstood the text. It meant quite simply, a Georgia Baptist explained, "that it is our duty to do unto others as it would be *reasonable* for us to wish others to do unto us, were our situations reversed."[17] The slave owed obedience to his master, the master humanity to the slave.

Equipped with the intellectual architecture of a proslavery millennialism, southern evangelicals pursued their own course toward social reform. Thus, Alabama Baptists urged masters to recognize their responsibilities as Christians; they should correct "the most erroneous abuses" of the slave system and prepare "to give an account to their master in heaven."[18] Slaveholders had a responsibility for their slaves' physical welfare as well as their spiritual development: when properly acquitted, this put masters on the moral high ground that northern employers of free labor, driven solely by money and the market, could never occupy. Missions to the slaves burgeoned through the 1840s and 1850s as planters lost their fear that missionaries were abolitionists in disguise. Even in South Carolina, where chronic white concern over the possibility of slave rebellion ran deepest, most of the slaves were under religious instruction by the eve of the Civil War, thanks to the vigorous leadership of such self-consciously benevolent slaveholding ministers as Charles Colcock Jones and William Capers.

Southern evangelicals' public agreement that slavery was benevolent, scriptural, and civilizing was not the full story. As John C. Calhoun learned in 1849, "many religious people at the South" had "strong misgivings" in private.[19] A handful of these were emancipationists, largely from the upper South, for whom slavery was a rank sin. Much more

16. Iveson L. Brookes, *A Defence of Southern Slavery* . . . (Hamburg, SC: Robinson and Carlyle, 1851), 5.

17. Patrick H. Mell, *Slavery: A Treatise* (Penfield, GA: Benjamin Brantley, 1844), 19.

18. *Christian Index* [Penfield, GA], May 23, 1850.

19. Charles Grier Sellers Jr., ed., *The Southerner as American* (Chapel Hill: University of North Carolina Press, 1960), 48.

typical of evangelical unease, however, were expressions that deemed human bondage not a sin, but a "curse" or a natural evil. What troubled these observers were slavery's day-to-day cruelties, its assault on the family, its debilitating moral influence on white and black alike, and its blighting effect on economic enterprise. Not least, they had to face up to the scriptural truth of the common humanity and unitary origins of the races: slaves, too, were created in the image of God; they had everlasting souls. Few expressed their anguish more earnestly than the Virginia Presbyterian minister Benjamin Smith, personally trapped in selling, hiring, and disciplining slaves. "O what trouble, running sore, constant pressing weight, perpetual wearing, dripping, is this patriarchal institution!" he lamented. "What miserable folly for men to cling to it as something heaven-descended."[20] Yet whatever their internal debate over whether slavery was an absolute good, a relative benefit, or a tolerable evil, southern evangelicals generally agreed that their institutions were scriptural and that owning slaves was no barrier to church membership.

This collapse into sectional divergence of the early republic's broad national consensus over Christian slaveholding, and the growing assertiveness of antislavery and proslavery millennialists, took institutional form in the schisms that shook the countrywide evangelical churches during the late 1830s and the 1840s. The slavery issue was inextricably bound up in the theological dispute that split Presbyterianism into Old and New School churches after 1838, southerners regarding abolitionism as the offspring of new-school heresy. Among Baptists the issue came to a head over the question of the employment of slaveholding ministers by the denomination's missionary bodies. In Augusta, Georgia, in May 1845, ministers joined governors, congressmen, and other leading public figures in forming the Southern Baptist Convention. Northern Baptists followed by reorganizing their own missionary bodies.

No schism, however, was as profound or as dangerous for national unity as the bitter split within the country's largest denomination, the Methodist Episcopal Church. One of the church's bishops, James O. Andrew of Georgia, had married a slave-owning widow. A majority of delegates at the General Conference meeting in New York in 1844 called on him to "desist from the exercise of his office" for as long as he remained "connected with slavery": although the church embraced thousands of

20. Francis Rosebro Flournoy, *Benjamin Mosby Smith, 1811-1893* (Richmond: Richmond Press, 1947), 57-59.

slaveholders, to accept one of them as an officer exercising nationwide authority would concede that slavery was a national, not local, institution.[21] Rather than surrender to what they judged the false doctrine of the sinfulness of slaveholding, southerners moved toward schism. The Conference overwhelmingly approved a Plan of Separation under which resources would be divided, and the annual conferences in the slave states set up an independent church, organized as the Methodist Episcopal Church, South, in 1845.

Mistakenly, some on both sides of the Mason-Dixon Line expected these schisms to strengthen the Union, by closing down forums where sectional champions could collide. Conservative evangelicals, however, North and South, took a less hopeful view. The North Carolinian Thomas Meredith despaired that Baptist separatists, in "frittering away the bonds of national union," invited "the horrors of civil war."[22] The Richmond Presbyterian William Plumer predicted that church divisions would "rend the star-spangled banner in twain . . . and the Potomac will be dyed with blood."[23] Methodists such as Nathan Bangs also saw rupture as a national disaster, by destroying a system of ministerial interchange that had a "natural tendency to do away with those prejudices which grow out of local circumstances and habits."[24] Many shrewdly understood that fracture would weaken the centrists: unity provided the best guarantee that northern moderates would defend southern interests.

Separation introduced new sources of bitterness and mutual stereotyping that further eroded evangelicals' sense of belonging to a Union impelled by a single, shared millennial vision. Quarreling and abrasion continued to mark North-South relations within Baptist and Presbyterian ranks throughout the 1840s and 1850s, but nothing in the experience of these two denominational families matched the trauma that schism visited on the Methodists. The Methodists' Plan of Separation, instead of providing a basis for the harmonious coexistence of the two branches of a divided church, gave rise instead to a chronic and ugly conflict that presaged the Civil War. The twelve hundred–mile line through the Border States from Maryland to Missouri produced split congregations, litiga-

21. Donald G. Mathews, *Slavery and Methodism: A Chapter in American Morality* (Princeton: Princeton University Press, 1965), 264.

22. *Biblical Recorder* [Raleigh, NC], January 4, 1845.

23. Thompson, *Presbyterians in the South*, 1:393–94.

24. *Pittsburgh Christian Advocate*, April 30, 1840; *Christian Advocate and Journal* [New York], May 14, 1845.

tion over local property, vilification in the press, and vigilante action. Invective once reserved for the other section's radicals was directed at all departed members. Magistrates seized and burned Methodist newspapers, their actions sustained by statute, grand juries, and vigilance committees. Physical violence, notably against antislavery preachers, scarred communities in Missouri, Kentucky, Virginia, and the eastern shore of Maryland. Each side was convinced of the righteousness of its own reforming impulse and the defective morality of the other.

The reform impulse and the conflicts it engendered would eventually engulf the American political arena and split it in two. For most evangelicals the separation of church and state posed no obstacle to their becoming politically engaged: the state, they agreed, should not support particular denominations through tax levies or preferential laws, but that did not prevent churches, or elements within them, from mobilizing in support of moral and faith-related issues. When Finney cemented his fame as an evangelist with his *Lectures on Revivals of Religion* in 1835, he uttered what had become an evangelical orthodoxy when he declared, "*The church must take right ground in regard to politics.*" During the founding era of mass democracy, during the 1820s and 1830s, Finney was just one of many religious voices that recognized the Christianizing potential of politics but also warned against the demoralizing effects of electioneering and the threat to individual conscience of blind loyalty to a political party. Candidates should be supported for their honesty and other personal qualities, not their party label. Christians were guilty of behaving "as if they thought God did not see what they do in politics." But in politics, "as on the subject of slavery and temperance, . . . the church must act right or the country will be ruined. . . . Politics are a part of religion in such a country as this."[25]

Finney was not proposing to set up a specifically Christian party, but he wanted—as did many others—to see Christian principles guiding government policy and shaping the political platforms that parties put before the public. Nurturing and maintaining a moral republic meant using the democratic arena to promote reform. The chief political division when Finney spoke out was the ideological fault line between the party of the president, Andrew Jackson, and the disparate coalition of opposition Whigs. Not all Whigs were reform-minded, but the party was the natural

25. Charles G. Finney, *Lectures on Revivals of Religion* (New York: Leavitt, Lord, 1835), 274.

home for the most dedicated monitors of public morality: the defenders of the Christian Sabbath against its trespass by Sunday mail-carriers; humanitarian opponents of Jackson's policy of forcible Native American removal, one that expelled from the South the Christian Cherokees and other "civilized tribes"; and the evangelical elements whose opposition to Masonry had earlier made them the allies of the Whigs' predecessors, the Antimasons. The millennialists and moral improvers who led the "evangelical united front" were overwhelmingly Whig.

Party leaders in Washington sought during the 1820s and 1830s to keep slavery off the public political agenda, fearing the damage it could do to national unity. But as cotton culture expanded into the Southwest, further entrenching slavery, it became increasingly difficult to gag political debate about its future. From the outset, most members of the AASS called for political action to supplement moral suasion: petitioning Congress, questioning candidates for office, voting only for antislavery men. Jackson's Democrats—tailoring their appeal to reach race-conscious northern poor whites (including Irish Catholics) and proslavery southerners who cherished states' rights—held little attraction for abolitionist evangelicals. Whigs' sympathy for reform and benevolent action made them a more natural political home, although the party's socially conservative, paternalist view of the world made it an uneasy berth for the most radical antislaveryites. For those who saw the two major parties as mere "divisions of the pro-slavery party"[26] there was a simple solution: a separate political organization, devoted to abolition.

The political force that then emerged, the Liberty party, put up an antislavery candidate—the Presbyterian James G. Birney—for the presidency in 1840 and 1844, and ran candidates for a raft of local and state offices. In its program, activities, and composition the new party was an expression of socially concerned, revivalist Protestantism. Its leaders ("ministers—not statesmen or politicians," one Libertyman noted) spoke for members who deemed slavery a moral corruption as well as a social evil. Acknowledging that Congress could not constitutionally interfere with slavery within individual states, they still insisted that the federal authorities treat it as a mere local institution, and make the interests of equality and free labor the controlling consideration in government action. Liberty meetings took on a revivalist character. "The Liberty party,"

26. William G. W. Lewis, *Biography of Samuel Lewis* (Cincinnati: Methodist Book Concern, 1857), 3:327.

one of its members later maintained, "unlike any other in history, was founded on moral principles—on the Bible, originating a contest not only against slavery but against atheistic politics from which Divine law was excluded."[27]

As a one-idea movement of "reformer politicians," the Liberty party achieved little electorally. Its successor, however, the Free Soil party of 1848, more effectively capitalized on the sharpening of northern evangelicals' reform sensibilities. By the second half of the 1840s, according to the Methodist John McClintock, "the division of Northern men into abolitionists and anti-abolitionists exists no longer. . . . In a word . . . the CONSCIENCE of the great Northern race is aroused."[28] That arousal resulted from political developments judged to expose the cumulative power of the so-called "slaveocracy": congressional laws that gagged discussion, the annexation of the Texas Republic, and territory seized by force from Mexico. President James K. Polk's warmongering provoked the particular hostility of evangelical forces in the Northeast: Congregationalists, New School Presbyterians, and Free Will Baptists, together with a determined minority of Baptists, Methodists, and Old School Presbyterians. Never doubting the wickedness of the Mexican conflict's origins, they saw in its outcome the acquisition of a vast domain standing at the mercy of the Slave Power. Ministers called on their congregations to reverse the "regular and constant progression" of slavery. "God himself consecrated the Soil of earth to Freedom," an Indiana pastor declared, "to be tilled only by the Sons of Freedom."[29]

As the movement for free soil gathered pace, Liberty clergy joined with thousands of evangelical defectors from the two main parties, Democrats and Whigs, to form a new third force. The organizing political convention of that Free Soil party, at Buffalo in August 1848, had more the character of a protracted revival meeting than a secular gathering. Twenty thousand supporters—men and women, black and white—under the canvas of "the great Oberlin canopy," encouraged the official delegates with prayers and hymns, imploring God to forgive the nation's complicity in slavery and racial intolerance. Speakers saw God's hand at

27. Austin Willey, *The History of the Antislavery Cause in State and Nation* (Portland, ME: B. Thurston, 1886), 236-39, 260.

28. John McClintock to Stephen Olin, December 31, 1846, McClintock Papers, Drew University.

29. B. F. Morris, *Our Country: Three Discourses . . .* (Lawrenceburgh, IN: J. B. Hall, 1848), 26-29.

work in making their convention the founding event of "a real Republic, to diffuse its light and truth to all Nations, until every member of the great human family shall know and rejoice in this great Salvation." The joyous expressions of millennialist hope that ended the convention ("The day of Freedom dawns at length—The Lord's appointed day!") swept evangelicals—clergy and laypeople—into the campaign. God, they knew, had called them to serve in the apocalyptic struggle between "the dark hellish principles of the past unholy war, and of slavery extended" and "the rights of man, the rights of God, and the claims of Jesus Christ on earth."[30]

The Whigs, as the self-styled party of Christian benevolence, were more vulnerable than the Democrats to evangelical defections. In 1848, however, they survived the electoral insurgency of the Free Soilers and, thanks to their strength in the South, saw the presidential victory of their candidate, the slaveholder Zachary Taylor. That result gave them false hope. Over the next few years the party suffered a continuing leakage of evangelical support, as Whig leaders appeared to temporize over Protestants' reform initiatives: the prohibition of drink, the place of the Bible in common schools, and the defence of Protestant values against a high tide of Irish and German Catholic immigration. For a brief period it appeared that it would be the anti-immigrant American, or Know Nothing, party that would benefit most from the haemorrhaging of the Whigs' millennialist support. But a new slavery-related crisis in 1854, over the Act that opened up the territories of Kansas and Nebraska to slave labor, drew antislavery Protestants into a variety of new fusion movements that eventually cohered into the Republican party. On a platform headlined as "Free Soil, Free Speech, Free Labor, Free Men," Republicans established themselves in the presidential election of 1856 as the chief opposition to the victorious Democrats, now seen as the best defenders of southern interests.

Much of the Republican party's early impetus derived from the energies of zealous evangelicals impelled by conscience, obedience to a higher law, and a powerful sense of public duty to find a political route to the kingdom of God. This brew of inter-sectional struggle and millennial religion found earnest expression in the diary of a Methodist itinerant preacher during the 1856 campaign. "The Lord came in power among the people and our souls rejoiced in the Lord," he exulted after a Connecticut

30. *New York Tribune*, September 7, 1848; *Oberlin Evangelist*, August 16, September 27, October 25, 1848.

revival meeting. He would soon register another Christian responsibility: "Election. Today the battle is to be fought between right & wrong. I went to the polls and did my duty. . . . May God aid the right!"[31]

Four years on, in 1860, the Republicans again presented themselves as the conscience of the nation in an election whose key issues once more aroused evangelicals' moral concern: the spread of slavery, the growth of Catholicism, and evidence of serious corruption in the national administration. Abraham Lincoln's presidential victory was widely judged the redeeming triumph of "the Lord's side." Although the Democrats had their own evangelical strongholds, particularly in the South, enough northern evangelicals stood as Republican candidates, acted as Republican local organizers, used their pulpits, and cast their votes to prompt the conclusion that they exerted "a most controlling power in electing Mr. Lincoln."[32]

If no understanding of Lincoln's election is complete without reference to the reform activity of *northern* evangelical Protestantism, then the final act in the prewar drama of national disintegration—the secession of the lower South and the setting up of a Confederacy—makes full sense only if we recognize the role of millennialist *southern* clergy in that process. Southern Protestantism provided a framework of understanding that encouraged political separation and gave it religious meaning. The most radical proslavery evangelicals rejoiced that the denominational schisms had purged their churches of subversion and error. Likewise, political secession became an act of purification, the righteous withdrawing from the ungodly. That crisis they judged a divine visitation on an ungodly nation. Secession offered escape from the tyranny of false constitutional doctrine and gave the reformers a route to a new birth, sacred and secular. A New Orleans minister defined the South's "providential trust": the "duty *to ourselves, to our slaves, to the world, and to Almighty God . . . to preserve and transmit our existing system of domestic servitude . . . wherever Providence and nature may carry it.*"[33]

In this crisis of the old Union, southern ministers abandoned their conventional political quietism for "active interposition." The calamity of Lincoln's election, they insisted, meant that clergy as well as politicians

---

31. Benjamin Adams, Diary, October 17, November 4, 1856, Drew University.

32. W. Hamilton to M. Simpson, February 23, 1861, Matthew Simpson Papers, Drew University; W. Nast to M. Simpson, February 23, March 4, 1861, R. Ricketts to M. Simpson, April 17, 1861, Matthew Simpson Papers, Library of Congress.

33. B. M. Palmer and William Thomas Leacock, *The Rights of the South Defended in the Pulpits* (Mobile: J. Y. Thompson, 1860), 8-9.

had a duty "to avert evil."[34] Secessionist clergy rode into the political
arena with all the zeal of the Republican ministers they had previously
rebuked for mixing religion and politics. In South Carolina, well before
the state adopted its ordinance of secession, church bodies themselves
called for a cleansing separation. Ministers took to the stump to win
election to secession conventions; one of them, the wealthy slaveholder
and Alabama Baptist Basil Manly, would soon be the serving chaplain at
Jefferson Davis's inauguration as President of the Confederate States.
Crusading northern evangelicals who saw in Lincoln's call to arms the
opening of a holy war would face southern troops equally sure that they
marched under the banner of God.

The "millennialist turn" of the pre–Civil War era saw revival-inspired
evangelicals rushing to serve in the numerous agencies of moral and social reform. These men and women took with them a definition of righteous action shaped in part by their hopes for the nation as a whole and
their belief that the young republic had a special role to play in God's
plan for the world at large. In its early phases, millennialist activism had
a unifying purpose: What evangelical could doubt that the moral health
of all the nation's citizens required religious instruction, deep knowledge of the Scriptures, temperance, self-control, and an appetite for
self-improvement? But these reform-minded evangelicals also developed
a view of righteous action shaped by their regional needs, experience,
and loyalties. As the contested place of slavery in God's plan became the
dominating moral question of the antebellum era and thrust itself into
the political arena, the "millennialist turn" gave rise to the "sectional
turn." The conflict between North and South—the free and slave sections of the nation—had at its heart the issue of the political protection
properly due to a peculiar institution of massive economic and material
consequence. In no simple sense was the ensuing Civil War caused by
American evangelicals' conflicting understandings of the imperative to
reform. But the moral intensity of their confrontation gave peculiar urgency to a political crisis that would brook no compromise. It ensured,
too, that when the battlefield conflict came it would be savage and bloody
beyond the prewar imagination.

34. *Biblical Recorder*, November 29, 1860; *North Carolina Presbyterian*, December
1, 8, 1860, January 5, 1861.

CHAPTER 5

The Rise of the Domestic Ideal
in the United States and Canada

Marguerite Van Die

"Our mothers direct us to heaven while they live, then when dead again their spirits hover over us & beckon us upwards," William McCampbell, a young Tennessee lawyer, reminded his fiancée, Sue Heiskell, in 1858.[1] McCampbell's tribute to his mother's role in his religious nurture was far from unique and formed part of a discourse of domesticity that helped courting evangelical couples grow in intimacy. That same year, far to the north, in the tiny border town of Stanstead, Quebec, Charles Colby, another young lawyer, experienced a profound conversion shortly after his engagement to Hattie Child, a Vermont schoolteacher. Although raised in the Christian faith, he confessed to his fiancée and her mother that his knowledge of God had always been intellectual rather than experiential. Suddenly his relationship with the divine had changed; now that he had realized God's goodness and love, all the barriers that had formerly separated him from his Savior had come down. For the first time in his life he was able to enter into prayer as an intimate dialogue with God.[2]

Both men and their fiancées were members of a growing middle class, both couples were young evangelical Christians, and both would draw

1. Scott Stephan, *Redeeming the Southern Family: Evangelical Women and Domestic Devotion in the Antebellum South* (Athens: University of Georgia Press, 2008), 4, 150-51, and 238.
2. Marguerite Van Die, *Religion, Family and Community in Victorian Canada: The Colbys of Carrollcroft* (Montreal, Kingston: Queen's University Press, 2005), 54-56.

The historiography on which this chapter is based is extensive, and for the sake of economy I will refer the reader only to relevant summaries.

84

on the domestic ideal as an anchor in their marriage and family life. For William McCampbell and Sue Heiskell, the language of evangelical domesticity softened the gender distinctions that were part of southern patriarchy and its code of honor, bringing them closer to the northern middle-class ideal of the companionate marriage.[3] For Canadians Charles Colby and Harriet Child, a shared family experience rooted in a loving and forgiving God became the sustaining force in a turbulent economic world racked by litigation, bankruptcy, and unpredictability. In each case they were acknowledging that the primary site of religious socialization was not the church but the home, lovingly tended by the mother. This domestic ideal, sometimes referred to as "the cult of domesticity," had become widely accepted among middle-class white evangelicals by the middle of the nineteenth century. While earlier periods such as the Puritan had acknowledged the importance of a godly household, the home had never been presented as a redemptive site. To some historians this sacralization of the home and the accompanying feminization of religion represent a major turning point and a break with Christian tradition.[4] On the other hand, the early Victorian period has also been described as a time when evangelical Protestants began to attain significant cultural authority in the Anglo-American world. This chapter addresses this contradiction between private devotion and public authority by examining the evolving relationship between the domestic practice of evangelical religion and the unique conditions of the North American economic and cultural environment in the first half of the nineteenth century.

In its personal call to repentance and a new way of life, evangelical experience was by nature dynamic and thus deeply influenced by such turning points in the daily life of its practitioners as conversion, becoming a church member, courtship, marriage, births, illness, and the nurture and preparation of children for adulthood. These personal turning points were experienced in a society also undergoing profound transformation. Especially in the northeastern United States, the years 1820 to 1860 were a boom time, punctuated by periodic financial collapses, a time when the country's population tripled from 10 million to

---

3. Stephan, *Redeeming the Southern Family*, 59-62. For a summary of the historiography on southern and northern marital differences see 259-60, notes 5-7.

4. Margaret Lamberts Bendroth, *Growing Up Protestant: Parents, Children and Mainline Churches* (New Brunswick, NJ: Rutgers University Press, 2002), 13; Leonore Davidoff et al., *The Family Story: Blood, Contract and Intimacy, 1830-1960* (London: Longman, 1999), 81.

30.1 million, accompanied by the rapid expansion of national territory, commerce, and industrialization aided by new technologies and means of transportation. Evangelicals, who dominated the Protestant churches, were active participants in this commercializing economy, but also promoted the ideal of a moral economy, a Christian society in keeping with their understanding of true religion as experiential, biblical, and socially activist. As observed by Candy Gunther Brown in a thoughtful study of evangelical print culture: "Evangelicals living in mid-nineteenth-century America . . . struggled with an inherent tension between their goal of purity, or keeping that which they considered as sacred uncontaminated by the profane world, and their goal of presence, or infusing the world with sanctifying influences."[5] Accordingly, in order to determine how and to what extent the domestic ideal in the antebellum period marked a religious turning point, we must take seriously the inherent tension evangelicals faced between purity and presence, between personal conversion and social transformation.

As was evident in the two vignettes introducing this chapter, and as Mark Noll has so often persuasively demonstrated, a comparative approach that crosses national boundaries draws attention to the multifaceted nature of changes in Christian thought and experience.[6] With a high rate of literacy and a burgeoning print culture, evangelicals formed an international textual community that invited exchange. Evangelicals in the northern and southern United States, and in British North America (after 1867 the Dominion of Canada), read the same literature extolling the nature and importance of domestic religion. Contemporary writers presented the ideal of domestic religion in terms of a universal morality assumed to be applicable in the Anglo-American world everywhere regardless of context. Their sermons, theological discourses, and didactic works provide important insight into the family structure and values that were intended to shape evangelical identity. Though often only implicitly, their teachings were also, however, addressing the social changes evangelicals and the wider population were experiencing in the antebellum period. Hence, though the image of the home as church struck deep roots in the American South and North, as in British North

5. Candy Gunther Brown, *The Word in the World: Evangelical Writing, Publishing, and Reading in America, 1789-1880* (Chapel Hill: University of North Carolina Press, 2004), 6.

6. Mark Noll, *A History of Christianity in the United States and Canada* (Grand Rapids: Eerdmans, 1992), 1-8.

America, the causes and results were significantly different. What follows is a brief examination of how the ideal of domesticity was constructed in the literature and the extent to which evangelicals in varied settings drew on it to shape their identity. As will be evident at various instances and addressed specifically in the conclusion, when assessing historical continuities and discontinuities in different social and political contexts, the theme of "turning points" acquires added complexity.

The importance of married life and a godly household had been a longstanding Protestant teaching since the days of the sixteenth-century Reformation. In New England a 1642 Massachusetts law, amplified in 1648, mandated masters of families at least once a week to catechize their children and servants "in the grounds and principles of Religion."[7] In keeping with this tradition, eighteenth-century evangelical leaders such as John Wesley and Jonathan Edwards frequently extolled family religion in order to ensure religious continuity from one generation to the next. Edwards's admonitions reflected concerns about the transformations of a world experiencing the emergence of a market-oriented economy and the breakdown of the patriarchal family once parents were no longer able to provide farms for all their sons. As offspring left in search of new land, he reminded parents of their crucial religious responsibilities to read the Bible aloud to their children, help them memorize the catechism, lead family prayer, and be a model of Christian virtue.[8] John Wesley, acutely aware that his followers needed to transmit Methodist faith and practice to the next generation, also preached on the duties of parents to provide religious instruction for their children, and rhetorically asked, "What will the consequence be, if they adopt not this resolution? if family religion be neglected?—if care be not taken of the rising generation? Will not the present revival in a short time die away?"[9]

The intense revivalism that swept rural pioneer communities in North America during the early decades of the nineteenth century emphasized the need for individual conversion and an abrupt break with a sinful past, and in so doing undermined the traditional family on which

7. Colleen McDannell, *The Christian Home in Victorian America, 1840-1900* (Bloomington: Indiana University Press, 1986), 5.

8. Catherine A. Brekus, "Children of Wrath, Children of Grace: Jonathan Edwards and the Puritan Culture of Child Rearing," in *The Child in Christian Thought*, ed. Marcia J. Bunge (Grand Rapids: Eerdmans, 2001), 321.

9. John Emory, ed., *The Works of the Reverend John Wesley, M.A.* (New York: B. Waugh and T. Mason, 1835), 2:301.

evangelical religious nurture had depended. Though less the case in the northeastern United States (where until the 1830s evangelicals were overwhelmingly Congregational and Presbyterian), itinerant Baptist and Methodist preachers were the most active in bringing evangelical religion to the southern states, the Ohio Valley, and the British North American colonies.[10] Gathered in such small intimate groups as Methodist class meetings and "love feasts," the converted entered into new familial bonds, based not on blood but on religious affection, addressing one another as sisters and brothers, allowing women to preach and even to select their marriage partner.[11] The 1829 Discipline of the Methodist Episcopal Church in Canada, for example, made one exception to the rule of female obedience in the case of a woman who "saw it her duty to marry" but whose parents refused "to let her marry any Christian." What mattered in marriage, the Discipline asserted, was not the denomination of the prospective partners but that they "have the form, and are seeking the power of godliness."[12]

Within several decades, however, with a view to gaining a larger public presence and Christianizing the wider society, such countercultural practices began to give way to more inclusive expressions of evangelical family identity. Focusing on Methodists in the Ohio Valley, historian A. Gregory Schneider has described a trajectory where converts domesticated their revivalist practice, with the result that the "secluded-but-transformative religious community was identified increasingly with the home circle."[13] In his view this transition and the accompanying enhancement of women's role in the home represented a declension in evangelical vitality, "a fall from Eden." Lost was the innocence and purity of the Methodist "quest for a holy community" in favor of a more ambiguous journey resulting in domestication, feminization, and

10. For revivalism in the North see Shelby H. Balik, *Rally the Scattered Believers: Northern New England's Religious Geography* (Bloomington: Indiana University Press, 2014), 110-47.

11. John H. Wigger, *Taking Heaven by Storm: Methodism and the Rise of Popular Christianity in America* (Urbana: University of Illinois Press, 1998), 80-103; Cynthia Lynn Lyerly, *Methodism and the Southern Mind, 1770-1810* (New York: Oxford University Press, 1998), 73-93.

12. Methodist Episcopal Church in Canada, *Doctrine and Discipline* (York: E. Ryerson and W. J. Coates, 1829), 80.

13. A. Gregory Schneider, *The Way of the Cross Leads Home: The Domestication of American Methodism* (Bloomington: Indiana University Press, 1993), xxvii.

the compartmentalization of private and public life.[14] Focusing on the "little families of love" that had ruptured kinship networks among early-nineteenth-century Baptists and Methodists in the South, Christine Heyrman observes a similar turning point, but offers a different interpretation. Her conclusion is that evangelical rhetoric had shifted by the 1830s to restore patriarchal authority within the household. Evangelical churches were no longer countercultural communities, and having dropped their unconventional practices and opposition to slavery became important bulwarks of the traditional slaveholding family and the southern code of honor.[15] In eastern and central British North America, a brief period of exuberant revivalism, or what one historian has termed the "Canada Fire," also gave way by the 1830s to a more sober evangelical piety that reflected the large influx of British immigrants of evangelical background after the Napoleonic wars and the conservative leadership of the British parent denominations.[16]

Some have seen a desire for respectability as the motivation for these evangelical turning points. More in keeping with the nature of religious continuity is the simple fact that evangelical presence depended on re-directing the goal of religious revival from the salvation of individuals to the formation of godly households. None were more aware of this than evangelical clergy and their female congregants. As has been well documented, women had formed a majority of church members in Protestant churches since the colonial period.[17] In pioneer conditions, homes and female hospitality had been indispensable for community worship until a church had been built. Long thereafter, through the trope "a mother in Israel," clergy would continue to acknowledge women's special role within the congregation. Select local studies of the converts in revivals during the period 1800–1830 in the northeastern United States, and a

14. Schneider, *Way of the Cross Leads Home*, 196–208.

15. Christine Leigh Heyrman, *Southern Cross: The Beginnings of the Bible Belt* (Chapel Hill: University of North Carolina Press, 1997), especially 117–205.

16. George Rawlyk, *The Canada Fire: Radical Evangelicalism in British North America, 1775–1812* (Montreal, Kingston: McGill-Queen's University Press, 1994); Todd Webb, *Transatlantic Methodists: British Wesleyanism and the Formation of an Evangelical Culture in Nineteenth-Century Ontario and Quebec* (Montreal, Kingston: McGill-Queen's University Press, 2013).

17. Anne Braude, "Women's History *Is* American Religious History," in *Retelling U.S. Religious History*, ed. Thomas A. Tweed (Berkeley: University of California Press, 1997), 87–107.

few decades later in British North America, reveal the predominance of women and youth, as well as a pattern in which husbands shortly afterward followed their wives into church membership. Mary Ryan, for example, in examining the religious revivals that swept through the evangelical churches of Oneida County, New York, from 1814 to 1838 in the wake of the construction of the Erie Canal, has noted a "story of domestic evangelicalism" in which first wives and mothers, then daughters, sons, and husbands joined in full church membership.[18]

Evangelical religion's emphasis on the experience of the heart, and the use of special means by revivalists such as Charles Finney, enhanced the role of women and the home in the process of salvation, and clergy frequently made reference to the prayers of women that had preceded such seasons. The wives and mothers who had gathered to pray for a religious revival in anticipation of Finney's tour of the Oneida area in the winter of 1825-26 had been accompanied by small children and had formed denominational maternal associations. Their constitutions pledged that each member would perform parental and religious duties, which included "praying for each child daily, attending meetings semimonthly, renewing each child's baptismal covenant regularly, reading systematically through the literature on the Christian education of children, setting a pious example to children at all times, and spending each child's birthday in prayer and fasting."[19]

As wives and mothers, women were especially attuned to the volatile impact on their sons and husbands of the economic revolution in commerce, transportation, and communication. Although by the mid-nineteenth century most of the United States and British North America continued to depend on farming, old ways were changing with the spread of a commercial market economy and the beginnings of industrialization. In the northern states, the attraction of commercial and industrial life and the decline of arable farmland brought many families and youth into urban centers, replacing the home with the workplace as the focus

18. Mary P. Ryan, *Cradle of the Middle Class: The Family in Oneida County, New York, 1790-1865* (Cambridge: Cambridge University Press, 1981), 60-104. Canadian studies locate this pattern in the 1850s. See Hannah M. Lane, "Tribalism, Proselytism, and Pluralism: Protestants, Family, and Denominational Identity in Mid-Nineteenth-Century St. Stephen, New Brunswick," in *Households of Faith: Family, Gender, and Community in Canada, 1760-1969*, ed. Nancy Christie (Montreal, Kingston: McGill-Queen's University Press, 2002), 103-37.

19. Ryan, *Cradle of the Middle Class*, 89.

of production. Between 1820 and 1860 the percentage of people in the United States living in urban areas (defined by the census as places with a population of 2,500 or over) tripled from 7 to 20 percent. During these same years the country emerged as a major industrial power, with manufacturing accounting for one-third of all commodity output. The creation of a wage-earning system replaced an earlier reliance on informal networks of kin or fellow workers with more impersonal regulations and relationships. Wealth, not aristocratic privilege, was now the measure of a person's status, and as one antebellum historian has observed, "Much more so than in Europe, *democracy* and *capitalism* very nearly became synonymous terms in the United States."[20] Free to pursue prosperity and unchecked by former personal and legal restrictions, property-holding groups in the middling ranks, who comprised approximately one-third of the population, began to shape the tone of society as a whole. Comprised of farmers, businessmen, professionals, and independent artisans, this third of the population controlled most of the businesses, the churches, the schools, and the press, and their spokespersons were the cultural leaders of the nation. It was in this new middle class where one found the majority of evangelicals, many tracing their conversion to the religious revivals between 1800 and the early 1830s (which in the United States had doubled the percentage of church members). Its male members were self-made individuals, assertive but self-disciplined in their pursuit of a livelihood.[21]

Not least among the values and way of life being reshaped by a turbulent marketplace were gender and family relations. The shift from agriculture to commerce had removed fathers from such everyday tasks in the home as child rearing and food production. Instead of land, the patrimony parents were now able to give their children was an education that emphasized self-restraint and moral behavior as conditions for success. In an aggressive economic environment that put moral values at risk, no site was considered better suited to train a child than the home, and none was considered better equipped to take on this task than the mother.

20. William L. Barney, *The Passage of the Republic: An Interdisciplinary History of Nineteenth-Century America* (Lexington, MA: D. C. Heath, 1987), 88.

21. Daniel Walker Howe, *What Hath God Wrought: The Transformation of America, 1815-1848* (New York: Oxford University Press, 2007), 165-202, 525-69. Richard Carwardine estimates that in the mid-1850s about 40 percent of the US population was "in close sympathy with evangelical Christianity." Carwardine, *Evangelicals and Politics in Antebellum America* (Knoxville: University of Tennessee Press, 1997), 44.

Feminist historians have coined such terms as a "separation of spheres" and a "cult of domesticity" to signify woman's new role in this emerging middle-class identity as guardian of home life and nurturer of children. Her retreat from the farm and workplace to the privacy of the home was made possible by the mechanized production of household goods, which reduced her time previously spent in such tasks as making soap, spinning and weaving, butchering meat, and laundering. The ability to purchase goods now depended on the father's wages rather than on the mother's productive farming skills. Even for modest middle-class families, the availability of cheap, often immigrant labor allowed the mother to shift some of her chores to a young hired girl and to devote more time to her family and to benevolent work. A major innovation was the promotion of homes with private, specialized rooms instead of the single interior prevalent in colonial America. In the ideal middle-class Victorian home, men, women, and children now had their own areas, while a parlor and library reflected the family's respectability and status.[22] Evidence shows that these changes were also accompanied by a decline in the estimated size of the nuclear family, with the average number of children borne by a white woman moving from 7.04 in 1800 to 5.42 in 1850.[23]

The lives of middle-class women were daily redefined by a host of other influences that helped turn the domestic ideal into a cultural construct. Romanticism, for example, ascribed to women a natural sensitivity and piety that, aided by new consumer goods and some relief from traditional tasks, could now help her turn the home into a place of daily religious practice and moral training. Originating in industrializing Victorian Britain, Romantic sentimentality about the home, whether as "humble cottage or royal residence," extolled its divinely appointed status in song, poetry, visual arts, and fiction. By the 1840s and 1850s male clergy and middle-class female writers such as Catharine Beecher, Harriet Beecher Stowe, Sarah Hale, and Lydia Sigourney were providing a stream of didactic literature proclaiming home and family as God-given institutions.[24] Noting that the apostle Paul in his letter to Timothy had recommended "that piety be shown at home," the Reverend George Weaver, a Unitarian, rhetorically wondered, "Is religion good? Then where is it

22. McDannell, *Christian Home in Victorian America*, 20-28; Peter Ward, *A History of Domestic Space: Privacy and the Canadian Home* (Vancouver: University of British Columbia Press, 1999).

23. Barney, *Passage of the Republic*, 75.

24. McDannell, *Christian Home in Victorian America*, 128-36.

needed more than at home? The world will go on without religion; but can man's dwelling places be real places without religion?" Advertised in the Christmas 1854 issue of the *Ladies Repository*, Weaver's *The Christian Household, embracing the Christian Home, Husband, Wife, Father, Mother, Child, Brother and Sister*, was intended as a practical manual to address "the absence of Christ in our households." The cause, he believed, lay not in a lack of sound preaching and theology, but in too little attention to the daily practice of "Christian principle and life."[25] Female writers agreed. To Catharine Beecher the home was the primary site of religious activity where women through "a religion of love" turned the life of the nursery and kitchen into a ministry aimed at the eternal salvation of their family. In her book *American Woman's Home: Or the Principles of Domestic Science*, written in collaboration with her sister, Harriet Beecher Stowe, she provided visual representation in the form of a home designed in the Gothic style, where a single building served as "a small church, a school-house, and a comfortable family dwelling."[26] There is no evidence that the dwelling was ever built, but her use of Gothic design was part of a widespread revival that associated domestic architecture with religion. The Methodists in 1864 built three hundred Gothic cottages at their summer retreat in Martha's Vineyard, an example followed in other locations, including ten years later in Canada West (later Ontario) at Grimsby Beach, on the northern shore of Lake Ontario. The prevalence of Gothic architecture in homes, churches, and public buildings throughout the English-speaking world strengthened the impression that, despite rising smokestacks, growing slums, and an impoverished working class, religion and the home were part of an unchanging moral order.

In the quite different agrarian slave economy of the American South, where patriarchal authority remained unchallenged, evangelicals likewise considered women and the home to play an important part in ensuring social stability. As managers of a large household, evangelical women worried and prayed about the salvation of their children while also considering themselves responsible for the eternal destiny of their slaves.[27] In British North America, with its small and scattered population and largely staple-exporting economy, women also continued to

25. George S. Weaver, *The Christian Household* (Boston: A. Tompkins and B. B. Mussey, 1856), 17 and vii.

26. McDannell, *Christian Home in Victorian America*, 37.

27. Stephan, *Redeeming the Southern Family*, 133–82. For a summary of disagreements among historians on the impact of evangelicalism on women's roles, see 15–17.

divide their energy between the family economy and the home.[28] As with their American counterparts, their every activity was seen to carry grave moral implications. During the 1842 Christmas season, the Congregationalist mother in Canada West, for example, was sternly admonished that even such a simple choice as spending time preparing her children's dress instead of attending to the needs of the Bible, Tract and Missionary Societies might leave a lasting negative impression upon a youthful mind.[29] Constantly watching over their children's every word and action, evangelical mothers regardless of their geographic setting were called to take on the role of minister in the home, gently reproving, correcting, and instructing as the occasion and the specific child warranted. Their divinely appointed task was to shape the conscience of their children and elevate them from their natural state to become Christians in word and deed.

To help mothers in this task was a new genre of juvenile fiction. Like the home, this literature (which made no mention of such divisive topics as slavery) depicted, as one scholar has observed, "a twilight world, a world that seems at first almost wholly sheltered from the robust life around it."[30] As in ideal childhood nurture, juvenile fiction assumed that children were by nature open to gentle but constructive correction. Summarizing the virtues recommended to young readers, historian Anne Scott Macleod notes that these uniformly tended toward "order, restraint, stability, and a strong sense of social responsibility as the age determined it. Obedience was the most fundamental virtue for a child to acquire: few stories closed without one salute to its importance."[31] Rather than ascribing efforts at social control to such stories, she considers their moral didacticism to be a reflection of the prevailing optimistic view that stressed human dignity and therefore took children seriously as moral beings.[32]

In its hopeful view of childhood, juvenile fiction mirrored an understanding of the human condition that was also influencing evangelical theology and practice. In a revivalist framework that called for repen-

28. Marjorie Griffin Cohen, *Women's Work, Markets, and Economic Development in Nineteenth-Century Ontario* (Toronto: University of Toronto Press, 1988).

29. "To Mothers," *Harbinger*, December 15, 1842, 179.

30. Anne Scott Macleod, *American Childhood: Essays on Children's Literature of the Nineteenth and Twentieth Centuries* (Athens: University of Georgia Press, 1994), 89.

31. Macleod, *American Childhood*, 96.

32. Macleod, *American Childhood*, 97–98.

tance and conversion, children and youth, as Margaret Bendroth and others have pointed out, were especially at risk at a time of high child mortality.[33] The values of the family and home were important in middle-class formation, but for evangelicals they also had eternal implications in preparing children for salvation. The Christian nurture promoted so strongly in the denominational press and prescriptive literature was intended to prepare children for conversion by gradually cultivating in them the religious and moral sensibilities formerly generated in the intensity of revival meetings. Such high expectations imposed heavy burdens on believing parents while also leaving them no reassurance on the ultimate salvation of their children. Though there was a general assumption that infants (anywhere from age three to seven) could not be held morally accountable, the failure of older children to experience conversion could tear families apart in this life and most definitely in eternity.

In the democratic, egalitarian ethos of an American society becoming more child-centered, the moral situation of the child and the duties of parents inevitably therefore became a matter of acute theological concern. The maternal associations and mothers' magazines established in the wake of the revivals of the 1820s and 1830s had been aimed at ensuring the eternal safety of the young. They were among the first to question why those who since infancy had been shaped by the religious influence of the home still needed to undergo conversion.[34] Their concern became part of a larger theological debate. Timothy Dwight (1757–1817), although still firmly rooting his thought in the tradition of his grandfather, Jonathan Edwards, had already placed a new emphasis on the receptivity of the child to Christian nurture and on the mother's special gifts for this task. As well, New Haven theologian Nathaniel Taylor (1786–1858) had challenged the Calvinist concept of total human depravity. Such developments opened a way for others such as Henry Ward Beecher and his literary sisters, Catharine and Harriet, to insist that God "was a God of love—intimate, immanent and concerned about human welfare."[35] Beecher continued to mount religious revivals in his New York congregation, but other theologians questioned whether revivalism was even a necessary part of evangelical religion and argued that greater attention should be devoted instead to normalizing the process

33. Bendroth, *Growing Up Protestant*, 20.
34. Ryan, *Cradle of the Middle Class*, 101.
35. McDannell, *Christian Home in Victorian America*, 18.

of sanctification. Foremost was the Congregationalist minister Horace Bushnell (1802–1876), whose book *Christian Nurture*, first published in 1847, has been seen as another major turning point, in this case toward a liberal evangelicalism.[36] Bushnell did not question that children were born with a sinful nature, but he believed that their openness to environmental influences could work positively.[37] Rather than breaking a child's will in preparation for conversion (as had been the approach of earlier evangelical educators such as Francis Wayland, well-known Baptist minister and president of Brown University), parents who surrounded their children with Christian influences from infancy could eliminate the need for conversion entirely and help them grow into mature Christians. In Bushnell's words, "The child is to be trained, not for conversion at some advanced age, but [is] expected to *grow up a Christian*. . . . God offers grace to make it possible."[38] God's grace now worked primarily not through the emotion-laden revival service but through the natural setting of home, motherhood, Sunday schools, and all the available agents of Christian nurture.

Bushnell was not alone in taking such a stance; theologians within other evangelical traditions were also rearticulating theology to address the place of the child within their denominational moral economy. Already in 1842, F. G. Hibbard, for example, a Methodist Episcopal minister in the Genesee Conference, had gone further in a lengthy treatise directed at Baptist teaching on adult baptism. Seeking to expunge any traces of baptismal regeneration from John Wesley's writings, Hibbard contended that as a result of Christ's atonement children were in a state of innocence at birth, and therefore the main concern of the church was not conversion but Christian nurture to keep them in their original state of innocence.[39] Hibbard's views on the moral status of the child, along with similar teachings by another American Methodist, Robert Olin, encountered strong resistance in Canada in the 1870s. There the leading Wesleyan theologian, Nathanael Burwash, echoing the warnings of the British parent denomination, reminded parents that for the sake of their children's eternal safety their aim was "not simply to have them moral

36. Bendroth, *Growing Up Protestant*, 27.

37. For the role of the Sunday school see Anne M. Boylan, *Sunday School: The Formation of an American Institution* (New Haven: Yale University Press, 1988), 133–65.

38. Horace Bushnell, *Christian Nurture* (New York: Charles Scribner, 1861), 10.

39. F. G. Hibbard, *A Treatise on Infant Baptism* (New York: G. Lane and P. P. Sandford, 1843), 5–6.

but by the help of God to have them converted."[40] That notwithstanding, when in the space of one week he and his wife, Margaret Proctor, lost four children under the age of ten to black diphtheria, and presumably before they had experienced a definite conversion, both parents believed without question that one day all would be reunited in heaven.

Not surprisingly, at such times when a family experienced illness and death, the tension between official doctrine and personal experience was acute. These experiences, with only a few exceptions, notably in the American Civil War, took place in the home and became part of the ritual of domestic religion. In their unpredictable and often physically alienating aspects, they challenged the orderliness of daily existence and brought families face-to-face with the chaotic side of nature. Evangelicals countered this with an experiential faith that provided a hedge against the uncertainty of eternal destiny and offered some confidence in proclaiming those who had been saved. This confidence was based not only on the ill or dying person's previous experience of conversion, for that could be "sinned away." Just as important was evidence of his or her subsequent moral life and its culmination in "a good death" as attested in a deathbed narrative.[41] Hence, although theological assurance of salvation rested with a sovereign God, in practical terms evangelicals were comforted by the narrative in which the dying person provided testimony of complete reliance on forgiveness through Christ's atonement and peacefully, sometimes even joyfully, accepted death. Obituaries attesting to such a good death were most often authored by clergy who fully drew on their didactic potential for the conversion of the living.

Of special concern in an age of high child mortality were children and youth, whose susceptibility was targeted by books such as the slim volume offered by the American Tract Society, *Narratives of Pious Children*, which presented in painstaking detail the exemplary lives and deaths of seventeen British children, some of whom were surprisingly happy to die. In his parting admonition, the author, the Reverend George Hendley, advised his young readers that "If you become like these dear children ... then you will be happy, your parents and your friends will love you, and God will love you; and when you die you will go to heaven, and dwell

40. Cited in Marguerite Van Die, *An Evangelical Mind: Nathanael Burwash and the Methodist Tradition in Canada, 1839-1917* (Montreal, Kingston: McGill-Queen's University Press, 1989), 28.
41. Stephan, *Redeeming the Southern Family*, 191-202.

with God, in whose presence there is fullness of joy, and at whose right hand are pleasures for evermore."[42] As in the juvenile fiction of the time, rather than warning children of their fate in the hands of an angry God, his assumptions were optimistic, relying on their moral malleability and guilt-shaped conscience.

The prevalence of illness and lack of effective medical intervention tended to make women as primary caregivers the source of the oral and, less often, the written testimony of a family member's spiritual encounter with life-threatening illness and death. There were many times, however, when evidence of a good death was unavailable. When the deathbed ritual could not unfold as prescribed, as in the case of sudden death, loss of consciousness or speaking ability, or questions about the deceased's moral behavior and preparedness, women caregivers could help with improvisation. Adding or subtracting details were ways whereby the eternal safety of the deceased could at least be intimated to the bereaved. As Drew Gilpin Faust has documented in *This Republic of Suffering*, the deaths of an estimated 620,000 soldiers far away from their families in the course of the American Civil War gave a heightened urgency to such reconstructions. Frequently authored by clergy and male relatives, these accounts of a good death served as a kind of lifeline between the new world of battle and the familiar world of home.[43]

Heaven, too, was reconceptualized when, in the late 1860s, writers such as Elizabeth Stuart Phelps in *The Gates Ajar* confidently began to describe an afterlife where mountains, trees, and homes filled with pianos, books, and pictures comfortably reflected middle-class materialism and taste. Narratives of the good death and the construction of a heaven that immortalized the Victorian family and domesticity were forms of consolation that promised the bereaved reunion with the deceased in a more perfect replica of earth.[44] In a study of southern evangelicalism, Scott Stephan has noted that, well before Phelps's work, women were putting their own expectations of heavenly happiness and family reunion into writing. Such expectations, however, were also laced with anxiety, for, since God was the final judge of a person's life on earth, hope of heaven was always in tension with fear of hell. One could never be absolutely

42. George Hendley, *Narratives of Pious Children* (New York: American Tract Society, n.d.), 62.

43. Drew Gilpin Faust, *This Republic of Suffering: Death and the American Civil War* (New York: Vintage Books, 2008), especially 4–33.

44. Faust, *This Republic of Suffering*, 185.

certain of a loved one's eternal destiny, as is evident in the number of accounts of women anxiously exhorting and praying at a family member's sickbed.[45] Given the prevailing cultural context, evangelical laypeople most often resolved the tension with a sensibility that favored the good death over the terrors of hell and replaced ambiguity with hope-filled certainty and trust in a loving God. Nothing tested this trust more than the death of an innocent child. For some, such as Harriet Beecher Stowe, who had abandoned a manifestly capricious Calvinist deity for an immanent loving God, the sudden cholera and death of her beloved infant Charley in 1849 could make sense only by believing that God had selected certain "special children" for a brighter and better future.[46]

For middle-class women and men, the hope in a brighter future when families would be reunited found material expression in the rural cemetery movement. By the mid-1840s well-to-do urban Protestants in Europe and North America were replacing older downtown, cramped, and unsanitary church graveyards with rural cemeteries unconnected to churches and under private control. Set apart from the smoke and stench of industry, cemeteries such as Laurel Hill (Philadelphia, 1836), Greenwood (Brooklyn, 1838), Allegheny (Pittsburgh, 1844), St. James (Toronto, 1844), Spring Grove (Cincinnati, 1845), Hollywood (Richmond, Virginia, 1849), and Mount Royal (Montreal, 1852) provided quiet places of remembrance, reflection, and communing with the spirit of the deceased. With their delicately carved angels, funeral urns, crosses, open Bibles, and other religious symbols, individual tombs set in a manicured landscape reinforced the message that death was not an end, but the beginning of an ordered eternal life with Christ.[47] Female images in the form of angels gave lasting evidence of women's role in gently guiding family members to heaven, while cherubs attested to the innocence of childhood. In keeping with the ideals of domestic religion, the rural cemetery offered narratives of immortality that reflected an orderly life, material comfort, and commerce, all of which had made these cemeteries possible. In the words of one of the movement's historians, "Victorian cemeteries were the material expression of the common ideal that heaven was home and home was heaven."[48]

45. Stephan, *Redeeming the Southern Family*, 185–87.

46. Joan D. Hedrick, *Harriet Beecher Stowe: A Life* (New York: Oxford University Press, 1994), 190–92.

47. Colleen McDannell, *Material Christianity: Religion and Popular Culture in America* (New Haven: Yale University Press, 1995), 103–31.

48. McDannell, *Material Christianity*, 130.

Rural cemeteries were only one outstanding expression of the evangelical pursuit to sacralize the mundane. Though the prevailing romanticism influenced the integration of the sacred and secular, its main driving force was the evangelical aspiration to Christianize every aspect of life, private as well as public. Organic unity had always been the ideal of Christendom, and until the eighteenth century in a predominantly agrarian society it had found expression in a religious establishment. In the antebellum period this ideal had been fractured by the separation of church and state, the expansion of the market economy, and the urbanization and industrialization that followed. Although churches retained their stabilizing function, the primary burden for maintaining a Christian society under voluntarism rested with the home, whose sanctity in turn required a dependable moral environment. The previous chapter in this volume has detailed how this concern found expression in evangelical efforts at moral reform. For evangelical women, especially in the urban North and in British North America, participation in moral reform offered an opportunity to make a meaningful contribution to public life and to transcend the "separation of spheres" that consigned them to the private sphere.[49] In keeping with the domestic ideal, female action was specifically aimed at protecting home and family from such public threats as Sabbath breaking, sexual offenses, gambling, and drunkenness.[50] In Rochester, evangelical women swept up in the Finney revivals organized a Female Moral Society in the mid-1830s; its committee "on the treatment of licentious men" was intent on exposing and eradicating adultery and licentious behavior.[51] In New York City, Margaret Barrett Allen Prior (1775-1842), hired as a missionary by the New York Female Moral Reform Society, for fifteen years walked the streets and visited the poor and the ill in slums, rescuing girls from brothels and aiding them to find respectable employment.[52]

Nothing, however, galvanized evangelicals of both sexes more than the abuse of alcohol, arguably the greatest financial and emotional threat to the family, when a wage earner could easily consume a week's wages

49. For the historiography on the limitations southern women experienced, see Stephan, *Redeeming the Southern Home*, 134, and 265n3.

50. Ryan, *Cradle of the Middle Class*, 116-27.

51. Nancy Hewitt, *Women's Activism and Social Change: Rochester, New York, 1822-1872* (Ithaca: Cornell University Press, 1984), 86-87.

52. Rosemary Radford Ruether and Rosemary Skinner Keller, eds., *Women and Religion in America*, vol. 1 (San Francisco: Harper & Row, 1982), 322-24.

in a few hours spent in the multitude of grog shops and taverns found in every town. In Montreal, Canada's largest urban center, elite Protestant women, influenced by American examples and by such evangelical "family" papers as *The Montreal Witness* and the *Canada Temperance Advocate*, were among the most active founding members of the Montreal Temperance Society in 1836. Five years later its Ladies Committee had succeeded in raising funds for a fulltime temperance worker, soon boosted to six traveling agents all engaged in province-wide temperance evangelism. Moved by idealism, sentimentality, and painful realities seen or experienced in homes and neighborhoods, women swelled the temperance ranks, and often received praise for their organizing, funding, and speaking abilities. "We do not know who could better describe the sad scenes occasioned by intemperance than those who have been its innocent victims," concluded one newspaper editor in Hamilton, Canada West, in 1851, commenting on the "rather novel thing" of a female temperance lecturer. By that date women on both sides of the border had begun political action through forming delegations to appeal to local authorities for stricter tavern laws.[53] One of the strongest calls for female suffrage in the latter decades of the nineteenth century would come from women in support of legislation aimed at protecting home and family from the ravages of alcohol and the power of the liquor industry.

At a time when politics remained a male prerogative, women's presence in the temperance cause reinforced an image of shared gender roles that was also increasingly informing the evangelical ideal of domesticity. In vaunting moral motherhood and woman's unique spiritual endowment, scholarly literature on domestic religion has at times downplayed the father's role, and some female writers, such as Catharine Beecher, wrote men entirely out of their constructions of the Christian home.[54] As clergy in the nineteenth century knew all too well, however, male participation was critical to the material infrastructure of the evangelical enterprise. Times of revival were measured not by the number of female and youthful converts, but by the entry of a greater number of men than usual into church membership.[55] Their presence was as es-

53. Jan Noel, *Canada Dry: Temperance Crusades in Canada before Confederation* (Toronto: Toronto University Press, 1995), 98–102.

54. McDannell, *Christian Home in Victorian America*, 114–15; Amanda Vickery, "Golden Age to Separate Spheres? A Review of the Categories and Chronology of English Women's History," *Historical Journal* 36 (1993): 384–414.

55. Terry D. Bilhartz, "Sex and the Second Great Awakening: The Feminization

sential for evangelical continuity as the mother's Christian nurture of the young. The evangelical ideal of a life of active service and acceptable moral conduct was best met if home, church, and civic life were closely integrated. Select local studies in the northeastern United States and in several British North American towns indicate that this became the case during and after religious revivals in the years 1830 to 1860. Increasingly, prominent male converts combined civic and church leadership by serving on church disciplinary committees, organizing a range of voluntary societies and charitable institutions, and managing missions and Sunday schools. At the same time their wives and daughters were indispensable fundraisers, served as active Sunday school and mission workers, and opened their homes to cottage prayer groups. Together, therefore, evangelical women and men worked to surround their children with Christian influences inside and outside the home.[56]

Contrary to historiography that has assumed the secular male world to be a moral wasteland, evangelical writers also constructed a concept of Christian manhood in keeping with the new ideal of domestic religion.[57] By the mid-nineteenth century, alongside extolling the virtue of the praying mother in the home, they exhorted male readers to practice such Christian virtues in the world of commerce as restraint, honesty, and a sense of moral responsibility, virtues also modeled in the juvenile literature of the period. Appearing at a time when denominational expansion called for increased lay involvement in time and money, this new construct of masculinity, the "Christian businessman," by the 1850s began to figure prominently in the columns of denominational papers and in prescriptive and biographical literature.[58]

---

of American Religion Reconsidered," in *Belief and Behavior: Essays in the New Religious History*, ed. Philip R. Vandermeer and Robert P. Swierenga (New Brunswick, NJ: Rutgers University Press, 1991), 116-35; John Tosh, *A Man's Place: Masculinity and the Middle-Class Home in Victorian England* (New Haven: Yale University Press, 1999).

56. Marguerite Van Die, "'The Marks of a Genuine Revival': Religion, Social Change, Gender and Community in Mid-Victorian Brantford, Ontario," *Canadian Historical Review* 79, no. 3 (1998): 524-63; David W. Bebbington, *Victorian Religious Revivals: Culture and Piety in Local and Global Contexts* (New York: Oxford University Press, 2012), chap. 6.

57. Clyde Griffen, "Reconstructing Masculinity from the Evangelical Revival to the Waning of Progressivism: A Speculative Synthesis," in *Meanings for Manhood*, ed. Mark Carnes and Clyde Griffin (Chicago: University of Chicago Press, 1990), 183-91.

58. Mark A. Noll, "Protestant Reasoning about Money and the Economy, 1790-1860: A Preliminary Probe," in *God and Mammon: Protestants, Money, and the Market, 1790-1860*, ed. Noll (New York: Oxford University Press, 2002), 274-75.

Its practical expression can be traced to the interdenominational "businessmen's revivals" held in major northern United States and Canadian urban centers in the fall and winter of 1857-58. Occurring at a time of financial crisis, high unemployment, and political strife over the extension of slavery with the Kansas-Nebraska Act, the revivals were a lay event that for the first time acknowledged and celebrated the affinity between evangelical religion and an emerging corporate culture. Into the 1850s, congregational revivals had followed the internal rhythm of the various denominations: Presbyterian "holy fairs," Methodist quarterly meetings and "watch night" services, and Baptist "protracted services." Novel this time were the interdenominational cooperation among urban churches, the prominent role of laymen, and the inclusion of noon-hour meetings held in the secular business district. In an urban landscape where public and private spaces were becoming more differentiated, the extensive advertising, tightly controlled schedule, and specific time allotment for prayers all reflected middle-class methods and values.

Occurring at a critical time in both the northern United States and British North America, the revivals modeled a new public role for evangelical laymen as active participants in the extension of religion to the workplace and to the nation. Among those drawn to a deeper faith were Philadelphia's "merchant prince" John Wannamaker and evangelist Dwight Moody, both of whom in different ways succeeded in blending business culture with late Victorian sentimentalism in ways that appealed to their middle-class constituencies.[59] Accelerated by the Civil War and Reconstruction, the synergy of northern evangelicalism and business helped provide missionaries, reformers, teachers, evangelists, and clergy with a public forum from which to proclaim and implement the Christian-home ideal as key to the moral transformation of the South, the nation, and the world beyond.[60] In the South, white evangelicals resisted such postmillennialism and instead followed their own trajectory of redefinition as women turned their personal self-sacrifice for family members, and the sacrifice in war of their sons and husbands, into a

59. For the discussion of the revival in New York City and its aftermath I am indebted to Kathryn Teresa Long, *The Revival of 1857-58: Interpreting an American Religious Awakening* (New York: Oxford University Press, 1998). John Corrigan, in *Business of the Heart: Religion and Emotion in the Nineteenth Century* (Berkeley: University of California Press, 2002), examines its gendered impact on the Boston area.

60. Bendroth, *Growing Up Protestant*, 39-59.

collective righteous "Cause" whose conservative family values would become associated in time with the "Bible Belt."[61]

Unlike the American South, British North America had begun by the 1850s to experience a pattern of accelerated economic growth resulting from extensive railway and canal construction, population increase, and rising farm output. Thanks to trade reciprocity with the United States, its economy had become more integrated into the American one, and thus it also shared the ill effects of that country's 1857 financial crisis. Several months before the start of the "businessmen's revivals," American Methodist revivalist Phoebe Palmer and her husband Walter had visited the industrializing city of Hamilton, on the shores of Lake Ontario. During their two-week stay, using the slogan "a laity for the times," the Palmers combined an emphasis on holiness with a practical piety that would have a far-reaching impact on the country's growing evangelical middle class.[62] Here, however, the turning point differed in a number of significant ways from the American. Unlike in the United States, where denominations had fractured over slavery in the 1840s, followed by bloody civil war in the 1860s, British North America's slower social and economic change and small, scattered population (less than a tenth of the American population in 1860) led to urgent demands for unification. This found political expression in Confederation in 1867, and denominational expression in the 1870s and 1880s in national Presbyterian and Methodist unions, to be followed by further efforts at union among the major evangelical denominations.[63] Although a shared emphasis on religious nurture in the home had been a factor facilitating union, Canadian evangelicals were unable to follow the American model and translate the values associated with the "Christian home" into a national construct. Engaged in bitter

61. Drew Gilpin Faust, "Altars of Sacrifice: Confederate Women and the Narratives of War," *Journal of American History* 76 (March 1990): 1200–1228; Kurt O. Berends, "Confederate Sacrifice and the 'Redemption' of the South," in *Religion in the American South: Protestants and Others in History and Culture*, ed. Beth Barton Schweiger and Donald Mathews (Chapel Hill: University of North Carolina Press, 2004), 99–123.

62. Marguerite Van Die, "A March of Victory and Triumph in Praise of 'The Beauty of Holiness': Laity and the Evangelical Impulse in Canadian Methodism, 1800–1884," in *Aspects of the Canadian Evangelical Experience*, ed. G. A. Rawlyk (Kingston, Montreal: McGill-Queen's University Press, 1997), 73–89.

63. For the unions and their culmination in the formation of the United Church of Canada see Phyllis D. Airhart, *A Church with the Soul of a Nation: Making and Remaking the United Church of Canada* (Montreal, Kingston: McGill-Queen's University Press, 2014), 1–29.

rhetorical warfare with the country's "priest-ridden" Roman Catholics, who in 1871 formed 40 percent of the population, the best they could achieve was to uphold the domestic ideal as a touchstone of Protestant moral superiority.[64]

As is evident from these comparisons, the evangelical ideal in domestic religion and its various turning points elude simple generalization, for each varies with place and time. Because it asks how people actually practiced religion in their daily lives, the study of domestic religion is more fluid and less clearly defined than that of doctrine and institutions. When the home becomes the site of religious nurture, such constructs as "declension," "evangelicalism," and formulaic definitions such as David Bebbington's "biblicism, conversionism, crucicentrism, and activism" (the classic definition of "evangelicalism") lose some of their interpretive force.[65] Instead, more attention has to be given to the structures that define everyday lives, to material culture, and to the tensions and contradictions people experience when they try to make connections between their own family situation, the wider society, and God.[66] Their efforts to address these tensions and contradictions can be seen as turning points, and they are intimately related to time and place. Though timing and results differed in the slave-holding South, among the northern middle class, or in colonial British North America, the various turning points all reflected a shared impulse by evangelicals to make meaningful connections between their faith and their daily lives. In every instance in this study, acceptance of the domestic ideal resulted in evangelical integration into the mainstream.

Evangelicals in the antebellum years were not the first to value family religion, but the separation of church and state, the move to religious voluntarism, and the demands of an expanding economy placed a new burden on believing parents. To cite historian John Gillis in his aptly entitled book *A World of Their Own Making,* "to the challenge of sustain-

64. J. R. Miller, "Anti-Catholicism in Canada: From the British Conquest to the Great War," in *Creed and Culture: The Place of English-Speaking Catholics in Canadian Society, 1750-1930,* ed. T. Murphy and G. Stortz (Montreal, Kingston: McGill-Queen's University Press, 1993), 25-48.

65. David W. Bebbington, *Evangelicalism in Modern Britain: A History from the 1730s to the 1980s* (London: Unwin Hyman, 1989), 3.

66. For an introduction to religion as lived experience see Robert Orsi, *Between Heaven and Earth: The Religious Worlds People Make and the Scholars Who Study Them* (Princeton: Princeton University Press, 2005).

ing the material basis of family life was now added the awesome task of providing for its spiritual requirements."[67] Breaking a child's will as the way to conversion had once fit with the values of a patriarchal, agrarian world. In the turbulent democratic and industrializing North, as well as in southern plantations and middle-class Canadian homes, gradual conversion in the home through a mother's moral training shaped a child to practice self-restraint and responsibility as an adult. With children raised in this way, notes another historian, "their actions, their beliefs, and their temperaments reveal, as nothing else could, that their earliest and most formative experiences still shaped and influenced their lives throughout youth and adulthood."[68] Culturally conditioned values appeared to them as natural, especially when supported by such material forms as Gothic architecture, rural cemeteries, and high-toned literature. Forming a further extension of the domestic ideal were a host of voluntary societies and missions, all dedicated to Christianizing society, the nation, and ultimately the world.

Presence is never abstract but always culturally conditioned. By adopting the domestic ideal as a first step in sanctifying all of life, evangelicals in the antebellum period implicitly addressed the inherent contradiction between maintaining purity and extending presence in a constantly changing society. Although collectively evangelicals considered home and family central to their identity, the religious worlds they constructed in the Deep South, in the urban North, and in British North America were therefore also distinctly different.

67. John Gillis, *A World of Their Own Making: Myth, Ritual, and the Quest for Family Values* (New York: Basic Books, 1996), 72.

68. Phillip J. Greven, *The Protestant Temperament: Patterns of Child-Rearing, Religious Experience, and the Self in Early America* (New York: Alfred A. Knopf, 1977), 64-65.

CHAPTER 6

The Civil War and the Making of Conservative American Evangelicalism

Luke E. Harlow

On Saturday, March 4, 1865, Abraham Lincoln addressed a crowd of more than 30,000 who had come to Washington, DC, to hear the US president speak on the occasion of his second inauguration. Most auditors failed to hear a single word Lincoln uttered that day, but his seven-hundred-word oration has nonetheless gone down as the most significant speech in American political history. Hindsight tells us that the American Civil War was nearing its end, but much remained unresolved militarily at that moment. The wave of Confederate surrenders would not begin for another month, starting on April 9 with Robert E. Lee at Appomattox Courthouse. Moreover, although some 1.2 million slaves had found freedom by that date, especially through military service, the emancipation of the country's remaining 2.75 million enslaved would not happen for several more months as US Army occupation continued to spread throughout the South. The Thirteenth Amendment ultimately ended slavery legally, but it was working its way through the states, and it would not be ratified until December.[1]

Four years earlier, Lincoln's election had prompted the secession of seven slaveholding states: South Carolina, Mississippi, Florida, Alabama, Georgia, Louisiana, and Texas. Virginia, Arkansas, North Carolina, and

---

1. Richard Carwardine, *Lincoln: A Life of Purpose and Power* (2003; New York: Knopf, 2006), 244–48; Gregory P. Downs, *After Appomattox: Military Occupation and the Ends of the War* (Cambridge, MA: Harvard University Press, 2015), 41–42.

With special thanks to Rusty Hawkins, Karl Gunther, Laura Porter, and Heath Carter.

Tennessee joined the Confederacy after Lincoln called on April 15, 1861, for 75,000 volunteers to suppress the southern rebellion that began at Fort Sumter, South Carolina. The war that followed would claim 750,000 soldiers'—and an untold number of civilians'—lives, more than 2 percent of the American population.

With the carnage still unfolding at the time of his second inaugural address, Lincoln explained directly how he saw the moral stakes of the conflict. In the most cited and quoted passage from that speech, Lincoln said the following:

> Both read the same Bible and pray to the same God, and each invokes His aid against the other. It may seem strange that any men should dare to ask a just God's assistance in wringing their bread from the sweat of other men's faces, but let us judge not, that we be not judged. The prayers of both could not be answered. That of neither has been answered fully. The Almighty has His own purposes. "Woe unto the world because of offenses; for it must needs be that offenses come, but woe to that man by whom the offense cometh." If we shall suppose that American slavery is one of those offenses which, in the providence of God, must needs come, but which, having continued through His appointed time, He now wills to remove, and that He gives to both North and South this terrible war as the woe due to those by whom the offense came, shall we discern therein any departure from those divine attributes which the believers in a living God always ascribe to Him? Fondly do we hope, fervently do we pray, that this mighty scourge of war may speedily pass away. Yet, if God wills that it continue until all the wealth piled by the bondsman's two hundred and fifty years of unrequited toil shall be sunk, and until every drop of blood drawn with the lash shall be paid by another drawn with the sword, as was said three thousand years ago, so still it must be said "the judgments of the Lord are true and righteous altogether."[2]

Despite his own profound religious sensibilities, Abraham Lincoln rarely darkened the door of a church. Yet he sounded very much like an evangelical Christian on this occasion, quoting Matthew 7:1, Matthew 18:7, and Psalm 19:9, and elsewhere in the speech employing biblical para-

---

2. Abraham Lincoln, "Second Inaugural Address," March 4, 1865, online at http://avalon.law.yale.edu/19th_century/lincoln2.asp.

phrase. Here Lincoln followed in the footsteps of an abolitionist tradition that for the last three decades had drawn on evangelical moral reasoning to condemn American slavery. His message was not vindictive. Lincoln argued that the entire United States—not merely the southern rebellion—was complicit in the sin of slavery. The war was thus fought to reckon with the nation's original sin: slavery. Because Americans had proven so unwilling to give up slavery—including those in the Border States who stayed in the Union and retained their claims to hold slaves well after the Emancipation Proclamation (1863)—there was no peaceful way to avoid the conflict. In this abolitionist view, which Lincoln clearly held in this moment, the war was not pointless or needless. It was a national atonement. The Civil War was a kind of blood sacrifice that led to redemption.

In articulating this interpretation of the war, where both Unionists and Confederates saw righteousness for their causes because of the ways they read Holy Scripture, the non-evangelical Lincoln spoke to a major fissure that ripped apart American evangelicalism and changed its character forever. For the abolitionist view of the Civil War's moral meaning conflicted directly with another evangelical vision. Indeed, as Lincoln explained, the Civil War had come about in large part because of two diametrically opposed ideas about the future of evangelical America: one antislavery and one proslavery. The Civil War resolved the great question of nineteenth-century American politics and culture: it determined that the United States would move forward as a country free from slavery. But it left unresolved a core tension that had in large part brought about the war itself: the religious struggle over slavery. That struggle turned on the way in which antislavery and proslavery Christians read the Bible.

In the proslavery vision held by white southerners, and even some white northerners, "redemption" did not connote atonement for slavery. As they saw it, slaveholding was no sin. Theirs was a righteous and biblical institution, a "divine trust" as New Orleans Presbyterian minister Benjamin M. Palmer had called it in 1860. Furthermore, the Confederate States of America's 1861 constitution "invok[ed] the favor and guidance of Almighty God" to bless the slaveholding republic it governed. And in December 1865 the Southern Presbyterian Church strikingly argued that, even though the war ended slavery in its "civil aspects," the fact remained that "the lawfulness of the relation as a question of social morality, and of Scriptural truth, has lost nothing of its importance." Abolitionism was still an "insidious error," "unscriptural and fanatical," "condemned not only by the word of God, but by the voice of the Church in all ages." As these white southern evangelicals explained, abolitionism proved "one of the most pernicious heresies of modern times." For white Christians in the South, in other words, slavery was not sinful; destroying slavery was.[3]

The Civil War could not resolve this conflict between antislavery and proslavery visions of the Christian faith. But because the Civil War brought the death of American slavery, it represented a major turning point in the history of American evangelicalism. To that moment, evangelicalism had been diffuse and diverse, which is why so much turmoil persisted among the godly over a range of social questions up to the Civil War: a variety of constituencies vied to establish the shape of the movement. The Civil War, and especially the emancipation it brought, removed the most significant cause of evangelical infighting in the middle of the nineteenth century. In so doing it streamlined the movement into one far narrower and far more conservative.

The Civil War and emancipation reordered the evangelical landscape in three ways. First, the slavery debates paved the way for the rise of liberal Protestantism, which would find itself outside the evangelical mainstream. Second, for African Americans, emancipation proved the culmination of a process long under way: the liberation of black believers from white churches. Even as African American Protestants remained overwhelmingly "evangelical" in tone and theology, evangelicalism after the Civil War, institutionally considered, would be a movement for whites only. Third, mainstream postwar evangelicalism, in large part because of the absence of more "liberal" Protestants and African Americans, abandoned a commitment to social activism—especially the kind espoused by antislavery evangelicals before the war, which connected revivalism with social reform. This chapter explains how the Civil War created this new conservative American evangelicalism.

Evangelicals of all types throughout nineteenth-century America drew their faith from a commitment to the primacy of the Bible as the divinely inspired, authoritative guide for the shaping of Christian life and practice.

3. Benjamin M. Palmer, "Slavery a Divine Trust," in *Fast Day Sermons; or The Pulpit on the State of the Country* (New York: Rudd & Carleton, 1861), 57–80; *Provisional and Permanent Constitutions, Together with the Acts and Resolutions of the Three Sessions of the Provisional Congress of the Confederate States* (Richmond, VA: Tyler, Wise, Allegre, and Smith, 1861), 3; *The American Annual Cyclopedia and Register of Important Events of the Year 1865*, vol. 5 (New York: Appleton, 1870), 706.

Moreover, evangelicals shared a common method of biblical interpretation. Emphasizing a literalist hermeneutic—inherited from the Reformed theological tradition, influenced by the common sense moral reasoning of the Scottish Enlightenment, and steeped in the American principle of democratic individualism—American evangelicals believed the Bible to be an eminently readable book that contained easily understandable, God-given teachings, which applied to all people at all times.[4]

With this understanding of the Bible, white southerners crafted a Christian argument that justified slavery. And by the time of the Civil War, that proslavery argument had been sharpened by decades of disputation with antislavery believers over the biblical merits of slavery. A stable of texts appeared in proslavery evangelical writings, proving that the Bible sanctioned slaveholding as integral to the divine economy. Jesus of Nazareth lived in a world of slaveholders but never discussed slavery in the Gospels—despite condemning many other sins. But other biblical texts were loaded with accounts of divine mandates for slaveholding. The Old Testament Pentateuch explained very carefully how the Hebrew people of God were to treat slaves (Exodus 21; Leviticus 25; Deuteronomy 5, 15, 23). In the New Testament, both Paul (Ephesians 6; Colossians 3; 1 Timothy 6) and Peter (1 Peter 2) called on slaves to obey their masters as they would obey their God. In the epistle to Philemon, Paul sought to effect the reconciliation of two Christian believers: the letter's recipient, a master, and his fugitive slave named Onesimus. Paul instructed Onesimus to return to his condition of bondage, but he hoped Philemon might treat the returned slave "above a servant." In a nineteenth-century American context in which slaveholders assured critics that their chattel were part of an extended family, and in which fugitive slave laws compelled escaped slaves to return to their masters, the application of the epistle could not be missed.[5]

The proslavery argument did not simply hang on proof texts. As

---

4. On the "Reformed, literal hermeneutic" and its significance for religious debates over slavery in antebellum America, see Mark A. Noll, *America's God: From Jonathan Edwards to Abraham Lincoln* (New York: Oxford University Press, 2002), 367-401. The broad conclusions of the present chapter are indebted to *America's God* and also to Mark A. Noll, *The Civil War as a Theological Crisis* (Chapel Hill: University of North Carolina Press, 2006), and Mark A. Noll, *God and Race in American Politics: A Short History* (Princeton: Princeton University Press, 2008).

5. Molly Oshatz, *Slavery and Sin: The Fight against Slavery and the Rise of Liberal Protestantism* (New York: Oxford University Press, 2012), 5-9.

proslavery theologians contended, the whole biblical witness endorsed slavery, for the biblical writers simply assumed slaveholding would be part of the world. After running through a litany of texts on the question, Virginia Baptist minister Thornton Stringfellow put it this way in 1850: "all the [New Testament] churches are recognized as composed of masters and servants; and . . . they are instructed by Christ how to discharge their relative duties." As Stringfellow explained about biblical Christianity, the early faith "did not abolish [slavery], or the right of one Christian to hold another Christian in bondage," but instead "adds to the obligation of the servant to render service with good will to his master, and that gospel fellowship is not to be entertained with persons who will not consent to it!" In such a conservative biblicist reading, the idea that slavery—in and of itself—might be sinful was unimaginable. Such a case proved nearly unassailable for anyone committed to common nineteenth-century evangelical "orthodoxy." Slavery was a biblical institution; that fact could not be denied.[6]

But many believers looked at American slavery and saw substantial deviations from that of Scripture. It was true that a number of antislavery evangelical clergy accepted the force of the proslavery biblical argument. When Rhode Island Baptist Francis Wayland squared off against South Carolina Baptist Richard Fuller in 1845, the biblicist Wayland conceded, "Never before . . . has the defence [sic] of slavery on Christian principles been so ably conducted." But that did not mean Wayland accepted the proslavery argument. When it came to the way the slave trade violated biblical mandates to preserve families, or the denial of literacy and education that marked southern slave law, the failure to uphold the requirement for a jubilee manumitting slaves every seven years, the frequent rape of enslaved women by predatory masters, or the ongoing violence of the system itself, antislavery biblicists saw a system justly deserving condemnation.[7]

6. Thornton Stringfellow, "A Brief Examination of the Scripture Testimony on the Institution of Slavery," in *The Ideology of Slavery: Proslavery Thought in the Antebellum South, 1830-1860*, ed. Drew Gilpin Faust (Baton Rouge: Louisiana State University Press, 1981), 165.

7. Oshatz, *Slavery and Sin*, 61-65; Richard Fuller and Francis Wayland, *Domestic Slavery Considered as a Scriptural Institution: In a Correspondence between the Rev. Richard Fuller of Beaufort, S. C., and the Rev. Francis Wayland, of Providence, R. I.* (New York: Lewis Colby, 1845), 226. On the central contradiction of modern slavery, how it sought to dehumanize human beings who by definition could never be dehumanized, see David

Slavery's defenders, for their part, often agreed with aspects of such critiques and contended that there needed to be a campaign, as Georgia Presbyterian planter Charles C. Jones called it, for "the religious instruction of the negroes." Such proslavery evangelicals contended that they worked to reform the system from within. As evidence for this assertion, proslavery believers pointed to the churches in the American South: they were overwhelmingly populated with enslaved believers and claimed that they received African Americans as spiritual equals. Churches, unlike anywhere else in the South, permitted enslaved members to testify against whites. They recognized and sanctioned Christian marriages among slaves. Because biblical literacy and the exposition of the Word were both central to the evangelical faith, churches taught enslaved believers to read and also encouraged the rise of African American ministers. Sometimes white evangelicals even sponsored separate black congregations, albeit under white oversight. As proslavery believers saw it, they had engaged throughout the eighteenth and nineteenth centuries in a successful program of outreach to the "heathen" enslaved—"slave missions"—that had resulted in a Christianized southern African American population.[8]

It was true that by the time of the Civil War significant numbers of southern African Americans—perhaps one million of the Bible Belt's four million enslaved—worshiped with whites or in separate black churches under white authority. But as former Kentucky slave Henry Bibb explained in 1850, "the slaves, with but few exceptions have no confidence at all in [white] preaching, because they preach a pro-slavery doctrine." Therefore it was also true that an "invisible institution" flourished among the enslaved, where evangelical Christian categories fused with African traditions to create a religious system free from the control of the southern master class. Guarded as a secret among its adherents, and practiced in the remove of "hush arbors" to avoid drawing attention from whites, a fragmentary historical record attests to this "slave religion." There is

---

Brion Davis, *Inhuman Bondage: The Rise and Fall of Slavery in the New World* (New York: Oxford University Press, 2006).

8. See Charles C. Jones, *The Religious Instruction of the Negroes. In the United States* (Savannah: Thomas Purse, 1842); Charles F. Irons, *The Origins of Proslavery Christianity: White and Black Evangelicals in Colonial and Antebellum Virginia* (Chapel Hill: University of North Carolina Press, 2008); Eugene D. Genovese, *A Consuming Fire: The Fall of the Confederacy in the Mind of the White Christian South* (Athens: University of Georgia Press, 1998), 3-33; John B. Boles, ed., *Masters and Slaves in the House of the Lord: Race and Religion in the American South, 1740-1870* (Lexington: University Press of Kentucky, 1985).

no doubt, however, that enslaved African Americans overwhelmingly desired to throw off white supremacist religious authority. That aspiration would become manifest after emancipation, when they left southern biracial churches in droves for autonomous black churches. By their own actions, enslaved believers gave the lie to the professed positive good of the slaveholders' Christianity.[9]

And so did proslavery believers. Despite their arguments that the power of the Christian gospel ameliorated the worst aspects of American slavery, none of slavery's defenders challenged its most fundamental reality: that enslaved people were commodities who could be bought and sold at any time. As the leading historical estimates suggest, 875,000 enslaved Americans endured forced migration between 1820 and 1860. While many of that number traveled with owners who headed west to the fertile soil of the Mississippi Valley and beyond, the majority—60 to 70 percent—moved because of the domestic slave trade. Biblicist white evangelicals read the sacred words of Galatians 3:28—"there is neither bond nor free . . . ye are all one in Jesus Christ"—and suggested that such spiritual equality existed with their churches' enslaved members. In some otherworldly sense that may have been true. But in the material context occupied by nineteenth-century evangelical Americans, a traffic in Christian souls thrived with Christian sanction.[10]

The anti-Christian aspects of American slavery were plain for any outsider to see. As the Yankee Congregationalist Moses Stuart argued in 1850, nothing like the modern notion of racism—an *"unbiblical,* if not *anti-biblical,* theory"—existed in the Bible. Citing a favorite text of antislavery lights, Acts 17:26, Stuart argued that "GOD HAS MADE OF ONE BLOOD [all nations of men]." Reaching more broadly into the biblical witness, Stuart contended, "by the offence of Adam *all men* were made sinners, (Rom. 5:19); also that in Adam *all* have died, (1 Cor. 15:22). There is one God, one Mediator, one Sanctifier of all." Manifold sins shot through American slavery in this biblicist antislavery argument, not least of which was the pretense that justified its basis, white supremacy. "There is not a man in

9. Henry Bibb, *Narrative of the Life and Adventures of Henry Bibb,* ed. Charles Heglar (1850; Madison: University of Wisconsin Press, 2001), 24; Boles, *Masters and Slaves in the House of the Lord,* 9; Albert J. Raboteau, *Slave Religion: The "Invisible Institution" in the Antebellum South* (New York: Oxford University Press, 1978); Irons, *Origins of Proslavery Christianity.*

10. Steven Deyle, *Carry Me Back: The Domestic Slave Trade in American Life* (New York: Oxford University Press, 2005), 289.

all the South, (that believes there is a God and a Bible of sacred authority), who would dare" to argue that he was following the golden rule in holding slaves. Certainly that claim could not be made "in the presence of that God *who is no respecter of persons*. This is enough." As Stuart contended, slavery's abstract sanction in Scripture did not justify its existence in practice.[11]

This sort of antislavery biblicism never persuaded proslavery believers. It nonetheless revealed much about how far the antislavery biblical argument could be carried. Read straightforwardly and plainly, no reader could avoid the conclusion that slavery was part of the divine order. For slavery's evangelical defenders, that truth clinched their case. To question slavery was to question everything. It meant questioning divine revelation.[12]

The proslavery argument furthermore drew much of its force from the biblical record's roots in antiquity. Antislavery was a new idea in the history of Christianity. For more than eighteen hundred years, the voice of the church had spoken clearly and in the affirmative on slavery. It was not proslavery believers who deviated from tradition; it was those who attacked slavery. Slavery's defenders knew their church history. They proved that point over and over to their antislavery opponents. And they were not wrong. By the time of the Civil War, many antislavery believers—aware of the theological novelty of their position—innovated to develop a Christianity that could accommodate direct condemnations of the evil institution.[13]

Indeed, one of the most impressive things about the modern antislavery movement was how quickly it coalesced and achieved its goals. While challenges to slavery emerged in pockets in the North American colonies—often from enslaved Christians themselves—nothing like an organized antislavery movement developed in the Atlantic world until the late eighteenth century. But within the span of a century, Haitians threw off the chains of French masters (Haitian Revolution, 1791-1804); Britain ended slavery in its colonies (1833, with the exception of India, where slaveholding was legal as late as 1860); the American slave system came to an end (1865); and Cuban slavery ceased by royal decree (1886). When Brazil abolished slavery in 1888, no slaveholding regimes remained in a

11. Oshatz, *Slavery and Sin*, 61-65; Moses Stuart, *Conscience and the Constitution* (Boston: Crocker and Brewster, 1850), 101.

12. Elizabeth Fox-Genovese and Eugene D. Genovese, *The Mind of the Master Class: History and Faith in the Southern Slaveholders' Worldview* (New York: Cambridge University Press, 2005), 505-27.

13. Davis, *Inhuman Bondage*, 27-47; Oshatz, *Slavery and Sin*, 61-71.

Western Hemisphere that a century earlier had been entirely dependent on the institution. In proslavery perspective, it was as if the world had changed overnight.[14]

It is important to underscore the central role of believers in bringing down these slaveholding regimes. The British antislavery movement, led by Quakers and evangelicals, profoundly influenced developments on the other side of the Atlantic. But American antislavery took on a somewhat different shape thanks to the democratized, market-driven—and evangelical republican—nature of American society between the Revolution and the Civil War. Because of the theologies of the Second Great Awakening that swept the northern United States during the 1820s and 1830s, many evangelicals on free soil came to believe that the society around them needed to be perfected through social reform, which would serve to bring about the millennial kingdom of God on earth and in their midst. As the most famous evangelist of the period, Charles Grandison Finney, explained, it was the duty of all right-thinking Christians to destroy any and all sins that might prevent souls from achieving perfection in this life. Finney taught a post-Calvinist evangelical doctrine that emphasized the free moral agency of believers to change their circumstances as well as the world they found themselves in. Since alcohol consumption, Sabbath labor, urban blight and poverty, and slavery all imposed barriers that limited moral freedom, Finney called for their eradication. Although Finney was not the most prominent American abolitionist, his teachings provided a theological foundation for northern evangelicals in the movement.[15]

Finney's antislavery doctrine of Christian perfectionism developed in conjunction with a rising wave of organized black Christian protest against slavery and white supremacy. In 1816, Daniel Coker, Richard Allen, and Absalom Jones led the incorporation of the United States' first African Amer-

14. Paul Harvey, *Through the Storm, through the Night: A History of African American Christianity* (Lanham, MD: Rowman and Littlefield, 2011), 21-25; Davis, *Inhuman Bondage*, 1-11, 231-49, 323-31; Eric Foner, *Nothing but Freedom: Emancipation and Its Legacy* (1983; Baton Rouge: Louisiana State University Press, 2007).

15. Charles G. Finney, *Lectures on Revivals of Religion* (New York: Leavitt, Lord, and Co., 1835), 274-80; Keith J. Hardman, *Charles Grandison Finney, 1792-1875: Revivalist and Reformer* (Syracuse: Syracuse University Press, 1987), 253-57; Douglas M. Strong, *Perfectionist Politics: Abolitionism and the Religious Tensions of American Democracy* (Syracuse: Syracuse University Press, 1999), 12-43; Timothy L. Smith, *Revivalism and Social Reform: American Protestantism on the Eve of the Civil War* (1957; Baltimore: Johns Hopkins University Press, 1980); Davis, *Inhuman Bondage*, 250-52.

ican denomination, the African Methodist Episcopal Church (AME). The church's roots extended to the 1790s, when Allen and Jones founded the Bethel Methodist Episcopal Church in Philadelphia as a protest against the city's segregated Methodist houses of worship. From the outset, the AME cultivated a visible critique of white American society, and especially its Christianity. For some, such as Daniel Coker, who served as a missionary to Liberia, African American destiny resided outside the United States, in Africa. But to most AME members, and to African Americans more broadly, the idea of leaving the United States proved unpalatable and impossible.[16]

That had everything to do with the nature of the American Colonization Society (ACS), the primary white organization committed to sending American blacks to Liberia. Founded in 1816 and led by southern slaveholders and northern white racial separatists, the ACS rejected out of hand the idea that blacks would ever coexist equally with whites in the United States. Its stated goals included removing the country's entire black population. The colonization scheme could in fact be deployed for antislavery ends, because for whites everywhere in the United States until the Civil War the dominant approach to ending slavery was what was called "gradual emancipation." Though every colony held slaves at the time of the American Revolution, the northern states had all moved by 1800 to end slavery through a slow process, gradually freeing enslaved children as they aged. The end of slavery in the North did not happen overnight—not until 1827 in New York, 1847 in Pennsylvania, 1848 in Connecticut, and 1857 in New Hampshire. In New Jersey the last slaves did not find freedom until 1865. Furthermore, most northern states enacted some form of a "black exclusion law," designed to limit black mobility and protect white supremacy. With that context in mind, colonization seemed to many whites the logical conclusion to the only emancipation process they believed in. Blacks and whites could not exist on equal terms in the United States.[17]

For African Americans, gradualism and colonization were nonstarters. As free black communities in the North increasingly realized that whites' best idea for black freedom meant removal, they responded by asserting their own claim to equal citizenship in the republic. That rev-

16. Harvey, *Through the Storm, through the Night*, 37-39.

17. Nicholas Guyatt, *Providence and the Invention of the United States, 1607-1876* (New York: Cambridge University Press, 2007), 203-7; Luke E. Harlow, *Religion, Race, and the Making of Confederate Kentucky, 1830-1880* (New York: Cambridge University Press, 2014), 22-23; Steven Hahn, *The Political Worlds of Slavery and Freedom* (Cambridge, MA: Harvard University Press, 2009), 7-9.

olutionary idea was given its most focused and concerted expression in 1829 by a Boston AME member named David Walker in his *Appeal to the Colored Citizens of the World*. Born free in 1796 in Wilmington, North Carolina, Walker spent some time in the 1810s in Charleston, South Carolina, where he worshiped at the city's AME church. In 1822, Charleston whites claimed that a leading free member of the church, Denmark Vesey, had organized an insurrection designed to spread from the church to enslaved blacks in the city before spilling into the South Carolina Low Country. It is possible that Walker himself was a participant in the plan, though it never got off the ground and historians widely debate whether or not it actually existed. The result was that 131 Charleston blacks were arrested with thirty-five hanged, including Vesey. The AME church was closed, and southern whites grew increasingly vigilant about regulating black assemblies. Walker himself left Charleston shortly thereafter and made his way to Boston, where he set up shop around 1825 selling used clothes.[18]

Four years later, Walker published his *Appeal*. It drew deeply on biblical chapter-and-verse to show the error of white American Christianity. Walker quoted Matthew 18:6:

> "Whoso shall offend one of these little ones which believe in me, it were better for him that a millstone were hanged about his neck, and that he were drowned in the depth of the sea." But the Americans with this very threatening of the Lord's, not only beat his little ones among the Africans, but many of them they put to death or murder. Now the avaricious Americans, think that the Lord Jesus Christ will let them off, because his words are no more than the words of a man!!!

Walker excoriated the "enlightened white Christians of America" for assuming the country was a white man's republic when "we have enriched it with our *blood and tears*." In this understanding, colonization was nothing more than a delusion that assuaged white anxieties and forestalled a true reckoning with the evils of slavery and white supremacy.[19]

---

18. Stephen Kantrowitz, *More Than Freedom: Fighting for Citizenship in a White Republic, 1829-1889* (New York: Penguin, 2013), 27-29; Peter P. Hinks, "Introduction," in David Walker, *Appeal to the Colored Citizens of the World*, ed. Hinks (University Park: Pennsylvania State University Press, 2000), xiv-xxv; Michael P. Johnson, "Denmark Vesey and His Co-Conspirators," *William and Mary Quarterly*, 3rd ser., 58, no. 4 (October 2001): 915-76.

19. Walker, *Appeal*, 67-69.

Walker's antislavery, anticolonizationist, antiracist argument for the full inclusion of African Americans in the United States registered a decisive impact. Scandalous to white southerners, Walker's *Appeal* was condemned for its purported influence on the self-trained Baptist preacher Nat Turner's August 1831 slave uprising in Southampton County, Virginia, which slayed sixty whites. If that connection was a stretch, it did directly influence the shape of the radical abolition movement that coalesced earlier that same year. On January 1, a white Bostonian named William Lloyd Garrison began publishing the *Liberator*, a weekly newspaper dedicated to the immediate—not gradual—abolition of slavery. Garrison knew well the pastor of Walker's AME congregation, Samuel Snowden, and despite his earlier support for gradualism and colonization he came to endorse Walker's arguments. Anticolonizationism became a staple of Garrrison and the *Liberator*'s output. It moreover became the defining trait of abolitionism. After 1830, gradualism and immediatism followed divergent paths. The difference hinged on what each side thought the end of slavery would mean for the place of African Americans in the United States. Yet just as important were the answers each side reached about how the Bible might be applied to the slavery question.[20]

From the outset, manifest religious divisions beset immediatism. In 1833, Garrison joined with Finneyite evangelical financier Arthur Tappan to create the American Anti-Slavery Society, which gave immediatism an organizational home. Like Tappan and his brother Lewis, as well as Theodore Dwight Weld and James G. Birney, many abolitionists came to their positions through the teachings of Charles Finney. These individuals were instrumental in the early years of Oberlin College (founded 1833), where Finney became a theology professor in 1835. Others came from Quaker, Unitarian, and freethinking backgrounds. Garrison himself had been Baptist, and at one point attended evangelical Congregationalist stalwart Lyman Beecher's congregation in Boston, but ultimately he embraced freethinking skepticism—questioning the authority of the Bible and emphasizing human reason. In 1840, the American Anti-Slavery Society splintered into competing factions. Central to that division were questions of gender and race, but religion was also predominant. The

---

20. Hinks, "Introduction," xlii–xliv; Kantrowitz, *More Than Freedom*, 13–83.

Tappans and their associates hoped to preserve a more robustly evangelical movement.[21]

Yet, despite that very real fissure among immediatists, nearly all abolitionists agreed that the American churches were, as James G. Birney argued in 1840, "bulwarks of American slavery." The southern churches that emerged from the church schisms of the 1830s and 1840s overtly sanctioned slaveholding, but the opposite was not true in the North. Thanks to a regnant moderation and concern about fidelity to church history and the biblical witness, northern churches were not strongly antislavery. They would increasingly move in that direction by the mid-1850s, but by that point many abolitionists had made up their minds about the established American churches' lack of a prophetic voice on the slavery question.[22]

For many abolitionists, nineteenth-century evangelical biblicist orthodoxy became increasingly impossible to accept. In 1837, Theodore Dwight Weld anonymously published a widely read treatise, *The Bible against Slavery*. Even antislavery readers found Weld a simplistic exegete, and the arguments failed to convince any but those already on Weld's side. Within a decade, Weld himself thought the Bible argument against slavery was impossible, and he rejected evangelicalism for freethinking rationalism.[23]

William Lloyd Garrison pushed even further. By 1845, he had concluded that, in truth, the Bible did explicitly sanction slavery. Unlike proslavery believers or antislavery moderates, that fact meant not that slavery was right, but that the Bible was wrong. Garrison came to conclude, "The God, who in America, is declared to sanction the impious system of slavery . . . is my ideal of the Devil." Rather than the authoritative source of truth most Americans saw in the Bible, Garrison read the book to be "a lie and a curse on mankind." He argued elsewhere that, "To say everything contained within the lids of the Bible is divinely inspired," such as the notion, for example, that slavery was a necessary part of God's

21. Ronald G. Walters, *The Antislavery Appeal: American Abolitionism after 1830* (Baltimore: Johns Hopkins University Press, 1976), 37-53.

22. John R. McKivigan, *The War against Proslavery Religion: Abolitionism and the Northern Churches, 1830-1865* (Ithaca: Cornell University Press, 1984); Lawrence J. Friedman, "Confidence and Pertinacity in Evangelical Abolitionism: Lewis Tappan's Circle," *American Quarterly* 31 (Spring 1979): 87-106; James G. Birney, *The American Churches: The Bulwarks of American Slavery*, 3rd ed. (Newburyport, MA: Charles Whipple, 1842); C. C. Goen, *Broken Churches, Broken Nation: Denominational Schisms and the Coming of the American Civil War* (Macon, GA: Mercer University Press, 1985).

23. Noll, *America's God*, 391-92; Oshatz, *Slavery and Sin*, 61-65.

ordained social order, "is to give utterance to a bold fiction, and to require the suspension of the reasoning faculties."[24]

The period's most prominent African American abolitionist, Frederick Douglass, echoed Birney and Garrison in what is arguably the most famous antislavery speech ever delivered. Douglass, a former Maryland slave, defiantly asked on July 5, 1852, "What to the Slave is the 4th of July?" Arguing that the freedom of Independence Day did not apply to the United States' enslaved—or even free black—population, Douglass particularly indicted the American church for teaching that "the relation of master and slave is ordained of God." Like Garrison, Douglass found that all too much to accept. In the face of such Christianity, he contended: "I would say, welcome infidelity! welcome atheism! welcome anything! in preference to the gospel, *as preached by those Divines*! They convert the very name of religion into an engine of tyranny and barbarous cruelty, and serve to confirm more infidels, in this age, than all the infidel writings of Thomas Paine, Voltaire, and Bolingbroke put together have done!" Douglass furthermore sounded much like David Walker as he denounced American Christianity as a "religion which favors the rich against the poor; which exalts the proud above the humble; which divides mankind into two classes, tyrants and slaves; which says to the man in chains, stay there; and to the oppressor, oppress on; it is a religion which may be professed and enjoyed by all the robbers and enslavers of mankind." For Douglass, "the popular worship of our land and nation" was "an abomination in the sight of God."[25]

Skeptics understandably saw churches as beyond the pale of influence, but so too did evangelical abolitionists. They argued for "come-outerism"—that is, for antislavery believers to leave traditional churches for those that refused fellowship with slaveholders. Rather than maintain links to northern churches, even in the wake of the church splits over slavery, evangelical abolitionists created an alternate path. In 1846, Lewis Tappan, George Whipple, Gerrit Smith, Joshua Leavitt, and other Fin-

24. J. Albert Harrill, "The Use of the New Testament in the American Slave Controversy: A Case History in the Hermeneutical Tension between Biblical Criticism and Christian Moral Debate," *Religion and American Culture* 10 (2000): 149–86, quotes 159–60; and quotes from William Lloyd Garrison, "No Union with Slaveholders!," *The Liberator*, September 19, 1851; "Thomas Paine," *The Liberator*, November 21, 1845.

25. Frederick Douglass, "What to the Slave Is the 4th of July?," in *American Antislavery Writings: Colonial Beginnings to Emancipation*, ed. James G. Basker (New York: Library of America Press, 2012), 614–15.

neyites founded the American Missionary Association (AMA) for just that purpose. The AMA was nonsectarian, evangelical, and abolitionist.[26]

More complicated were the evolving attitudes of antislavery moderates who remained in the established northern churches. They understood—as Weld and Garrison did—that it was impossible to attack slavery using the Bible alone. It was true, as David Walker, Frederick Douglass, and Moses Stuart claimed, that the message of Jesus and the "spirit" of the Bible stood against human oppression. But there was no getting around slavery's abstract biblical sanction. Rather than jettison the faith, however, they innovated. Following the lead of an earlier Unitarian method of biblical interpretation, antislavery moderates placed the Bible in the span of human history and determined that the Christian God revealed himself "progressively" over time. In each successive generation, humans developed better moral sensibilities and became more adept at realizing God's will. Thus, many antislavery but also anti-abolitionist northern ministers and theologians—among them Horace Bushnell, E. P. Barrows, and Albert Barnes—historicized Scripture and developed a Protestantism that did not depend on the Bible alone. This new "liberal" faith sublimated the plain word of Scripture to human experience. And with that understanding, antislavery Protestants had a belief system at the ready to celebrate the North and condemn the slaveholding South. Liberal Protestantism—before it was known as such—helped bridge the divide between gradual emancipationists and abolitionists to support the Union cause in 1861.[27]

Thus, when the war came, as much as Confederates invoked Christian sanction for their cause, so too did Unionist believers. Plenty remained of the old revivalist and millennialist impulse to eradicate slavery and usher in the kingdom of God. But earlier Finneyite arguments against slavery had depended on a kind of moral suasion that emphasized that changes of heart preceded social change. The triune God of grace was indeed the God of armies, but evangelical antislavery activists had not imagined that a modern state—capable of raising two million soldiers, creating a common currency, and developing a national tax system—would be required to eradicate slavery. In the end, that is precisely what was necessary to defeat the Confederacy. And northern believers were happy to champion the cause.

26. McKivigan, *War against Proslavery Religion*; Friedman, "Confidence and Pertinacity."

27. Oshatz, *Slavery and Sin*, 61–147.

Before the war itself was even over, northerners called for the South's "religious Reconstruction." All the major northern churches passed overtly nationalistic resolutions demanding loyalty to the United States above all else. Contrary to earlier patterns, they also all denounced slavery as sin. As northern Methodist bishops argued in 1864 in language echoed by other northern denominational mouthpieces, it was their "solemn judgment that none should be admitted to [northern Methodist] fellowship who are either slaveholders or are tainted with treason." In the mode of antebellum revivalism, they saw the war as an opportunity to destroy the sin of slaveholding and pave the way for God's millennial reign. Following the lead of the AMA, they furthermore commissioned missionaries to labor in the South among former slaves and in churches devastated by the war. Confident in their ability to change the shape of American society, these Christians proceeded boldly into the fray. America would be redeemed from slavery.[28]

After the war, northern Methodists and Presbyterians were especially keen to reunite denominations fractured by slavery. White southerners were not. And they made their case by reasserting their theological fidelity. As southern Methodists explained in 1874 about the denominational schism thirty years earlier, "The existence of slavery in the southern States furnished an occasion, with its connected questions, fruitful of disturbance; and to this division has been mainly attributed. The position of southern Methodism on that subject was scriptural." Because northern Methodists refused to acknowledge that white southerners in fact held a monopoly on biblical orthodoxy, a breach in American Methodism—as well as the Union's other evangelical Protestant denominations—became inevitable and irreparable. At that late date white Methodists in the South were direct about their views: "Our opinions have undergone no change." The death of slavery by military force and law had not destroyed the faith of these white southerners: "The causes which led to the division in 1844

28. *Journal of the General Conference of the Methodist Episcopal Church, Held in Philadelphia, Pa., 1864* (New York: Carlton & Porter, 1864), 279; Timothy L. Wesley, *The Politics of Faith during the Civil War* (Baton Rouge: Louisiana State University Press, 2013), 67-72, 78-80; James H. Moorhead, *American Apocalypse: Yankee Protestants and the Civil War* (New Haven: Yale University Press, 1978); Daniel W. Stowell, *Rebuilding Zion: The Religious Reconstruction of the South, 1863-1877* (New York: Oxford University Press, 1998), 30-31; George C. Rable, *God's Almost Chosen Peoples: A Religious History of the American Civil War* (Chapel Hill: University of North Carolina Press, 2010), 330-34.

... have not disappeared. Some of them exist in their original form and force, and others have been modified, but not diminished."[29]

Southern Presbyterians were even bolder in 1871:

> The dogma which denies the lawfulness of [slavery] under any circumstances; which condemns it as always contrary to the Divine will; which asserts its inherent sinfulness, is completely contradicted by the plainest facts and teachings of the Old Testament and New; is a doctrine unknown to the Church until recent times; is a pernicious heresy, embracing a principle not only infidel and fanatical, but subversive of every relation of life, and every civil government on earth.[30]

These statements should not be read outside of their political context. From the perspective of white southerners, far worse than the destruction of slavery was what came after: Reconstruction. In that moment, according to racist interpretation, a vindictive North sought to rub the former Confederacy's nose in defeat. Thanks to the Reconstruction Acts of 1867, which reduced the former Confederate states (except Tennessee) to the status of territories—therefore under the control of Congress and required to establish new state constitutions for readmission to the Union—the US Army ensured that more than 1.3 million black (703,400) and white (660,000) voters went to the polls in the South. That allowed for the emergence of a southern Republican party in a region historically dominated by Democrats. The Fourteenth (1868) and Fifteenth (1870) Amendments made multiracial birthright citizenship and the elective franchise for men regardless of race the laws of the land. Combined with the Thirteenth Amendment, these three "Reconstruction Amendments" served as the constitutional foundation for what historians call the "Second American Revolution." At its core, the American slave system was a set of property rights and a political regime—both blessed by the white South's dominant evangelical culture. Prior to the

29. *Formal Fraternity. Proceedings of the General Conference of the Methodist Episcopal Church and of the Methodist Episcopal Church, South, in 1872, 1874, and 1876, and of the Joint Commission of the Two Churches on Fraternal Relations, at Cape May, New Jersey, August 16-23, 1876* (New York: Nelson and Phillips, 1876), 37, 38.

30. *The Distinctive Principles of the Presbyterian Church in the United States, Commonly Called the Southern Presbyterian Church, as Set Forth in the Formal Declarations, and Illustrated by Extracts from Proceedings of the General Assembly, from 1861-70* (Richmond: Presbyterian Committee of Publication, [1871]), 131-32.

Civil War, slaveholders in the American South enjoyed full protection of their right to hold some four million people as property under the law. In 1860, that slave property was collectively worth more than three billion dollars and was responsible for higher wealth per capita in the South than in the North. Slavery was incredibly profitable, central to the shape of the American economy, and showed no signs of ending. But within five years, that wealth in slaves had been confiscated through the Civil War; by 1870 former slaves were no longer property but citizens, landowners, students, voters, and in some cases officeholders. The United States that existed from 1789 to 1861—built upon whites-only citizenship and dominated by slaveholders, with slaveholding presidents for fifty of the republic's first seventy-two years—was no more.[31]

Nowhere was that reality clearer than in the departure of African American believers from the South's biracial churches. Though white southerners would call for the ongoing salience of the proslavery argument and white religious oversight for the age of emancipation, freedpeople rejected such claims out of hand. Liberated from the coercive power of slaveholders, they drew deeply on the biblical motif of the exodus narrative and created new churches or established linkages to the autonomous black churches founded in the antebellum North.[32]

Basic statistics highlight the overwhelming African American rejection of white southern congregations. In 1860, the proslavery Methodist Episcopal Church, South (MECS), had claimed nearly 208,000 African American members. But in 1869 less than 10 percent of that membership remained (fewer than 20,000). Those numbers continued to drop; by the last decade of the nineteenth century the MECS counted just 357 African Americans on the rolls. Because of the localized nature of Baptist ecclesiology, national and regional statistics are harder to determine, but state-level conventions recorded a similar pattern of African American exodus. As one key example, Southern Baptists in Georgia claimed more

31. John Hope Franklin, *Reconstruction after the Civil War*, 3rd ed. (Chicago: University of Chicago Press, 2013), 79–80; James M. McPherson, *Abraham Lincoln and the Second American Revolution* (New York: Oxford University Press, 1991), 3–22; and Gavin Wright, *Slavery and American Economic Development* (Baton Rouge: Louisiana State University Press, 2006), esp. 60 for data on wealth in slaves.

32. Stowell, *Rebuilding Zion*, 80–99; Irons, *Origins of Proslavery Christianity*, 247–60; and Katherine L. Dvorak, *An African-American Exodus: The Segregation of the Southern Churches* (New York: Carlson, 1991).

than 27,000 black members in 1860, but that number dwindled to just over 10,000 by 1870. By 1877, almost no African American Baptists continued to worship with whites in that state.[33]

For African Americans who had lived under slavery, the chance to create independent churches recalled the prophetic words of Micah 4: "But they shall sit every man under his vine and under his fig tree; and none shall make *them* afraid: for the mouth of the LORD of hosts hath spoken *it*." The Micah text addressed a righteous remnant who had remained faithful to the God of Israel in spite of many travails. It foretold a time when oppressive forces would "beat their swords into plowshares" and "nation(s)" would not "learn war any more." But that biblical promise was not yet fulfilled, and similarly the future of African American Christianity would not be a utopian one. There would be trouble from a white supremacist America outside these churches, and regular controversy within them. Internecine squabbles over politics, theology, ecclesiology, and relationships with white denominations would shape postemancipation religious life. But all these debates would be had among African Americans themselves, independent of the white supremacist church authority that once deigned to dictate the shape of their faith and lives. As a result, black congregations would become fertile grounds for the cultivating of African American aspirations into the twentieth century.[34]

In stark contrast to freedpeople's invocation of the exodus narrative, southern whites grasped for another biblical metaphor to explain their position after the Civil War: redemption. For the Christian abolitionist tradition, like the one Abraham Lincoln voiced in his second inaugural address, the sense of a need for redemption was imbued with a hope that the Civil War might make right the longstanding wrong of American slavery. Like Lincoln's, the white southern vision was also blood-soaked with evangelical meaning. But redemption meant something else to those be-

33. Stowell, *Rebuilding Zion*, 80–81; Dvorak, *African-American Exodus*, 87, 121, 168.

34. Reginald F. Hildebrand, *The Times Were Strange and Stirring: Methodist Preachers and the Crisis of Emancipation* (Durham: Duke University Press, 1995); John Giggie, *After Redemption: Jim Crow and the Transformation of African American Religion in the Delta* (New York: Oxford University Press, 2008), 3–22; and William E. Montgomery, *Under Their Own Vine and Fig Tree: The African-American Church in the South, 1865-1900* (Baton Rouge: Louisiana State University Press, 1993). The biblical quotes are from Micah 4:3–4.

lievers who cast their lot with the Confederacy. Instead of atoning for the sin of slavery, it referred to atoning for the North's sins of the Civil War and Reconstruction. The war to destroy slavery was a war against the Christian God's biblical design for the ordering of human societies. Thus the tragedy was that the war had to occur at all—as if the once-enslaved millions had nothing to say about it.[35]

"Redemption" therefore meant what started in the 1870s: the restoration of southern "home rule," shorthand for white Democratic governments that would restore white supremacy in the South. It happened through nothing less than a terrorist counter-revolution against interracial democracy. Tennessee gave birth to the Ku Klux Klan in 1865, and that Christian organization served as the military arm of a Democratic ascendancy in the state, which came to dominate Tennessee politics by 1870. In other ex-Confederate states, US military occupation succeeded in protecting African American voters for a few more years. But white supremacist violence similarly manipulated elections elsewhere in the South—and particularly targeted the region's emerging autonomous African American churches as primary sites of black independence. Between 1874 and 1876, white Democratic dominance was made possible in Mississippi by leaving a trail of dead opponents—especially from the state's black majority—surrounding political affairs and election seasons. In one of the most notorious but also representative examples, in December 1874 whites slayed an unknown number of African Americans—perhaps three hundred—in Vicksburg. White Democrats throughout the South followed the lead of this "Mississippi Plan," and the former Confederacy found itself "redeemed" by the mid-1870s.[36]

Southern "redemption" could not have happened without white sup-

---

35. Harlow, *Religion, Race, and the Making of Confederate Kentucky*, 187-89; Daniel W. Stowell, "Why 'Redemption'? Religion and the End of Reconstruction, 1869-1877," in *Vale of Tears: New Essays on Religion and Reconstruction*, ed. Edward J. Blum and W. Scott Poole (Macon, GA: Mercer University Press, 2005), 133-46.

36. George C. Rable, *But There Was No Peace: The Role of Violence in the Politics of Reconstruction* (1984; Baton Rouge: Louisiana State University Press, 2007), 66-80, 144-91; Nicholas Lemann, *Redemption: The Last Battle of the Civil War* (New York: Farrar, Straus, and Giroux, 2006); Edward J. Blum, *Reforging the White Republic: Race, Religion, and American Nationalism, 1865-1898* (Baton Rouge: Louisiana State University Press, 2005), 76-82; and Margaret M. Storey, "The Crucible of Reconstruction: Unionists and the Struggle for Alabama's Postwar Homefront," in *The Great Task Remaining before Us: Reconstruction as America's Continuing Civil War*, ed. Paul A. Cimbala and Randall M. Miller (New York: Fordham University Press, 2010), 84-86.

port from elsewhere in the United States. By the 1880s and 1890s, whites across the country had turned to another metaphor with deep biblical roots: reconciliation. As it played out in late-nineteenth-century America, "reconciliation" concerned northern and southern whites agreeing to ignore the war's emancipationist consequence. The Civil War era drastically expanded American democracy, for its constitutional amendments applied not merely to the South, but to the whole nation. Yet many of these advances were undone by a Jim Crow America that emerged in the 1880s. Broad disenfranchisement—brought into being through poll taxes, literacy tests, and "grandfather" clauses—became standard in the South. The Supreme Court's 1896 *Plessy v. Ferguson* decision established the constitutionality of racial segregation through "separate but equal" facilities. And by the turn of the century the southern Jim Crow system was matched by northern and western "sundown towns" for minorities excluded from white-only communities.[37]

A variety of legal instruments made the rise of the Jim Crow era possible. And extra-legal instruments did as well. As was the case with southern "redemption," the violent context for "reconciliation" should not be ignored. Southern whites—as well as some northern—lynched, as public spectacle, on average more than one African American per week from 1890 to 1930 (and from 1890 to 1910 it was nearly two per week). Lynching became a fixture, and race riots in Wilmington (1898), Atlanta (1906), East St. Louis (1917), Chicago (1919), Knoxville (1919), Omaha (1919), Washington, DC (1919), and Tulsa (1921) came to mark this late-nineteenth- and early-twentieth-century "reconciled" land. While white Americans ignored slavery as central to the Civil War, racist violence established the parameters of American freedom.[38]

There was no mistaking the close affinity between a particularly conservative theology embraced by many evangelical whites in America—which grounded the Christian gospel in a sense of retributive violence for innate sinfulness—and the widespread assaults on African

37. David W. Blight, *Race and Reunion: The Civil War in American Memory* (Cambridge, MA: Belknap Press of Harvard University Press, 2001); Blum, *Reforging the White Republic*; James W. Loewen, *Sundown Towns: A Hidden Dimension of American Racism* (New York: New Press, 2005).

38. Amy Louise Wood, *Lynching and Spectacle: Witnessing Racial Violence in America, 1890-1940* (Chapel Hill: University of North Carolina Press, 2009); W. Fitzhugh Brundage, *Lynching in the New South: Georgia and Virginia, 1880-1930* (Urbana: University of Illinois Press, 1993).

American people widely considered innately inferior by whites. To be sure, evangelicalism was just one of many contributing factors to a white southern moral culture that facilitated lynching, but it was impossible to miss the strong influence of what can accurately be called a "theology of racial violence." Such was the case for white Methodist evangelist Sam Jones, who held deeply to the values of the "old-time religion" emphasizing human sinfulness and divine judgment. Jones also subscribed to a commonplace sacralized white supremacy, arguing that the racist hierarchy of white over black had been "so far preserved" by "Nature, God, and the best interests of mankind." Because of a biblical sense of social order, Jones generally opposed the lawlessness of mob action. But Jones's position had its limits. After the brutal lynching of Sam Hose outside Newnan, Georgia, in April 1899—where a crowd of more than two thousand witnessed Hose's castration and burning—Jones initially condemned the extralegal vigilantism that guided Hose's killers. But shortly thereafter Jones reversed course: "Sam Hose deserved to be burnt," he argued. "I am in favor of the sheriff executing the criminal, except in cases like Sam Hose, then anybody, anything, anyway to get rid of such a brute." Hose had killed a local white farmer and purportedly raped his wife. Hose admitted to the former, out of self-defense, and outside investigators concluded that the latter did not occur. But for the evangelist Sam Jones, as was the case for all white supporters of lynching, the facts of the case did not matter. In this view, Hose was born wont to sinful ends and had desecrated the sacred realm of the white family. Extreme actions required extreme retribution. At best, evangelical whites remained mute on racist violence. But a clearer-eyed and more honest assessment shows that, in a country dominated by evangelicals, evangelical sensibilities pervaded spectacle lynching. This was not just a matter of cultural symbolism: believing whites also carried the torch and the rope.[39]

Reconciliation among whites, in short, was only possible at the cost of black bodies. It was in this violently oppressive, deeply evangelical, emerging segregated America that whites remembered, not a struggle over the fate of slavery, but instead a war where brothers fought brothers. Envisioning the Civil War and Reconstruction as a great "tragic era,"

39. Darren E. Grem, "Sam Hose, Sam Jones, and the Theology of Racial Violence," *Georgia Historical Quarterly* 90 (Spring 2006): 35–61, quotes 40, 58; Wood, *Lynching and Spectacle*, 45–68.

whites could compliment both sides for honorably laying down their lives for basic principles such as hearth and home. While the United States had won the Civil War and ended slavery in the process, many could legitimately ask if the white South had won the peace.[40]

The same could be said for the history of nineteenth-century American evangelicalism. African Americans were absolutely indispensable to the building of the early American republic, but for most whites they were indispensable insofar as they were disposable. That was plainly the case for conservative white evangelicals. From the history of slaveholding, along with colonization and gradual emancipation, through redemption and reconciliation, white believers were clear about their ambition to exploit black lives. And when those lives proved unexploitable, they sought their removal. In the broader relief of nineteenth-century American history, the course of the Civil War and emancipation meant that African Americans would be woven into the American republic with citizenship rights. There would not be a whites-only United States. But American evangelicalism would take that form.

That move happened with recourse to old theological positions. The biblicism that split evangelicalism over the slavery question proved the means of reconciling the movement's more conservative adherents. The emancipation of four million enslaved African Americans also led to the emancipation of "common sense" biblicism from its bondage to the slavery question. Liberal Protestantism had emerged because of the debate over slavery and the Bible, but it was no longer necessary to innovate theologically to deal with slavery. Slavery had been dealt with. Evangelicals outside the South who were never comfortable with liberal approaches to Scripture found a natural kinship with biblicist southerners—who by their own admission never changed on the Bible or slavery. Where before the war biblical literalism was the hallmark of the proslavery argument, northern and western evangelicals were now liberated from its defense of slavery and free to make common cause with white southerners in religious matters of "orthodoxy." A new set of issues—"fundamentals" such as the historicity of Scripture, the creation of the world, biblical miracles, and much else—would take center stage. But the specter of slav-

40. The phrase "tragic era" is from white reconciliationist journalist Claude Bowers, *The Tragic Era: The Revolution after Lincoln* (Cambridge, MA: Houghton Mifflin, 1929). Blight, *Race and Reunion*; Blum, *Reforging the White Republic*.

ery would shade everything that was to come. The result was a far more conservative evangelicalism, with an attenuated voice on public matters. Most plainly, that voice had little to say about the era's racist strife.[41]

Against its antebellum pattern in the North, the reformist element of evangelicalism became privatized and individualistic. Where Charles Finney had called for the transformation of society as a whole, postwar evangelists such as Dwight L. Moody focused on personal piety. Before the war, evangelicals sought to usher the millennial kingdom of God into the here and now. Afterward, evangelicals embraced pessimism about social change and prayed for the Christian God to rapture them out of their current dispensation, that they might enjoy the millennium in the sweet by and by.

And perhaps most significantly, the new evangelicalism would remain a movement almost exclusively for whites. Black Protestantism would be something else. There were no African American contributors to *The Fundamentals* (1910-1915), and leading northern fundamentalist J. Gresham Machen was quite clear that his project leaned on conceptions of "Anglo-Saxon liberty." By contrast, B. B. Warfield, Machen's colleague at Princeton Theological Seminary, wrote from a biblicist perspective on the "unity of the human race," notably questioned segregation, and clashed with Machen over integration at their institution. But that was as far as it went for Warfield. He never challenged his Presbyterian Church U.S.A.'s segregated structure, and certainly made little mention of racial violence in America. Indeed, most white evangelicals did not write on the race question at all, which was in keeping with a reconciliationist white America that preferred not to discuss the issue even as it was erupting all around. Instead, they emphasized the church's "spirituality" and non-political nature, a doctrine not surprisingly developed in the heat of the slavery struggle by white southern theologians seeking to undermine the claims of abolitionists. The "spirituality of the church" would have a long

---

41. The classic accounts of the origins of fundamentalism and modern evangelicalism do not discuss the Civil War, slavery, or race. See Ernest R. Sandeen, *The Roots of Fundamentalism: British and American Millenarianism, 1800-1930* (Chicago: University of Chicago Press, 1970); and George M. Marsden, *Fundamentalism and American Culture: The Shaping of Twentieth-Century Evangelicalism, 1870-1925* (New York: Oxford University Press, 1980). Though not attuned to the role of the slavery question, more recent work has shown expressly the role of racial division in the shaping of fundamentalism, especially Matthew Avery Sutton, *American Apocalypse: A History of Modern Evangelicalism* (Cambridge, MA: Belknap Press of Harvard University Press, 2014), 109-12.

life in white evangelical circles, and it proved key in keeping white evangelical support—South, North, and West—of civil rights to a minimum.[42]

As antislavery critics contended, "the Bible alone" was always a lie. Believers of all varieties always brought myriad assumptions to the text. That truth continued to permeate American evangelicalism well into the twentieth century. Like evangelicals before the Civil War, whose conservative biblicism and sense of church history undermined civil-rights activism, so too would later generations follow the proslavery path. Their appeals to "biblical authority" had much to say about the origin of the species and the virgin birth, but they had little to say about a society that lynched at least one person per week over a forty-year period. A straightforward reading of the Bible could not sustain support for white supremacy. But a straightforward reading of the Bible was seemingly also unable to offer aid and comfort to anti-lynching campaigns. Though there always existed the possibility of an "evangelical left" in American history, so long as conservative believers remained committed to strict biblicism, white evangelical supporters of progressive causes and civil rights would be nothing more than a moral minority.[43]

Many twentieth-century observers scratched their heads and pondered why 11 o'clock Sunday morning was the most segregated hour of the week in American society. But the answer to that question was hidden in plain sight. It resided in the history of nineteenth-century evangelicalism and its struggle to interpret the meaning of the Civil War and emancipation.

42. J. Gresham Machen, *Christianity and Liberalism*, ed. Carl Trueman (1923; Grand Rapids: Eerdmans, 2009), 12; B. B. Warfield, "On the Antiquity and Unity of the Human Race," *Princeton Theological Review* 9 (January 1911): 1-25; James H. Moorhead, *Princeton Seminary in American Culture* (Grand Rapids: Eerdmans, 2012), 254-55; Peter Slade, *Open Friendship in a Closed Society: Mission Mississippi and a Theology of Friendship* (New York: Oxford University Press, 2009), 103-6. On later developments, see Carolyn Renée Dupont, *Mississippi Praying: Southern White Evangelicals and the Civil Rights Movement, 1945-1975* (New York: New York University Press, 2013). On twentieth-century evangelicalism as a white movement, see Molly Worthen, *Apostles of Reason: The Crisis of Authority in American Evangelicalism* (New York: Oxford University Press, 2013), 5; and on the defining significance of race in evangelicalism to the recent past, see Michael O. Emerson and Christian Smith, *Divided by Faith: Evangelical Religion and the Problem of Race in America* (New York: Oxford University Press, 2000). On the spirituality of the church's proslavery origins, see Harlow, *Religion, Race, and the Making of Confederate Kentucky*, 136-40.

43. David R. Swartz, *Moral Minority: The Evangelical Left in an Age of Conservatism* (Philadelphia: University of Pennsylvania Press, 2012); and Brantley W. Gasaway, *Progressive Evangelicals and the Pursuit of Social Justice* (Chapel Hill: University of North Carolina Press, 2014).

CHAPTER 7

The Rise of Fundamentalism

George M. Marsden

On May 7, 1915, a German U-boat torpedoed a British ocean liner, the *Lusitania*, near the coast of Ireland. More than one thousand civilians died, including 128 Americans. President Woodrow Wilson, though eager to stay out of the war, protested in the strongest terms, demanding "strict accountability" for such infringement of the rights of Americans. Wilson's secretary of state, William Jennings Bryan, the famed three-time Democratic presidential candidate and fervent Christian champion of negotiating peace, felt forced to resign. Under Wilson's policy, he believed, American entry into war would be inevitable. Two years later, events proved Bryan correct. In the spring of 1917 Germany began engaging in unrestricted submarine warfare and soon sank five American merchant vessels. Woodrow Wilson declared war on April 2, 1917.

Among the many momentous consequences of that reluctantly taken action was that it proved to be one of the major turning points in the history of American evangelicalism. Prior to the war, a visitor from another country would have found Protestantism to be the default religion of the United States and evangelicalism to be the predominant form of Protestantism. In fact, the more diverse the population became, especially as Roman Catholic immigrants flooded into the cities, the more Protestant the nation seemed in its public self-understanding. Schoolbooks celebrated the nation's Pilgrim origins. Protestant Americans shaped almost everything in the wider culture. Many who were Protestant by birthright were hardly pious. Yet social reformers and their conservative opponents each still often framed their outlook as "Christian." The "social gospel" was the progressive reform movement at prayer. Democrats Woodrow

Wilson and William Jennings Bryan were two of the most devout Protestant leaders the nation ever had. In the 1912 presidential campaign, Wilson's most formidable opponent was Theodore Roosevelt, whose Progressive party used "Onward Christian Soldiers" as its theme song.

Our observer would not have said that prewar American Protestantism was unified or uniform. One of its most conspicuous traits was that it was divided into all sorts of denominations and agencies and was further divided ethnically and regionally, especially between North and South. Protestants were almost all segregated racially as well, so much so that public Protestantism meant, without having to say it, white Protestantism. Politically, Protestants could be found everywhere on the spectrum, and typically their voting patterns reflected their regional, ethnic, or social location more than specific religious teachings. Upon close examination our observer might also have noticed some portentous differences in beliefs, especially about the Bible and the nature of salvation, within some of the largest northern denominations.

Yet despite these differences there was a wide spectrum of white Protestant groups that thought of themselves as part of the same extended family and could present something of a united front. There was the Federal Council of Churches, organized in 1908 to speak especially for the progressive elements of the largest northern white denominations. Most of these same denominations studied a common set of weekly Sunday school lessons. Their teachings and their worship would be a mix of biblicist and conversionist themes and uplifting moral themes, considering how best to follow Jesus each day. Whichever of these emphases took precedence, most Protestant denominations still spoke of themselves as "evangelical." Almost all of them had their roots in awakenings and revivalism and still emphasized evangelism and missions. The most remarkable manifestation of a united Protestant front was the temperance movement. That had enough momentum to convert wartime enthusiasm into a constitutional amendment for the prohibition of alcoholic beverages.

Yet, within a few years of the end of World War I, the most conspicuous trait of white American Protestantism was that it was divided into warring factions between "fundamentalists" and their more liberal opponents. Just ten years after resigning as secretary of state, William Jennings Bryan was engaged in a fervid campaign to ban the teaching of biological evolution in American public schools. That campaign culminated in the Scopes Trial of July 1925 in Dayton, Tennessee. Despite being technically on the winning side of the conviction of a young biology professor, John Scopes, for having taught evolution, Bryan was subjected to merciless ridicule from the liberal northern press for his "obscurantist" views. He died a few days later, still as much the champion of the common people as he had been during his three runs for president as the progressive "Great Commoner." But now he and his many supporters were characterized by the mainstream press as fighting to hold back progress in the name of outmoded, anti-intellectual biblicist "fundamentalism."

William Jennings Bryan was not a typical fundamentalist, but then fundamentalism, like the white Protestantism it affected, was not one unified movement. Rather, fundamentalism was a common attitude of militancy that spread among various sorts of Bible-believing white Protestants after World War I. Changes in churches and American culture were happening so fast that an infectious mood spread among many that it was time to stand up and fight in defense of one's faith. Fundamentalists can be most easily defined as militantly biblicist evangelicals. They are militant in that they are ready to fight for their faith and practices against contrary trends in modern churches and culture.

Wars often act as catalysts that speed social changes, and that was certainly the case regarding the impact of World War I on the United States. In retrospect we can see that the potentialities for these changes were already in place, but it took the added ingredient of American engagement in a terrible overseas conflict to suddenly bring them out. Or to change the metaphor, prior to World War I we can see some serious cracks opening up in the edifices of America's major social, intellectual, and religious structures, but it took the pressures of the floodwaters released by the war to open these cracks into major irreparable breaches. From our vantage point, having seen the breaches, we can go back and examine the cracks. So, to understand the rise of fundamentalism as a turning point in American Protestantism, we need to go back and look more carefully at the prewar rumblings that weakened the flood walls.

Our prewar visitor to the United States would not have found a fundamentalist movement or even much evidence that such a major development was about to occur. She could have found, however, some significant pockets of militantly biblicist evangelicals here and there. Many Protestant denominations, especially those of the Reformed tradition, such as the Presbyterians and Baptists, had long housed doctrinal purists who were ready to fight and sometimes to split over a departure from what they considered an essential doctrine. Conservative Presbyterians were most notorious for such disputes. So, not surprisingly, they were in the forefront of standing up against the rise of liberal theologies in their midst. In 1910 the General Assembly of the major northern Presbyterian denomination adopted a five-point declaration of essential doctrines to be held by candidates for the ministry: (1) the inerrancy of Scripture, (2) the Virgin Birth of Jesus Christ, (3) his substitutionary atonement, (4) his bodily resurrection, and (5) the authenticity of biblical miracles. Southern Baptists and southern Presbyterians could take such teachings for granted without having to spell them out. Although a few southern professors had been disciplined over the years for teaching even a mild form of divinely guided biological evolution, the region was so solidly conservative doctrinally that there was not much ongoing controversy. The same was true of many conservative denominations North and South. At the other end of the spectrum were more liberal denominations, such as the Congregationalists and the Disciples of Christ, which, despite the presence of some conservatives, were more accepting of doctrinal innovation and varieties of points of view. They emphasized open-mindedness to new ideas as a major Christian virtue.

Denominations in the Methodist tradition were more likely to have divisions over practice rather than doctrine. Throughout the nineteenth century there had been a number of movements that sought to renew the intensity of Methodist holiness teachings. As part of the revivalist tradition, they not only put strong emphasis on being born again but also cultivated experiences of dramatic outpouring of the Holy Spirit, resulting in a life dedicated to holiness. Among the denominations shaped by the holiness movement were the Wesleyan Methodists, the Church of the Nazarene, the Salvation Army, and many varieties (white or African American) of the Church of God. These all took biblical literalism for granted and demanded strict standards of personal behavior from their members, especially renunciation of vices such as drinking, smoking, dancing, card-playing, and expensive or immodest dress. One issue regarding which both mainline Methodists and holiness offshoots were militant was the temperance crusade.

Pentecostal groups, which sprang up on the fringes of American evangelicalism after 1900, put even more emphasis on dramatic experience of the Holy Spirit. As Edith Blumhofer describes in her chapter in this volume, they were more innovative, teaching that the last days before Jesus's return to earth would be marked by a great outpouring of the Holy Spirit, or "latter rain." For true believers, then, the emerging era would be an overwhelmingly spiritual time when the ideal for the church would be the primitive practices of the New Testament church, including dramatic healings, speaking in tongues, and other spiritual gifts. Early Pentecostals had their greatest appeal among less prosperous white and black American Protestants. They were militant in rejecting the worldliness of modernity and the tepidness of other churches, but they resisted those trends largely by separating from them into their own organizations and by observing strict rules of lifestyle. Their emphasis on spiritual gifts and starting new organizations invited strong local leadership and led to many varieties and factions. While strictly biblicist and conversionist in the tradition of American revivalism, their combination of doctrinal innovations, extravagant worship, and social location kept most of them from much direct association with most other Bible-teaching evangelicals.

These breakaway holiness and Pentecostal movements pointed to a volatile feature of American evangelicalism. Our astute observer might have noticed that evangelicalism resembled the American free-enterprise system. While most of the business of American Protestantism was done by the large brand-name denominations, enterprising evangelists kept springing up with competing and novel ways to gain a clientele. The American tradition of revivalism went back to the Great Awakening and the evangelistic tours of George Whitefield of the mid-1700s that Harry Stout describes in his chapter. Talented evangelists who could attract a following typically founded their own organizations. Sometimes they saw their work as simply supplementing the established denominations. Often, though, their message that the times called for greater spiritual intensity led to innovative doctrines and to new church institutions. As revivalists, they were in one sense hyper-conservatives who insisted on Bible-based doctrines of conversion. Yet, paradoxically, they were in another sense agents of rapid change, who developed not only their own organizations and promotional techniques, but also new doctrines that intensified the old gospel message.

In the era between the Civil War and the First World War, of the scores of successful enterprising evangelists the most influential had been Dwight L. Moody (1837-1899). Moody conducted huge revival campaigns in many American cities and was successful in Great Britain as well. He turned out to be one of the main progenitors of fundamentalism in that a number of the younger evangelists who worked with him became leaders in the later movement. But Moody himself, although he worked through his own organizations, was friendly to all evangelical denominations and a peacemaker rather than a fighter. He was dedicated to preserving evangelism or soul saving as the top priority. In 1886 he founded in Chicago what would become a very influential school, the Moody Bible Institute. Its single purpose was to train Christian workers and teachers, especially for evangelism and missions, and it would become the prototype for scores of other such Bible institutes. In Moody's time, and in part because of his irenic nature, a sharp line was not yet drawn between more conservative biblicist evangelists, such as Moody and his followers, and the more liberal evangelicals who still valued evangelism. The clearest example of this was the Student Volunteer Movement that Moody helped to found, also in 1886. This agency urged college students to give their lives to missions. Its motto was "the evangelization of the world in this generation," and it flourished on major Ivy League campuses such as Princeton and Yale, where right up to World War I evangelicalism enjoyed status among elites even as the intellectual world was changing.

Moody was quietly associated, however, with one innovative doctrine, and it was a bona fide time bomb that would explode in the fundamentalist era. That was the teaching of dispensational premillennialism, which had been developed in the early nineteenth century by the Irish Plymouth Brethren evangelist John Nelson Darby and became popular among American revivalists after the Civil War. This teaching was based on a very literal reading of the Bible and especially of its prophecies. Dispensationalists divided world history into seven dispensations, with each distinguished from the others by God's method of interacting with humans. Starting with the Garden of Eden, each dispensation culminated in sinful human failure and God's judgment. Currently, according to this teaching, we are living in the next-to-last era, or Church Age. Humans once again have massively rebelled against God. Moreover, current events fit patterns of prophecy found especially in Daniel and Revelation, which indicate that the end of the age and the judgment of God are very near. The first manifestation of that end of the age will be "the secret rapture of the church," when all true believers will mysteriously disappear as they are caught up into the air to meet Christ. Following that (in the most prevalent version) there will be seven years of tribulation, as the forces of Antichrist do their worst, and then there will be the triumphant return of Christ with his saints to defeat those forces and set up a millennial kingdom for a literal one thousand years on earth. Moody himself, with his emphasis on keeping to a simple gospel message, did not emphasize the specifics of these teachings. He was, however, convinced that Jesus was returning soon, and that the modern age was getting alarmingly worse, not progressively better, as some more liberal Protestants would have it. Moody's appropriation of dispensationalism was best encapsulated in his famous saying, "I look upon this world as a wrecked vessel. God has given me a lifeboat and said to me 'Moody, save all you can.'"[1]

The more detailed teaching that was becoming popular among Moody's associates was a time bomb because, along with being an impetus for evangelism, it had some additional implications. Most of the younger evangelist friends and associates of Moody, such as Reuben Torrey, James M. Gray, A. C. Dixon, A. J. Gordon, Arno C. Gaebelein, and C. I. Scofield, believed that they had found in dispensational premillennialism the key to unlocking the meaning of Scripture. These men were all instrumental in shaping the later fundamentalist movement through both their writings and a network of Bible institutes that emphasized dispensational biblical interpretation. One major influence was C. I. Scofield's *Reference Bible* (1909), which contained extensive dispensationalist notes. By the 1920s "the Scofield Bible" became *the* standard Bible in many fundamentalist circles.

One implication of taking this method of interpreting Scripture as normative was that it committed its adherents to a literalistic, scientistic view of the Bible, as though it were a coded encyclopedia of precise propositions that needed only to be deciphered through the proper method. Prophetic numbers, such as the thousand-year reign of Christ or the seven years of tribulation, were taken to represent exact lengths of time. The historical accounts likewise had to be not only reliable but also precise. Thus dispensationalists insisted on the "inerrancy" of Scripture. So when, after World War I, many denominations debated naturalistic versus supernaturalistic views of the Bible, dispensationalists remained thoroughly committed to strongly supernaturalistic views.

A second potentially explosive implication of dispensationalism was that it taught that one of the marks of the present Church Age was that the major denominations had degenerated along with the rebellious wider culture. The Roman Catholic Church and the papacy were longstanding

---

1. As quoted in George Marsden, *Fundamentalism and American Culture*, 2nd ed. (1980; New York: Oxford University Press, 2006), 38; hereafter *FAAC*. Unless otherwise indicated, documentation for this essay and detailed documentation for quotations can be found in that volume.

examples of such prophesized corruptions, but the growing apostasy of the liberal Protestant churches was even more alarming evidence that the end was near. Such outlooks cultivated militancy in guarding against any inroads of liberalism. So when debates about modernism erupted after World War I, dispensationalists were ready both to condemn liberal teachings and to stay separate from them.

A third implication of dispensationalism was that its adherents were inclined to see the world and American culture itself getting worse rather than better. That put them at odds with the mood of much of American Protestantism of the Progressive Era prior to World War I. Only a generation earlier, before the Civil War, as Richard Carwardine describes in his chapter in this volume, most American evangelicals, including most biblicist revivalists, had been more optimistic about the modern age and had held a "postmillennial" view that the world would improve and become more Christianized and that Christ would return only *after* a culminating "millennial" age. That outlook had been more conducive to social reform movements such as antislavery, temperance, or women's rights, and faith in social progress was a trait of the social gospel movement of the Progressive Era. Dispensationalism's more pessimistic outlook encouraged expressions of alarm over cultural trends. So when, after World War I, and with the emergence of the roaring twenties, many Americans became unusually prone to cultural alarms, dispensationalists were prepared to react with heightened militancy and uncompromising apocalyptic rhetoric.

Prior to World War I these implications of dispensationalism were largely potentialities, and even a close observer might not have noticed them. While there were a few militants and scrimmages here and there, battle lines between strictly biblicist evangelicals and more liberal outlooks were not firmly drawn. Perhaps the best index of the dominant mood of the premillennial biblicist revivalists of the era is found in *The Fundamentals*, which were published between 1910 and 1915. Each of these twelve paperbound booklets, financed by Lyman Stewart, a dispensationalist and California oil millionaire, contained a collection of essays.[2] The editors were leading Bible teachers, such as Reuben A. Tor-

2. Timothy E. W. Gloege, *Guaranteed Pure: The Moody Bible Institute, Business, and the Making of Modern Evangelicalism* (Chapel Hill: University of North Carolina Press, 2015), offers important insights on the roles of wealthy businessmen in helping to shape this emerging movement. That is a feature that can be found throughout the history of the movement.

rey, founding dean of the Bible Institute of Los Angeles (also funded by Stewart), and A. C. Dixon, a noted pastor and evangelist. The booklets were sent free to every Protestant pastor, missionary, college professor, Sunday school superintendent, and religious editor in the English-speaking world. The editors sent out some three million individual copies in all. No doubt with this broad audience in mind, the series included little about dispensational premillennialism. Rather, the largest emphasis was on defending the authority and inerrant character of Scripture against scholarly "higher criticism," which raised questions about the Bible's historical reliability. In addition, the booklets presented traditional evangelical teachings, personal testimonies, criticisms of modernist theologies, general defenses of the faith, and polemics against Roman Catholicism and other "isms," such as Mormonism, Russellism, Eddyism, and modern spiritualism. The most striking evidence of the relative moderation of *The Fundamentals* was that they sent mixed messages regarding biological evolution. While one "occupant of the pew" suggested that all "evolutionism" in the pulpit was of the Devil, other prominent scholars allowed that the view that God might have used limited forms of evolution in creation was compatible with a conservative reading of Genesis.

While *The Fundamentals* did not spark overt controversy at the time, they did signal that a huge rift had been opening up in the Protestant world. The spread of higher criticism of Scripture was threatening to undermine traditional Christian faith, which for Protestants had been based on "the Bible alone" as the highest authority. Furthermore, new theologies denied central evangelical teachings of the necessity of being born again based on the atoning work of Jesus Christ on the cross. They emphasized instead "bringing Jesus into your heart" and following the ethics of Jesus as the way to bring out the best in humanity. Often they added the social gospel imperative to "Christianize the social order," and they implied that God worked through the best developments of modern science, culture, and morality. There would have been no dramatic emergence of fundamentalism after World War I had not there been a prior revolution: namely, the quiet acceptance of higher criticism and liberal modern theologies within many of the largest American Protestant denominations, especially in their theological schools and universities in the North.

Meanwhile, many other American Protestants, sometimes inhabiting the same denominations as theological liberals, had been moving in just the opposite direction in shoring up the faith in the face of the challenges of modern science, biblical criticism, and evolutionary thought. Rather than emphasizing how God worked through the best in history and human experience, they insisted all the more strongly that God worked through dramatic supernatural interventions into the natural order. So, in response to biblical criticism, they emphasized (as in the northern Presbyterian declaration of 1910) the supernatural, God-given, and therefore "inerrant" nature of the Bible and the authenticity of the biblical miracles, especially the Virgin Birth and bodily resurrection of Jesus Christ. Furthermore, premillennial evangelists—in stark contrast with modernists, who saw God's work unfolding progressively in the evolution of modern history—taught that historical change from one epoch to the next was driven by dramatic judgments and interventions from God. One could truly follow Jesus only if one's sinful heart was dramatically changed in a conversion experience. And most revivalists, including dispensationalists, affirmed the stringent holiness teaching that even after conversion one needed further dramatic experience of the supernatural power of the Holy Spirit in order to live a life of holiness.

Despite the relative peace that prevailed among America's divided "evangelical" Protestants, the outlooks of the parties on the extremes were so vastly far apart that they were ready to explode into controversy. Then came the cultural crisis precipitated by America's entry into World War I. That upset the equilibrium of American Protestantism and set off the explosion.

While Americans had been reluctant to enter a European war, once they did their flag-waving patriotism seemed to know no bounds. Protestant clergy were particularly strong in promoting the American cause. President Wilson had defined that cause as to "make the world safe for democracy," an ideal that fit closely with liberal Protestant optimism for worldwide reform. Most strikingly, especially in the light of later attitudes, some of the leading premillennial evangelists were initially cool toward the war, and some others even advocated pacifism. That led to a revealing controversy between some of the theologians at the Divinity School of the University of Chicago, a bastion of liberal Protestantism, and the Moody Bible Institute, which was a headquarters for the premillennial evangelistic movement. In 1918 University of Chicago theologian Shirley Jackson Case accused premillennialists of disloyalty akin to that of the Communist Industrial Workers of the World. Case suggested that premillennialists might be funded by German sources. "The American nation," he wrote, "is engaged in a gigantic effort to make the world safe for democracy." So "it would be almost traitorous negligence to ignore the detrimental character of premillennial propaganda."[3] By the time these accusations were published, the moment had already passed when they had much plausibility. After some hesitation in 1917, most premillennialists trumpeted the war effort with as much enthusiasm as other Americans. Some had never had any qualms about doing so. Billy Sunday, for one, was a showman who knew that super-patriotism and evangelism made a good combination. Sunday, who was the most popular evangelist of the day, often ended sermons by jumping on the pulpit and waving a flag. "If you turn hell upside down," he would say, "you will find 'Made in Germany' stamped on the bottom."[4]

In the war's immediate aftermath, America as a whole seemed gripped with a sense of cultural crisis. Rapid demobilization brought labor unrest, strikes, and bombings. These led to fears of foreign influence and to a "red scare" regarding Bolshevism, especially in the light of the 1917 Russian Revolution. The horrors of the World War made it clear that something had gone terribly wrong with European civilization. Modern science, rather than leading to inexorable progress, had led to unprecedented destruction. Rapidly changing moral standards made it easy to fear that America, too, was losing its moorings. For almost two years Americans had been fervently engaged in what seemed a righteous crusade. The armistice of November 1918 brought that cause to a sudden end and left many looking for new crusades on the home front. The upheaval of the war and the breakdown in Western civilization that it pointed to offered new impetus to mobilize to keep America strong. The movement for prohibition of alcoholic beverages, culminating in the ratification of the Eighteenth Amendment in 1919, was one manifestation of such hope for cultural reform. The passage and ratification just after the war of the Nineteenth Amendment, granting women the right to vote, was another. For conservative Protestants the mobilization of a militant movement to combat what they saw as destructive liberal theological trends fit the immediate postwar mood for strengthening American civilization.

The first organizational expression of a militant fundamentalist movement came with the founding in 1919 of the World's Christian Fundamentals Association, a premillennialist group under the leadership of

3. As quoted in *FAAC*, 147.
4. As quoted in *FAAC*, 142.

William B. Riley, a Baptist pastor in Minneapolis. Unlike some earlier dispensationalist predecessors, which dealt largely with how the prophetic signs of the times underscored the urgency of evangelism, this one prominently addressed the crisis in American civilization. The real question for America, Riley observed, was "who will rise, and when will he come to *make democracy safe for the world*."[5] Only "the blood of the Son of God" could do that, by remedying human sinfulness. In other words, the only thing that was going to save civilization was the preaching of the true gospel. The problem with German "Kultur" was that evolutionary doctrines had bred both theological modernism and militarism. Riley was a fit leader for the emerging fundamentalist movement because he did not believe that the premillennial expectation that Jesus was returning very soon meant that Christians should neglect caring for society today. Riley had been active in the campaigns for prohibition, and he maintained that Bible believers needed to combat moral evils in society and also trends such as evolutionism, theological modernism, and Bolshevism. Failure to fight these would undermine the primary task of proclaiming the gospel.

One front in this war was the major northern denominations. If these were taken over by modernists, then there would be little hope for a culture that needed first of all preaching of the truly biblical gospel of salvation through the atoning work of Christ alone. Battles over such issues were likely to be most intense in denominations that had both a strong traditionally evangelical wing and also a growing acceptance of theological liberalism. Especially in two of the largest Baptist and Presbyterian denominations of the north, the balance was right for some major conflicts.

The term "fundamentalists" originated in the midst of such a controversy in the Northern Baptist Convention. In the summer of 1920, Curtis Lee Laws, editor of the influential Baptist paper *The Watchman-Examiner*, coined the term to designate his own conservative party in the battles that were looming in the upcoming meeting of the Convention. "Fundamentalists," wrote Laws, were those who were ready "to do battle royal for the Fundamentals." It is important to note that this and other early uses of "fundamentalists" and "fundamentals" had to do first of all with defending fundamental biblical doctrines. Even if the cultural crisis precipitated much of the militance, fundamentalists did not lose sight of their major task of defending the Bible, as they understood it, against its

5. As quoted in *FAAC*, 152.

detractors. In the Baptist case, conflicts on the mission fields were also instrumental in precipitating a sense of a common cause among defenders of biblicist evangelism. Modernist missionaries were preaching a gospel of uplifting ideals for civilization, while more traditionally evangelical missionaries from many denominations, southern as well as northern, could be mobilized around defending the biblical fundamentals and a gospel of being "born again." It is worth noting that this emerging coalition was not coextensive with dispensational premillennialism, as Laws himself illustrated and was eager to point out. Premillennialists, such as Riley, were conspicuous in supporting the denominational battles. But fundamentalism was not a single unified movement. Rather, what Laws was describing was a mood of militancy that was spreading among anti-modernist biblicist evangelicals of many sorts.

Most Presbyterian fundamentalists were not dispensationalists, but Presbyterians nonetheless played a significant role among the diverse co-belligerents who were shaping the new mood of militancy. As their five-point declaration of essential doctrines in 1910 illustrated, conservative Presbyterians in the (northern) Presbyterian Church in the U.S.A. had already been fighting for fundamental doctrines before the war, so the new postwar mood only intensified their efforts. Like their Northern Baptist counterparts, they hoped that they could control the denominational machinery so as to rule out modernist theology as unacceptable heresy. In both of these denominations, conservatives had enough strength among rank-and-file clergy and church officers to have a reasonable chance of gaining control. Liberals counterattacked. The most famous instance was a widely published 1922 sermon, "Shall the Fundamentalists Win?" by renowned preacher Harry Emerson Fosdick, a Baptist serving a New York City Presbyterian church. Fosdick accused the fundamentalists of intolerance. The most effective conservative rebuttal came from Princeton Theological Seminary biblical scholar J. Gresham Machen in his 1923 volume *Christianity and Liberalism*. Machen argued pointedly that the new liberal theologies that advocated God-assisted cultivation of noble religious sentiments and virtue was really a different religion from historic Christianity in which salvation was dependent on Christ's atoning work on the cross on behalf of otherwise hopeless sinners. "A separation between the two parties in the Church," Machen declared, "is the crying need of the hour."[6] Many outside commenta-

---

6. As quoted in *FAAC*, 175.

tors, notably H. L. Mencken and Walter Lippmann, acknowledged that Machen had logic on his side.

Nonetheless, even in largely conservative denominations, including the northern Presbyterians and Baptists, many moderates feared the charge of "intolerance" and were not ready to provoke schism. So among the Presbyterians, where the militant party was strong, not much could be accomplished beyond a 1923 reaffirmation of the five points of "essential doctrines." Liberals countered with a protest petition, the Auburn Affirmation, for which they gathered some 1,300 signatures, including those of some moderate conservatives. The petition urged tolerance, saying that the five points represented only "certain theories" about inspiration, the incarnation, the atonement, the resurrection, and the miracles. Among both Baptists and Presbyterians, many conservatives backed away from taking hardline fundamentalist positions that would have led to schism. After all, they reasoned, the first task was to preach the gospel, and church splits and acrimony would detract from that.

Smaller fundamentalist protests flared up in other northern denominations, including the Methodists, Episcopalians, and Disciples of Christ, but had little impact in restraining inclusivist trends. In the South, fundamentalist attitudes meant only shoring up conservative lines of defense already in place. Fundamentalist attitudes also spread into many smaller denominations, including ethnic groups such as the Missouri Synod Lutherans, Christian Reformed, Evangelical Free, and Swedish Covenant, and holiness groups, such as the Wesleyans and Nazarenes, where conservative parties heightened efforts to fend off the slightest inroads of liberal approaches. Even Mennonites and Evangelical Friends felt the effects of militant fundamentalist teachings.

Fundamentalist militancy within denominations had its counterpart on another front: in all sorts of conservative evangelical reactions against changing cultural mores. Revivalist and biblicist evangelicals had long condemned social vices, but as the roaring twenties emerged after World War I there seemed to be more to combat. John Roach Straton, a premillennialist evangelist, became notorious in New York City for his campaigns against the new standards of dancing and women's dress, as well as against open expressions of sexuality in the theater and movies, all of which reflected the newer and more permissive standards of the jazz age. Many fundamentalists were alarmed when women were granted the vote in 1920, fearing that new feminine roles and attitudes would undermine traditional teachings regarding the family, gender roles, and sexuality.

Fundamentalists shared many other Americans' alarm over the threat of Bolshevism. Some fundamentalists openly expressed their prejudices against immigrants, Catholics, Jews, and African Americans, although those attitudes reflected their social location more than their theology.[7] Moreover, the teaching that Jesus would return very soon did not seem to inhibit many premillennialists from joining in political campaigns. Although politics, narrowly defined, was hardly the primary concern of the movement, these believers came from a Protestant tradition accustomed to trying to enlist the government for righteous causes. Fundamentalists were often ambivalent as to whether to characterize Jazz Age America as simply under judgment like ancient Babylon (as dispensational premillennialism implied) or as a new Israel that could be brought back to a godly heritage.

Aimee Semple McPherson, for instance, relished engaging in such fundamentalist cultural battles. Perhaps the most famous evangelist of the era, Sister Aimee came from a Pentecostal heritage that allowed women preachers. Pentecostals and other fundamentalists had some doctrinal differences, but they also shared many militant attitudes. McPherson found that controversy could aid evangelism. She often attacked modernists from her Los Angeles pulpit. She advocated cleaning up local vices, and she denounced local political officials. She promoted campaigns to ban the teaching of Darwinism in public schools. As a premillennialist she preached that the United States was under judgment, but she also loved to invoke American patriotism.[8] In the midst of the cultural tensions of the 1920s, McPherson had many male counterparts. Her principal non-Pentecostal fundamentalist antagonist in Los Angeles, just to cite one instance, was known as "fighting Bob Shuler."

Of the many different efforts to save America's Christian heritage, the most sensational was the anti-evolution crusade. The issue had compelling symbolic resonance for many biblicist Protestants. Secularists were using biological evolution to discredit the Bible's teaching regarding creation in Genesis, hence disparaging biblicist Christianity generally. Furthermore, evolutionary teachings were behind many anti-Christian secular philosophies, such as those that had led to German militarism.

---

7. Matthew Avery Sutton, *American Apocalypse: A History of Modern Evangelicalism* (Cambridge, MA: Harvard University Press, 2014), 114–47, documents these prejudices.

8. Edith L. Blumhofer, *Aimee Semple McPherson: Everybody's Sister* (Grand Rapids: Eerdmans, 1993); Matthew Avery Sutton, *Aimee Semple McPherson and the Resurrection of Christian America* (Cambridge, MA: Harvard University Press, 2007).

The resonance of the cause was greatly amplified when, very soon after the war, William Jennings Bryan took it up. Bryan thought that, since most Americans believed in the Bible, the democratic solution was to ban the teaching of biological evolution from public schools. A number of prominent premillennial evangelists also joined in the crusade, alerting their constituencies to the threat of Darwinism. In the South much of the citizenry was proud to be identified as "fundamentalist," and by the mid-1920s several southern states passed legislation banning the teaching of biological evolution in their schools and bills were pending in some other states, including in the North.

The Scopes Trial and the ridicule heaped upon Bryan catalyzed a reaction against fundamentalism as a national movement. After 1925 the strength of the militant parties in the major northern denominations began to decline precipitously. Nonetheless, the controversies of the 1920s left an indelible imprint on many conservative Protestants. Typically, one of the ways they thought of themselves was as those who were ready to stand up for the fundamental truths of the Bible without compromise. That militancy did not have to be expressed in national campaigns. More often it was manifested in militant gatekeeping to be sure that one's own group remained free from the taints of compromise. Nowhere is that more clearly illustrated than with regard to the anti-evolution movement itself. Whereas before World War I proto-fundamentalists allowed room for some very limited forms of God-directed evolution, after the Scopes Trial such views were ruled out of bounds in most fundamentalist circles. Even William Jennings Bryan had believed that each of the "days" of Genesis 1 might represent a long period of time. In the decades after his death the standard fundamentalist view became that of "creation science," which insisted that the "days" of Genesis were each twenty-four hours, that the earth was only some thousands of years old, and that the geological evidence was explained by the worldwide flood of Noah's time. Such hardline biblicist views, rather than receding after the 1920s, continued to grow in popularity.

In the decades after the 1920s, fundamentalists were similarly militant in gatekeeping on other issues. Typically, they enforced the strictest mores for their constituents: no smoking, drinking, dancing, use of makeup, card playing, or attendance at theater or movies. They were also on guard against the slightest doctrinal compromise in their midst. They insisted on strict doctrinal tests for their leaders, including subscription to the inerrancy of Scripture and other fundamental doctrines. By the mid-twentieth century many fundamentalists were also insisting on ecclesiastical separation from any denomination that allowed liberal theological teachings.

Yet, because fundamentalists were shaped by prior religious traditions, there was much more to outlooks than just militancy. They were dedicated to preserving and protecting the fundamental teachings of their particular heritage because they were convinced that the gospel message was a matter of eternal life or death. These high stakes steeled their passionate dedication to proclaiming the Good News. Evangelism and missions were top priorities. Some believed that, for the sake of promoting these aims, it was better to emphasize the positive elements of a simple gospel message rather than emphasize what they were against. So fundamentalists came in many varieties and with varying degrees of militancy.

The dispensational revivalist movement continued to be a driving force for much of fundamentalism. Even prior to World War I, that movement operated largely through schools such as the Moody Bible Institute. These, plus evangelistic organizations, Bible conferences, missions agencies, and a few colleges and seminaries, gave the dispensationalist movement virtual independence from major denominations, even for those who might retain such denominational affiliations. So even after 1925, when fundamentalism was declining as a movement to reclaim older denominations or American culture generally, dispensationalists were building parachurch networks promoting their own doctrines. It was these that made the *Scofield Reference Bible* the standard fundamentalist Bible. Dallas Theological Seminary became a leading center for dispensationalist teaching, as did Bob Jones University, Wheaton College, and an ever-growing network of Bible colleges. These educational institutions especially were influential in promoting dispensationalist teachings and fundamentalist attitudes in all sorts of denominations. Fundamentalists also founded some of their own denominations, such as the small but influential General Association of Regular Baptists and Carl McIntire's Bible Presbyterian Church. More often fundamentalists operated through largely independent local churches that might be affiliated with a larger quasi-denominational network. William B. Riley, for instance, long oversaw such a network of Baptist churches in Minnesota. The combative dispensationalist evangelist J. Frank Norris headed the World Baptist Fellowship, which eventually led to a breakaway offshoot, the Baptist Bible Fellowship.[9]

9. Joel A. Carpenter, *Revive Us Again: The Reawakening of American Fundamental-*

In the middle decades of the twentieth century, this loosely organized and often-feuding dispensationalist network was so influential (and so often used "fundamentalist" as a self-designation) that it sometimes seemed as though dispensationalism had become coextensive with fundamentalism as an ongoing interconnected movement. Yet throughout the country—in the Deep South, for instance[10]—there were many other militantly anti-liberal, Bible-believing, white Protestants who were not dispensationalists but would have recognized themselves as "fundamentalists."[11] While they were not all connected to each other institutionally, they shared the common mood of militancy. Bible-believing Christians were being confronted by real and massive twentieth-century cultural trends that threatened the fundamentals of their faith and practices, and many were ready to fight back. The dispensationalist movement itself had been transformed since the days of the irenic D. L. Moody. The cultural crisis following World War I was a true turning point after which the movement took on a new tone. Even if evangelism and missions were still its primary concerns, hard-liner militancy, alarmist characterization of cultural trends, and uncompromising gatekeeping were now among its most conspicuous traits.[12]

ism (New York: Oxford University Press, 1997), provides a fine characterization of the complexities of the mid-century movement.

10. Grant Wacker, "Uneasy in Zion: Evangelicals in Postmodern Society," in *Evangelicalism and Modern America*, ed. George Marsden (Grand Rapids: Eerdmans, 1984), 17-28, offers an insightful account of how southern "custodial" attitudes toward the predominantly evangelical cultures prepare adherents for resistance when they see those values threatened.

11. Like the term "evangelical" today, "fundamentalist" often was not the primary identification that many militantly conservative evangelicals would have used to describe themselves. Yet in the 1930s or 1940s many nondispensationalists would have been happy to be recognized as "fundamentalists" in the sense of being Bible-believing, born-again Christians willing to defend the fundamentals of the faith against liberal theologies and permissive practices.

12. Michael S. Hamilton, "The Interdenominational Evangelicalism of D. L. Moody and the Problem of Fundamentalism," in *American Evangelicalism: George Marsden and the State of American Religious History*, ed. Darren Dochuk, Thomas S. Kidd, and Kurt W. Peterson (Notre Dame: University of Notre Dame Press, 2014), 230-80, provides an impressive case for making dispensationalism rather than militancy the defining characteristic of fundamentalism. The present account implicitly answers those objections by providing a way of telling the story that keeps militancy as the distinguishing feature yet takes Hamilton's objections into account. Hamilton argues in part based on the fact that even during the 1920s not all leading dispensationalists were highlighting contro-

Fundamentalist militancy and defensiveness often brought reactions and splits within the loosely organized movement, and, perhaps not surprising, the largest long-term reaction was that against fundamentalist militancy itself. In this case the turning point coincided with World War II. Oddly, this second global conflagration had some opposite cultural effects compared with the first. World War II ushered in a period of greater cultural conservatism and a sense of national unity. For whatever reason, many conservative evangelicals who earlier had been drawn into hardline fundamentalist attitudes were by the 1940s ready to revert to emphasizing more positive and inclusive attitudes. Without giving up any core doctrines, leaders who had been associated with fundamentalism began to emphasize somewhat broader outlooks, which they characterized as "the new evangelicalism" or soon just as "evangelicalism." As Grant Wacker describes in his chapter in this volume, Billy Graham became the preeminent representative of this "evangelical" movement. The new evangelicalism was a coalition of loosely related groups that had fundamentalist backgrounds. Others rejected the new movement and remained militant fundamentalists. They condemned Graham and his ilk as compromisers. Typically they made separatism the issue. Graham, who was reviving the irenic spirit of Dwight L. Moody,[13] was willing to cooperate with the major mainline Protestant denominations rather than separating from those who tolerated theological liberalism. Some fundamentalists, such as at Bob Jones University, insisted not only on separating from liberal denominations but also on "second-degree separatism." That is, they broke fellowship with those, such as Graham, who fellowshipped with those who remained in churches that tolerated liberals. Those and others who continued to call themselves "fundamentalists" insisted all the more on remaining pure, both on fundamental doctrines and in lifestyle.

versialism in their publications. By way of contrast, Matthew Sutton, *American Apocalypse*, who also tends to equate fundamentalism with dispensationalism, highlights dispensationalist controversialism on a host of issues. In other words, the movement had more than one side. Ernest Sandeen, *The Roots of Fundamentalism: British and American Millenarianism, 1900-1930* (Chicago: University of Chicago Press, 1970), provides the classic argument for equating the fundamentalist movement with dispensational millenarianism. See *FAAC*, passim, for a critique of his formulation.

13. Hamilton's way of telling the story, "The Interdenominational Evangelicalism of D. L. Moody," helps explain the continuities between the more irenic (though still broadly dispensational) evangelicalism of Moody and that of Graham. But recognizing that continuity also highlights that the fundamentalist militancy of the era from about 1920 to 1940 had altered much of the dispensationalist movement.

By the end of the 1950s, new lines between "evangelicals" and the more militant "fundamentalists" were drawn, often on the basis of whether or not they liked Billy Graham.

Still another turning point followed the Vietnam War and the cultural upheavals of the 1960s and 1970s. By about 1980 "fundamentalism" had reemerged as a national movement, but in an altered form. In this new form it differed from both the nationally oriented fundamentalism of the 1920s and the separatist fundamentalism of the 1950s, in that it was most conspicuously a political movement. Earlier fundamentalism, like American evangelicalism generally, often had political dimensions. Despite premillennial teachings that Jesus would return within the current generation, and despite frequent condemnations of liberal Christians for being too political, fundamentalists retained an impulse to Christianize American society and sometimes joined in political movements. Yet these political forays had been occasional and haphazard. With the new "culture wars" fundamentalism that emerged by 1980, militant Republican party politics became a leading characteristic of the coalition. And while the coalition had some prominent separatist fundamentalist leadership, most notably Jerry Falwell, its political character drew in a whole new coalition of militant, mostly white, Protestants, Catholics, Mormons, and others. Emphasizing traditional family values in opposition to feminism, gay rights, abortion, and permissiveness generally, as well as anti-evolution, anti-Communism, and opposition to liberal, social-welfare, big government, they construed their cause as an effort to return the United States to its Christian roots.

This new fundamentalism was especially strong in the South, among southerners moving elsewhere in the Sun Belt, and in the American heartland generally where white Protestants had long been dominant. It helped precipitate a split in America's largest Protestant denomination, the Southern Baptist Convention. As in the 1920s, doctrinal issues versus theological liberalism played a major role in the conflict, but in this case these were typically mixed with political allegiances and attitudes on culture-war issues. Unlike the 1920s, the conservative party (which was called "fundamentalist" by opponents, but seldom by themselves) won and took over and excluded liberals from major seminaries and denominational structures.

The events of 9/11 precipitated another turning point for the term "fundamentalist," as in the years after that event the word seemed to lose some of its appeal as a self-designation. During the 1990s the American term "fundamentalist" had often been generalized by journalists and scholars to designate any militantly anti-modern religious group. So the 9/11 terrorists were sometimes called "Islamic fundamentalists," even though their militancy took a very different form from that of American Protestant fundamentalists. "Fundamentalism" was already used widely in liberal American circles as an equivalent for "mindless intolerance." Perhaps related to these factors, by the second decade of the twenty-first century the word seemed to have quietly receded from emphasis as a way of advertising one's self or institution. Nonetheless, the diminishment of the term does not take away from the ongoing reality of conservative evangelical militancy against liberal theologies, lifestyles, permissive mores, and politics. Even if fundamentalism is not always an easily iden-tifiable movement, fundamentalist militancy has left a host of legacies.

CHAPTER 8

Urban Pentecostalism: Chicago, 1906–1912

Edith L. Blumhofer

As the twentieth century dawned, some Americans anticipated a new "move of God" for a new century. A few resolute souls among them found what they anticipated and forged a movement destined to influence the course of global Christian history. They called themselves "Apostolic Faith" people, but before long their focus on the New Testament narrative of the Day of Pentecost (Acts 2) made it logical to dub them "Pentecostals." Their assertion of the importance of a "know-so" baptism with the Holy Spirit set them apart. The "know-so" part referred to speaking in tongues, which they saw as the biblical evidence of a spiritual empowerment available to every Christian that would enable a global end-times revival. Most Americans ignored them, and so Apostolic Faith people inhabited the margins of the margin of American evangelicalism. A century later, though, the explosion of world Christianity brought them prominence. Pentecostalism had multiple global origins. The story of early Chicago Pentecostals demonstrates the easy blending of global and local in a grassroots religious movement with an end-times evangelistic imperative. Chicagoans had a formative influence on the emergence, spread, and contours of Pentecostalism in the United States and abroad, and their story illustrates the extraordinary vitality and flexibility of grassroots Christianity in turn-of-the-century urban America.

"The Lord is doing wonderful things here in Chicago," Mrs. E. W. Stirling wrote early in 1907. "Even the children are receiving the baptism with the Holy Ghost and speaking in tongues. On the 21st of December [1906] in a little mission on Halsted Street, the Lord baptized me with the Holy Ghost at one o'clock in the night. I began to speak in tongues.

There were many present at that time, and I went around shaking hands and speaking in tongues. O, the deep settled peace in my soul."[1]

Here and there across Chicago's diverse neighborhoods, small groups of people shared Mrs. Stirling's wonderment: God was at work in Chicago in 1907, not in the city's stately churches but in the storefront missions and homes where people gathered to encourage one another to "know God" with supernatural certainty. The faithful described New Testament spiritual gifts such as speaking in tongues or healings as "wonderful," "miraculous," an entirely "new thing," but in fact such experiences made sense in particular networks that had flourished for at least a decade on the city's evangelical margins. When Pentecostals from elsewhere brought their news of an end-times restoration of New Testament power to Chicago's radical evangelicals, they found that the Spirit seemed already to be on the move. Separate and overlapping local religious stirrings had created a grassroots context that made Pentecostal assertions of revival and spiritual power plausible.

Between 1907 and 1912, Chicago was perhaps the most influential hub for American Pentecostals. In Los Angeles, where a revival in humble quarters on Azusa Street drew wide attention in 1906, enthusiasm and attendance ebbed. The fervor in Chicago, however, steadily increased. In Chicago, neighborhood preachers not only shaped Pentecostal beliefs and practice; they also exported their views abroad. Home to two of Pentecostalism's nationally circulated monthlies as well as to people who influenced the movement's identity, Chicago also provided the context for the spread of Pentecostalism among European immigrants and their connections abroad.

Why did Pentecostalism establish itself so readily in Chicago? Where in the city did it find its niche? The answer is complex. Chicago's strategic location, its transportation links, and its rich ethnic and religious mix made the city hospitable to religious variety. But Pentecostalism took root in particular places on the Chicago religious landscape while it neglected others. One answer may be that it flourished first where existing grassroots networks had prepared the ground.

At least four distinct but overlapping and interwoven webs of grassroots piety nurtured faith hospitable to the supernatural, and Pentecostal ideas spread in these existing connections. Each was sensitive to women's voices and racial inclusivity and consisted of restless religious

1. *The Apostolic Faith* 1, no. 6 (February-March 1907): 8.

"insiders" and perennial religious "outsiders": (1) the remnants of John Alexander Dowie's Christian Catholic Church; (2) the Christian and Missionary Alliance; (3) the World's Faith Missionary Association; and (4) immigrant Protestant missions, especially Scandinavian, Italian, and German. A brief introduction to these networks suggests the grassroots infrastructures that gave the first Pentecostals a place on Chicago's religious landscape.

The troubles that beset John Alexander Dowie after 1901 in Zion City, his holy community just north of Chicago, tend to overshadow his astonishing rise on the Chicago religious scene. A native of Scotland and graduate of the University of Edinburgh, Dowie began his professional life as a Congregational pastor in Australia and migrated with his family to the United States in 1888. By then he had discovered his vocation as a healing evangelist. Outspoken and controversial, he began in Chicago in 1893 by praying for the sick in a crude tabernacle not far from an entrance to the World's Fair.[2] This choice of venue was no accident: both Dowie and the Fair were in the entertainment (as well as enlightenment) business. Dowie thundered against vice, the clergy, "dead" churches, the pope, the press, secret societies, politicians, and the city's medical establishment. The thousands who crowded his meetings found him an entertaining if bombastic performer.

Dowie's rallies were carefully orchestrated and unfailingly colorful. What people heard proved infinitely more engaging than the typical fare in the city's churches. Before long a surprising number of ordinary Chicagoans, blacks, native born, and immigrants, testified to extraordinary healings. As his crowds grew, Dowie filled the Chicago Auditorium, the city's largest hall.[3] He next opened several large tabernacles in crowded neighborhoods and purchased a vacant church on Michigan Avenue near Sixteenth Street. This became Zion Tabernacle no. 1, the hub for Dowie's new Christian Catholic Church.[4] Dowie called his collective efforts "Zion." He operated several divine healing homes on Chicago's South Side where he welcomed the sick who came for his prayers. In 1895, the homes set the stage for a blitz of free publicity when, in a colorful court

2. See photo, *Leaves of Healing* 1, no. 1 (August 31, 1894): cover; and in the same issue, John Alexander Dowie, "Zion Tabernacle," 2.
3. "Zion's Onward Movement: The Chicago Auditorium," *Leaves of Healing* 2, no. 15 (January 17, 1896): 239.
4. "Zion's Onward Movement: Organization of the Christian Catholic Church," *Leaves of Healing* 2, no. 19 (February 28, 1896): 292-300.

battle, he fought charges that in them he practiced medicine without a license. Dowie published the proceedings as *Zion's Holy War with the Hosts of Hell in Chicago*. In response to constant requests for accommodation from people who wanted instruction and prayer for healing, he purchased a 150-bedroom hotel at Michigan Avenue and Twelfth Street.[5]

Zion's creed was simple. Only those who had had a definite conversion experience were Christians, and Christians showed their faith by abstaining from pork, medicine, and secret societies as well as from the usual list of worldly pleasures. Dowie labeled the vast majority of Christians hypocrites, idolaters, or worse, and he acknowledged only those who adhered to his rules and submitted to rebaptism by triple immersion as full-fledged members of Zion. Surprising numbers of people—thousands each year in Chicago alone—made their way into the water at Zion Tabernacle where Dowie regularly featured testimonies like that of one who exulted in salvation from both "Lutheranism and infidelism." To Zion's faithful, that claim made perfect sense.[6]

The thousands of Chicagoans who made Zion Tabernacle their religious home lived in all the city's neighborhoods, with the largest concentration on Chicago's South Side. African Americans mingled with native-born and immigrant whites, and Dowie mobilized them by organizing two "rings around Chicago," an "inner" and an "outer" circle. The inner ring consisted in 1901 of 320 weekly house meetings in twelve languages that circled the city from Evanston on the north to the far South Side.[7] Meetings in the surrounding suburbs constituted the outer ring. The faithful opened their homes, creating a grassroots network that linked Chicago's neighborhoods and close-in suburbs. A weekly publication, *Leaves of Healing*, reported on every service in Zion Tabernacle and gave the names and addresses of those recently healed or baptized. It listed house meetings, provided detailed directions to Zion Tabernacle, and proved an invaluable tool for building a constituency.

Dowie's faithful made much of personal holiness and radical faith in a God who was powerfully present and eager to be known and experienced. By 1901, Dowie himself had moved north to his new community, Zion City. From 1906, his increasingly radical claims about himself com-

5. *Leaves of Healing* 4, no. 1 (October 30, 1897): 19.
6. For basic information about Zion, see Gordon Lindsay, *John Alexander Dowie: A Life Story of Trials, Tragedies and Triumphs* (Dallas: Christ for the Nations, 1986).
7. John G. Speicher, "Zion Cottage Meetings," *Leaves of Healing* 8, no. 23 (March 30, 1901): 732–33.

bined with allegations of moral failings and the financial ruin of his uto-
pia to erode his personal following, yet his Chicago followers remained
staunchly loyal to his core message and were ready to be mobilized when
Pentecostals came to town.

Sermons at Zion Tabernacle occasionally vented Dowie's distaste for
another grassroots network that overlapped his own, the Christian and
Missionary Alliance, and its founder, Albert B. Simpson, who prayed for
the sick but did not ban medicine.

The Chicago Alliance was affiliated with the national movement that
Simpson created in the 1880s to spread a message he called the fourfold
gospel. With headquarters in New York, the Alliance gathered evangelicals who shared Simpson's yearning for "deeper" Christian experience
of prayer, Bible study, testimony, and support for foreign missions. In
1906, the Alliance had 150 organized branches and 250 additional regular meeting points at which the faithful explored weekly the practical
dimensions of experiencing Christ as savior, healer, sanctifier, and coming king.[8] It attracted middle- and working-class people who worshiped
in traditional Protestant churches on Sunday mornings and pursued a
deeper spiritual life at weekday gatherings.

In 1900, William MacArthur dominated the Chicago Alliance. A
charismatic figure, MacArthur was the son of Scottish immigrants.[9] (His
enduring claim to fame in Chicago has more to do with his children than
with his preaching. William MacArthur was the father of two prominent
Chicagoans—John MacArthur of the John and Catherine T. MacArthur
Foundation, and Charles MacArthur, journalist, Pulitzer prize–winning
playwright, and the first husband of Helen Hayes.) The central Alliance meeting at Willard Hall at Monroe and Clark Streets convened on
Thursday afternoons. Three meeting places on the South Side—a United
Brethren church and two residences, one in Hyde Park and the other in
Englewood—served rapidly growing neighborhoods. On the North Side,
Alliance groups met weekly at Dr. William Gentry's People's Indepen-
dent Church and in homes. The Gospel Tabernacle, an independent
church on St. Louis Avenue near Twenty-First Street in sympathy with
Alliance views, served the West Side. The MacArthurs owned adjacent
homes that they opened to the public for daily morning prayer and Bible

8. *The Christian and Missionary Alliance* 25, no. 22 (June 9, 1906): 353.
9. For biographical information, see John Sawin, "Alliance History Notes," unpub-
lished typescript, Canadian Theological Seminary, Regina, Saskatchewan.

study, Friday afternoon healing services, a daily quiet hour of prayer at
6 p.m., and a monthly day of prayer.[10]

Alliance faithful could be found on the membership rolls of many of
Chicago's Protestant churches. A network within other networks, they
were deeply committed to helping the needy and saving the lost, but
they were also driven by concern for the quality of their relationship with
God. They wanted "God's best," and they devoted themselves to pursuing whatever that meant. They had many similarities and occasional
close ties to a third web of independently minded evangelicals inside
and outside established congregations, the World's Faith Missionary
Association.

The World's Faith Missionary Association grew out of the religious
longings of its founders, Charles and Minnie Hanley. Devout Protestants,
the Hanleys found themselves yearning for a greater awareness of spiritual vitality, and in the 1880s they launched a ministry shaped by their
reading of the times and the Bible.

Charles Hanley was the successful editor of the *Shenandoah (Iowa)
Post* and a deacon in the Congregational Church in that southwestern
Iowa county seat when he began associating with people consumed with
the desire to be "wholly given up to God, and entirely free from everything that would hinder or grieve the Spirit in His workings."[11] His wife,
Minnie George, had grown up Methodist, been immersed by Baptists,
and shared her husband's longing to experience God. The couple had
dramatic religious experiences (Minnie called hers a "baptism with the
Holy Ghost and fire"), reevaluated their priorities, and decided to become full-time Christian workers. Hanley began by transforming the *Post*
into his idea of a Christian paper. He found that he could not "conscien-
tiously advertise cigars and tobacco, theaters, publish town gossip, and
engage in party and wire pulling politics."[12] In keeping with this new
approach, he changed the paper's name to *The Firebrand*. Prominent on
the first page of each issue were the words "Holiness unto the Lord."

Their newfound zeal colored the language of the Hanleys' memories
of this dramatic reinvention of themselves: "The devil was on hand to
make the good people think we were crazy and some of them are con-

10. "The Work in Chicago," *The Christian Alliance* 24, no. 27 (July 15, 1905): 444.

11. Clara Lum, "The Living Gospel, or A Missionary Family," *The Firebrand*, June
1901, 1.

12. Lum, "The Living Gospel," 1.

vinced. But we continue with God's help to keep pouring salvation, red hot, right into the ranks of formality and hypocrisy."[13] People canceled subscriptions to the paper and greeted the Hanleys on the street with "'Amen' and 'Hallelujah' in jeering tones." Shunned by former acquaintances and struggling to live "by faith" (without salary from secular employment), the Hanleys opened a faith home and missionary training school, expanded the reach of *The Firebrand*, and sponsored evangelistic endeavors.

In 1896, they began offering ministerial credentials to people eager to engage in Christian work outside of denominations. Their network came to include a variety of rescue missions and foreign missionaries, but its largest constituency comprised evangelists who tirelessly crisscrossed the country, preaching in small towns and out-of-the-way villages as well as in large cities. This loose association was interracial and tolerated a range of doctrines and styles.

The Association attracted a changing group of Chicagoans, some with ties to Moody Bible Institute. The Hanleys endorsed Beulah Rescue Mission on North Clark Street as well as various evangelists and city missionaries. Two missions on North Avenue were part of their circle. Although the Hanleys did not cooperate with Dowie, they did provide some supportive commentary, and Dowie reciprocated with an endorsement of their paper.[14] It is not surprising, then, that in Chicago and elsewhere these networks overlapped.

A fourth web of like-minded Protestants emerged in Chicago's swelling immigrant communities. Immigrants arrived in startling numbers. In 1890, some 78 percent of the population was either foreign-born or the children of immigrants, often living in neighborhoods where the old language and customs prevailed. A range of foreign-language newspapers and religious publications served new arrivals and nurtured a sense of community. Two of Chicago's many immigrant groups illustrate how the immigrant experience created space for a radical evangelical witness: Italian Protestants and Swedish Baptists.

Chicago's Italian neighborhoods were home to a handful of Italians of Waldensian heritage as well as to some who converted to Protestantism soon after their arrival. Led by evangelist Michele Nardi, those of Waldensian heritage organized a small congregation. In March 1892, sixty-three of these created an Italian Presbyterian church. A $10,000

---

13. Lum, "The Living Gospel," 1.
14. "Editorial Notes," *Leaves of Healing* 4, no. 27 (April 30, 1898): 536.

donation from Chicago's Fourth Presbyterian Church helped to construct First Italian Presbyterian Church on the corner of West Ohio and Halsted Streets in 1894.[15]

Italian Protestants evangelized within their extended families, and whole families joined the new church. Among the converts was Luigi Francescon, who arrived in Chicago in 1890, converted to Protestantism in 1891, and became a charter member and elder at First Italian Presbyterian Church. Before long, he stirred up dissension over infant baptism. In 1903 he took advantage of the pastor's absence to immerse twenty Presbyterians. Forced out of the church, Francescon opened his own mission, which soon divided over the proper observance of Sunday. Despite such differences, these Italian Protestants kept in touch. They lived and worked together and shared family ties. When the Pentecostal movement arrived in the city, it spread easily and rapidly among this constituency.

Swedish Baptists had a different story. They prospered in Chicago, supporting thriving neighborhood congregations. The presence of their seminary in Morgan Park on the city's far South Side made Chicago a hub for this small immigrant denomination.

Early in 1906, Second Swedish Baptist Church became the local center for a revival known as the "new movement." Located in the heart of a Swedish community at Wentworth Avenue and Twenty-Fifth Street, Second Swedish Baptist had as its pastor in 1905 the Rev. J. W. Hjerstrom. He invited Swedish Baptists eager for revival to gather on Mondays for prayer. People came from around the city, and in February 1906 Second Swedish Baptist Church became the setting for emotional revival scenes, including speaking in tongues.[16]

Reports of revivals in other parts of the world—especially Wales and India—circulated widely among evangelicals in 1905, and Hjerstrom's interest in renewal echoed in many Swedish hearts. Remembered as a "fiery orator" with unusual "power" over the Swedish language, Hjerstrom became the chief advocate among American Swedish Baptists for expressive forms of prayer, repentance, and worship and for baptisms with the Holy Spirit.

Speaking in tongues, prayer for the sick, and other evidences associ-

15. Louis DeCaro, *Our Heritage* (Sharon, PA: General Council, Christian Church of North America, 1977), 20.

16. Adolf Olson, *A Centenary History* (Chicago: Baptist Conference Press, 1952), 263-66; "Fran missionskaltet: Illinois," *Nya Weck-Posten*, February 6, February 13, March 20, 1906, 4.

ated with revival, though hardly universal, were certainly not unknown among pietist Scandinavians in America.[17] Now they appeared in most of the city's Swedish Baptist congregations. The people—and especially the pastors—of Second Baptist, Humboldt Park Swedish Baptist, and Lake View Swedish Baptist proved most amenable and would soon find affinities for the Pentecostal movement.[18]

These four networks informally linked Chicago citizens and neighborhoods and had much in common. Each network mobilized people who were restless inside the establishment as well as those who inhabited a sprawling and often invisible army of Christian spiritual seekers. In these circles women found greater freedom for self-expression. Dowie ordained a few women as elders and many more as evangelists and deaconesses. Minnie Hanley was as much a leader of the World's Faith Missionary Association as her husband, and they credentialed hundreds of females. Blacks and whites mingled daily in these circles, and immigrants and the poor were welcome.

Though national in scope, such networks cultivated a strong sense of community and mission among their adherents in Chicago neighborhoods. With meeting places scattered throughout the city and periodicals to cultivate their followings, this independent religious world provided a hospitable context in which yet another grassroots Christian movement could emerge and compete. The four by no means exhaust the long list of the city's grassroots religious circles with which Pentecostals would soon interact. Chicago was home to various holiness groups as well as to efforts that extended out from the Moody Church and Moody Bible Institute. The four networks discussed above, then, illustrate the workings of a larger evangelical subculture that existed within and outside the city's denominations.

Word of revival stirrings in Los Angeles reached Chicago in the summer of 1906 by mail, both in the pages of religious periodicals and via personal letters.[19] Within a few weeks, people arrived from Los Angeles to report in person. Participants in Chicago's grassroots evangelical

17. "Fined $35: Evangelist Who Has Been Holding Frenzied Meetings Is Taken to Court," *Daily Journal* (Fergus Falls, MN), March 11, 1905, 3.

18. E. Ruden, "The Baptist Witness in Scandinavia and the North," *Baptist Quarterly* 27 (1979): 76-83.

19. The best summary of early Pentecostalism in Chicago is included in Robert Mapes Anderson, *Vision of the Disinherited* (New York: Oxford University Press, 1979), 128-30.

circles learned separately but simultaneously about a California revival marked by dramatic experiences and spiritual gifts, and the news piqued interest in the gospel missions that dotted the city.

The Apostolic Faith had gained a hearing in Los Angeles during the late spring and early summer of 1906. With its emphasis on the restoration in the end times of New Testament miracles and spiritual gifts, the Apostolic Faith movement had curious features that drew the press and the public to a nondescript building on Azusa Street where people spoke in tongues, prayed for the sick, and gave uninhibited expression to their emotions. Letters of inquiry poured in, people traveled long distances to see for themselves, and the convinced left to spread the word: Pentecost had come; New Testament Christianity had been restored in the last days. Azusa Street leaders began chronicling the revival in September 1906, and copies of its paper, *The Apostolic Faith*, reached Chicago.

Pilgrims from Azusa Street had already passed through. In July 1906 A. G. and Lillian Garr, members of a holiness group, the Burning Bush, arrived to announce their separation from the Burning Bush and their imminent departure for India as Apostolic Faith missionaries.[20] In August another band of missionaries en route from Azusa Street to Jerusalem passed through Chicago, telling any who would listen of their new religious experiences.[21] One, a restless worker named Lucy Leatherman, had long been a familiar figure on the Chicago storefront mission scene.[22] Then in September 1906, Chicago's curious had an opportunity to hear the founder of the Apostolic Faith movement, Charles Parham, at Volunteer Hall in the Ravenswood section of the city. Parham was in the midst of a visit to nearby Zion: Dowie's city was in receivership and his followers in disarray, and Parham briefly seemed poised to sweep Dowie's flock into the Apostolic Faith movement.[23] Parham's co-evangelist, Mabel Smith Hall, broke away from the Zion meetings to share her version of the Apostolic Faith in Chicago storefront missions.[24] When four Azusa

20. "Good News from Danville, VA," *Apostolic Faith* 1, no. 1 (September 1906): 4.

21. "Missionaries to Jerusalem," *Apostolic Faith* 1, no. 1 (September 1906): 4; Mrs. E. D. Whitnall, "Pentecostal Experience," *Word and Work* 30, no. 10 (October 1908): 303.

22. "Notes," *The Missionary World*, September 1904, 5; *The Firebrand*, September 1900, 1; *The Missionary World*, September 1902, 3; "Another Missionary, Once at the Training Home," *The Missionary World*, December 1906, 1.

23. "Effect of the Tongues Movement," *Free Methodist*, November 6, 1906, 9.

24. Bennett F. Lawrence, *The Apostolic Faith Restored* (St. Louis: The Gospel Publishing House, 1916), 67.

Street participants announced their call to preach Pentecost in Chicago in the spring of 1907, then, the "call" they professed seemed somewhat belated: the city already had several thriving Pentecostal missions and a growing roster of energetic Pentecostal evangelists.[25]

A Mrs. D. E. Whithall was the first Chicagoan on record to speak in tongues in response to news from Los Angeles. As she told it, while riding the elevated railroad on August 31, 1906, she felt "the power" come on her, and she spoke in an unknown tongue. Her husband's response was hardly surprising: "[He] thought I was losing my mind."[26] The earliest Chicago mission to identify with the revival was led by John Sinclair, an independently minded son of the Scottish Highlands who migrated to Chicago in the 1880s. He married the Roman Catholic Mary Ellen Bie, converted to Catholicism, and opened a blacksmith shop on Chicago's South Side.[27] In the late 1890s, the Sinclairs joined Dowie's Zion Tabernacle. Mary Sinclair testified to a healing, and soon Sinclair began preaching at an independent mission at 328 West Sixty-Third Street in the Englewood section of Chicago.[28] He supported his family by continuing his trade.

When he heard in July 1906 about revival in Los Angeles, Sinclair urged his congregation to pray specifically for a baptism in the Holy Spirit marked by speaking in tongues. He spoke in tongues (the accepted "proof" of such baptism) on November 20, and the mission quickly became a magnet for seekers and the curious. Sinclair's preaching colleague, William Howard Durham, held back, wanting to see the Apostolic Faith movement in Los Angeles for himself before making up his mind about its teaching.

Durham, a restless pilgrim destined to help shape the larger identity of American Pentecostalism, had pastoral responsibilities in two mission congregations. He lived on the premises of his North Side meeting hall,

25. *Apostolic Faith* 1, no. 8 (May 1907): 2.

26. Whitnall, "Pentecostal Experience," 303.

27. Larry Martin, *In the Beginning* (Duncan, OK: Christian Life Books, 1994), 57-59; "Instantly Healed of Catarrh of the Stomach, Heart Trouble and Hemorrhage. Delivered from Rome," *Leaves of Healing* 6, no. 23 (March 31, 1900): 734.

28. "Obeying God in Baptism," *Leaves of Healing* 4, no. 34 (June 18, 1898): 675. Sinclair may have been ordained an elder by Dowie in 1897. His application for credentials with the Assemblies of God cites an 1897 ordination by Dowie, but his name is not listed among those ordained in Zion in 1897. He was known as Elder Sinclair, a title that those ordained as elders by Dowie frequently used for the rest of their lives.

the Full Gospel Assembly on West North Avenue, with which he had been associated at least since 1904. A familiar face among Chicago's radical evangelicals, Durham held ministerial credentials from the World's Faith Missionary Association. He was deadly serious, direct, uncompromising, and utterly committed to holiness and evangelism.[29]

Born on January 10, 1873, in Rockastle County, Kentucky, William Durham arrived in Chicago in 1892 and then moved on to southwestern Minnesota. There he came under the influence of local evangelists with ties to the World's Faith Missionary Association (WFMA), revival streams in the Scandinavian Free Mission, and the Christian and Missionary Alliance. G. L. Morgan of Windom, Minnesota, an acknowledged leader networked into all three groups, convened annual camp meetings and winter conventions. Under the tutelage of such WFMA evangelists, Durham embraced the Hanleys' understanding of holiness and the "deeper" Christian life and made his first attempts at preaching. He soon traveled a circuit defined by the WFMA that brought him new contacts in the little-known but thriving world of upper-Midwest radical evangelicalism.[30]

Durham returned to Chicago in about 1903, but he continued itinerant evangelism in the WFMA. In June 1905 he married Bessie Mae Whitmore of Tracy, Minnesota, and brought her to live in the mission on North Avenue.[31] Ideally located directly across from Humboldt Park on a wide thoroughfare served by an elevated train line, the mission was in the heart of a neighborhood of modest private residences and shops owned by Germans and Scandinavians.

In 1906 Durham puzzled over the new excitement about speaking in tongues:

I had labored in Chicago for four years, in the missions at 943 West North Ave. and at 328 West 63rd Street, and, as both missions stood for the full Gospel, and were made up of deeply spiritual people, I never doubted that most of them had the same experience I had; and I had believed for years that I had the Holy Ghost. But when the Spirit be-

29. His first ministerial credentials were issued in January 1902 by the World's Faith Missionary Association. On file in Marshall, Lyon County, Minnesota.

30. G. L. Morgan, *Sketch of My Life, with Some of My Experiences in Evangelistic Work* (privately published, n.d.), held by the Cottonwood County Historical Society, Windom, Minnesota.

31. "Editorial Notes," *Bethel Trumpet* 2, no. 2 (March 1901): 12.

gan to fall in 63rd Street and then in North Avenue Mission, to my surprise, the most spiritual persons were the first to be baptized and speak in tongues, but I said to my wife, "You will see some get just what the rest do, that will not speak in tongues." But, when nearly forty in 63rd Street Mission and some fifteen in North Avenue Mission had received the Holy Spirit and every one of them had spoken in tongues, it made me stop and think, especially as I had never doubted that at least two-thirds of these people had exactly the same experience as I had myself.[32]

Early in 1907, friends in Los Angeles wired train fare and offered Durham hospitality, enabling him to visit Azusa Street. He spent three weeks at the mission "seeking his Pentecost." He described what happened to him on March 2, 1907, as "strange and wonderful and yet glorious":

[The Holy Ghost] worked my whole body, one section at a time, first my arms, then my limbs, then my body, then my head, then my face, then my chin, and finally at 1 a.m. Saturday, March 2, after being under the power for three hours, He finished the work on my vocal organs, and spoke through me in unknown tongues. I arose, perfectly conscious outwardly and inwardly that I was fully baptized in the Holy Ghost.[33]

When Durham returned to Chicago, the impact of his embrace of the revival in the missions on North Avenue and Sixty-Third Street was immediate. Durham took a "clear stand" for the baptism in the Holy Spirit, and the North Avenue Mission could not hold the crowds. He moved his family out and opened their living quarters in the rear of the mission for overflow. Meetings ran day and night. Nightly prayer meetings had begun before Durham's trip, and the congregation was primed for what followed his return. One participant, C. N. Arensbach, explained: "Since January 13th we have had meetings every night, and expect to keep them up till Jesus comes." When Durham returned, Arensbach continued, "it became necessary to seek larger quarters, as the people come from near and far to witness the mighty works of God. . . . Thursday is set apart for

---

32. *The Pentecostal Testimony*, Winter 1909, 5.

33. "A Chicago Evangelist's Pentecost," *The Apostolic Faith* 1, no. 6 (February-March 1907): 4.

all day meetings, and Tuesday afternoon for workers' meeting. There has been much interpretation. Hallelujah!"[34]

By the summer of 1907, there were at least six Pentecostal missions in Chicago. At the end of the year, the number had doubled, augmented by an unknown number of house meetings.[35]

In the spring of 1907, Luigi Francescon passed a street meeting where he heard talk of the baptism with the Holy Spirit. Directed to the North Avenue Mission, he promptly brought other Italians. Durham later reminisced: "I noticed a number of Italian people in the meeting one night.... It was blessed to hear them speak in tongues and sing in the Spirit. The addition of these dear people to our work was a great help to us. They were filled with the Spirit, and with faith and power." During the summer of 1907, Francescon spent his spare time at the mission. He brought Pietro Ottolini, the leader of another Italian group that had seceded from First Italian Presbyterian Church, and his congregation into the North Avenue Mission.

Chicago's Italian Protestants taxed the facilities of a congregation already bursting its seams. "God has a plan," Durham insisted, though scores were often turned away for lack of space. Francescon's and Ottolini's groups met on September 15, 1907, to form an Italian Pentecostal Mission. By 1908, about one hundred Italians had spoken in tongues. Francescon, Durham noted, had been "transformed into a flaming minister of Christ."[36] In 1910, Franceson left Chicago for evangelistic work among Italians in Brazil. His efforts resulted in the Congregação Crista do Brasil, which grew into a thriving denomination claiming well over 3 million adherents.[37] Chicago Italian Pentecostals evangelized Italy as well. A local Protestant wrote: "From this community in Chicago arrived in 1908 the Christian Gospel to our nation."[38] Francescon and Ottolini played prominent roles in the mission to Italy where, generations later, the country's more than 500,000 Pentecostals trace their origins primarily to the efforts of men and women from Chicago.[39]

---

34. "Mission in Chicago," *The Household of God* 3, no. 11 (November 1907): 10–11.

35. E. N. Bell, "Testimony of a Baptist Pastor," *The Pentecostal Testimony*, Winter 1909, 8.

36. "Letter from Brother W. H. Durham," *The Apostolic Messenger* 1, no. 1 (February-March 1908): 1.

37. See Walter Hollenweger, *The Pentecostals* (Minneapolis: Augsburg, 1972), 85ff.

38. Roberto Bracco, quoted in DeCaro, *Our Heritage*, 58.

39. DeCaro, *Our Heritage*, 57–61; William Durham, "Foreign Missions and Missionaries," *The Pentecostal Testimony* 1, no. 8, 14.

Norwegians and Swedes came to the North Avenue Mission, too. Ferdinand Sandgren, an editor of *Folke-Vennen*, a Norwegian weekly, took responsibility for the mission's publishing. *Folke-Vennen*, meanwhile, helped to spread revival news. One reader, a missionary to China identified as B. Berntsen, wrote often to *Folke-Vennen*, urging the claims of the new movement and reporting on his contacts with Spirit-baptized people around the world. *Folke-Vennen* carried stories of the beginnings of Pentecostalism in Norway and letters from Thomas Ball Barratt, a Norwegian Methodist who spoke in tongues in New York and became the movement's enthusiastic promoter in Oslo.[40]

Swedish Baptists, with fresh memories of their own "new movement" of 1905, also flocked to the mission.[41] Martin Carlson, pastor of the nearby Humboldt Park Swedish Baptist Church, embraced Pentecostal teaching, and Swedish Baptist historian Adolf Olson notes that "all the characteristics of Pentecostalism were present" in Carlson's church.[42] Between 1907 and 1910, the Swedish Baptist Church of Lake View lost 115 members, many to Pentecostal missions.[43] The Swedish Baptist press carried reports from Sweden where a young Baptist pastor, Lewi Pethrus, led a notable Apostolic Faith revival in Stockholm. Reports from abroad and events in Chicago forced Swedish Baptists to take sides. In 1908 the North Avenue Mission established a Swedish-language Pentecostal mission. Early in 1909 the *Apostolic Faith* (Portland, OR) published a letter describing the Chicago mission's fervor: "God has opened up a little Swedish mission here. . . . God talks and sings in tongues and prophesies, and all is about our dear Bridegroom's soon coming. . . . There are so many seeking ones here now."[44]

Among Swedish Baptists turned Pentecostals were Daniel Berg and Gunnar Vingren. Berg lived and worked in Chicago. Vingren, a 1908 graduate of the Swedish Baptist theological school in Morgan Park, served a congregation in Menominee, Michigan, until the fall of 1909 when he

40. For example, Thomas Ball Barratt, "En Praedikants Beksendelse," *Folke-Vennen*, December 13, 1906, 1; Hans Lehne, "De nye Foreteelser i Kristiania," *Folke-Vennen*, January 24, 1907, 1; "Pastor Barratts Moder i Kristiania," *Folke-Vennen*, February 14, 1907, 4; Berntsen letter, *Folke-Vennen*, April 24, 1907, 5.

41. Frederick Link to Robert Cunningham, March 9, 1951, in Link's ministerial file, Assemblies of God Archives.

42. Olson, *Centenary History*, 278.

43. Olson, *Centenary History*, 275.

44. *Apostolic Faith* (Portland, OR), January 1909, 1.

spoke in tongues during a convention at First Swedish Baptist Church in Chicago.[45] Consecrated to Pentecostal ministry by William Durham, Berg and Vingren departed Chicago in 1910 to bring the Pentecostal revival to Swedish immigrants in Brazil.[46] When they turned the results of their independent efforts over to the Assemblies of God a generation later, the work initiated by these independent Swedish Pentecostals had generated the largest Pentecostal movement anywhere in the world, the Assembleias de Deus, with over 14.4 million adherents.[47]

On December 12, 1907, the North Avenue Mission purchased the mission property for $8,000.[48] Durham added an extension, nearly doubling the seating capacity. The congregation installed a baptistery, and in the next two years Durham immersed eight hundred people.[49] He began issuing an occasional paper, *The Pentecostal Testimony*, published and distributed free of charge "as the Lord provided." By 1912 he had published 367,000 copies as well as 250,000 tracts.[50]

Early in 1908 Durham wrote: "The meetings are getting better all the time." Hundreds from Chicago, and more hundreds from a distance, had come and been baptized in the Spirit, among them promising Christian workers. Notable among these were several future Pentecostal leaders, such as well-to-do businessman Andrew Argue of Winnipeg, and Southern Baptist pastor Eudorus Bell of Ft. Worth, Texas.[51] Robert Semple and his bride, Aimee Kennedy (later McPherson), came from Ontario to spend a year with Durham before setting out as missionaries to China.[52]

---

45. Gunnar Vingren, manuscript autobiography translated from the Swedish and owned by Ivar Vingren, in the author's possession.

46. For their story, see E. Conde, *Historia das Assembleias de Deus no Brasil* (Rio de Janeiro, 1960); Daniel Berg, *Enviado por Deus, Memorias de Daniel Berg* (São Paulo, 1959); I. Vingren, *O Diario do Pioneiro* (Rio de Janeiro, 1973); *The Apostolic Revival in Brazil: A Short Overview of the Swedish Pentecostal Mission* (Stockholm, 1934).

47. Today the Assemblies of God of Brazil alone claims at least 17 million members, while the total number of Pentecostals in the country exceeds 25 million. For an assessment, see Hollenweger, *The Pentecostals*, 79.

48. Cook County Record Book, 1907, 608, 29. Copies in possession of the author.

49. Durham, "A Glimpse of a Gracious Work of God in Chicago," 156.

50. "Interpretation of Tongues," *The Bridegroom's Messenger* 2, no. 23 (October 1, 1908): 1.

51. E. N. Bell, "Testimony of a Baptist Pastor," *The Pentecostal Testimony*, Winter 1909, 8.

52. Aimee Semple McPherson, *This Is That* (Los Angeles: Echo Park Evangelistic Association, 1923), 58–61.

Durham and Aimee Semple formed a team of note in Pentecostal circles: he uttered messages in tongues, and she responded instantly with interpretations that seemed so remarkable that they were often published and circulated in Pentecostal papers.[53]

Meanwhile, Durham's erstwhile colleague, John Sinclair, had been ordained to Pentecostal ministry by itinerant Pentecostal evangelist William Manley, and one James A. Bell had come to assist him in the Sixty-Third Street Mission, now known as the Christian Apostolic Assembly.[54] Durham concentrated his efforts on the city's North Side.

Durham had responsibility for several meeting points, one of which was Mrs. Maria D. Buddington's House of Prayer at 3520 Forest Avenue. The Buddington home had gracious double parlors that for years had been at the disposal of the Chicago Alliance. He preached regularly at a mission at 325 South Clark Street.[55] By 1912 the North Avenue Mission had helped to form at least ten other Chicago Pentecostal congregations. In part, this was Durham's way of dealing with cramped quarters at North Avenue. "God," he reported, did not "let us enlarge our borders." Rather, "ministers and workers come and get their baptism; but in almost every instance they go out to labor in other fields. But still the old home mission is crowded to the doors, and many have been turned away."[56]

In addition to associated Italian and Swedish "works" (as the Pentecostals called them), a Persian mission opened at 821 North Clark Street. Chicago had the largest Persian population in the United States, and Andrew Urshan, a young immigrant from Iran, showed interest in Pentecostal practice.[57] The son of an evangelical pastor, Urshan was educated at the American Presbyterian Training College near Urmiah City and migrated to the United States in 1902. When someone introduced him to Chicago's independent evangelical networks, his spiritual yearnings awakened and he made his way to Sinclair's mission. All the while, he gathered compatriots for weekly Persian services in a room at Moody Church.

53. "The Great War," *The Upper Room* 1, no. 10 (May 1910): 2; "God Appointed Convention," *The Promise*, March 1910, 1–2.

54. For Sinclair's ordination information, see his ministerial file, Assemblies of God Archives, Springfield, Missouri.

55. William H. Durham, "The Latest News," *The Bridegroom's Messenger*, October 15, 1910, 4.

56. Durham, "A Glimpse of a Gracious Work of God in Chicago," 155.

57. Andrew Urshan, *The Life Story of Andrew bar David Urshan: An Autobiography of the Author's First Forty Years* (Portland, OR: Apostolic Books, 1967), 1.

When Urshan and friends passed a street meeting at Clark Street and Chicago Avenue, an intersection in the neighborhood favored by Persian immigrants, they were intrigued. The meeting's organizers came from the North Avenue Mission, and Urshan and his friends visited Durham's meetings and began praying for the baptism with the Holy Spirit. When some spoke in tongues, Moody Church pastor Amzi Clarence Dixon preached a sermon exposing the errors of the tongues speakers and asked the Persians to move out.[58] In 1909 they established the Persian Pentecostal Mission. Their Sunday afternoon, Tuesday, Friday, and Saturday evening services gained a reputation among Pentecostals for fervor and spiritual power.[59] Within a few months, Durham baptized twenty-two Persian men, and three immediately set out to evangelize their homeland.[60] Before long, Persian Pentecostals needed larger quarters and moved to a five-hundred-seat hall nearby at 717 North Wells Street.

Informal associations among Chicago's missions meant that the faithful could be found in services at one mission or another every night. Durham's congregation met for scheduled services ten times every week, and sometimes these lasted well into the night. Durham described them as follows:

> Sometimes the services might be said to be conducted in the ordinary way, that is, there will be little or no speaking in tongues, and the pastor will preach a sermon. Again, as soon as we come together, we feel the mighty power of God upon us, and at times it increases till there can be no regular order of service, but all is turned over to the Holy Ghost, who runs things as He wills, and at such times one need not leave the earth to be in heaven.[61]

---

58. Frank Ewart reported that Durham visited Dixon and challenged him to accept the Pentecostal message. Frank Ewart, *The Phenomenon of Pentecost* (Hazelwood, MO: World Aflame Press, 1975), 98; Andrew Urshan, "Pentecost among the Persians in Chicago," *The Bridegroom's Messenger*, September 1, 1910, 3; A. C. Dixon, *Speaking with Tongues* (Chicago: The Bible Institute Colportage Association, 1908).

59. William H. Durham, "The Latest News," *The Bridegroom's Messenger*, October 15, 1910, 4.

60. Durham, "A Glimpse of a Gracious Work of God in Chicago," 156; "A Remarkable Letter," *The Pentecostal Testimony* 1, no. 8, 9–10.

61. Durham, "A Glimpse of a Gracious Work of God in Chicago," 156; "A Remarkable Letter," 9–10.

In August 1909 Durham's wife died, leaving him with a newborn and two toddlers. Two sisters, Gertrude and Ethyl Taylor, moved into the household, one as housekeeper, the other as Durham's secretary. Durham spent weeks at a time on the road. During a trip to Canada in January 1910, he stopped in London, Ontario, for meetings in the home of William Wortman, a socially prominent businessman and member of a Methodist church. The level of response surprised everyone. Three weeks of evangelistic services laid the groundwork for one of Canada's largest and most successful Pentecostal churches, London Gospel Temple.[62]

Durham returned to Chicago in February just in time to bury his six-month-old daughter who died of pneumonia. Durham responded by redoubling his efforts. In the throes of his grief and worn by the intensity of constant revival, he opted to challenge Pentecostals' dominant assumptions about sanctification, a practical doctrine for Pentecostals. What followed permanently altered the contours of North American Pentecostalism.

Most Pentecostals believed that sanctification was a second definite work of grace, an instantaneous experience of cleansing that followed conversion and preceded the baptism in the Holy Spirit. Many deemed a crisis experience of sanctification a prerequisite for the baptism with the Holy Spirit. In the Chicago networks that nurtured early Pentecostals, opinions about sanctification were perhaps less structured than elsewhere, but they tended toward the "second work" theory. Durham took on the majority view when he advocated what he called "the finished work of Calvary."

What Durham now endorsed resembled closely the position of his colleagues in the World's Faith Missionary Association.[63] After 1910 Durham insisted that the "central truth" of the gospel was the believer's identification with Christ at conversion and thereafter: "We come to Christ by faith, and it is only by faith that we abide in him. . . . As soon as a man believes, he is saved, but it requires just as much faith to keep right with God as it did to get right in the first place."[64]

More than a century later, it is difficult to understand just how divisive Durham's ideas became. He described what followed as a battle and

62. "Londoners Claim the 'Gift of Tongues' (Led by Chicago Missionary)," *Evening Free Press* (London, ON), February 1, 1910, 1, 8; "32 People Now Claim to Have 'Gift of Tongues' at Pentecost Meeting," *Evening Free Press* (London, ON), February 2, 1910, 1.

63. "It Is Finished," *The Firebrand*, January 1901, 2.

64. William H. Durham, "Sanctification," *The Pentecostal Testimony* 1, no. 8 (1911): 2.

claimed that he found himself the object of accusations and slander.[65] God, he said, had revealed to him that the time had come "to establish in all the earth the simple, primitive Gospel of our Lord and Savior Jesus Christ, and that the Finished Work of Calvary was the central theme, yea, the very germ and life of that gospel."[66] In the end, Durham won his point in many places. The "finished work of Calvary" left a permanent rift in North American Pentecostalism.

In the fall of 1910, Durham preached a three-week convention at Glad Tidings Tabernacle in New York, "dealing death to sin and striking terror to everything that savored with compromise."[67] He returned to Chicago for the holidays, then departed again in January for Minneapolis and California. He spent much of 1911 in Los Angeles, contending for the "finished work" and planting a congregation of nearly one thousand adherents.[68] Others assumed responsibility for the North Avenue Mission.[69] On the South Side, John Sinclair's Christian Apostolic Assembly prospered. In 1908 the congregation built a large tabernacle on Wentworth Avenue with a spacious hall seating seven hundred. Its dedication on December 6, 1908, drew representatives of the various networks that Pentecostal experience had woven together. William MacArthur represented the Chicago Christian and Missionary Alliance (which, for several years, was essentially Pentecostal in experience if not fully so in doctrine). Several of Dowie's elders, now Pentecostal ministers familiar in Chicago's missions (W. E. Moody, F. A. Graves, Harry Robinson), participated in the occasion, as did William Gentry, a popular lay preacher, homeopathic physician, and editor of *The Word*. The occasion provided opportunity for a show of strength and unity.[70]

65. Charles Parham, *The Apostolic Faith*, Supplement, July 1912; Bartleman, *How Pentecost Came*, 145ff.; William Durham, "The Great Battle of 1911," *The Pentecostal Testimony* 2, no. 1 (1912): 6; William Durham, "Concerning Self-Defense, Misrepresentations, Etc.," *The Pentecostal Testimony* 2, no. 2 (Spring 1912): 12.
66. Durham, "The Great Battle of 1911," 6.
67. "The Lord's Convention," *The Midnight Cry* 1, no. 1 (March-April 1911): 8.
68. Frank Bartleman, *How Pentecost Came to Los Angeles* (Los Angeles: privately published, 1925), 145-53; William Durham, "The Great Revival at Azusa Street Mission—How It Began and How It Ended," *The Pentecostal Testimony* 1, no. 8, 3-4; "Important Notice," *The Pentecostal Testimony* 1, no. 8, 15.
69. See "Notice Concerning the Heavenly Messages," *Elbethel* 1, no. 3 (1914): 15; "Important Notice—Our Headquarters Removed," *The Pentecostal Testimony* 1, no. 8, 1; William Durham, "Warning," *The Pentecostal Testimony* 1, no. 8, 14.
70. "The Chicago Assembly," *The Household of God* 5, no. 2 (February 1909): 4.

MacArthur was there because the Chicago branch of the Alliance had been swept—at least for the moment—into the Pentecostal movement. MacArthur first reported on the tongues movement in Chicago in January 1907.[71] He started a weekly meeting open to all who wanted "to pray especially that we might receive all that God was willing to bestow."[72] On June 12, Chicago Alliance people began speaking in tongues.[73] For the next few years, evangelists from other Alliance branches who welcomed Pentecostal practices participated in Chicago Alliance conventions, and Alliance people found their way to the city's Pentecostal missions.[74]

Also on the South Side, in an area close to the Black Belt, was another congregation that came to rival the North Avenue Mission as a hotbed of Pentecostal vitality. Opened in 1906 by a former overseer in Dowie's Zion, the Stone Church reached out to former members of the Christian Catholic Church as well as to its neighborhood around Thirty-Seventh Street and Indiana Avenue, a part of the city experiencing rapid ethnic transformation.

Stone Church pastor William Hamner Piper and his wife, Lydia Markley, had been ordained by Dowie, he as an elder and overseer, she as an elder. On December 9, 1906—with Dowie disgraced and his followers scattered—the Pipers conducted their first service.[75] The congregation quickly swelled to about six hundred, many of whom had been Dowieites in the past. Piper knew that Pentecostal teaching was rife among Chicago's grassroots evangelicals. He decided neither to oppose nor to endorse it until declining numbers convinced him that his reluctance amounted to opposing God. In June 1907 he invited three friends from Zion City to talk about Zion's Pentecostal revival.[76]

Piper recalled an eager response. "God gave us very deep and precious meetings every night in the week for many weeks," Piper remi-

71. W. T. MacArthur, "The Promise of the Father and Speaking with Tongues in Chicago," *The Christian and Missionary Alliance*, January 26, 1907, 40.

72. W. T. MacArthur, "The Promise of the Father and Speaking with Tongues in Chicago," *The Christian and Missionary Alliance*, July 27, 1907, 44.

73. MacArthur, "The Promise of the Father and Speaking with Tongues in Chicago," *The Christian and Missionary Alliance*, July 27, 1907, 44.

74. See, for example, "Chicago Convention," *The Christian and Missionary Alliance* 30, no. 6 (July 18, 1908): 267.

75. William Hamner Piper, "Long Weary Months of Spiritual Drought Broken by the Gracious Coming of the Holy Spirit," *The Latter Rain Evangel* 1, no. 1 (October 1908): 3.

76. Gordon P. Gardiner, "Out of Zion . . . into All the World," *Bread of Life* 31, no. 4 (April 1982): 5-12.

nisced. "Soon the Spirit of God was poured out, and from week to week people were baptized."[77] By the time Piper spoke in tongues in February 1908, a large percentage of the congregation had already done so.[78]

The commodious facilities of the Stone Church now became a favorite venue for protracted meetings that attracted people prominent in the small but growing national and international Pentecostal circles. At the Stone Church, former Christian and Missionary Alliance teacher David Wesley Myland, now a Pentecostal, delivered the series of sermons that made the biblical image of the "latter rain" part of American Pentecostal identity.[79] Piper called his monthly publication *The Latter Rain Evangel*. Like Durham's *Pentecostal Testimony*, the *Latter Rain Evangel* played a role in making Chicago a prominent national center for the new movement. Carrying news, sermons, announcements, and missionary reports, these papers encouraged the faithful, evangelized outsiders, and raised support for the faith workers who carried the Pentecostal message around the world.

Whereas from 1907 Durham strongly insisted that tongues speech always manifested the baptism with the Holy Spirit, Piper chose to be decidedly less dogmatic on the subject. This difference apparently prevented full cooperation between Durham and Piper.[80] They moved within the same networks in Chicago and the Pentecostal conventions beyond, but there is little evidence of direct cooperation between the two in Chicago.[81]

In the summer of 1911, the Pipers reached out to the growing ranks of Pentecostals in Chicago with an invitation to a convention that featured Chicago leaders rather than the usual roster of guests from elsewhere. For several years, the Pipers had expressed concern about a lack of unity among the Chicago missions.[82] They gave each mission leader "liberty

77. Gardiner, "Out of Zion," 5–12.

78. "Notes," *The Latter Rain Evangel*, July 1909, 14; "An Important Announcement," *The Latter Rain Evangel*, March 1910, 2; "Home News," *The Latter Rain Evangel*, August 1910, 14.

79. D. Wesley Myland, *The Latter Rain Covenant and Pentecostal Power with Testimony of Healings and Baptism* (Chicago: Evangel Publishing House, 1910).

80. In the summer of 1909, Piper did publish an announcement of Durham's upcoming convention, *The Latter Rain Evangel*, August 1909, 10.

81. See, for example, William H. Piper, "The Third Anniversary of the Stone Church," *The Latter Rain Evangel*, January 1910, 3.

82. Durham wrote an article called "False Doctrines" that enumerated several issues troubling Pentecostals. Note that one "false doctrine" already agitating was

in the Spirit" to speak. "Wherein were differences in doctrine," Piper reported, "God overruled and enabled us to be patient with each other."[83] Durham's associate, Frederick Link (formerly a German Methodist pastor), who had taken charge of the North Avenue Mission when Durham left for California, participated. This was the first recorded occasion in which the two leading Pentecostal congregations in the city joined forces.

Late in 1911, Piper suddenly developed a blood infection. He died on December 29, 1911, at the age of forty-two.[84] Lydia Piper faced her bereavement with fortitude and continued the ministries of the Stone Church. Within a few years, though, she relinquished the pulpit to others and moved her family to California.[85]

In its early years, a few African Americans became regular attenders at the Stone Church. Among those who found their life's direction in its pews was Lucy Smith, a woman who later gained a wide following in the city's Bronzeville neighborhood. Shortly after Piper's death, Smith, recently arrived from Georgia, began attending Stone Church. Stone Church suited her, and she testified to a baptism with the Holy Spirit in 1914.

When a sense of her own calling came, she left to begin healing and prayer services in her home. These services grew and moved several times until 1926, when Lucy Smith, now known as Elder Lucy Smith, began building a tabernacle in the heart of Bronzeville. She attracted mainly new arrivals from the South.[86] An untutored, humble, and simple woman, Lucy Smith manifested deep sympathy with people in need.

---

baptism in Jesus's name only, an innovation usually dated two years later. Other "false doctrines" included marital purity, abstaining from marriage, and the necessity of Spirit baptism to salvation. On all of these, as well as on tongues as "uniform" initial evidence of the baptism with the Holy Spirit, opinions ranged widely. Durham's article is included in a pamphlet issued by Elbethel, a Pentecostal ministry in Chicago established by Durham's close friends, the MacIlvarys, called "Articles Written by Pastor W. H. Durham Taken from Pentecostal Testimony," n.d. In the Assemblies of God Archives, Springfield, Missouri.

83. "The Chicago Convention," *The Latter Rain Evangel*, June 1911, 2.
84. Anna C. Reiff, "Asleep in Jesus," *The Latter Rain Evangel*, January 1912, 2.
85. "Minutes of Meeting of The Stone Church Congregation, May 26, 1916," 1.
86. Herbert M. Smith, "Three Negro Preachers in Chicago: A Study in Religious Leadership," M. A. Thesis, The University of Chicago Divinity School, 1935, 7-20; Allan Spear, *Black Chicago: The Making of a Negro Ghetto* (Chicago: University of Chicago Press, 1967), 174; Mrs. Isaac Neeley, "Seeking the Old Paths," *The Latter Rain Evangel*, January 1912, 19-20.

Her large congregation, the Pentecostal Church of All Nations—made up largely of the poor—fed and clothed the needy through the Depression and beyond. When she died in 1952, more than 50,000 people filed past her coffin to pay tribute.

Another Stone Church member was a printer and preacher named George C. Brinkman. With his wife, Klazien Balkema, Brinkman opened the Pentecostal Herald Mission on Halsted Street. In 1915 the Brinkmans began issuing a paper, *The Pentecostal Herald*, which by 1919 had a monthly circulation of 45,000.[87] In 1919 the Brinkmans, Sinclairs, James Bell, and others in Chicago founded a Pentecostal denomination, the Pentecostal Church of God.

In January 1912, a month after William Piper died, William Durham returned to Chicago. He had been eager for several months to reestablish his base of operations in Chicago. The Persian mission offered its premises for revival meetings that began in mid-February 1912. Crowds came and services ran from morning until well into the night every day of the week. In one local mission, 177 received the baptism in the Holy Spirit.[88] Sometime that spring, Durham opened yet another mission, the Full Gospel Assembly, at 2623 Florence Avenue. He wrote enthusiastically of powerful meetings and many conversions and Spirit baptisms among the "old and young, black and white, Italians, Persians, Scandinavians, Germans, Indians, Baptists, Methodists and Salvationists who came."[89]

The future appeared bright until he suddenly took ill. Stricken with pneumonia, Durham left Chicago in July 1912 "to visit his dear ones" in Los Angeles. The day after he arrived, he died at the age of thirty-nine. By mid-1912 the two strongest personalities of early Chicago Pentecostalism had died in their prime, leaving the city's leading Pentecostal congregations in transition. Durham's *Pentecostal Testimony* ceased publication, although the *Latter Rain Evangel* remained a leading Pentecostal periodical until 1933. Without their two dominant personalities, Chicago Pentecostals became a vital network that overlapped others on the city's religious margins. The next significant surge in Chicago's Pentecostal ranks accompanied the black migration and featured the rapid growth on the city's South Side of the predominantly black Church of God in Christ.

87. Martin, *In the Beginning*, 39–44.
88. "Editorial Note," *The Pentecostal Testimony* 2, no. 2 (Spring 1912): 1.
89. William H. Durham, "The Great Chicago Revival," *The Pentecostal Testimony*, July 1912, 14.

The migration of southern blacks to Chicago was already under way in 1912, while European immigration was diminishing, and these patterns altered the city's landscape in the next decade. Between 1906 and 1912, Chicago's first Pentecostal missions were, at least to some degree, integrated, a reality that visitors from Europe thought noteworthy.[90] Around World War I, for the first time, separate black Pentecostal missions began to appear and proliferate. By 1928 (after the black migration), by some estimates, Chicago had at least forty-five black Pentecostal missions.[91]

The congregations established during the early days of Chicago Pentecostalism networked in different ways around ethnic groupings, doctrinal points, and polity preferences. Some—but by no means all—of the city's Italian Pentecostals helped to form what became the Christian Churches of North America, an Italian Pentecostal denomination.[92] Scandinavian Pentecostals generally resisted denominational organization, but some cooperated to form the Independent Assemblies of God.[93] Some of the city's German Pentecostals joined the Assemblies of God, a denomination formed in 1914 with which the Stone Church affiliated in the 1940s. Already in the 1920s, the North Avenue Mission left behind Durham's aversion to denominations and affiliated with the Assemblies of God. Andrew Urshan found a home in a nontrinitarian form of Pentecostalism that came to prominence in the World War I years.

If Chicago's heyday as a defining center for American Pentecostal identity, doctrine, and practice was brief, the city's Pentecostal missions neither disappeared nor diminished. Rather, the movement—by now scattered through more of the city's neighborhoods—took its place among the dense networks that functioned beneath the radar of the city's religious pundits, retaining its ethnic diversity but shedding its racial inclusivity. Elsewhere, the influence of Chicago's first Pentecostals

90. Pastor J. Paul (Berlin, Germany), "Pastor Paul's Journey in America," *Confidence*, December 1912, 271; Alexander Boddy, "Chicago the Mighty," *Confidence*, March 1913, 53.

91. Anderson, *Vision of the Disinherited*, 130. The religious censuses and city directories are notoriously inaccurate on Pentecostalism. See St. Clair Drake and Horace R. Clayton, *Black Metropolis*, 2 vols. (New York: Harper & Row, 1962), 2:414.

92. DeCaro, *Our Heritage*, 63–72.

93. *The Fellowship of Christian Assemblies* (Los Angeles: Fellowship Press, 1978), 2. Chicago Scandinavian congregations played a role in the mid-twentieth-century movement known as the Latter Rain. The papers of J. Mattson-Boze in the David DuPlessis Center at Fuller Theological Seminary in Pasadena document this era.

helped to shape the larger Pentecostal landscape: Durham's embrace of "the finished work of Calvary," Piper's reticence about a "uniform initial evidence" of the baptism with the Holy Spirit, and Andrew Urshan's later defense of a "Jesus only" doctrine that denied the orthodox understanding of the Trinity described three major streams within worldwide Pentecostalism. And Chicago Pentecostals, lay and ordained, shared their Pentecostal views around the world, where their descendants are numbered in the millions.

In Chicago, Pentecostalism spread first through dense and overlapped independent webs of Protestant restlessness on the margins of the city's respectable Christianity. Those networks not only enabled it to establish itself; their elasticity also permitted it to form new combinations of association and practice.

The first Chicago-based Pentecostals were always part of something global. Pentecostalism had multiple global points of origin, and the American story is a chapter in a larger whole. Like many other local stories, Chicago's story blended immediately into an emerging global Christian movement. Through the force of personality, travel, the printed word, institution building, and networking between 1906 and 1912, the first Chicago Pentecostals contributed in vital ways to the shape of global Christianity.

CHAPTER 9

The Great Migration

Dennis C. Dickerson

The Institutional Church and Social Settlement in Chicago, a bold initiative in the social gospel in 1900, anticipated a new direction in black religious development. Reverdy C. Ransom, the pastor and warden, in a report to the 1904 African Methodist Episcopal (AME) Church General Conference, observed that African American clergy "have long been seriously concerned over the social and moral concern of the large and rapidly increasing Negro population in our cities." With regard to the Institutional Church it was "in the midst of a Negro population numbering over forty thousand" and "its doors are open all day every day," offering a broad range of social services. Similarly, Richard R. Wright Jr., a student at the divinity school at the University of Chicago and Ransom's assistant, echoed his mentor in saying, "the church should help the community in practical daily living." This steady flow of black migrants settling in Chicago and other northern cities became after 1916 a massive flood of humanity populating these same municipalities through the 1920s. Ransom, for this reason, stayed attuned to these demographic developments. While residing in New York City as editor of the *AME Church Review*, he moved to the "Black Tenderloin" in lower Manhattan and in 1918 founded the Church of Simon of Cyrene. He and his wife, Emma, with a core of thirty members, "visited the sick, the saloons, the houses of prostitution, the gambling joints," and other venues that black churches usually avoided. Additionally, the police precinct whose support Ransom sought arranged "to parole" prisoners to his oversight. Increasingly, Ransom and a growing number of black clerical contemporaries viewed their social gospel ministries as biblically mandated and as effective evangelism. Moreover, these developments emanating from the black religious culture spilled over onto the American religious landscape and became turning points in its twentieth-century evolution.[1]

Between 1916 and 1930, the Great Migration, which increased the need for religious ventures like those that Ransom inaugurated, also created the modern urban black church and unprecedented diversity in black religious expressions. The shift of multiple thousands of African Americans from the agricultural South to the urban North swelled their presence in major urban areas and transformed their religious institutions and culture. The proletarianization of blacks challenged churches to address workplace issues and to encounter corporate influence within black communities. Many adopted the model of Chicago's Institutional Church and offered more than worship to those who lived in their urban environs. Additionally, the sacred within black religious life met the urban "blues" and produced new genres in music and worship rituals. Because of demographic, class, and cultural pressures, established black churches yielded to new expressions of religiosity, which led to the creation of new religious bodies, some of which were non-Christian. These developments culminated in a multifaceted black religion with four defining attributes: (1) churches stratified by class and culture, (2) renewed social gospel ministries, (3) the rise of the gospel "blues" and the transformation of black religious culture, and (4) increased diversity in religious expression, belief, and ritual. Because of the Great Migration, black religion, a product of the slave background and its original agricultural setting, moved into a secularized urban environment that transformed the belief, culture, and institutions that sustained the religious expression of an African American proletariat.

The massive movement of blacks from southern farms to northern factories had nothing to do with religious factors except in how their migration was characterized. The "exodus," a biblical term used by some contemporaries, implied efforts of an oppressed people to make their way to a Promised Land far away from the site of their subjugation. There was surely a parallel set of circumstances for African Americans in 1914 at the outbreak of World War I. The European conflict, unprecedented in scope

1. *First Quadrennial Report of the Pastor and Warden of the Institutional Church and Social Settlement to the Twenty-Second Session of the General Conference and the Connectional Trustees of the African Methodist Episcopal Church*, convened at Quinn Chapel, Chicago, Illinois, May 1904, 6; Richard R. Wright Jr., *Eighty-Seven Years behind the Black Curtain* (Philadelphia: Rare Book Company, 1965), 94; Reverdy C. Ransom, *The Pilgrimage of Harriet Ransom's Son* (Nashville: AME Sunday School Union, n.d.), 231-32.

and carnage, sharply reduced the regular supply of unskilled workers coming out of Southern and Eastern Europe to America for ample employment in the industrial areas of the Northeast and Midwest. European immigration fell precipitously just as American industry geared up for defense production to aid its Allies and, in 1917 and 1918, to supply military ordnance for US troops. Hence, recruiters for northern employers and the Division of Negro Economics in the US Department of Labor mobilized African Americans, a substitute pool and a large untapped source of unskilled laborers, to take the place of foreign-born workers.

These "pull" factors combined with compelling "push" factors indigenous to the South that stirred black migration out of the region. A brutal recent history of lynching and other barbaric forms of racial violence, a new regime of legalized Jim Crow, and a cruel and exploitative crop lien system convinced African Americans that social and economic opportunities in northern industrial communities, where higher wages were available, compared favorably to certain degradation in the South. Delegates to the 1915 Allegheny-Ohio Annual Conference of the AME Zion Church meeting in Pittsburgh confirmed black discontent about violent and segregationist practices. "We have heard," they said, "of some very unpleasant happenings in our country such as lynchings" and the "inhuman and barbarous treatment" of an AME Zion bishop and general officer who "were forcibly ejected from a Pullman sleeper and carried into the jim crow car." The 1920 General Conference of the AME Church acknowledged that, "by reason of these untoward conditions, thousands upon thousands of our racial group have migrated to the Northland. It has been an exodus, the like of which has not been witnessed within the bounds of any nation since history began. From hamlet and village and city; from farm and factory; catching inspiration apparently overnight, yet with a vigor and resolution; fresh and irrepressible, our people have arisen and gathering together their belongings when possible moved like the tramp of an invading army toward the promised land of better education, good wages, unrestricted use of the ballot and a larger measure of freedom." In recognizing conditions pushing blacks out of the South, AME delegates declared, "the people of African descent in America registered their eternal protest against proscription, peonage, disfranchisement, Judge Lynch and Ku Kluxism."[2]

2. *Minutes of the Sixty-Seventh Annual Session of the Allegheny-Ohio Conference (of the) AME Zion Church Held in John Wesley Church (Pittsburgh, Pennsylvania), September 29–October 3, 1915, 40; Journal of the Twenty-Seventh Quadrennial Session of the General*

Northern employers, who capitalized on these sentiments, actively facilitated the migration through agreements with railroads to offer "transportation" to prospective black workers, whose fares would be deducted from their wages after they accepted employment in a mill or factory. These employers often hired black recruiters to travel throughout the South to beckon blacks to migrate to Chicago or Pittsburgh or Detroit. Later, these same recruiters became black welfare officers who supervised housing, recreation, athletics, and religious activities for migrants and their families. These efforts resulted in swelling black populations throughout the urban and industrial North. One scholar noted that "of the ten Northern cities with more than 25,000 Negroes in 1920, all but two—Pittsburgh and Kansas City—registered gains of over 50% in the decade." He added that the black population in Detroit grew by 611 percent, while the increase in Cleveland was 308 percent and in Chicago 148 percent. The Department of Labor in 1923 estimated the migration out of the South numbered 478,700.[3]

Scholars at that time, such as Charles H. Wesley, a historian and AME pastor, viewed the migration as a watershed in black economic history that heralded a new era for African Americans in industrial labor. Additionally, in his landmark work *Negro Labor in the United States, 1850-1925*, a study based on his Harvard PhD dissertation, Wesley described the migration as mainly occurring in two stages: the period from 1916 to 1919 and another from 1921 to 1923. The census, according to Wesley, told the story of its regional impact. The 1920 enumeration showed that states in the North and West experienced an increase of 472,418 blacks since 1910. The South's black population, during the same period, had grown by only 2 percent. According to Wesley, these demographic shifts meant that black churches should offer vigorous responses to the exodus. Hence, he and other clergy in the Baltimore Annual Conference admonished their denomination to provide aid to those settling within their church jurisdiction. They said pastors and parishioners should "seek out and bring into the church the migrants" and assist their adjustment to their new environs.[4]

Conference of the African Methodist Episcopal Church, held in Louisville, Kentucky, May 5, including the 21st, 1924, 397.

3. Allan Spear, *Black Chicago: The Making of a Negro Ghetto, 1890-1920* (Chicago: University of Chicago Press, 1967), 140; Charles H. Wesley, *Negro Labor in the United States, 1850-1925: A Study in American Economic History* (New York: Vanguard, 1927), 285.

4. Wesley, *Negro Labor in the United States*, 283; *Minutes of the One Hundred and Sixth*

Dramatic membership growth was the immediate and concrete consequence of the black migration. Blacks, for example, poured into New York City's Harlem during the exodus. A steady influx brought the black population from 91,709 in 1910 to 152,467 in 1920, spearheading additional growth to 327,706 in 1930, including 54,754 West Indians. Abyssinian Baptist Church, which moved from lower Manhattan to Harlem, like other black congregations during the 1910s, dedicated a mammoth new edifice in 1922 thanks to the harvest of new members mainly from the South. Between 1908 and the 1930s, the socially conscious Adam Clayton Powell Sr. grew the membership from more than one thousand to seven thousand. In Pittsburgh the large Ebenezer Baptist Church swelled from 1,500 to 3,000. The neighboring Central Baptist Church, during the first stage of the migration, drew 544 new members. The AME Zion General Conference of 1920 acknowledged that the migration included "thousands of members of our own church." Consequently, "[i]n Chicago, two churches were bought . . . in Detroit two, (and) one in Braddock, (Pennsylvania)." Additionally, the Zion denomination "profited largely in Buffalo, Pittsburgh, Cincinnati, St. Louis, Indianapolis, Philadelphia, Newark, Washington, D. C., and quite a number of other places." Construction started in 1923 for a new edifice for Mother AME Zion Church in New York City because of "the increase of the colored population." At John Wesley AME Zion Church in Pittsburgh, for example, 1,200 new members were attracted between 1920 and 1926. Also, in Pittsburgh the Colored Methodist Episcopal Church (CME) appropriated $2,000 to Bishop Randall A. Carter to establish that denomination in the Smoky City. From this initiative emerged three new CME congregations. A CME historian observed that a mission began in Cleveland in 1902, but because of the migration "the entire Connection made a concerted effort to purchase a magnificent Jewish synagogue to house the growing congregation." Moreover, in 1922, as a result of the exodus, St. Paul CME Church in Chicago boasted two thousand members, while a newly housed second congregation, Carter Chapel, drew two hundred communicants.[5]

Session of the Baltimore Annual Conference of the African Methodist Episcopal Church, held in Trinity AME Church (Baltimore, Maryland), April 25-29, 1923, 60-61.

5. Gilbert Osofsky, Harlem: The Making of a Ghetto (New York: Harper and Row, 1963), 128-29; Genna Rae McNeil, Houston B. Roberson, Quinton H. Dixie, and Kevin McGruder, Witness: Two Hundred Years of African American Faith and Practice at the Abyssinian Baptist Church of Harlem, New York (Grand Rapids: Eerdmans, 2014), 88, 117-22,

Wesley's advice to Baltimore AMEs had been heeded already in several northern churches that followed the Ransom example at Chicago's Institutional Church and Social Settlement. Moreover, AMEs, at their 1920 General Conference, admonished clergy to "aid our people to rehabilitate themselves in their new Northern home." They added, "we are glad to note the opening of the factories and shops of the North to workmen of African descent." Therefore, the AME Church should "not flag in the effort to save from the vice and iniquity surrounding life in the large city, the men and women of our group who have sought to avail themselves of these industrial and other civic opportunities. May our ministry not fail in its effort to employ all the arms of effective social service to this end." Powell at Abyssinian in Harlem, like other pastors who espoused the social gospel, also declared that churches had obligations to respond to the migration. As early as 1911 his sermons adhered to the theme "A Model Church," which aimed "to minister to the whole person." He told fellow Baptists that the migration required them to provide "a great community center" and to create educational opportunities for black adults who were either illiterate or semi-literate because of substandard southern schooling. The Abyssinian Community House, a part of the church's new physical plant, offered classes in English, physical education, dressmaking, and drama.[6]

With blacks flocking into northern cities and neighboring satellite communities, housing shortages became an urgent concern. To address this pressing need J. C. Austin, pastor of the growing Ebenezer Baptist Church in Pittsburgh, established a Home Finder's League. Pastor Harrison G. Payne, in nearby Homestead, Pennsylvania, formed at Park Place AME Church a real estate agency to provide lodging to migrants at low rental and purchasing rates. Charles Albert Tindley, at the populous East Calvary Methodist Episcopal Church in Philadelphia, led fellow pastors in starting housing committees to find lodging for newcomers. He urged his own members to charge "a fair weekly rental." They also

---

145–46; cited in William J. Walls, *The African Methodist Episcopal Zion Church: Reality of the Black Church* (Charlotte: AME Zion Publishing House, 1974), 251, 254; Dennis C. Dickerson, *Out of the Crucible: Black Steelworkers in Western Pennsylvania, 1875–1980* (Albany: State University of New York Press, 1986), 65, 67; Othal H. Lakey, *The History of the CME Church* (Memphis: CME Publishing House, 1985), 427.

6. *Journal of the Twenty-Seventh Quadrennial Session of the General Conference, AME Church, 1920,* 397; McNeil et al., *Witness,* 101, 108, 113, 130.

invited migrants to attend church services at East Calvary, and many of them joined.[7]

Additionally, employers pulled clergy and active laymen into black worker recruitment and also hired them as staff to supervise housing and recreational and religious activities. Philadelphia, for example, had multiple industrial and military facilities needing large pools of unskilled labor. To meet these war and postwar personnel needs, the vice president of operations of the Pennsylvania Railroad shifted Reverend James Henry Duckrey, a Baptist minister, from messenger to labor agent. Duckrey, starting in 1916 in Jacksonville, Florida, boarded trainloads of black workers and brought them to eager employers in Philadelphia. Grover Nelson, another Baptist minister, functioned in a similar role at the Carnegie steel works in Homestead, Pennsylvania. Nelson, a native of Columbus, Ohio, and a graduate of Wilberforce University, recruited black workers mainly in Virginia and North Carolina and paid their fares to western Pennsylvania. At the same time that he operated the mill community center, Nelson entered the ministry. To support his aspiration, steel officials arranged his schedule so he could attend Western Theological Seminary. He served as pastor of several area churches, including one in Ford City that had been established by the Pittsburgh Plate Glass Company.[8]

Select clergy, such as Duckrey in Philadelphia and Nelson in the Pittsburgh area, were gatekeepers for employers who wanted reliable black laborers. Pastors Robert L. Bradby at Second Baptist Church, Everard Daniel at St. Matthew Episcopal Church, and, to a lesser extent, William Peck at Bethel AME Church, all leading congregations, served as liaisons for the Ford Motor Company. Those seeking jobs at Ford increased their chances if a recommendation was forthcoming from one of these ministers. Bradby, for example, an immigrant from nearby Chatham, Ontario, became pastor at Second Church in 1910. By 1925, because of the black migration and his exuberant preaching, the congregation expanded from less than three hundred to nearly four thousand members. Growth in Second Church also benefited from Bradby's proactive posture toward the exodus. Evangelizing people by going door to door and preaching on street corners made both him and his church accessible to newcom-

---

7. Dickerson, *Out of the Crucible*, 57; Ralph H. Jones, *Charles Albert Tindley: Prince of Preachers* (Nashville: Abingdon, 1982), 81.

8. Jones, *Charles Albert Tindley*, 80-81; Dickerson, *Out of the Crucible*, 105-6, 109, 111.

ers. During the height of the migration, from 1917 to 1919, for example, Bradby deployed church teams to meet trains bringing migrants to the city. Second Church also had a Social Service Department that offered classes in dressmaking, home health care, stenography, and electronics. Ford officials tapped Bradby to suggest "very high type fellows" to work for the firm. Father Daniel at St. Matthew, Bradby's competitor, served the other congregation that many joined "with an eye to securing a job at Ford." Moreover, Daniel's parishioner, Donald Marshall, worked in the Ford Service Department as a policeman, and eventually he hired blacks and functioned like a "straw boss." These Detroit clergy showed that evangelism realized through social gospel outreach easily blended with the workplace objectives of employers. Employees, socialized through the evangelical culture of black churches, likely would become reliable, non-union laborers.[9]

Though these middle-class ministers usually interacted with employers in selecting fit employees for their industrial facilities, they shared access with a rising cadre of mostly migrant preachers who became bi-vocational pastors. They preached to their congregations on Sundays and labored with them during the week in mills, mines, and factories. This phenomenon occurred prevalently in western Pennsylvania but also characterized clergy profiles elsewhere in the industrial North. For example, J. H. Flagg, an Alabama migrant, organized Bethel AME Church in Johnstown, Pennsylvania, and Isaac S. Freeman, a Georgia migrant, started Ebenezer AME Church in Woodlawn (Aliquippa), Pennsylvania. Each labored in the steel industry at Jones & Laughlin and Bethlehem in their respective milltowns. Another Georgia migrant, J. L. Simmons, worked at Lockhart Iron & Steel in McKees Rocks, Pennsylvania, and later, while still an employee, became a pastor at various Baptist congregations in Pittsburgh and neighboring Carnegie, Pennsylvania.[10]

Employers tightened their grip on clergy and their congregations through strategic contributions that encouraged expectations for additional philanthropy. Henry Ford, an Episcopalian, donated funds to help build a parish house at St. Matthew Church, and in 1929 he started annual visits to the congregation. In the 1920s in Woodlawn (Aliquippa), in the

9. Cara L. Shelly, "Bradby's Baptists: Second Baptist Church of Detroit, 1910–1946," *Michigan Historical Review* 17, no. 1 (Spring 1991): 2, 4–7, 16–17; August Meier and Elliott Rudwick, *Black Detroit and the Rise of the UAW* (New York: Oxford University Press, 1981), 10.

10. Dickerson, *Out of the Crucible*, 69.

Beaver Valley in Pennsylvania, the Jones and Laughlin Steel Corporation commenced yearly contributions of $150 to Bethel Baptist Church, Tried Stone Baptist Church, Emmanuel AME Zion Church, Jones Chapel Methodist Episcopal Church, and the Church of God in Christ. In Johnstown, Pennsylvania, Bethlehem Steel provided a building for Bethel AME Church and Mt. Sinai Baptist Church to share. When Alabama migrants organized Shiloh Baptist Church, the company donated another building to this congregation. The Carnegie Steel Works in Homestead, Pennsylvania, in 1924 gave to Clark Memorial Baptist Church a matching donation of $5,000 for its mortgage liquidation on its new edifice.[11]

The presence of black labor recruiters and social service employees also extended the reach of employers into black churches. George Foster Jones, for example, the manager of the community center for the Carnegie steel plant in Clairton, Pennsylvania, served as chorister at First AME Church and as the sponsor of the "colored community chorus." Charles Broadfield, a Hampton Institute graduate who supervised the community center for the Carnegie steel facility in Duquesne, Pennsylvania, was a member and later an officer in Payne Chapel AME Church. When the congregation, mainly because of the migration, outgrew its building in the late 1920s, he allowed fellow members to hold their worship services on the mill property.[12]

The migration exposed the vulnerability of black churches to the encroachments of corporate power, especially when a harvest of new members and fresh funds became available to expand their property holdings. Despite their espousal of a social gospel, a set of programs that they sometimes shared with employer-sponsored initiatives, black churches could scarcely present themselves as unambiguous defenders of black interests. Though black laborers found improved economic conditions in northern industries over what they experienced in the agricultural South, racial discrimination maintained barriers that kept them unequal to white and immigrant workers. Black ministers, grateful to employers for drawing migrants into these communities as potential members, easily encouraged parishioners to shun unions because of their well-known antipathy to black workers. As long as African American laborers eschewed white-dominated unions, employers gained a pliant workforce

11. Meier and Rudwick, *Black Detroit and the Rise of the UAW*, 10; Dickerson, *Out of the Crucible*, 114.

12. Dickerson, *Out of the Crucible*, 110–11.

and black churches benefited from new members to populate their pews with parishioners whose wages helped to build or purchase new buildings. These ironies led one scholar, Sadie Tanner Mossell, self-described as "a true daughter" of the AME Church, to admonish black churches in 1921 that they could help migrants more by building houses for them rather than "expensive church edifices at a cost of hundreds of thousands of dollars."[13]

Mossell identified the proverbial thread that unraveled a social order that white workers vowed to protect from this invasion of black migrants. Though employers sought and welcomed black newcomers as a fresh supply of unskilled and non-unionized workers, white laborers viewed African American incursions into the workplace and racially exclusive neighborhoods as unwelcome developments. Consequently, there was widespread violence throughout the Northeast and Midwest between 1917 and 1919. Race riots erupted in East St. Louis, Illinois, from May through July in 1917 because blacks arrived to replace striking white laborers at the Aluminum Ore Company. Accompanying the white-perpetrated violence was the lynching of some African Americans. The Chicago race riot in 1919 occurred because blacks trespassed upon a beach that whites claimed as their own. The drowning of a black youth resulted, and during the rioting fifteen whites and more than twenty blacks were killed. The Chicago riot was one of nearly three dozen upheavals of violence happening during the "red summer" of 1919. These events drew directly from the migration and the rapid growth of a northern black working class newly settled in innumerable industrial communities.

Though AMEs, like other black religious bodies, were beneficiaries of the migration, they viewed the race riots as the northern counterpart to ongoing "mob violence" against black southerners. Emma Ransom, a veteran social gospel practitioner with her husband, Reverdy C. Ransom, addressed the 1919 meeting of her denomination's Women's Parent Mite Missionary Society. She denounced the violence against blacks, and she advised clergy to condemn the "recent race riots" and to stir "the conscience of the country" in defense of the African American population. AME Bishop Charles S. Smith observed: "the new Negro does not hate any element of the white people in this country. What he does hate and

13. See Sadie Tanner Mossell, "The Standard of Living among One Hundred Negro Migrant Families in Philadelphia," *Annals of the American Academy of Political and Social Science* 98 (November 1921): 175, 217-18.

that with bitter hatred are the wrongs from which he suffers. He hates injustice, oppression, discriminatory laws and practices, unequal opportunity in the field of industrial and economic endeavor."[14]

The AME North Ohio Annual Conference in 1919 blamed the race riots on "the influence of Southern propaganda upon the irresponsible white men of these northern communities and the presence of Southerners of decided Southern spirit in our midst." It was "their's to terrorize the colored people and leave the impression that the Negro is no more safe in the North than in the South." Though blacks were advised not to be the "aggressors" and to seek "a friendly relationship with the other race," there was no suggestion that the migration should be halted or that the opportunities that the exodus opened for African Americans should be stopped. The delegates also supported a congressional bill to investigate the "Race Riots." Moreover, the AME bishops in their episcopal address to the 1920 General Conference declared that their denomination "marshals every fiber of its Christian manhood and all its moral and intellectual strength against the burning, mutilating, or lynching of any human being of any race by mob violence."[15]

What the migration offered to mainstream black churches, primarily within established Baptist and Methodist bodies, were opportunities for institutional development and for showing themselves as defenders of black rights. Those within smaller but significant ecclesiastical groups also capitalized on the dynamic demographic changes within growing black northern communities. Black Presbyterians, for example, grew their presence in the Northeast and Midwest by a respectable twenty-four churches in Rochester, Boston, Indianapolis, and Kansas City. In Pittsburgh, for example, Charles H. Trusty, pastor at Grace Memorial Presbyterian Church in the city's Hill District from 1910 to 1925, more than doubled his membership during this period from two hundred to 488. Moreover, he facilitated the founding of two other Calvinist congregations: Bethesda Church in the East Liberty area and Bidwell Street

14. *Minutes and Reports of the Seventh Quadrennial Convention of the Women's Parent Mite Missionary Society of the African Methodist Episcopal Church*, held in Mt. Zion AME Church, Jacksonville, Florida, October 14-19, 1919, 53-54; Charles S. Smith, *The First Race Riot Recorded in History* (1920), 9.

15. *Minutes of the Thirty-Eighth Annual Session of the North Ohio Conference of the African Methodist Episcopal Church*, held in Payne's Chapel AME Church, Hamilton, Ohio, October 8-12, 1919, 75; *Journal of the Twenty-Seventh Quadrennial Session of the General Conference*, AME Church, 1920, 190.

Church on the North Side. Broader forces, however, undermined the mainstream denominations' seeming predominance in the religious loyalties of the African American population.[16]

A decade before the start of the wartime migration, the Azusa Street revivals in Los Angeles, featuring a fiery, effective black preacher, William J. Seymour, unleashed an unprecedented outpouring of Pentecostal energy among hundreds of holiness seekers. Out of this unpretentious site of exuberant glossolalia and intense spirituality came evangelists, both white and black, who launched new denominations such as the Assemblies of God and the Church of God, Cleveland, Tennessee. Some of them, especially the Assemblies of God, drew their initial credentialing from the oldest of the denominations coming out of Azusa Street, namely, the Church of God in Christ. Its leader, Charles Harrison Mason, and his counterpart, Garfield T. Haywood of the Pentecostal Assemblies of the World, started with an interracial vision for their denominations, but ultimately they presided in all-black religious bodies. These and other black holiness and Pentecostal groups either came northward with the migrants or awaited the arrival of newcomers who affiliated with these rapidly growing organizations.[17]

The religious energy and surge of evangelical fervor emerging from California's urban camp meetings poured into urban America new and growing sectarian bodies. Though white city residents were similarly affected by the religious reach of the Azusa Street mission, they stayed socially aloof in their separate religious communities. Nonetheless, holiness and Pentecostal movements visited upon black urban sites in Chicago, Detroit, and numerous other cities an unprecedented evangelical transformation.

Migrants sometimes encountered a cold formality and aloofness in established black churches in Chicago, Cleveland, Pittsburgh, and Philadelphia. Caught in unfamiliar surroundings both at white-dominated worksites and then within black social spaces that seemed either indifferent or condescending, some migrants preferred the smaller and more

16. Dennis C. Dickerson, "Charles H. Trusty: Black Presbyterian Missionary and Denominational Leader," *American Presbyterians: Journal of Presbyterian History* 67, no. 4 (Winter 1989): 289-91.

17. David D. Daniels III, "Charles Harrison Mason: The Interracial Impulse of Early Pentecostalism," and David Bundy, "G. T. Haywood: Religion for Urban Realities," in *Portraits of a Generation: Early Pentecostal Leaders*, ed. James R. Goff Jr. and Grant Wacker (Fayetteville: University of Arkansas Press, 2002), 237-70.

hospitable settings of storefront churches that better satisfied their religious yearnings. The southern-based Church of God in Christ (COGIC), whose head, Bishop Mason, received the gift of speaking in tongues at Azusa Street, spread quickly in this new northern soil. The experience of Otha M. Kelly, a migrant and eventually a COGIC leader, typified these experiences.

Kelly, born in 1897 in Mississippi, attended both Baptist and Methodist churches. His parents joined the Evening Light Saints, a holiness group who believed in "clean living." A white group who had been to Azusa Street and received baptism with the Holy Ghost convinced Kelly's parents that they too should seek the gift of speaking in tongues. Kelly recalled that his parents were "'saved' people before but there was something radically different about them now." These experiences pulled the Kelly family into the Church of God in Christ and moved the elder Kelly to allow the construction of a COGIC church on family land. At the same time Kelly, his two brothers, and their pastor grew disenchanted with rural southern life. They also hated the white supremacy and racism embodied in Mississippi governor Theodore Bilbo. They migrated to Chicago in 1917, and Kelly secured employment at the Union Stockyards. Moreover, he remembered, "I found out Elder William Roberts from Memphis, Tennessee was in charge of the mission" in Chicago and that it was affiliated with COGIC. At a revival Kelly himself "received the baptism with the Holy Ghost." After working in a glass factory, a foundry, and a rug company, Kelly entered the ministry in 1927 and initially preached in a tent in Chicago. Next, he became a traveling evangelist with several stops throughout the Midwest and in New York. These experiences reflected that of other ministers and members of COGIC. They eschewed established Baptist and Methodist churches and spread new holiness and Pentecostal bodies in numerous northern communities.[18]

The Church of God in Christ, while it had existed for a shorter time than venerable black churches whose founding stretched back into the eighteenth and early nineteenth centuries, espoused doctrines and beliefs that lay within the key parameters of Christian orthodoxy. COGIC flourished mainly because of its freedom in worship, spiritual excitement, and vigorous expressions of religiosity. Though pneumatology

18. Otha M. Kelly, *Profile of a Churchman: The Life of Otha M. Kelly in the Church of God in Christ* (Jamaica, NY: K. & C. Publishing, 1976), vii, 18, 27–30, 32–37, 55, 59–60, 62–63.

figured more prominently in COGIC and other holiness and Pentecostal bodies than among Baptists, Methodists, Presbyterians, or Catholics, none within these mainstream churches could legitimately find anything that was theologically offensive in Mason's or Haywood's religious bodies. At the same time, the migration created religious space for newly founded orthodox bodies such as COGIC and various nontraditional, iconoclastic movements that broadened the boundaries of black belief. Their origins drew from eclectic sources, some of which reflected submerged strands of faith-claims already embedded in the African American religious heritage. These newer religions thrived because of their cultic characteristics centered around leaders who were personally compelling. These founders possessed the same charisma that characterized larger-than-life preachers such as Powell at Abyssinian Baptist in Harlem or J. C. Austin at Ebenezer Baptist in Pittsburgh and later at Pilgrim Baptist in Chicago. The principal difference lay in the unconventional beliefs of the progenitors of what one scholar described as the "Black Gods of the Metropolis."[19]

These newer religions included various sects that were familiarly known as black Jews. In 1923 Arnold Josiah Ford started the Beth B'nai Abraham congregation. For a time Ford was involved with Marcus Garvey's nationalist Universal Negro Improvement Association, where he tried to convince the Jamaican leader and others that Judaism was the real religion of blacks. They were actually a lost tribe, a description that one sect called American Falashas. In 1925 Timothy Drew started in Chicago the Moorish Science Temple, on the premise that African Americans were descended from the Moors of North Africa. This meant that the authentic religion of blacks was Islam. To buttress his view, Drew, who became Noble Drew Ali, published in 1927 the *Circle Seven Koran*, which codified his portrait of African Americans as ethnically Asiatic and religiously Muslim. He also declared that Jesus was a Moor. Additionally, he asserted that various nationalities in humankind should separate themselves geographically. Perhaps the appeal of the Moorish Science Temple drew in part from those remnants of Islam that were found in the well-established black fraternal orders. The Black Shriners in the Ancient Egyptian Arabic Order of the Nobles of the Mystic Shrine, for example, may have been a source for Ali. This organization claimed broad

---

19. See Arthur Huff Fauset, *Black Gods of the Metropolis* (Philadelphia: University of Pennsylvania Press, 1944).

membership among traditional black Christians. Maybe the appeal of the Moorish Temple was less exotic than it appeared. From popular mainstream churches to newer holiness, Pentecostal, and spiritualist groups to congregations of black Jews and black Muslims, the spatial and social possibilities that large urban geographies provided to migrants stretched the range of religions that were available for newcomers to embrace.[20]

Even as the migration enlarged the space for religious belief and expression, the broader faith culture of African Americans was similarly expanded. The exodus, in pouring thousands into urban settings, also transformed the role that gender played in ministry, redefined religious music, and commodified black religion. Traditionally, masculinity constituted the persona of ministers in major northern churches. The deep resonance and authority of the male voice, the manly attire of their clerical robes and suits, and the scene of majority female congregations shouting "amens" on the delivery of spiritually animated sermons of male pulpiteers functioned as the primary tropes of ministerial masculinity. Whether they were Chicago pastors such as L. K. Williams at the overflowing Olivet Baptist Church or Archibald J. Carey Sr. at the crowded Institutional AME Church, black preachers, at congregations both large and small, constructed themselves as talented preachers and as undisputed leaders of their largely female following. Though their ascendancy was scarcely undermined during the migration, the gender component of ministry became increasingly contested. Women, despite ingrained sexism in all sectors of black religious life, took advantage of opportunities that the migration offered.

Women who pursued ministry in the AME and AME Zion denominations were further along with regard to formal credentialing than their counterparts in other religious bodies. In these respects black religious bodies, both traditional and newly established, surged ahead of their white evangelical colleagues. At the same time as the migration, some women, such as Martha Jayne Keys and Mary G. Evans, already had been trained along with men at Ohio's Payne Theological Seminary, a flagship institution of their denomination. Keys and Evans, after the short-lived

20. Nora L. Rubel, "'Chased Out of Palestine': Prophet Cherry's Church of God and Early Black Judaisms in the United States," and Edward E. Curtis IV, "Debating the Origins of the Moorish Science Temple: Toward a New Cultural History," in *The New Black Gods: Arthur Fauset and the Study of African American Religions*, ed. Edward E. Curtis IV and Danielle Brune Sigler (Bloomington: Indiana University Press, 2009), 58–59, 71, 73, 83.

ordination of Sarah Ann Hughes in the North Carolina Annual Conference in 1885, were designated as evangelists and allowed to preach and to serve as pastors at small and fledgling congregations. Similarly, the AME Zion Church, despite official ordination of women in 1898, gave them no appointments to major churches. Nonetheless, in the official minutes of annual conferences scores of women filled the roster of evangelists and ordinands-in-waiting. The 1915 Allegheny-Ohio Annual Conference of the AME Zion Church had three women noted as ministerial candidates "on trial." The AME 1917 North Ohio Annual Conference had available for service three women from Delaware, Cleveland, and Xenia, Ohio. The 1917 Ohio Annual Conference also listed three female evangelists from Cincinnati, Ironspot, and Columbus, Ohio. The 1920 Philadelphia Annual Conference, on the other hand, included nearly thirty women listed as evangelists. These rosters appeared in AME jurisdictions throughout the denomination and showed the pent-up demand of women for official ministerial standing.[21]

Because AME, AME Zion, and holiness women of an earlier generation remained visible in the North during the migration, their achievements became an indication of what already had been gained. Nora Taylor was perhaps the best known of AME evangelists. Aside from preaching widely in the Midwest, Taylor served as first vice president of the Women's Parent Mite Missionary Society. When visiting the meeting of the Pittsburgh Conference Branch in 1922 in the mill town of New Castle, Pennsylvania, Taylor preached a sermon on "Prejudice, Conversion, and Influence." The Eucharist was celebrated following her sermon, but, because she was barred from ordination, male clergy consecrated and distributed the bread and wine to eighty "communicants." When Taylor

21. "Martha Jayne Keys," in Richard R. Wright Jr., compiler, *Who's Who in the General Conference 1924*, comp. (Philadelphia: Book Concern of the AME Church, 1924), 151-52; "Miss Mary G. Evans," in Richard R. Wright Jr., editor-in-chief, *Centennial Encyclopedia of the African Methodist Episcopal Church* (Philadelphia: Book Concern of the AME Church, 1916), 88-89; *Minutes of the Sixty-Seventh Annual Session of the Allegheny-Ohio Conference*, AME Zion Church, 1915, 2; *Minutes (of the) Thirty-Sixth Annual Session of the North Ohio Annual Conference of the African Methodist Episcopal Church*, held in North Street AME Church, Springfield, Ohio, September 19-23, 1917, 3; *Journal of the Eighty-Seventh Annual Session of the Ohio Conference of the African Methodist Episcopal Church*, held in St. Paul AME Church, Columbus, Ohio, September 12-16, 1917, 6; *Journal of Proceedings of the One Hundred and Fourth Session of the Philadelphia Annual Conference of the African Methodist Episcopal Church*, held in Bethel AME Church, Steelton, Pennsylvania, June 9-15, 1920, 6.

died in 1923, Ransom, still editor of the *AME Church Review*, explained how she created clerical space for herself in a male-dominated ministry. "She was an obscure member of Quinn Chapel, Chicago Ill(inois), with limited education, without influence, or influential friends," he observed. "Yet, despite these handicaps, by sheer forcefulness of her personality and by complete consecration to God of her physical strength and her natural gifts of mind and spirit, she arose to be the most popular, the most influential and the most universally beloved woman of her day," Ransom concluded.[22]

Florence Spearing Randolph, ordained as an AME Zion deacon in 1900, had long been a pastor in New York and New Jersey, most notably at Summit, New Jersey, starting in 1925. Also active in the Women's Christian Temperance Union and the National Association of Colored Women's Clubs, Randolph's clergy profile, like that of Taylor, was well known in the Northeast at the time of the migration. Mary Magdalena Lewis Tate, a holiness preacher after her conversion in Tennessee, subsequently experienced glossolalia in 1908. Because of these profound spiritual encounters, Tate established the Church of the Living God, the Pillar and Ground of Truth, of which she became bishop. A split in 1919 led to the founding of a derivative body in Philadelphia in 1919 with a similar name. Congregations with these affiliations spread throughout the North in the migration era.[23]

These women feminized church leadership and positioned their female successors to broaden a religious space for themselves during the migration. They presented themselves as nonthreatening, modest, restrained, and feminine. Evans was pictured in the 1916 *Centennial Encyclopedia of the African Methodist Episcopal Church*, in which she was referred to as "Miss." Her hair was stylishly coiffured and tastefully displayed. A full white collar trimmed with white lace circled the top of her black robe, covering her neck modestly. She also wore a cross that

22. *Minutes of the Twenty-Sixth Annual Convention of the Woman's Mite Missionary Society, Pittsburgh Conference Branch (of the) African Methodist Episcopal Church*, held in Bethel AME Church, New Castle, Pennsylvania, July 5-9, 1922, 5; Reverdy C. Ransom, "Nora Taylor," *AME Church Review* 40, no. 158 (October 1923): 91-92.

23. Bettye Collier-Thomas, "Minister and Feminist: The Life of Florence Spearing Randolph," in *This Far by Faith: Readings in African American Women's Biography*, ed. Judith Weisenfeld and Richard Newman (New York: Routledge, 1996), 180-81; "Mary Magdalena Lewis Tate," in *Encyclopedia of African American Religions*, ed. Larry G. Murphy, J. Gordon Melton, and Gary L. Ward (New York: Garland, 1993), 740-41.

stretched downward over her clerical garb. Wallace D. Best, whose analysis of female ministerial presentation influences this discussion, insightfully portrayed Evans later in her ministry as robing and styling herself so that her feminine form was deemphasized. Taylor, whose photograph appeared on a 1923 memorial cover of the *AME Church Review*, was bespectacled and dressed in a plain, dark robe adorned with a white collar circling around a high V-neck; the Missionary Evangelist Saint also wore a cross hanging on a short chain. Keys, who wore a clerical robe with a long-chained cross, was pictured in *Who's Who in the General Conference (of) 1924*; the photograph highlighted her plain ministerial attire but scarcely hid her buxom form and impressively coiffured hair.[24]

As migrants flooded into Chicago and Philadelphia, their choice of churches included those that were female founded. Georgia-born Elder Lucy Smith arrived in Chicago in 1910 and started the All Nations Pentecostal Church; she also became overseer of derivative congregations in the All Nations Pentecostal Conference. Smith, a former Baptist and a member of Chicago's Olivet and Ebenezer Churches, left these black congregations and affiliated with a white Pentecostal church. After she accepted her call to preach in 1914, Smith left to found her own congregation in 1916. Her authority for ministry, she said, came from being "raised up pastor by the mighty hands of God." In Philadelphia there was Bishop Ida Robinson. Georgia born and Florida raised, Robinson arrived in Philadelphia in 1917 and was converted in a holiness church. She started preaching and was assigned as pastor to the Mount Olive Holy Church in 1919. Because some males in the denomination, the United Holy Church of America, objected to women preachers, Robinson left and began her own congregation in 1925 called the Mount Sinai Holy Church. She also presided over branch congregations elsewhere in the Middle Atlantic.[25]

African American church women possessed multiple avenues to assert authority beyond the ministry itself. Black Methodist and Baptist women had long established international missionary societies. Though

24. "Miss Mary G. Evans," *Centennial Encyclopedia*, 88; Wallace D. Best, *Passionately Human, No Less Divine: Religion and Culture in Black Chicago, 1915-1952* (Princeton: Princeton University Press, 2005), 158; Ransom, "Nora Taylor," *AME Church Review*, October 1923, cover; "Martha Jayne Keys," in *Who's Who in the General Conference (of) 1924*, 151.

25. Best, *Passionately Human, No Less Divine*, 151-52, 162-64; Harold Dean Trulear, "Ida B. Robinson: The Mother as Symbolic Presence," in *Portraits of a Generation*, 312-14.

named as auxiliaries, they actually functioned autonomously with their own officers and sources of funding. COGIC's Women's Department, authorized in 1911 by Bishop Charles Harrison Mason, followed the black Baptist and Methodist pattern of self-government. On various levels within COGIC, especially within congregations, the church mother, an honorific title, set standards of conduct for younger women and exercised power like a church elder. Often the church mother exhibited such wisdom and judgment that males and females deferred to her for advice, prayer, and scriptural insight.[26]

Though church leadership lay principally with male clergy, their traditional grip was increasingly uncertain. The continued rise of women in ministry and the expanded significance of church mothers and so-called auxiliary women's groups contributed, at least in part, to the unsettling of the black population. These movements also compelled churches and their clergy to engage the black secular culture in unprecedented ways. That black religion increasingly became a commodity in the marketplace of religious consumers and that religious music was redefined showed that forces beyond the control of traditional male clergy were moving African American churches where they had never been before.

Just as twentieth-century evangelists used the latest technology to present Christianity to a mass culture through records, radio, and other media, black religion was similarly produced, packaged, and presented to a black public. Either as a substitute or as a supplement to church attendance, phonograph records containing sermons, songs, and other elements of the black religious culture engaged African Americans recently arrived to the city. The phonograph, invented in 1877 by Thomas A. Edison, became the principal instrument used to convey religion to black newcomers. Records played on the phonograph featuring blues and jazz performers entered African American communities in 1920. Some black clergy recoiled at this development and redoubled their efforts to convert their churches to venues of morally approved entertainment. This strategy to nullify the effects of the phonograph may have worked temporarily in various mainline congregations, but savvy black preachers instead successfully harnessed this medium to their religious purposes. For example, Evangelist Calvin Dixon, known as a black Billy Sunday, in 1925 recorded ten of his sermons in New York City. This act, says his-

---

26. Anthea D. Butler, *Women in the Church of God in Christ: Making a Sanctified World* (Chapel Hill: University of North Carolina Press, 2007), 2–3, 43–44.

torian Lerone A. Martin, marked "the emergence of black sermons as a modern commodity." Ads in the popular and nationally circulated *Chicago Defender* aided this process of dissemination of the Dixon sermons, and music companies, both black and white, also played a large role in popularizing this new presentation of black religion. "The phonograph," Martin argues, became "a new and necessary means to preach the gospel to the black masses."[27]

Holiness and Pentecostal preachers, more than their Baptist and Methodist counterparts, were first to record and disseminate their sermons and worship services "on wax." One Church of God in Christ minister, F. W. McGee, promoted exuberant preaching and music as his means to establish a congregation in Des Moines, Iowa. Next, in 1925, he moved on to Chicago, where he pitched a tent and unleashed a music band to play "lively music." His evangelistic successes helped to grow COGIC in the area and led Charles Harrison Mason to appoint him as a bishop. A representative of Victor Records signed him to a contract to record such popular sermons as "My Wife's a Holy Roller" and "Jonah in the Belly of the Whale." About seven women during this period recorded their sermons. Reverend Cora Hopson, for example, preached a rendition of Paul Laurence Dunbar's poem, "Antebellum Sermon," in Chicago in 1926 for Paramount Records. In 1927 Reverend Leora Ross, accompanied by the Church of the Living God singers, preached in a Chicago studio for Okeh Race Records sermons entitled "Dry Bones in the Valley" and "A Gambler Broke in a Strange Land."[28]

The genre of religious music also changed during the migration period. Though this development would also affect evangelical whites, experimenting with new musical forms, which were often owing to black secular blues, energized black evangelical worship and culture. Traditional worship in mainline black churches usually was anchored in singing the hymns of Charles Wesley, Isaac Watts, and other classic hymnologists. There was also folk religious music derived from the African American experience, including the slave spirituals and other songs of unknown authorship and improvisation of historic hymns. Already back in 1897, hymnologist Henry M. Turner, the AME bishop, said that "the time

27. Lerone A. Martin, *Preaching on Wax: The Phonograph and the Shaping of Modern African American Religion* (New York: New York University Press, 2014), 11, 32, 62–63, 71, 84, 90.
28. Martin, *Preaching on Wax*, 110–14, 116–19.

had come for the Negro to preserve and write his own hymns." Hence, he was pleased when his Georgia Annual Conferences began to sing the compositions of Charles Albert Tindley, the black Methodist Episcopal Church pastor in Philadelphia who wrote "Stand By Me" and "By and By When the Morning Comes." Tindley copyrighted several hymns in 1901, including "The Lord Will Make a Way" and "I'll Overcome Some Day." Another group of hymns followed in 1905, including "The Storm Is Passing Over" and "Nothing Between." Tindley's hymnody spread rapidly among a range of African American churches and won supporters such as Turner and many others. Tindley's repertoire of religious music enabled him to attract an ample share of Philadelphia's black migrants into his East Calvary Methodist Episcopal Church, later renamed Tindley Temple, into an enviable membership of seven thousand.[29]

Thomas A. Dorsey, the son of a Baptist preacher, added another dimension to black religious music. Born in Georgia in 1899, Dorsey grew up in a Baptist church in his hometown of Villa Rica, but moved with his parents to Atlanta and Forsyth, Georgia, and then back again to his birthplace, all within the first four years of his life. He learned to play the organ like his mother. From her he imbibed attachment to traditional black religious music, and through his maternal uncle, a guitar player, Dorsey was exposed to the country blues. Dorsey, who had become proficient with the piano, migrated in 1915 to Atlanta, where he played in dance halls. He migrated to Chicago in 1917 to realize his ambition to become a professional musician.[30]

In the Windy City, Dorsey was exposed to jazz and to the blues, and he adapted a version of a blues song, "A Good Man Is Hard to Find." After a relative invited him to the Chicago meeting of the 1921 National Baptist Convention, Dorsey resumed his church involvement. First, he met and interacted with the compiler of the recently released *Gospel Pearls*, Reverend W. M. Nix, and he became the director of music for a Baptist congregation on the city's South Side. In 1922 he wrote the religious song "If I Don't Get There." Throughout the 1920s, however, Dorsey vacillated between religious music and the secular blues that Ma Rainey, Bessie Smith, and others popularized within black migrant communities in Chi-

29. Dennis C. Dickerson, *A Liberated Past: Explorations in AME Church History* (Nashville: AMEC Sunday School Union, 2003), 64; Jones, *Charles Albert Tindley*, 40, 103.

30. Michael Harris, *The Rise of the Gospel Blues: The Music of Thomas Andrew Dorsey* (New York: Oxford University Press, 1992), xix, 15, 19-20, 43-44, 47.

cago and elsewhere in the Midwest and Northeast. Dorsey himself copyrighted in the blues genre compositions such as "Riverside Blues" and "Miss Anna Blues." The secular blues, with their slow meter and expressions of sadness, tragedy, misfortune, and unrequited love, later merged with a new musical form called the "gospel blues." Dorsey decided in 1928 to compose music with styles and lyrics that reflected his blues background and his familiarity with this secular musical genre. He continued to play and compose the secular blues until his wife's death in childbirth in 1932. This tragedy, a kind of Damascus Road experience, pushed him into a full-time engagement in developing the "gospel blues" and popularizing this new genre of religious music. His composition "Precious Lord, Take My Hand" and his founding of the gospel choir movement, though initially opposed by mainline black churches, transformed the landscape of black religion.

The Great Migration scrambled what seemed to be normative in black religion. Thrust into urban and industrial geographies in the Northeast and Midwest, where a broader range of religious choices was available, black migrants selected faith affiliations that suited their particular social, economic, and cultural needs. Some joined churches with interlocking connections with employers, while others selected religious communities that merged the sacred and secular culture through music. Whatever they chose, their selections represented another aspect of the freedom they sought beyond the danger and disenfranchisement they had encountered in the segregated South.

Evangelicalism within the African American religious community became a turning point in American religious history. It exposed those economic factors and alignments that blended the interests of black churches and white employers. Although black ministers offered insurgent critiques of the racial and economic deprivations that afflicted black migrants, they allied with mill and factory managers who wanted reliable workers for their plants and who would provide them with plentiful parishioners for their congregations. Additionally, migrants created cultural space through evangelicalism for a new musical genre whose impact affected general American religion. The gospel blues, derived from the secular urban blues and arising out of the migration, permeated the black religious culture and would later influence white evangelical music. Moreover, the rise of black women preachers, contemporaries of Aimee Semple McPherson, the prominent white female evangelist and founder of the International Church of the Foursquare Gospel, increasingly undermined male dominance in the pulpit. Martha Jayne Keys, Mary G. Evans, and Lucy Smith, who became far more widespread than their white female counterparts, introduced gender dynamics in preaching within the evangelical culture. These developments in the history of twentieth-century American evangelicalism became turning points that the Great Migration generated and poured into the broader landscape of American and African American religion.

CHAPTER 10

The Global Turn in American Evangelicalism

Mark Hutchinson

In 1994, to my surprise, I found myself addressing a conference in Tiranë, Albania, on the life and contribution of national cultural hero Gjerazim Qiriazi. I knew nothing about Qiriazi, or indeed about Albania—which was only fair, as they also knew nothing about me. I was there to provide some context: Qiriazi (1858–1894) was an evangelical educator (and founder of Kosovo Protestant Evangelical Church) who established the basis for modern Albanian schools. It was something that the local British missionary John Quanrud, of the Ichthus Fellowship, was attempting to help Albanians, afflicted by seventy years of state atheism, rediscover about themselves. I was functionally there, however, because Mark Noll couldn't be: Australian availability from the other end of the earth filled in for American expertise at a British-sponsored function in the immediate aftermath of the collapse of the Iron Curtain, at a conference run in multiple Eastern European languages. At precisely the same time, Quanrud noted to me, American missionaries were dropping into medieval mountaintop villages by helicopter to run "crusades" among people who had yet to achieve running water and domestic electricity. Which of these, if any of them, was an example of a global turn in American evangelicalism?

As Mark Noll points out with his usual subtlety in *The New Shape of World Christianity*, the instance of a "global turn" is not simply about a subject "discovering" the world or incorporating the international as one in a series of content items.[1] This was the failure of first-generation

---

1. Mark A. Noll, *The New Shape of World Christianity: How American Experience Reflects Global Faith* (Downers Grove, IL: InterVarsity, 2009).

203

courses in "World Christianity"—by which American institutions meant "those bits of Christianity which are not us." Ugandans and Mongolians (and, when they were remembered, Australians and Canadians) were all "World Christians" in such courses, because they were not American. Unless, of course, they were dealt with as part of "Western" Christianity, in which case they were treated as if they were merely either British or American colonies. Likewise, this was the weakness of otherwise helpful texts such as *Exporting the American Gospel: Global Christian Fundamentalism*, and the strength of the work of Andrew Walls. The former left unexplored an understanding of what constructed the "other" category, while the latter incorporated a historical insistence on the importance of the particular.[2]

This chapter takes a synthetic approach, combining the broad generalizations of social scientists with the respect for the "distributed particular" that is the strength of the historian. It suggests that to take a "global turn" is to shift frames—to transform the still life of the common, the ordinary, into the mobile, fluid extraordinary by reenvisioning what appears to be self-contained as part of a larger movement in "the space of flows."[3] It is important to be careful of implicit metaphors: to suggest that history "turns" is to impose a spatial metaphor on the flow of time that may be more or less useful, depending on its application. With regard to American Christianity, this chapter will suggest, the global "turn" came not in the recognition that there were other ways of being Christian (something that is constantly breaking on the shores of the "immigration nation"), or that there is an American Christian role in the international space (something that has been present from the country's very earliest days); rather, the global "turn" came when American Christians held as intrinsic the possibility that they themselves were not a consolidated reality, but rather (as the globalization theorist Arjun Appadurai calls it) an "ethnoscape": a geographic area made up of a mobile and transforming population that comprises a multitude of ethnic and national origins. Such an analysis has the advantage of making "World Christi-

2. Steve Brouwer, Paul Gifford, and Susan D. Rose, *Exporting the American Gospel: Global Christian Fundamentalism* (New York: Routledge, 1996); Andrew Walls, *The Cross-Cultural Process in Christian History: Studies in the Transmission and Appropriation of Faith* (Maryknoll, NY: Orbis, 2002).

3. For this, see Manuel Castells, *The Rise of the Network Society* (Oxford: Blackwell, 1996); and Arjun Appadurai, "Disjuncture and Difference in the Global Cultural Economy," in *Global Culture*, ed. M. Featherstone (London: Sage, 1991).

anity" not about "them," but rather about the "us" that relationship to "them" creates. It respects the particular and connects historic time with geographical space in reflexive ways that do not close out the methods by which others calculate times and spaces. It does not, in short, assume that there was a single moment or even decade in which things "turned," but rather that there were moments/periods of rising consciousness of change. Reflecting back on the Albanian experience, the unintentional hegemony of helicopter-borne Southern Baptists was not a "global turn," despite the fact that they were working internationally (and sometimes transnationally). Neither, as Linford Stutzman notes, was it *merely* American nationalism.[4] Rather, processually it might be seen as part of the globalizing of an *internationalized* American evangelicalism, prior to the arrival of the global turn proper.

Shifting out of the determinative metaphor of "turning points" broadens our understanding of the dynamics of social transformation. Appadurai himself posits broader applications of his concept of "ethnoscape," and Malcolm Waters has suggested that scholars of global religion use the word "sacriscapes" instead. This and the term "spiritscapes" have been used in this way by a number of scholars to refer to the construction and flow of ideas related to spirituality.[5] It is only now being used by scholars of American evangelicalism, who have had several decades to incorporate ideas about indigenization from their missiologist colleagues and are now applying these lessons in relatively blunt concepts such as "reverse mission." The delay in the uptake of such social-theoretical approaches is natural among historians, whose discipline is defined by empirical assumptions embodied in sources. When pouring the "stuff" of history into metaphorical containers such as "turning points," however, it is worth considering the form imposed by the container as much as the contents themselves.

As a way of narrowing the focus, the key question might be rephrased as follows: How do we distinguish between American Christianity abroad, and American Christianity that has taken a "global turn"? The idea of *sacriscapes* (*pace* Castells and Appadurai) points to a useful

4. Linford Stutzman, "Evangelical Missions in Albania: Is It a Case of Culture War?" *East-West Church and Ministry Report* 3, no. 1 (Fall 1995), http://www.east westreport.org/articles/ewo3104.htm.

5. Maureen Ann Hinkley, "An Exploration of Inculturation: The International Jesuit Education Leadership Project for Central and East European Educators" (DEd, Teachers College, Columbia University, 2001).

distinction: a sacriscape is present when a religious form or idea is trans-
ferred to a different sociocultural context, absorbed and indigenized, and
then transformationally presented back to the originating culture. This
process—which in globalization terms is known as "reflexivity"—implies
that we can look for the "global turn" in American evangelicalism when
it becomes self-consciously reflexive toward its own practice flowing
around the world, and is changed thereby. A movement or institution
has made a "global turn," then, when it participates in or exemplifies:

- a permutable community of transethnic, transnational beings
- physical and metaphysical worlds that have porous ethnic, geographic, cultural, and national boundaries
- sacriscaped domains that are under constant reconstruction, deconstruction, and de-territorialization
- permeability through the renegotiation of images, intents, and identities of local and foreign origin according to local needs.

Returning to our interim example, one might say that the *absence*
of the American scholar from the Qiriazi commemoration in 1994 was,
perhaps, a better example of a "global turn." Quanrud was appropriating
(i.e., transferring) knowledge from the American context, indigenizing it,
and then presenting Qiriazi (a British and Foreign Bible Society colpor-
teur) back both to his own culture and to the Albanian culture in which
he was working. It is a facile example, but useful prior to exploring more
substantial cases in the globalization of American evangelicalism. Many
such examples might be chosen (indeed, perhaps *need* to be chosen, in
order to sustain the understanding that a "turn" is not necessarily a moment in time, but a shift in self-conception). Given the demands of space,
the one example given here is that of the emergence of the major evangelical nongovernmental organization World Vision International (WVI).

Inevitably, as nongovernmental organizations or NGOs have moved
into the global spaces, they have been caught up in, and have been cre-
ators of, the dynamics of globalization. Unlike states, they are not defined
by the need to protect borders (or their related tax-bases), but, like states,
they develop bureaucratic systems and constituencies that they need to
diversify and adapt in order to work internationally. Through the twentieth century, the international space became increasingly regulated (and,
at the time of writing in the aftermath of the murder of twelve people in
a Paris-based satirical magazine, contested). International actors have

had to become transnational actors, in a diplomatic space increasingly defined and inhabited by global organizations such as the World Bank, the International Monetary Fund, the United Nations, the International Labor Organization, and many others besides. Simple risk reduction and the demands of operational efficiency meant that over the longer term they needed to "master a range of new skills,"[6] both hard and soft, including security assessment (many WVI operations are in dangerous settings, such as Darfur, where staff can be, and indeed are, killed, kidnapped, or injured),[7] and determine "how best to engage in international diplomacy."[8] Such diplomacy is the lifeblood of organizations that, on the one hand, need to protect their "floating" (i.e., nonterritorial) corporate identity while at the same time leverage the resources of nation-states for transnational purposes. In authoritarian settings, as in Zimbabwe in 2005, the NGO can even become the meat in the sandwich in intergovernmental disputes, with harrassment through administrative "investigations" acting as a signal to state actors in the international space.[9]

This transition can be seen in the case of the young Herbert Hoover, entangled in trying to facilitate the movement of neutral American citizens out of the pathway of the oncoming First World War. He quickly discovered that, in their responses to international crisis, nation-states were too readily tied up in national value structures of reputation, class, and self-image. Hoover was frustrated that "the capital sent high salaried officials who knew nothing of local conditions to stay in expensive hotels instead of relying on local residents with local knowledge."[10] Hoover, the Quaker engineer committed to religious liberty, public efficiency, and volunteerism, and later leader of *the* archetypical modern technological society, thus discovered in Belgium the Faustian codependency between nation-states and international actors. Over the next century, NGOs would become a preferred mechanism for nation-states to construct "civil society" in places beyond the reach (for reasons of law, ef-

6. Larry Winter Roeder and Albert Simard, *Diplomacy and Negotiation for Humanitarian NGOs* (New York: Springer, 2013), x.

7. World Vision, "NGOs 'Assessing Security' Before Resuming South Darfur Ops," https://www.dabangasudan.org/en/all-news/article/world-vision-ngos-assessing-security-before-resuming-south-darfur-ops.

8. Roeder and Simard, *Diplomacy and Negotiation*, x.

9. "Zimbabwe Starts Investigating NGOs," Xinhua News Agency, CEIS [Woodside], May 11, 2005, 1.

10. Roeder and Simard, *Diplomacy and Negotiation*, 367.

ficiency, or effectiveness) of governmental agencies (in the voluntary sector, for instance, or in transnational spaces where international convention carried little weight).[11] It was thus definitional for those NGOs to learn how to negotiate a dynamic space for their continued existence that did not bring them into conflict with their sponsoring governments or coopt the rights of their constituencies. For evangelical agencies, the latter has historically meant "denominational bodies," but over time it has also come to include the agency of local congregations (which can find their missional identities contractualized in much the same way that secular critics have noted that NGOs have become "part of a neoliberal service sector of state-devoluted activity" and so "part of an extended state").[12] The disillusionment that has emerged in recent years between the academic commentariat and non-state actors can also occur among local churches. Should a successful WVI program in, say, Rwanda, undermine the spontaneous charity traditionally provided to a church's local community, there are consequences for its external reputation and its ability to maintain internal motivation toward local community rather than merely collective private spirituality. Professionalization and elite patronage can, as Craig J. Jenkins and Craig M. Eckert note with regard to African American social movement organizations (SMOs), lead to local demobilization.[13] Evangelical voluntary agencies (such as InterVarsity, for example) have long had to learn to tread a narrow line between the local church and global need. Likewise, the story of World Vision follows the arc from individual charisma, to international agency, to transnational citizen, with the seemingly inevitable tensions and transformative conflicts along the way.

It is a story that also demonstrates the importance of not over-laboring the "turning point" metaphor when approaching world history. If one were to pay attention to the narrative of World Vision founder Bob Pierce, the "turning point" would be his 1948 Youth For Christ campaign in China, during which Dutch orphanage director Tena Hoelkeboer challenged him to consider the consequences of conversion for young people in China. The story, as told and retold, focuses in (camera-like) on a single girl, White Jade, whose confession of faith to her parents after

11. Sabine Lang, *NGOs, Civil Society, and the Public Sphere* (Cambridge: Cambridge University Press, 2012), 61.

12. Lang, *NGOs, Civil Society, and the Public Sphere*, 61.

13. Quoted in Lang, *NGOs, Civil Society, and the Public Sphere*, 69.

an emotional Pierceian challenge resulted in her being expelled from her home: "The child's back was bleeding from the caning her father had given her when she announced that she was now a follower of Jesus Christ."[14] That, along with Hoelkeboer's pragmatic response, "What are you going to do about it?," bear all the hallmarks of a historical moment converted to pulpiteering theatrics. The question placed Pierce in a co-nundrum: prewar fundamentalist American evangelicalism was strongly anti–social gospel in orientation. Rather than "sell" good *social* works, however, Pierce told and retold the *personal* story of White Jade in pulpits, on radio, in film, in broadcasts, etc. In so doing, he relocated his mission on the safer ground of the core planks of universalizing evangelicalism. Following the framework described by British historian of evangelicalism David Bebbington,[15] White Jade's story is conversionist (wrapped in the larger story of evangelical success by Pierce, "China's Billy Graham"), crucicentric (the scripturally tuned evangelical "ear" is drawn to the blood on the child's back), Christocentric (she is now "a follower of Jesus Christ" rather than the gods of her forebears), and pragmatic ("What are you going to *do* about it?," a challenge to both Pierce as unreflective activ-ist and to audiences hearing the story on his return, where the emphasis moves to the "you" in the question). For someone looking for a "turning point," this story is the armchair historian's delight: visual, emotional, rhetorically useful, linked to direct personal account.

And it is probably wrong. Pierce, after all, was excluded from China along with the thousands of other missionaries after the Communist take-over in 1949. Those who retell the story have no idea what happened to "White Jade"—and even those who are interested (Bob Brown, for exam-ple, of Xiamen University) have found it impossible to relocate the child central to the story.[16] In terms of historical method, then, the facts of the story are much less accessible than at first appears to be the case in popu-lar evangelical representations. What is left is a personal justification after the fact as to what inspired later action, the significance of which was not visible for years to come. Brown and others do not doubt that something

14. Marilee Pierce Dunker, "White Jade: The Story of the First Sponsored Child," various locations.

15. David Bebbington, *Evangelicalism in Modern Britain: A History from the 1730s to the 1980s* (New York: Routledge, 1989), 2-3.

16. See Brown's blog, "Off the Wall," where he describes the intense local inter-est that the search for White Jade provoked in Xiamen: http://offthewallchina.blogspot.com.au/2013/10/search-for-white-jade-world-vision-true.html.

like this happened; the significance of the story, however, is its function as an "organisational origin myth."[17] The filmic clarity subsequently elicited by dozens of evangelical authors and activists is not inherent in the event.[18] At best, what was *an* event was later reified into "the" event. Historically, Pierce's China story obtains its significance from Korea, which (after the Kuomintang [KMT] collapse in 1949) became entangled in American politics and America's sense of national mission amid the more general internationalism unleashed by World War II. This is a story of significance for the postwar emergence of the neo-evangelicals, who were seeking to break out of the ghetto partly chosen by them, partly forced upon them, by their withdrawal from major American institutions during the 1930s. The crucible was the dislocation and mobility created by the events of World War II: mass meetings of soldiers in transit and in camps were led by itinerant evangelists such as Torrey Johnson, Paul Guinness, and Jack Wyrtzen.[19] This effort was consolidated in the formation of Youth for Christ (YFC), which Bob Pierce joined in 1944 as a traveling evangelist, quickly rising to the position of vice president.[20] Torrey Johnson was elected chairman, and Billy Graham became the organization's first full-time evangelist. The organization followed the armed forces overseas, at first in serving and chaplaincy roles, and then increasingly as evangelists in the postwar world. Local chapters of YFC were founded around the world, even as Graham's massive global success (the origins of which are outlined in this volume by Grant Wacker) made way for new ventures and new countries.[21] Not surprisingly, the language of the US military flowed

17. Erica Bornstein, *Spirit of Development: Protestant NGOs, Morality, and Economics in Zimbabwe* (New York: Routledge, 2004), 148.

18. E.g., "One Child Inspires a World Vision: Today, Millions Have Hope," *The Globe and Mail,* January 15, 2000; Richard Stearns, *The Hole in Our Gospel* (Nashville: Thomas Nelson, 2009), 249; Robert Wuthnow, *Boundless Faith: The Global Outreach of American Churches* (Berkeley: University of California Press, 2009), 123; and dozens of blogs, such as http://lifeisreallybeautiful.com/tag/tena-hoelkeboer/.

19. Joel Carpenter, "Youth for Christ and the New Evangelicals' Place in the Life of the Nation," in *Religion and the Life of the Nation: American Recoveries,* ed. Rowland A. Sherrill (Chicago: University of Illinois Press, 1990), 144.

20. David P. King, "Heartbroken for God's World: The Story of Bob Pierce, Founder of World Vision and Samaritans Purse," in *Religion in Philanthropic Organizations: Family, Friend, or Foe?* ed. Thomas J. Davis (Bloomington: Indiana University Press, 2013), 71.

21. M. Hutchinson, "The Forgotten Front: The Palermo Brothers and American Evangelical Expansion in Post-War Italy," *Canadian Journal of Pentecostal-Charismatic Christianity* 5, no. 1 (2014): 1.

over into the language and practice of YFC and the Graham organization. YFC established "invasion teams" deployed for three- to six-month
evangelistic tours to win the world for Christ. They "exported a largely
American gospel and returned to interpret the world to their American
audience at home. YFC became both a mission society and a model of
American triumphalism."[22]

The consequences for World Vision (when it was founded in 1950)
were formational. While it would be some years before it could even be
considered to have a formal organizational structure and culture, World
Vision in its earliest phase was an extension of the charisma of Bob Pierce.
His politics were not that different from Billy Graham himself, who declared what every right-thinking American evangelical (Republican or
Democrat) thought at the time: Communism was of the Devil, and the
fall of China was the result of blunders by the Truman administration. "I
do not think the men in Washington have any grasp of the Oriental mind.
Alger Hiss shaped our foreign policy and some of the men who formulate
it [now] have never been to the East."[23] Graham prayed, and provoked
Eisenhower when he met him, to "go to Korea" and make a stand.[24] That
was certainly what Bob Pierce did, mobilizing American support for the
victims of the Korean War. His military model, however, was perhaps less
the organizational stability of Eisenhower than the charismatic personalism of Douglas MacArthur. The two generals, one spiritual, the other
military, would share similar difficulties in their relationships with their
host institutions.

By 1953, even before he introduced the idea of child sponsorship,
Pierce was funneling over $100,000 per year to causes in Asia.[25] Child
sponsorship not only caused that income to multiply over the subsequent
years, but it solved a significant problem for evangelicals nervous about
the threat of a resurgent social gospel. Almost all accounts of WVI's rise
agree on two points: first, that, by directly linking the donor with the
recipient, Pierce made the subsidization of development *personal*; and
second, he dispersed the personal in ever-larger circles by the adoption
of new media and information technologies—particularly telethons and

22. King, "Heartbroken for God's World," 74.
23. Quoted in David Aikman, *Billy Graham: His Life and Influence* (New York:
Thomas Nelson, 2007), 184.
24. Marshall Frady, *Billy Graham: A Parable of American Righteousness* (New York:
Simon and Schuster, 2006), 255.
25. King, "Heartbroken for God's World," 77.

film,[26] but eventually also computerized mailing lists that enabled direct address across large geographic volumes).[27] The fact that all of these (new media, the linkage of the global to the local, the rise of the image) are markers familiar to readers of globalization theory raises the question: Is the WVI of the early 1950s indicative of a global turn in American evangelicalism?

Probably not (yet). Engagement with the problems of his time didn't change Pierce's theology—and despite the fact that he was fundamentally pragmatic (as seen in his adaptation to the needs that fell across his path and his stellar reputation in Asia), much of his impact related to the ups and downs of postwar American expansion. While he built a community, the only transnational being who inhabited it was Pierce himself. His conscientious individualism functionally separated the increasing need for resources at one end from the need for accountability and management at the other. Neither the physical nor the metaphysical world of the WVI of the early 1950s was "porous," except in the sense that Pierce created direct relationships between sponsor and recipient. The metaphysical worlds remained separate: there was, for example, very little that Asia had to say to America in terms of the way it understood evangelicalism. American foreign policy in Asia was still a form of forward defense up until the early 1960s: no deterritorialization here in the sense used by nineteenth-century imperialists when their colleagues absorbed elements of their colonial settings. The "Ugly American," however much Pierce railed against it, was still a result of "my country right or wrong" projected out to the frontiers of the Cold War and expanding trade. There would be no "re-negotiation of images, intents, and identities of local and foreign origin according to local needs" until WVI representatives went beyond simply funding individuals and began to engage in the broader development work that required them to associate with the subjects of their work for extended periods in often difficult circumstances.[28] It would not be too much to say that, while Pierce's financial

26. John R. Hamilton, "An Historical Study of Bob Pierce and World Vision's Development of the Evangelical Social Action Film" (PhD diss., University of Southern California, 1980).

27. See Ted W. Engstrom, "The Use of Technology: A Vital Tool That Will Help," in *One Race, One Gospel, One Task*, ed. Carl F. H. Henry and W. Stanley Mooneyham, vol. 1 (Minneapolis: World Wide, 1967), 315-16.

28. See R. Coeller, "Beyond the Borders: Radicalized Evangelical Missionaries in Central America from the 1950s through the 1980s" (PhD diss., American University,

impact was upon Asia, the major impact of his broader practice was upon his domestic constituency, who for the first time were provided with a nondenominational, personalized, and theologically neutral mechanism for engaging in the social consequences of broader "new evangelical" expansion.

What Pierce's evangelical pragmatism didn't account for was that success (which entailed becoming a historical actor of significance) had consequences. On the one hand, growth in income and impact resulted in a growing organizational framework that needed leadership of the sort that Pierce was ill suited to provide. He could rally support, "glad hand" politicians, and break down doors, but he couldn't provide the sort of embracing worldview that could "in-spire" a bureaucratic form with a sense of its necessary coherence in pursuit of a goal. In 1956 World Vision's budget passed $1 million, and by 1962, with American entanglement in Vietnam accelerating after the demonstrable complicity of the White House in regime change, the organization took the portentous step of registering with the US Agency for International Development. This was a step simultaneously away from Pierce's advanced voluntarism, into a political maelstrom, and toward expanded needs and development demands, which would see WVI for the first time take on expanded development operations (such as "Christian refugee centers") beyond child sponsorship.[29] Pierce was restrained both by his operational context and by his upbringing: he was "trusted . . . because of his fluency with the evangelical vernacular" and because of the primacy he placed on evangelism. "You can't preach to people whose stomachs are empty. First, you have to give them food."[30] The act was utterly in the realm of the concrete.

Comparison to a contemporary evangelical leader of like international impact, John Stott, is instructive. This highly privileged scion of the British establishment "knew he was privileged, knew that the gap between him and the lower classes was huge, and had little idea what to do

---

2012). As with Charles Troutman's involvement in caring for Latino refugees across the Mexican/American border, "Missionaries sent out as representatives of these evangelical groups, with the goal of converting others into the fold, were thus converted theologically or politically themselves and no longer 'fit' within their home communities" (Coeller, "Beyond the Borders," abstract).

29. King, "Heartbroken for God's World," 81.

30. David P. King, "The New Internationalists: World Vision and the Revival of American Evangelical Humanitarianism, 1950–2010," *Religions* 3, no. 4 (2012): 929.

about it."[31] He was different from Pierce, however, in that Stott was (via British meliorism, education, and a closer concern as to the drift away from Victorian values toward "Darkest England") culturally disposed toward intellectual integration, a disposition and set of intellectual skills that conditioned what one scholar calls the "manichean" tendencies of British proto-fundamentalism.[32] Stott was thus able to ride a rising tide of evangelical social concern consequent on the movement's expansion in numbers and in global reach. While the decline of the Anglican Evangelical Group Movement prior to the war had indicated a withdrawal from social concern,[33] neo-evangelicals were increasingly concerned to apply their energies to the pressing matters of poverty, marginalization, and social fragmentation. This was evident in Norman Anderson's appeal to the 1967 Keele Conference, but also in the emergence of an "evangelical left" in the USA around people such as Ron Sider and Jim Wallis.[34] Pierce staggered into growing conflict with his own organization. In 1964 he had a health breakdown related to his overexposure in the field—a sign that the organization was already well beyond the paternalist individual-ministry form around which it had been shaped. To add insult to injury, World Vision managed to get on quite well in his absence. The formalization of management under (from 1963) Ted Engstrom, and the introduction of critical-reflective practices through the Mission Advanced Research and Communication Center at Fuller Theological Seminary, were burrs under Pierce's saddle.[35] Though he was publicly supportive,

31. Alister Chapman, *Godly Ambition: John Stott and the Evangelical Movement* (Oxford: Oxford University Press, 2011), 114.

32. See Ian S. Rennie, "Fundamentalism and the Varieties of North Atlantic Evangelicalism," in *Evangelicalism: Comparative Studies of Popular Protestantism in North America, the British Isles, and Beyond, 1700-1990*, ed. M. Noll, D. Bebbington, and G. Rawlyk (New York: Oxford University Press, 1994).

33. Cf. Martin Wellings, "The Anglican Evangelical Group Movement," in *Evangelicalism and the Church of England in the Twentieth Century: Reform, Resistance and Renewal*, ed. Andrew Atherstone and John G. Maiden (Woodbridge: Boydell Press, 2014), 68–88.

34. David R. Swartz, "'Embodying the Global Soul: Internationalism and the American Evangelical Left," *Religions* 3, no. 4 (2012): 888–89.

35. King, "Heartbroken for God's World," 79–80. Pierce told an interviewer: "World Vision has a new complex computer system which diagnoses the failures of Christianity and prints them on a data sheet. . . . I can't stand it. I love the early days when I was walking with widows and holding babies. When I began flying over them and being met by committees at the airport it almost killed me." Quoted in King, "Heartbroken for God's World," 85.

the increasing rows with his leadership led in 1967 to Pierce's resignation. After another extended time of recovery, he relaunched Food for the World as Samaritan's Purse (SPI), in which he embodied the primacy of the sort of evangelism that he felt had been lost through the growth and institutionalization of WVI. As David P. King points out, the result of Pierce's indirect journeyings was the establishment of two out of the United States' ten largest NGOs, a uniquely large American evangelical presence in an international aid scene then otherwise dominated by the traditional denominations. It was an achievement that, King observes, potentially makes Pierce the "leading religious philanthropist of the twentieth century."[36]

Both institutions went off in different directions: the criticism they receive acts as a bellwether for the challenges each has faced in making a "global turn." Samaritan's Purse remained entrenched in the American evangelical heartland, and has consequently retained (after Pierce's death, under the leadership of Franklin Graham) its traditional, unblinking evangelistic focus. As a result, it has become something of a target for interests in both secular and non-Christian religious development: to the one, it is the creeping hand of American imperialism, to the other, a protagonist in the "fundamentalist quest." Particular criticism has arisen around SPI's "proselytism" in Africa and the Middle East.[37] While it is not necessary to take such critique literally (the same criticism does not, for example, seem to attach to similarly proselytizing but non-American or non-Christian charities, raising questions as to the color of the critics' "eyeglasses"), it is important to take it seriously. Such discourse is essential to the "space of flows," where identities are negotiated. Samaritan Purse's fault here is not its insistence on acting continuously with its faith statements. Rather, the problem is an issue of learning how to speak the polite language of the international market, a language that would enable Samaritan's Purse to balance its conversionism (read internationally as exclusivism) with its commitment to compassion toward *all* human beings.

World Vision, on the other hand, has adapted over time, maintaining its tight Pierceian focus on children and poverty through energetic local church representation and the creation of a non-church general social

---

36. King, "Heartbroken for God's World," 71.

37. Farzana Hassan Shahid, *Prophecy and the Fundamentalist Quest: An Integrative Study of Christian and Muslim Apocalyptic Religion* (Jefferson, NC: McFarland, 2008), 83.

identity and drawing base, but adding to that an integration of theological reflection and "listening," the division of its national/regional bodies into quasi-autonomous organizations,[38] and occasionally outsourcing to other SMOs and NGOs "voice and advocacy efforts that its board of directors would not deem appropriate for the image of World Vision itself."[39] Its organizational structure—emphasizing local agency and "supervision and support" rather than "command and control"—directly adds to the organization's ability to negotiate spaces for action with nation-states. World Vision's "remarkable global private fund-raising operation" has made it less dependent on US government funding, for example, than many other NGOs.[40] The operation was based on what Xu Yushan and Han Junkui have called a "dumbbell" model, acting as the mediator between communities of donation and communities of reception, its famous child-sponsorship model becoming the cause for inquiry among scholars from countries where philanthropy has been based (by way of illustration) on social (e.g., Confucian corporatism) or religious (e.g., Islamic *zakat*) duty.[41] The fact that World Vision's income from areas such as Hong Kong actually grew during periods of economic recession[42] points to the problem of purely class-based or economistic analyses of religious activity.

An example of this sort of arc of development can be seen in World Vision's changing activities in China. It will be remembered that it was China, and its entanglement in the globalizing American imagination, which attracted YFC and Bob Pierce in the first place. China and India were disproportionately central to the Protestant missionary mindset for a number of reasons: As "high cultures," they were (wrongly) assumed to be most aligned with the rational presuppositions of "true religion." Their mere size also made them appealing to Protestant pragmatism; the China Inland Mission's magazine, it will be recalled, was entitled *China's Millions*, the sine qua non for "mass" evangelism. As Grant Wacker notes with regard to William Randolph Hearst, mass media and concern for the development of the nation-state were essential contributors to

38. Susan McDonic, "Juggling the Religious and the Secular World Visions," in *Religion in Philanthropic Organizations*, 172ff.

39. Lang, *NGOs, Civil Society, and the Public Sphere*, 69.

40. Roeder and Simard, *Diplomacy and Negotiation*, 232.

41. Xu Yushan and Han Junkui, "A Dumbbell Pattern in NGO Fundraising: The Case of World Vision," *China Nonprofit Review* 3, no. 1 (January 2011): 121.

42. Xu and Han, "A Dumbbell Pattern," 121.

evangelical expansion.[43] Through the 1930s Chiang Kai-shek and the Kuomintang nationalists carefully developed civilizational politics to project a mythology of Chiang as "the Christian general." In this, he was abetted by the reflexive global missionary culture. In 1936 the "missionary kid" Henry R. Luce, "founder and publisher of *Time, Life* and *Fortune* [magazines], began to promote Chiang Kai-shek as China's hope for the future."[44] Luce, born in China and the son of a Presbyterian missionary, was only one among a global network of both Chinese and Western merchants, politicians, and cultural actors who found in Protestant Christianity a bridge between East and West. China would be the realization of the long-held postmillennial vision in which faith and reason were continuous with one another, and democracy and modernization were the natural outcome of Christianization. Luce's vision was no narrow Americanism: at the same time that Chiang (who, Fenby argues, was more of a "Confucian fascist" than the "Christian gentleman warrior" envisaged in the West)[45] was being "boosted" by Luce, Chinese Presbyterians such as John Young Wai and George Kwok Bew were rallying the financial resources and the cross-cultural and political skills of Pacific Rim expatriate communities to help fill the enormous gaps in China's ability to modernize.[46] Evangelical-style voluntarism was essential to the new regime, from mission agencies that dealt with particular social problems (such as the Chinese Mission to Lepers, founded by Australian Chinese expatriate William Yinson Lee in 1921)[47] to the Whampoa Academy Officers' Moral Endeavour Association (modeled on the YMCA).[48] As one Australian Presbyterian visitor reported on the eve of Sun Yat Sen's 1912

43. See Wacker's chapter in this volume, "Billy Graham's 1949 Los Angeles Revival."

44. Brenda A. Ericson, "The Making of an Ally: Chiang Kai-shek and American Foreign Policy, 1936–1941" (PhD diss., University of New Mexico, 2004), 4.

45. Jonathan Fenby, *Generalissimo Chiang Kai Shek and the China He Lost* (New York: Caroll & Graf, 2005). The phrase "Confucian fascist" is taken from George Fetherling, "Chiang Kai-shek: Portrait of a Confucian Fascist; New Biography Details Life of Nationalist China's Failed Champion," *Telegraph-Journal*, June 18, 2005.

46. Mei-Fen Kuo, *Making Chinese Australia: Urban Elites, Newspapers, and the Formation of Chinese Australian Identity, 1892–1912* (Clayton, Victoria, Australia: Monash University Publishing, 2013).

47. Angela Leung and Qizi Liang, *Leprosy in China: A History* (New York: Columbia University Press, 2008), 161.

48. Jeremy E. Taylor, "The Production of the Chiang Kai-Shek Personality Cult, 1929–1975," *The China Quarterly* 185 (March 2006): 99.

revolution in China, "the Holy Spirit was working in Korea as in no other country. He believed that once despised nation was destined to become the evangelist of the East, and to bring China and Japan to the feet of Jesus Christ."[49] It was a vision that appeared all the more righteous after the Japanese invasion of 1937. Protestant missionaries had by this stage been opposing Japanese imperialism in Korea for nearly half a century; the brutality of the colonial regime there was regularly highlighted by such events as the March 1 massacres of 1919. Here was an imperialism that itself had proven resistant to Protestantism, and was now oppressing a population in which Christianity was making rapid advances. When it came to China, the Rape of Nanking only strengthened Protestant determination to overlook Chiang's shortcomings (such as his brutality, his dependence on underworld figures to achieve his ends, and a personality cult that owed more to Leninism and Tai Ping syncretism than it did to Christianity).[50] Brenda Ericson notes,

> After the Japanese invasion of China in 1937, many former missionaries, businessmen, authors and academics worked together in various endeavors to bring to the attention of the American public the plight of the Chinese war victims, and to elicit financial and diplomatic support on behalf of the Nationalists.[51]

The postmillennial Christian internationalism that linked faith, democracy, and modernization proved a brief and fragile mirage that only barely survived the Second World War. When the KMT collapsed before the Communist offensives of 1948–49, the internationalist elements of the dialogue (along with Chiang's American-educated widow, Meiling Soong; his second wife, Jennie Chen; and many of the scions of the great urban merchant houses in Shanghai and Tianjiang) would retreat to the USA, where they continued to have an impact on Christian perceptions of the world.[52] By then, the old denominational supports for this sort of positive internationalism were already collapsing back in their heartlands. Bob Pierce's emergence as "the Billy Graham of China," therefore, wasn't a spontaneous emergence into a neutral space. China was a place

49. "Korea's Destiny to Evangelise the East," *Advertiser*, May 5, 1911, 8.
50. See Taylor, "The Production of the Chiang Kai-Shek Personality Cult," 97.
51. Ericson, "The Making of an Ally," 4.
52. See Jennie Ch'en Chieh-ju, *Chiang Kai-shek's Secret Past: The Memoir of His Second Wife, Ch'en Chieh-ju*, ed. L. E. Eastman (Boulder: Westview, 1993).

of struggle and ultimately of disappointed dreams, which inscribed responses to critical elements of the time—such as Chinese Communism, the post–World War II response to Stalinism, the critical place of Korea, and the like—on the American Christian imagination. Nor was it an emergence *from* a neutral space. China and, by extension, Korea were places where the pieces of the liberal postmillennial Christian dream lay scattered on the ground. A YFC "invasion team" in such places was an effective way of responding to the "liberals" who dominated the mainline denominational machinery after the fundamentalist-modernist debates of the 1920s and 1930s. The question China posed was how evangelicals such as Pierce would respond to entering into a "space of flows" where all identities were up for renegotiation.

The organization that Bob Pierce had quit in 1967 phrased this problem in terms of "incarnation." The Protestant flight from sixteenth-century Catholic realism, on the one hand, and from nineteenth-century social gospelers, on the other, left old-style fundamentalism in something of a bind. Its major global competitors, Pentecostalism and Catholicism, had resources to deal with the global/local conundrum through praxes of "presence/Presence." Neo-evangelicalism now needed to find an equivalent. After 1949 World Vision (like most of the more directly missionary agencies) was forced to develop its relationship with China at arm's length—through proxies, usually based in Hong Kong or Singapore. It was not until 1982 that World Vision returned to the country so deeply entrenched in its founding mythology. It was already quite a different organization from that which had been founded in the shadows of the Communist revolution to deal directly with the after-effects of Chinese involvement on the Korean peninsula. Partially through the relationships that it developed with the world of Christian colleges and seminaries, partially in response to the politics of postcolonial NGO-formation through the 1970s, the organization's operational staff developed a reflective, self-critical capacity that was rare in the evangelical world prior to 1960. As part of its move to a more federal, globally present form, in 1993 it formally reorganized its operations in China as an autonomous World Vision–China (WV-China) office. In 1997 it signed an agreement to launch a Child-Focused Area Development program in China, which enabled the organization to do more than distribute disaster relief. Within years, WV-China was demonstrating remarkable cultural sensitivity and adroitness in managing the complex tides of Chinese politics and global opinion, growing to deliver eighty-eight projects across fourteen provinces in China, with over 2.3 million beneficiaries.[53] Central to its success was the new federal form's ability to do more than simply put a Chinese face on a Western program. Federating as it spread around the world, WVI arrived at a global form that enabled it to be authentically Chinese in China, energetically international when testifying before the World Bank, and reflexively transnational when the regional units met one another to debate key issues. As Ho shows, for instance, the launch of the HIV/AIDS Awareness and Capacity Building project in 2001 was attended by an internal culture-change process, which involved the organization creating a situationally appropriate capacity before moving to roll out programs across the country. It was, in short, a new way of being present, of being a culturally appropriate implementation before attempting to multiply points of action. The lessons of child sponsorship had been learned, and (assisted by broader trends in evangelical theology, such as that emerging from the Lausanne movement) they were used as the basis for a global/local theology and organizational form. The organization founded by "the Billy Graham of China" was ultimately able to define itself around "Christian engagement by example" rather than by proclamation, assuring its supporters (non-evangelical and evangelical alike) that "we oppose proselytism and coercion of any kind."[54]

It was said of Chiang Kai-shek that he had a talent for defeating past enemies but a weakness in understanding what was needed to defeat those before him.[55] It is too early to say which of the paths taken by Bob Pierce's organizational offspring will ultimately prove most successful in engaging the new global realities. In the light of the rise of fundamentalist/essentialist movements around the world, the sort of declarative evangelicalism represented by Samaritan's Purse could easily entrench itself in a supranational network of local communities of like mind, and avoid the socializing pressures of the global NGO community. There is no end of need, and the organization will certainly find friends, for example, in the "underground" churches in China.[56] For Franklin Graham, Pierce's style of globe-trotting personal presence

53. Ho Wai Ip, "World Vision," *China Development Brief*, Spring 2002.
54. "Who We Are," World Vision Australia site, http://www.worldvision.com.au/AboutUs/WhoWeAre.aspx?lpos=top_drop_1_Whoweare.
55. Fetherling, "Chiang Kai-shek: Portrait of a Confucian Fascist."
56. See, for example, Geoffrey A. Fowler, "China Opens Doors to Quake Relief, but Not Missionaries," *Wall Street Journal*, May 31, 2008, Eastern edition, A-2.

seems to continue to work.[57] What Samaritan's Purse will find difficult is variegating its sources of financial and political power as the Western (including even "exceptional" American) public culture continues to squeeze that form of evangelicalism to the margins. Through its strategy, World Vision threatens to become detached from its evangelical support base; for Samaritan's Purse, the danger is that its evangelical support base will become disconnected from the new, relativized form of the American state.

Over the longer term, the ability of evangelicalism to produce such a range of responses to global problems is an indicator of its strength. By throwing up a range of responses, evangelical Christianity remains adaptive to unpredictable turns. A number of observations emerge. First, evangelical communities respond to globalization in various ways. This may include responding (as WVI has done) to the demands of global citizenship by absorbing and/or adapting to consensual restrictions and language and creating a "glocalized" institutional form and theology to match, or (as Samaritan's Purse has done) by maintaining a traditional declarative approach to the gospel, solving the problems of coherence and presence by organizing around Piercean organizational charisma (as embodied in Franklin Graham). The second observation is that not all global institutions solve the problems of inter/transnationalization by taking a "global turn." This suggests the need for a sophisticated approach to distinguishing between global evangelical forms and those that are merely present globally. Various evangelical forms may well be on a development arc between these poles: the fact that an African denomination, for instance, has off-shoots in America and Europe does not necessarily mean that it has taken on a global form. It may be the case in a generation or two, as its members become in(ter)culturated, but it will not happen without organizational, cultural, and ideological change. Glocal settings are locations of change, negotiation, and dynamism: as historians we need to develop analytical and rhetorical forms that are capable of capturing and communicating this.

One approach would be to use the definitions described in this chapter as a form of score card (see page 206 above). First, do we discover in World Vision *a permutable community of transethnic, transnational beings*? Both WVI's broader practices and the specific case study of WVI's work

---

57. Monte Mitchell, "Graham of Samaritan's Purse Was Near Beijing When Earthquake Hit," *Winston-Salem Journal*, May 14, 2008, 1.

would suggest so. WVI commences outreach by establishing local internal dialogue and culture change before it implements delivery on the
ground; that is, external action is predicated on internal culture change.
This is not merely an abstract virtue of WVI but an essential characteristic for continued effectiveness. As the 2006 Harwood Institute Report
on NGOs pointed out, the danger of Hoover's bugbear (i.e., government
reporting requirements) is internal bureaucratization. Nongovernmental
institutions can become "colonized by governmental ways of doing business," detaching them from their constituencies and blunting their ability
to "channel their voices," to undertake both diplomacy and advocacy.[58]
This may be more an application of Weberian theory than an observation
of reality on the ground, a reflection of the ironic instrumentalization that
the secular academy brings to its objects of inquiry. It is an observation
informed by the assumption that institutionalization will lead to both
bureaucratization and disenchantment, a "general homogenization of
language, practice, and organization."[59] While ignoring the reenchanting
capacities in the communities with which Christian NGOs interact, it is
a useful description of the problems faced by evangelicals in the transnational space, and it explains in part the success of some evangelical
strategies. World Vision's core operations connect individuals in developed countries with individuals in developing countries: "donors know
exactly whom they are supporting."[60] At the same time, the organization
has proved itself capable of change, moving from pure one-to-one relationships to "putting children first and [to] developing regions," to avoid
the problems of wealth disparity and social tension that individual sponsorship could create in developing settings. Given the resistance among
evangelical traditions to community-development models and the social
gospel, this has been a significant change, a "global turn."

Second, is World Vision marked by inhabiting *physical and metaphysical worlds that have porous ethnic, geographic, cultural, and national boundaries*? Again, the answer seems to be yes: the shift to a federated, globally
dispersed form, the national associations of which are free to choose programs that gain local traction and that directly engage local individuals
(Christian or not), families, and congregations, is an almost textbook
definition of "glocalization." In America, World Vision is American, but

58. Quoted in Lang, *NGOs, Civil Society, and the Public Sphere*, 60.
59. King, "Heartbroken for God's World," 71.
60. Xu and Han, "A Dumbbell Pattern," 123.

in Australia, China, New Zealand, or any of the ninety-six countries in which WVI works it can present a local or international or transnational face. It can present itself as "big" (22,500 staff members working in ninety-six countries; $2.5 billion in turnover; 100 million people impacted annually), or operate as a middle-rank "mediating institution" that can speak to issues of national policy (for instance, WV-USA's recent World Vision's "Hope for the Holy Land Tour" at Seattle Pacific University),[61] or work on a personal level (with local representatives, direct outreach into lounge-rooms through a wide range of media, and "get involved" resources that help people organize their spirituality for social action.)[62]

This latter point is directly related to the third criterion, *spiritscaped domains that are under constant reconstruction, deconstruction, and deterritorialization*. Through the provision of resources and channels for organizing personal evangelical spirituality, World Vision does not simply reflect existing evangelical spirituality but also relativizes national borders and rewrites international issues into individual and local spaces. None of this is foreign to evangelical tradition: from the *Short Account of God's Dealings with The Reverend Mr. George Whitefield* (which had the dual purpose of attracting support for the establishment of an orphanage), through William Carey's global conspectus in his *Enquiry into the Obligations of Christians* (1792), through Sunday school newspapers alerting young Americans to the needs of the Pacific Islands, and onwards, evangelicals have been assiduous users of media. World Vision, however, has moved from the more passive, if emotive, medium of telethons to active social media and community mobilization. Any schoolchild with Internet access can "Join the World Vision Advocate Network!" and agitate with their congressional representative or the White House for action against the problems of child soldiers, human trafficking, and child health issues. The problems of a village in Africa or even an individual refugee child in Syria become the problem of the local Christian in the USA or New Zealand. One is invited to make choices as Jesus would make them—with all the ambivalence about the power of the human state, the universality of the gospel proclamation, and the personalism of the gospel narratives that that implies.

Fourth, World Vision inculcates a spirituality that is "busy for both

61. Kat Wynn, "Forum Talks 'Hope for the Holy Land,'" *The Falcon*, November 5, 2014, http://www.thefalcononline.com/2014/11/forum-talks-hope-for-the-holy-land/.
62. http://www.worldvision.org/get-involved.

worlds,"[63] which by definition creates a spirituality that holds the two worlds—the spiritual and the material—in tension. In such a spirituality (as the final criterion suggests) the believer is involved in the constant *renegotiation of images, intents, and identities of local and foreign origin according to local needs.*

None of this is unique to World Vision. WVI is, rather, a leading case of successful adaptation to common globalizing forces. The permutable community, "porous worlds," renegotiated sacriscapes, and permeable local/foreign flows are also readily seen in other successful evangelical global adaptations. One merely has to stand in the multiethnic, mobile congregations of London, São Paolo, or Singapore, or track the development of global revival forms (such as Holy Trinity Brompton's Alpha course), or note the emergence of "virtual denominations" associated with megachurches or the emerging church movement to recognize that evangelicals have often made the "global turn" with energy and adaptability, "diversity and fluidity."[64] At the same time, however, it is equally possible to find traditional evangelical denominations that have failed to make the turn, among them fundamentalist Baptists, traditional ethnic denominations that have relocated physically but failed to create bridges into their host societies, and rural movements struggling to adapt to rapid urbanization and ubiquitous mobility. Many of these are declining or are fighting rearguard actions that occasionally spill over into the media.[65] Equally, it is possible to find (as with World Vision's sibling, Samaritan's Purse, or the late Charles Colson's Prison Fellowship) organizations that remain committed to forms of evangelicalism "born in the USA," while also expanding around the world.

These three scenarios, in addition to the myriad subcultural flows of evangelical energy that result in constant religious innovation, point to the problems associated with identifying any particular "global turning" in American evangelicalism. Here, the World Vision case study indicates

63. The phrase was that of British-Australian Congregationalist newspaperman John Fairfax. See Stuart Johnson, "'Busy for Both Worlds': John Fairfax as a Leading Evangelical Layman," *Lucas: An Evangelical History Review* 27, no. 8 (2000): 41–63.

64. Andrew Atherstone and John Maiden, "Anglican Evangelicalism in the Twentieth Century: Identities and Contexts," in *Evangelicalism and the Church of England in the Twentieth Century*, 2.

65. One could mention fringe irritant groups such as Dove World Outreach Centre or Westboro Baptist Church, which have invented extreme public images for themselves in order to break into the media space.

the necessity of considering how intercultural spatiality and interspatial culturality impact spiritualities as they globalize and glocalize. It suggests that the early twentieth century would be a useful time and space in which to explore the phenomenon of "global turning" in various American Christian communities. This is something that Mark Noll has arrived at, albeit along a different path. His comparative work with Canada and in transatlantic evangelicalism has, for many American evangelical historians, provided great impetus to look beyond their own backyard. His book *The New Shape of World Christianity* (which demonstrates Noll's remarkable insight by using the USA as a palette rather than as a normative framework) is more than simply a logical intellectual journey.[66] As with the World Vision story, the study of global evangelicalism has been a profoundly *personal* journey for Noll: each boundary crossed, each story told, has had a personal relationship on the other side of the line (Canada with George Rawlyk; Britain with David Bebbington, David Hempton, and many others; his global work with friends scattered around the world). There are many scholars who, as a result of being drawn into Mark Noll's scholarship and friendship, have found themselves (as I did in Tiranë in 1994) doing things they had not previously thought of in places about which they previously knew nothing. That, if anything, is an example of the global turning of a great evangelical mind, a scholar not immune to the embedded wisdom of human experience.

66. Mark A. Noll, *The New Shape of World Christianity: How American Experience Reflects Global Faith* (Downers Grove, IL: InterVarsity, 2009).

CHAPTER 11

Billy Graham's 1949 Los Angeles Revival

Grant Wacker

In 1997 Billy Graham was a year shy of his eightieth birthday. An extraordinary life it had been. In the previous half-century he had grown from an obscure itinerant preacher to a national leader of the emerging evangelical movement to an international icon accustomed to golfing with presidents and dining with prime ministers. By many accounts he ranked as the most influential evangelist since George Whitefield in the eighteenth century. So it is understandable that on the eve of his eightieth birthday he would accede to the requests of many people to put it all together in a memoir, *Just as I Am: The Autobiography of Billy Graham*.[1]

Yet the task was not easy. With a life so long and so filled with travel and events and people, where would Graham start? How would he find

---

1. *Just as I Am: The Autobiography of Billy Graham* (San Francisco: HarperSanFrancisco; Grand Rapids: Zondervan, 1997, revised 2007). In this chapter, I have not tried to cite sources for commonly known data about Graham or the 1949 Los Angeles campaign. For that, the best account remains William Martin, *A Prophet with Honor: The Billy Graham Story* (New York: W. Morrow and Co., 1991), chap. 7, "The Canvas Cathedral." Russ Busby, *Billy Graham, God's Ambassador: A Lifelong Mission of Giving Hope to the World* (Alexandria: Time-Life Books, 1999), 47–55, offers details and priceless photographs of the setting, crowds, advertising materials, and Graham in action.

With this chapter, I wish to express my profound appreciation to Mark Noll for a lifetime of wise counsel, loyal friendship, and Christian witness. Parts of this chapter draw on and occasionally quote my article "Watershed: Los Angeles 1949," *Christian History* 111 (October 2014): 4–9, and my book *America's Pastor: Billy Graham and the Shaping of a Nation* (Cambridge, MA: Harvard University Press, 2014). I wish to thank my research assistants, Katie Benjamin and Aaron Griffith, for their contributions throughout.

a storyline that cast even the main events, let alone the minor ones, into a coherent narrative? As it turned out, he judged that the fulcrum of his career—and thus the fulcrum of the memoir—lay in chapter 9. He called it, "Watershed: Los Angeles 1949."

That choice proved sound, for the tactics that Graham deployed in Los Angeles etched the template for virtually all of his campaign meetings for the next six decades.[2] Striking similarities marked the ministries of the great evangelists of the late nineteenth and early twentieth centuries—especially Dwight L. Moody, Billy Sunday, and Aimee Semple McPherson—and Graham. All of them spoke to millions in their crusade meetings and (in McPherson's case) over the radio. All of them appealed to emotions, but none of them were emotional, let alone histrionic, in their preaching. None was a prince of the pulpit but all were effective speakers who, with brilliant success, achieved their purpose of drawing thousands, perhaps millions, to Christ. And they all proved pragmatic and entrepreneurial, using advertising, prayer groups, publicity appearances, and follow-up procedures both aggressively and without hesitation.

The similarities took more specific forms, too. Both Graham and Moody appealed to middle-class and especially business people, with their esteem for propriety and the power of individual choice. Both Graham and Sunday used foreign threats—in Graham's case, Russia and Communism, in Sunday's case Germany and biblical criticism—as a foil against which they deployed evangelical Christianity as the only lasting solution for the world's problems. And both Graham and McPherson lionized mass communications and particularly electronic technology to herald their message to the far corners of the nation and many parts of the world.

But if Graham resembled his predecessors in many respects, he also differed from them, both individually and together. Unlike the stolid and rotund Moody, Graham was dashing and always took a great picture. Unlike Sunday's slang-drenched preaching, Graham's mannered diction bore the precision of "Carolina stage English." Unlike the flamboyantly Pentecostal McPherson, Graham downplayed talk about the Holy Spirit and skirted

2. I say "campaign" because Graham did not adopt the more common term "crusade" until the following year. He came to believe that "crusade" more aptly suggested the extensive preparation that took place before the meetings and the counseling with converts that took place after the meetings. About 1952 Graham started to use the term "inquirer" rather than "convert" to emphasize that only God could know who a true convert really was.

discussions of miraculous divine interventions. And unlike his forerunners, Graham routinely—the key word here is "routinely"—hobnobbed and schmoozed with many of the richest and most powerful men and women in the world, including nine successive presidents of the United States.

But the greatest difference between Graham and his predecessors was the sheer magnitude and complexity of his ministry. The number of people he addressed in person and in the media; the number of books, magazines, newspaper columns, and movies he produced; and the number of letters he received from grassroots admirers around the world dwarfed the ministry of any one of his predecessors. Indeed, though there is no way to quantify the claim, it is conceivable that Graham's reach exceeded that of his late-nineteenth- and early-twentieth-century evangelist predecessors put together. Though the distinctiveness of Graham's approach started to manifest itself in his Charlotte campaign in 1947, it emerged in full force in Los Angeles in 1949. The City of Angels revival marked a turning point both in his career and in the career of post–World War II evangelicalism.

When Graham hopped off the train in Los Angeles in mid-September 1949, he was bursting with energy. He had only enough revival sermons to last two weeks, plus some sketchy notes that he planned to turn into sermons for the final days of the scheduled three-week run. As things turned out, however, the revival would continue for eight weeks. Services ran full steam every night and Sunday afternoons from September 25 to November 20. In the course of seventy-two meetings, Graham preached sixty-five sermons to a cumulative audience of 350,000—maybe 400,000—souls. Though tabulations varied, something like three thousand persons committed and another three thousand recommitted their lives to Christ.[3] Along the way, Graham spoke to countless civic, school, and business groups. He made three to four appearances every day, gave dozens of interviews, and found time to schmooze with Hollywood celebrities such as Cecil B. DeMille, Spencer Tracy, and Katharine Hepburn.[4] The preacher even gave time to Hollywood gossip columnist Louella Parsons (who called him a "really naïve, humble man.")[5]

3. Graham, *Just as I Am*, 158; Mel Larson, "Tasting Revival—at Los Angeles," in *Revival in Our Time: The Story of the Billy Graham Evangelistic Campaigns, Including Six of His Sermons* (Wheaton, IL: Van Kampen Press, 1950), 13; [Larson], "Continuing Revival—at Boston," *Revival in Our Time*, 38.

4. Busby, *Billy Graham*, 47-55.

5. Parsons quoted in Martin, *Prophet with Honor*, 120.

The meeting site was a six-thousand-seat Ringling Brothers tent, pitched at the corner of Washington and Hill Streets, near the city's central shopping district. That prime location had not been easy to come by, but after complex negotiations it finally had opened up—providentially, it seemed to insiders. One partisan would later remember it as "a quarter . . . sacred to thousands."[6] The tent's dirt floor, covered with sawdust, gave it an aura of authenticity. Ushers eventually jammed an additional three thousand chairs into the space. They called it a "Cathedral of Canvas."[7]

In late November, the southern preacher finally boarded the train back to his new home in Minneapolis. Twenty pounds had disappeared from his already lean body, and he struggled with exhaustion. No one would have been surprised.

In *Just as I Am*, Graham characteristically insisted that the revival's success had been entirely "*God's* doing" (Graham's emphasis).[8] That claim lies outside the scope of historical analysis, but mundane factors that historians *can* judge played a role. At least four streams of influence are visible.

The first stream grew from the turbulence that rocked the political, social, and economic environment in the years just after the war. The battlefields in Europe and in the Pacific had quieted, but the rhythms of daily life had not. On Friday, September 23—just two days before the revival started—President Harry Truman announced that the Soviet Union had exploded an atomic bomb. The United States was no longer the sole possessor of nuclear weaponry. That turn of events was bad enough, but it felt even more ominous because the Soviets had also embraced the deadly, aggressive, atheistic ideology of Communism. The threat felt overwhelming. Six days after the revival started, Mainland China fell to Mao Zedong's "Red" Army. The Chinese calamity made clear that Communists possessed both the determination and the ability to—in Graham's words—"holster the whole world."[9] Graham brought the danger home. In his very first sermon, he warned that the Soviets had targeted Los Angeles, just behind New York City and Chicago.[10] He also warned

6. Larson, "Tasting Revival," 18.

7. Roland Wild, "Brother, Can You Spare a Prayer?" *Illustrated* (London), December 31, 1949, page number not shown.

8. Graham, *Just as I Am*, 158.

9. Billy Graham, "Christianity vs. a Bloodless Religion," Hollywood, CA, 1951, http://billygraham.org/audio/christianity-vs-a-bloodless-religion.

10. Billy Graham, "We Need Revival," in *Revival in Our Time*, 75.

that Communists had proved more "rampant" in Los Angeles than in any other city in America.[11]

The Soviet Union and Red China themselves were threats, hardly less ominous than the bomb and the ideology of Communism. For months, the *Los Angeles Times*'s headlines had trumpeted the Soviet threat. "RED LOCKS HOLD ARCHBISHOP IN PRAGUE PALACE," blared one.[12] "Russ Girls Made Bait for Luring Tito Aides," said another.[13] Banners linked the Soviet threat with racial fears. "REVOLT PLOT: Plan of Reds for Negro Nation Told" stirred white anxieties—and sold papers. So did: "NEW YORK. A Georgia Negro who said he was trained in Moscow today testified that a Negro nation was to have been forged from America's Deep South by the flames of violent revolution."[14] The Soviet Union's lackey nation, Red China, aroused fears too. On April 22, 1949, readers awoke to learn that "RAF Alerted as Chinese Reds Still Blast Warships."[15] Shortly afterward they learned that "China Reds Capture Key Rail Town."[16] In the face of such perils, who could rest?

At home additional dangers lurked, and they looked nearly as grim. Recurrent economic downturns and the spiraling threat of juvenile delinquency rattled Americans' self-confidence. Beyond those hazards, wherever Graham looked on the American landscape—and he looked everywhere—he saw multiple threats: suicide, divorce, materialism, militarism, racism, and rampant sexual immorality. Graham often threw boredom into the mix too.[17]

The second stream of influence grew from the fervent and systematic work of the Christian Businessmen's Committee of Los Angeles (hereafter, the Committee). Like Graham himself, the Committee understood that revivals had to be "worked up as well as prayed down."[18] Combining forces with local parachurch organizations, such as Gideons,

11. Graham cited in Marshall Frady, *Billy Graham: A Parable of American Righteousness* (Boston: Little, Brown, 1979), 198.

12. *Los Angeles Times*, July 11, 1949.

13. *Los Angeles Times*, May 31, 1949.

14. *Los Angeles Times*, April 19, 1949.

15. *Los Angeles Times*, April 22, 1949.

16. *Los Angeles Times*, May 9, 1949.

17. See, for example, the sermon Graham preached the first night, September 25, 1949, "Prepare to Meet God (Amos 4 [7]:12," Tape T5703, Sermons, http://www2.whea ton.edu/bgc/archives/exhibits/LA49/05sermons01.html.

18. This phrase, often used in American religious history, probably started with reference to Charles Finney's revivals in the middle nineteenth century.

Navigators, Christian Endeavor, Christian Men, Child Evangelism, Salvation Army, and, especially, Youth for Christ (YFC), the Committee had started to plant the seeds early in the decade.[19] Between 1943 and 1949, it sponsored seventeen city-wide evangelistic meetings, led by nationally known figures such as Hyman Appleman, Merv Rosell, Jack Shuler, and Graham's close friend Charles Templeton (who later lost his faith). Though some of those meetings—especially the ones led by Rosell—posted impressive results, the Committee sought more.[20]

So it was that in April 1949 the members of the Committee invited a relatively untested young preacher from North Carolina to try his hand.[21] They already knew Graham. The Committee had sponsored him at the Hollywood Bowl in the summer of 1947.[22] And the following year they asked him to hold an evangelistic campaign in Los Angeles. He turned them down, thinking the time was not ripe. In 1949 they asked again. This time he agreed—but with conditions. The conditions required adding clergy to the Committee, finding a bigger tent, winning the support of local churches, and beefing up the budget—mostly for advertising—from $7,000 to the then-unheard-of sum of $25,000 (equivalent to $244,000 in 2013).[23]

Reflecting the relentless expansiveness that marked all of Graham's campaigns, the Committee made no small plans. In the eighteen months preceding the meeting, the members enlisted support from the entire Southern California region. It organized thousands of prayer meetings. Some ran all night. The Committee initiated "concerts of prayer" (that is, people praying at the same time of the day in multiple places) as well. Graham insisted that supporters' prayers formed the most important ingredient in the revival's success.[24] How-

19. Committee letterhead, July 28, 1949, "Preparation 7," http://www2.wheaton.edu/bgc/archives/exhibits/LA49/03prep07.html.

20. Martin, *Prophet with Honor*, 113; "Timeline," http://www2.wheaton.edu/bgc/archives/exhibits/LA49/10timeline.html; "Introduction," http://www2.wheaton.edu/bgc/archives/exhibits/LA49/01readmore.html.

21. "Protestants Plan City Revivals," *Los Angeles Times*, April 30, 1949, A-3. The Committee had issued the invitation the day before.

22. "Introduction," http://www2.wheaton.edu/bgc/archives/exhibits/LA49/01readmore.html; "Preparation 1," http://www2.wheaton.edu/bgc/archives/exhibits/LA49/03prep01.html.

23. "Timeline," http://www2.wheaton.edu/bgc/archives/exhibits/LA49/10timeline.html. The Committee eventually raised the budget to approximately $30,000, mostly for advertising and promotion.

24. Billy Graham, "I Tasted Revival," *Youth for Christ Magazine*, January 1950, 14.

ever assessed, any outsider could see that concerted systematic prayer galvanized popular interest. Zealots took the message door-to-door, neighborhood by neighborhood.

The Committee left no public-relations stone unturned. It sent letters to radio stations asking them to invite their listeners to attend every service possible. It placed ads in papers, and even nailed down a press conference with Los Angeles mayor Fletcher Bowron on the eve of the meetings—the very first press conference of Graham's life.[25] Bowron warmly endorsed the revival for its "great benefit to the city"[26]—portending the civic commendations that would shower down on Graham in the coming decades. To be sure, the Committee's effort to win the attention of the secular press saw little success in the first three weeks, but not for lack of trying.

The Committee's adroit use of popular advertising merits special attention. Blanketing the region with flyers, posters, and banners, the group heralded the "mammoth tent," "6000 free seats," "inspiring music," "unprecedented demands," "dynamic preaching," and "America's foremost evangelist." Adjectives such as "huge," "vital," "young," "golden," "thrilling," "dramatic," "magnetic," "eloquent," "compelling," "persuasive," "tremendous," "outstanding," "enthusiastic," "international," "interdenominational," and, perhaps best of all, "free," proliferated. The press joined the Committee choir, describing Graham as "America's most glamorous young preacher" and as "the most flamboyant item in the national scene." Hyperbole took no vacation.[27]

This multi-pronged advertising blitz fostered a sense that a historic watershed had been—or soon would be—crossed. The promise of "6000 free seats," for example, signified that something truly extraordinary was taking place. And since the seats were free, everyone could be a part of the spectacle, regardless of class, race, age, or gender. (More on that later.) "Dramatic preaching" guaranteed attenders that they would not get bored, as they might in an ordinary church service. "Glorious Music" recognized the emotional power of music, certainly not new to revival-

25. Graham, *Just as I Am*, 143.
26. "Bowron Backs Dr. Graham's Revival Drive," *Los Angeles Times*, September 25, 1949, A-3.
27. I take this terminology from a variety of promotional documents. Many of them are reproduced in "Into the Big Tent" (title for digital archival display), http://www 2.wheaton.edu/bgc/archives/exhibits/LA49/entrance.html, Billy Graham Center Archives, and in Busby, *Billy Graham*, 47-55.

ism, but strongly featured in these meetings with a large choir, two grand pianos, a skilled violinist, and the nightly artistry of choirmaster Cliff Barrows and soloist George Beverly Shea.[28]

Other ads bore other shadings of meaning, but they all conveyed the same message of exuberant expectancy. Banners such as "An International and Interdenominational Movement" and "Strictly non-political, inter-racial, church-promoting" had heralded Graham's Hollywood Bowl rally back in 1947.[29] "Hundreds of Churches Uniting" heralded, with equal fervor, the breadth of Graham's appeal now. And they intimated respectability, too.[30] Though sawdust covered the floor and canvas the canopy, the meeting drew well-dressed partisans to the very center of a bustling city, not to a skid-row mission or a backwoods redoubt.

The Committee took no chances. For more than two centuries evangelicals had worshiped a God who worked not only fast but also conspicuously. So did their advertising. They set up a "steeple of light" shooting hundreds of feet up into the night sky from the tent grounds. Beyond that, their broadsides made clear that time counted. The eternal destinies of mortal souls counted. "IF YOU WISH TO HELP SAVE THIS GREAT COMMUNITY FROM THE CURSE OF GODLESSNESS," read one poster, "VOLUNTEER TODAY!"[31]

The blitz paid off. As things turned out, more than one-fourth of Los Angeles area churches ended up supporting the revival in one way or another. No wonder. Everyone stood to gain. Graham timed the revival's meetings so that they would not conflict with regular church services. Meetings took place every night (except Sunday) at 7:30, and on Sundays at 3:00 and 8:45. Children's services on Saturday morning, and the Saturday night service that catered to youth interests, expanded the revival's demographic range. But Graham did more than that. He also made clear that he was not competing with local preachers. There was "little jealousy," he observed, perhaps a bit too jauntily, "for they recognize there have to be racehorses and plough-horses in every busi-

28. "Media 4," http://www2.wheaton.edu/bgc/archives/exhibits/LA49/06 media12.html.

29. "Preparation 1.1," http://www2.wheaton.edu/bgc/archives/exhibits/ LA49/03prep01-1.html.

30. "Photograph 2," http://www2.wheaton.edu/bgc/archives/exhibits/ LA49/02pictures02.html.

31. "Preparation 11," http://www2.wheaton.edu/bgc/archives/exhibits/ LA49/03prep11.html.

ness."[32] A British journalist shrewdly discerned that the Committee "knew something when it hired a searchlight, in the Hollywood premier style, and called its tent the 'canvas cathedral.'"[33]

The third stream of influence involved outside voices. After the revival got under way, the Committee's promotional materials began to blend with similar materials churned out by the local press. The two tributaries grew from different motivations—converts for one and revenue for the other—but the product was the same: to promote the size and vitality of the meetings. Together they formed a common marketing front that might be called, simply, the media.

Though the Committee had made clear before the revival started that this would not be a pulpit-pounding circus, after it started the broader media made equally clear that the campaign was not only respectable but also glamorous. And glamor attracted crowds. The media emphasized the support of Hollywood celebrities. "Film Folk Attending Tent," boasted the *Hollywood Citizen-News* in mid-October. Film folk included stars, grips, extras, and cameramen. Never reluctant to throw in a teaser, the press noted too the "lovely Colleen Townsend" attended the meetings.[34] (Many years later a *Los Angeles Times* reporter recounted how the actress Jane Russell—"a sassy, brassy, buxom bomb shell"—also had been there, "'wheeling a former soldier, wounded in the war, down that sawdust aisle to meet Billy and receive the Lord.'"[35]) Respectability and glamor were not the sole attractions, of course, but they added to the allure. Photographers captured long lines outside the tent, anxious souls hoping to get in but too late for a seat. Lest anyone miss the point, journalists connected the dots. "Last Sunday more than 20,000 people came to the big tent. Thousands were obliged to stand outside at both services," ran a typical headline. "COME EARLY TO AVOID STANDING."[36]

The media also readily fell into the outlook that everyone everywhere had their eyes fixed squarely on events in Los Angeles, and the reverse. "This campaign has taken on nation-wide significance," one promoter

32. Graham quoted in Wild, "Brother, Can You Spare a Prayer?" page number not shown.

33. Wild, "Brother, Can You Spare a Prayer?" 29.

34. *Hollywood Citizen-News*, October 15, 1949, 7, "Media 5," 7, http://www2.whea ton.edu/bgc/archives/exhibits/LA49/06media05.html.

35. Cecilia Rasmussen, "L.A. Then and Now," *Los Angeles Times*, September 2, 2007.

36. Los Angeles *Daily News*, October 26, 1949, 21, "During 2," http://www2.whea ton.edu/bgc/archives/exhibits/LA49/04during02.html.

urged before the meetings started.[37] And after they started, the prospects grew even more impressive: "ALL THE WORLD IS TALKING ABOUT GREATER L.A.'s GREATEST REVIVAL!"[38] This outlook intimated explosive as well as implosive images: "7TH TRIUMPHANT WEEK!"—"AMERICA's FOREMOST EVANGELIST CONTINUES BY PUBLIC DEMAND"; or again: "BURSTING AT THE SEAMS WITH REVIVAL ENTHUSIASM."[39] Such reports, both visual and narrative, suggested something like a truck-stop-diner mentality: if a lot of cars are there, it must be good.

The media also showcased Graham's formal educational credentials. By the standards of the secular academy they proved modest: degrees from two unaccredited Bible institutes and a bachelor's degree from Wheaton College, a respected though fundamentalist institution near Chicago. And during the campaign he observed—perhaps a bit disingenuously—that God had chosen to use a "country boy," not someone with a fancy PhD or DD.[40] But in 1947 Graham had accepted an invitation to serve as president of another fundamentalist enterprise known as Northwestern Schools (a Bible institute, college, and seminary) in Minneapolis. He served that post for five years as the youngest college president in the nation.

Media coverage focused on the college president part of his working dossier. They stressed that Northwestern Schools enrolled fully 1,500 students. They pointed out that Graham held "two American honorary collegiate degrees, D.D. and Dr. of humanities, and two degrees from England, Fellow of the Royal Geographic Society and Master of the Royal Literary Society."[41] Before the revival even started, the *Los Angeles Times* introduced the preacher as "Dr. William Frank Graham," and soon the Associated Press did too.[42] Graham let people know that he had been to

37. C. C. Jenkins, Executive Director, the Committee, to [blank], September 6, 1949, "Media 1," http://www2.wheaton.edu/bgc/archives/exhibits/LA49/06media01 .html.

38. Newspaper ad, November 8, 1949, "During 7," http://www2.wheaton.edu/bgc/ archives/exhibits/LA49/04during07.html.

39. Ad in *Pasadena Independent*, November 15, 1949, "During 9," http://www2 .wheaton.edu/bgc/archives/exhibits/LA49/04during09.html.

40. Graham quoted in Frady, *Billy Graham*, 199.

41. "Thousands Throng Tent Site to Hear Evangelist Preach," *Los Angeles Evening and Herald Express*, October 27, 1949, B-9, "Media 6," http://www2.wheaton.edu/bgc/ archives/exhibits/LA49/06media06.html.

42. "Tent Crusader's Drive Likened to Billy Sunday," *Los Angeles Times*, September

Europe six times, invoking the authority of the seasoned traveler.[43] Despite his youth, the preacher implied, he knew what was going on in the world. He could be trusted.

The fourth stream of influence grew from the momentum released by Graham's own experiences just before the revival as well as his style of self-presentation once it began. In August 1949, he remembered, he had struggled through a terrible crisis of faith. His close friend and onetime associate Charles Templeton—who was going through a spiritual crisis of his own—badgered him about the Bible's authority in the face of modern higher criticism. Hoping to find clarity about his commitments, Graham decamped to a spiritual retreat center in the San Bernadino Mountains outside Los Angeles. Lost in prayer, he came to the conclusion that, even though the Bible said many things he did not understand, he would embrace it by faith—which was to say, by an act of raw volition. The narrative quickly gained wheels, and it reappeared ever after in virtually every account of Graham's spiritual pilgrimage. Though this story, like all creation stories, merits close analysis, the key point for present purposes is that Graham already had come to see himself and his ministry in crisis terms days before the tent meeting began.

And then there was Graham's style of self-presentation. Besides smashing good looks, he knew how to dress and play the part of a man destined to strike a mark on the historical record. Journalists called him—take your choice—"Barrymore of the Bible," "Gabriel in Gabardine," and "Hollywood . . . John the Baptist."[44] Outfitted in pastel suits, billowing kerchief, hand-painted ties, flaming argyle socks, and wide-brimmed hats, he came across—as his own advance billing put it—as "tall, slender, handsome." The billing went on: "[W]ith a curly shock of blond hair, Graham looks like a collar ad, acts like a motion picture star, thinks like a psychology professor, talks like a North Carolinian and preaches like a combination of Billy Sunday and Dwight L. Moody. . . . He uses few illustrations, no sob stories, absolutely no deathbed stuff."[45] One paper

24, 1949; AP News Release, November 2, 1949, "Media 12," http://www2.wheaton.edu/bgc/archives/exhibits/LA49/06media12.html.

43. "Evangelist Opens Revival Crusade," *Los Angeles Times*, September 26, 1949, 24.

44. For the first two see "Billy Graham: Young Thunderer of Revival," *Newsweek*, February 1, 1954, 44; for the third see Martin, *Prophet with Honor*, 186.

45. Quoted in Nancy Gibbs and Michael Duffy, "The Preacher and the Presidents: Billy Graham in the White House" (Miller Center for Public Affairs, University of Virginia, n.d.), 5.

said it more succinctly: "Graham . . . hypnotizes the six thousand nightly by a blend of good showmanship, common sense and a fine voice that lasts out two full hours of exhortation."[46]

But of course the main thing was not Graham's looks or dress or style but the theological content of his preaching. Few considered him a pulpit prince, but no one doubted his effectiveness. The substance of his memorized sermons proved predictable, night after night. Years later, one of Graham's close associates said, "If you have heard Billy ten times, you probably have heard all of his sermons."[47] Actually, if followers had heard Billy *one* time, they had heard them all. Sooner or later every one of them circled around to what was, in effect, the same text: John 3:16: "For God so loved the world that he gave his only Son so that whoever believes in him shall not perish but have everlasting life." In every sermon of every service, Graham would say, he drove for a verdict.[48]

The messages followed a familiar format. Graham began with a litany of national and international perils that people had brought on themselves—Communism, depressions, immorality, and crime, among others. Evangelists in other eras had spoken of the perils of the times, but Graham's evocation seemed broader in scope and fiercer in consequences. The unprecedented terrors of the atomic age heightened the gravity of the threat. In his very first sermon, delivered Sunday afternoon, September 25, 1949, Graham reminded his audience that just two days earlier the nuclear age had dawned. War was closer than they thought. "Russia has now exploded an atomic bomb!"[49] And though the dangers were natural in the sense that humans had brought them upon themselves, they also were supernatural in the sense that Satan stood behind them.

This litany of external perils paralleled internal ones of meaninglessness, loneliness, addictions, backsliding, and faithlessness. And all of those maladies ultimately grew from a single source: the sinful heart. Graham made clear that sin was innate—what theologians called original sin—but it manifested itself in sinful acts, which played themselves out right now, right here, in the present. Yet the good news was that cleansing

46. Roland Wild, "Brother, Can You Spare a Prayer?" page number not shown.

47. Gerald Beaven quoted in Deborah H. (Hart) Strober and Gerald S. Strober, *Billy Graham: An Oral and Narrative Biography* (San Francisco: Jossey-Bass, 2006), 135.

48. Stanley High, *Billy Graham: The Personal Story of the Man, His Message, and His Mission* (New York: McGraw-Hill, 1956), 52.

49. Billy Graham, "Why a Revival?" September 25, 1949, T5701, http://www2.wheaton.edu/bgc/archives/exhibits/LA49/05sermons01.html, at 13:43.

from both kinds of sin—inherited and actual—led to a new life in Christ. This new life was available to anyone simply for the asking. Believe that Christ died for your sins, he boomed, receive Christ into your hearts, and then live lives of faith and holiness.

If the content of Graham's sermons proved predictable, so did the manner of delivery. Graham never described himself as theatrical, but the adjective fit. One reporter later said that he revealed "the coiled tension of a panther."[50] He preached fast, as if fated never to preach again. One stenographer clocked him at 240 words a minute.[51] Many called him "God's machine-gun."[52] The speed was intentional. Graham self-consciously adopted the rapid-fire delivery of successful radio newscasters such as Walter Winchell and H. B. Kaltenborn. And then there was the volume. Many years later Graham remembered that one magazine had dubbed him "trumpet-lunged."[53] In Los Angeles, he really did "yell a lot," said one associate.[54] In later decades—when Graham's preaching more resembled an avuncular fireside chat—he freely admitted that back in those days he had preached very fast and very loud.

Throughout, Graham quoted the Bible from memory—rapidly, accurately, and frequently. An oversized cardboard poster of an open Bible, standing in front of the pulpit, underscored the Bible's centrality.[55] Equally important, the poster portrayed the Bible as open, making clear that it was available to anyone who chose to read and accept it. In a Bible-steeped culture, that strategy—born of deep conviction that the Bible contained God's authoritative answer to every problem—added layers of authority.

In an age when military heroes and dashing movie stars figured large, Graham exploited the wider culture's esteem for traditional images of masculinity, especially when he preached. He shook his right fist or aimed his right index finger at the audience like a cocked pistol. Quoting

50. Elizabeth Kaye, "Billy Graham Rises," *George*, December 1996, 140.

51. Martin, *Prophet with Honor*, 96.

52. For one of many references to this phrase see "Will Graham," in *Chicken Soup for the Soul: Billy Graham and Me; 101 Inspiring Personal Stories from Presidents, Pastors, Performers, and Other People Who Know Him Well*, ed. Steve Posner, Amy Newmark, and A. Larry Ross (Cos Cob, CT: Chicken Soup for the Soul Publishing, 2013), 174.

53. Graham, *Just as I Am*, 150.

54. Strober and Strober, *Billy Graham*, 41.

55. "Photograph 7," http://www2.wheaton.edu/bgc/archives/exhibits/LA49/02pictures07.html.

the Bible fifty to one hundred times in a sermon, Graham later allowed that he fired passages like "ammunition."[56] Elsewhere he switched the metaphor and spoke of the Bible "slashing into men's consciousness."[57] At the end of the sermon, he forthrightly invited individuals to stand up and walk to the front. No one doubted that he commanded the situation. There was, said one observer, "no sugary voice pleading for people to come to Christ. It was a manly approach." The invitations stopped only when the people stopped. In most services, hundreds of men and women made the long trek to the front.

But not in the first few weeks. The success of the revival has obscured our vision of how hard it was won. Despite concerts of prayer, meticulous organization, multiple neighborhood committees, and vast and intense publicity, the revival got off to a rocky start. Initially the Committee had scheduled it to run three weeks, from Sunday, September 25, to Sunday, October 16. In those weeks the crowds ran a respectable two to three thousand per night, but since the tent seated more than six thousand, ushers found themselves spreading out the chairs to make it look full. The Committee whipped up a press conference the day before the meetings started, but it was poorly attended. Except for one short article published way back on page 24 in the *Los Angeles Times* the day after the meeting started, the local papers initially paid little attention.[58] "As far as the media were concerned," Graham later remembered, "the Los Angeles Campaign—by far our most ambitious evangelistic effort to date—was going to be a nonevent."[59] The Committee placed ads, and neighborhood churches slipped notices into their usual spots on the church page, but otherwise the revival seemed destined to follow the path of most revivals: earnest support for a few days, maybe a few weeks, but nothing to make the history books. Unseasonably cold weather did not help.

Toward the end of the third week, Graham, song leader Cliff Barrows, soloist George Beverly Shea, and the Committee fell into consultation and prayer about whether the revival should stop or whether it should continue past the scheduled closing date. Uncertain, they, like Gideon in the Old Testament, decided on a "fleece" (or test) to see what God wanted them to do. The fleece was the weather. On Sunday, October

56. Graham, "I Tasted Revival!" 13.
57. Graham quoted in Martin, *Prophet with Honor*, 112.
58. "Evangelist Opens Revival Crusade," *Los Angeles Times*, September 26, 1949, 24.
59. Graham, *Just as I Am*, 143.

16—the very day the revival had been scheduled to close—God answered their request with warm winds. The flaps on the tent, initially lowered to conserve heat, now had to be raised.

On Monday, October 17, Stuart ("Stew") Hamblen came to faith in an early morning meeting with Graham at the hotel where he was staying. Hamblen, the son of a Texas Methodist preacher, was a storied country performer, radio show host, and local celebrity, not known for piety. The following day—October 18—Hamblen gave his testimony on his radio program, and later told the tent audience about his "return to the teachings of Christ."[60] With this exposure, the crowds grew and the Committee extended the campaign for another two weeks. Hamblen would write the *Hit Parade* favorites "Tis No Secret (What God Can Do)" and "This Ole House" to herald his new birth.[61]

Additional celebrity conversions and the resulting publicity fueled the revival. The most famous was Louis Zamperini. He was an Olympic track star and survivor of a brutal Japanese prisoner-of-war camp, but after his return home in 1945 his life had fallen apart. Facing divorce, alcoholism, and severe post-traumatic stress, he visited the tent sometime in the fifth week, found Christ, and spent the rest of his long life as a Christian speaker on the power of forgiveness. Zamperini's biographer, Laura Hillenbrand, tellingly said that when he returned to Japan and unsuccessfully offered to forgive his principal tormenter in prison, "the war was over." Zamperini remained closely associated with Graham's ministry for more than six decades. He died in 2014 at the age of ninety-seven.[62]

Even at this early stage of his career, Graham understood the power of celebrity testimonies. The word of the satisfied customer outpointed that of any debater, let alone any textbook writer. He knew too the power of trophy converts. In his first sermon he boasted that "movie people"

---

60. "Stuart Hamblen Hits Sawdust Trail at Revival," *Los Angeles Examiner*, November 1, 1949, front page.

61. Martin, *Prophet with Honor*, 117; Larson, "Tasting Revival," 15. The date Hamblen spoke to the campaign crowd is not clear, but probably within a week and not later than October 31, 1949. "Timeline," http://www2.wheaton.edu/bgc/archives/exhibits/LA49/10timeline.html; "Louis Zamperini, Stuart Hamblen Turn to Teachings of Billy Graham at Revival," newspaper clipping, November 1, 1949, "Media 11," http://www2.wheaton.edu/bgc/archives/exhibits/LA49/06media11.html.

62. "Timeline," http://www2.wheaton.edu/bgc/archives/exhibits/LA49/10timeline.html; Laura Hillenbrand, *Unbroken: A World War II Story of Survival, Resilience, and Redemption* (New York: Random House, 2010), 380.

were coming. And he discerned that people who had veered across polite society's boundaries, and then came back to safety, exerted a special appeal. One suspects that prodigal sons and daughters proved especially persuasive to Graham's conventional, middle-class, church-going audiences.

The improved weather and Hamblen's well-publicized endorsement saw powerful reinforcement in another event that transpired early in the fourth week. One night, walking into the tent, Graham found the scene swarming with reporters, notepads open and flash bulbs popping. When he asked what was going on, one journalist told him, "You have been kissed by William Randolph Hearst." Purportedly Hearst had told his reporters, "Puff Graham."[63] In the next few days the Los Angeles *Examiner* and the Los Angeles *Herald Express*, both owned by the publishing tycoon, showcased stories about Graham's revival. Soon the Associated Press, United Press, International News Service, and *London Daily Mail* ran accounts too. On November 14 *Time* magazine jumped in, with "Sickle for the Harvest." A week later *Time*'s cousin publication, *Life*, with a readership of 25 million, ran its own piece, "A Rising Young Evangelist." *Newsweek*, *Quick*, and the *Los Angeles Times* (which Hearst did not own) joined the parade. Graham and the press not only had found each other but also found the marriage enormously beneficial. Over the years Graham gained vast publicity—mostly positive—from the press. The press in turn gained a steady source of revenue from the stories about the invariably affable, photogenic, and loquacious evangelist.

Folded into this story was another one, not particularly important in itself, but one that gained importance for what it revealed about how legends develop and the impact they hold. Though Hearst had spent a year at an Episcopal prep school in New England,[64] he was not known as a man of deep religious, let alone evangelical, convictions. "[T]he fact that Mr. Hearst was involved . . . will be proof enough to some that the Lord was not," one editor quipped.[65] So three questions arose: How did Hearst hear about Graham, why did Hearst decide to promote Graham, and how did Hearst communicate his interest in Graham to his editors?[66]

---

63. Graham, *Just as I Am*, 150.

64. Kenneth Whyte, *The Uncrowned King: The Sensational Rise of William Randolph Hearst* (Berkeley, CA: Counterpoint, 2009), 18–19.

65. High, *Billy Graham*, 148.

66. My discussion of Hearst here and in the following paragraphs draws on Kevin K.

The answer to all three questions remains murky. As for the first one—how Hearst heard about the revival—one story held that one of his house-keepers had told him about it, another that the Holy Spirit had directed the housekeeper to do so, and still another that Hearst had caught wind of the meetings and slipped in, in disguise, with his mistress Marion Davies. Many years later Graham admitted that he did not know which story was true.[67] The most credible narrative is that the Committee as well as Graham himself had worked hard behind the scenes, through intermediaries, to win Hearst's attention.[68] In any event, the reason for Hearst's interest was more evident. The tycoon held robust political views: fiercely pro-American and fiercely anti-Communist. Less well known is that in some ways he was also progressive: he supported women's rights and opposed trusts, long hours, and racial stereotyping—anything that exploited ordinary people.[69] Most important, perhaps, he strongly supported a well-ordered society.

That final conviction, the need for a well-ordered society, likely had prompted Hearst to support Youth for Christ (YFC) at least as far back as 1946. The organization had emerged in the early 1940s, mainly in New York, Philadelphia, and especially Chicago. It aimed to provide "wholesome" entertainment, patriotic uplift, and evangelistic appeal to servicemen and women returned from military duty, as well as crowds of adolescents and young adults crowding city streets at night.[70] Graham actually got his start in big-city evangelism at a YFC rally at Orchestra Hall in Chicago, May 27, 1944—ten days before D-Day. He stayed with YFC for about four years, gradually mixing YFC meetings with ones he organized on his own. By the time of the 1949 Los Angeles meeting, Graham was working independently, but YFC had left its mark. His aggressive, flamboyant style and hard-hitting message had been forged on the anvil of YFC meetings in the United States and Europe. Many people

Wright, "Printing Graham's Gospel: William Randolph Hearst, Billy Graham, and the Good News of America," seminar paper, Duke University, 2008, in my possession.

67. Graham, *Just as I Am*, 150. Hearst's two sons affirmed the third story. Larry B. Stammer, "Billy Graham Is Frail, but Mission Is Strong," *Los Angeles Times*, November 17, 2004.

68. See Martin, *Prophet with Honor*, 115-20, 636n117.

69. David Nasaw, *The Chief: The Life of William Randolph Hearst* (Boston: Houghton Mifflin, 2000), 380; Ben Procter, *William Randolph Hearst: The Early Years, 1863-1910* (New York: Oxford University Press, 1998), 136, 147. I owe these references to my research assistant, Katie Benjamin.

70. Bruce L. Shelley, "The Rise of Evangelical Youth Movements," *Fides et Historia* 18, no. 1 (1982): 45-63.

who were not conspicuously religious, including President Harry Truman, liked YFC. Americans lived in perilous times, and YFC seemed to offer solutions, especially to the growing threat of juvenile delinquency. So it was not surprising that in 1946 Hearst sent a memo to his editors urging them to "Puff *YFC*" (my emphasis).

"Puff YFC" eventually became "Puff Graham." But it took time. Two early insider books about Graham, published in 1950 and 1951, did not mention Hearst, let alone the "Puff Graham" story.[71] Stanley High's 1956 biography, *Billy Graham: The Personal Story of the Man, His Message, and His Mission*, seems the first instance in which a serious biographer claimed that Hearst had sent his reporters a directive to "Puff *Graham*" (my emphasis).[72] Most subsequent biographies, including well-researched ones by William McLoughlin (1960) and John Pollock (1966), picked up the tale. Graham repeated it in his 1997 memoir, but he admitted that he did not know if it was true.[73] In 1983 Patricia Cornwell's biography of Ruth Bell Graham cast serious doubt. No hard copy of the directive ever materialized, and Hearst's son denied it, claiming that his father probably had said, "[G]ive attention to Billy Graham's meetings." William Martin's exhaustively researched biography of 1991 offered additional reasons to question the story.[74]

In one sense the "Puff Graham" tale is unimportant, but in another sense it is very important. It not only amplified Hearst's role but also created an impression that Graham's Los Angeles campaign owed its success to a random comment by a wealthy and powerful businessman who had a political and financial interest in the preacher's work. It erroneously implied, in other words, that the revival had just tumbled from the sky like a sacred meteor. That image served the purposes of hagiographers looking for divine intervention as well as debunkers looking for simple accidents.

After Hearst took notice, the Committee extended the revival another week, and then another, and then one more, for a total of eight. Some people wanted it to go on indefinitely, but Graham had reached his limit. He had preached all the sermons he knew, started borrowing ser-

71. The books are *Revival in Our Time* and *America's Hour of Decision: Including a Life Story of Billy Graham* (Wheaton, IL: Van Kampen Press, 1951). I owe this insight to Bob Shuster, Billy Graham Center Archives archivist, email to me, February 5, 2011.

72. High, *Billy Graham*, 148.

73. Graham, *Just as I Am*, 150.

74. Patricia Cornwell, *Ruth, a Portrait: The Story of Ruth Bell Graham* (New York: Doubleday, 1997), 86; Martin, *Prophet with Honor*, 115-20, 636n117.

mons from friends, and even replayed (with credit) Jonathan Edwards's eighteenth-century fire-breathing masterpiece, "Sinners in the Hands of an Angry God." The Committee had enlarged the tent to nine thousand, and additional thousands stood outside. One night fifteen thousand reportedly jammed the grounds.[75]

These considerations bring us finally to ask, why did the people come in the first place? Graham was disarmingly candid. "People came to the meetings for all sorts of reasons." Some were religious and some were not. "No doubt some were simply curious to see what was going on. Others were skeptical and dropped by just to confirm their prejudices." Graham admitted, with a wink, that a Los Angeles county judge "thought a night in the tent might do convicted offenders more good than a night in jail."[76] Yet in Graham's memory "many were desperate over some crisis in their lives and hoped they might get a last chance to set things right." The Rev. Edward O. Garver, a night watchman, echoed Graham's judgment that the revival offered visitors a life-changing experience. He "heard the shuffling of feet in the sawdust, sobs in the darkness," said the *Los Angeles Times* in 1949.[77]

Something like nostalgia undoubtedly played a role too. Photographic evidence suggests that the audiences were overwhelmingly white, middle aged, and middle class. For that matter, most dressed as if they had just come from Sunday school.[78] Many undoubtedly sought ratification of "main street" values that they held dear: family, neighborhood, thrift, and self-reliance.[79] There are good reasons to believe that many—perhaps a majority—of the people who streamed into Graham's tent night after night were recent migrants from the South and the Midwest, where those values remained strong.[80]

75. Graham, "I Tasted Revival!" 14.

76. Graham, *Just as I Am*, 153.

77. Edward O. Garver, paraphrased in William A. Moses, "Watchman in Night Prays with Strays," *Los Angeles Times*, November 5, 1949, A-2.

78. See, for example, "Tent Revival Ends after Eight Weeks," *Los Angeles Times*, November 21, 1949, 20; Busby, *Billy Graham*, 51.

79. The journalist/historian Lou Cannon, drawing on a *Newsweek* article, saw these values in Ronald Reagan. I see them in Graham, too. Lou Cannon, *President Reagan: The Role of a Lifetime* (New York: Public Affairs, 1991), 435.

80. Darren Dochuk, *From Bible Belt to Sunbelt: Plain-Folk Religion, Grassroots Politics, and the Rise of Evangelical Conservatism* (New York: Norton, 2011), xv–xvi, 106–10, 173. See also James N. Gregory, "The Southern Diaspora and the Urban Dispossessed," *Journal of American History* (June 1985): 113, 118.

However explained, Graham estimated that 82 percent of the people who made Christian commitments had never been church members,[81] but that figure probably was too high. If the pattern in Los Angeles replicated the pattern of later crusades—one well studied by historians and sociologists—a minority came to Christ for the first time, but the majority reaffirmed commitments grown cold.[82] For them, Graham did not so much convert them to something new as call them back to something old.[83] He reminded them of who they once were and who they now wished themselves to be, both individually and collectively as a society. They crossed a boundary.

In a variety of ways, Graham, the Committee, the press, and later observers seemed somehow to sense that what was taking place in the tent in Los Angeles in the fall of 1949 marked a turn to something definably different in the history of American revivalism. Graham could not peer into his own future, of course, nor did he pretend to do so. But from the outset he did sense that the 1949 meeting marked a new departure. "[T]his is going to be the greatest revival Los Angeles has ever seen," he trumpeted in the very first sermon. He soon realized, however, that it was easier to proclaim the revival's singularity than to live with it. He was dismayed when the newspapers started to quote him. "[S]omething has broken out that is way beyond me," he admitted to a friend. Graham found the frenzied attention that he and his wife Ruth received on the train heading home to Minneapolis unnerving. Reporting the events of the previous eight weeks to the students in Northwestern School's chapel the next day, he broke down. The preacher had just turned thirty-one.[84] "Almost overnight," he remembered a half-century later, "we became nationally known." "Everywhere we turned, someone wanted us to come and do for them what had been done in Los Angeles."[85] The stunning success of his next revival, which opened New Year's Eve in Boston, surely confirmed in his mind that Los Angeles had catapulted onto the arc of history.

81. Graham, *Just as I Am*, 157.

82. Wacker, *America's Pastor*, 263-64. In 2009 the Billy Graham Archives said that "3,000 inquirers" registered "first time" decisions, "3,000 more made other decisions, such as recommitting their lives," and 1,600 children made decisions at children meetings, although "it is unclear whether these were in addition to the 3,000 inquirers." "Statistics," http://www2.wheaton.edu/bgc/archives/exhibits/LA49/14statistics.html.

83. Frady, *Billy Graham*, 197.

84. Martin, *Prophet with Honor*, 120.

85. Graham, *Just as I Am*, xx, 158.

Other partisans too soon sensed that something special had taken place in the campaign in Los Angeles. Their comments helped to mortise that sense into memory. Within months, Fuller Theological Seminary founder Charles E. Fuller judged that the "harvest" was being "reaped all over the country."[86] At the same time, Mel Larson, one of Graham's first biographers, offered a similar observation: "Revival flowed through Billy Graham at that time until the whole world was conscious of it."[87] The first full-length biography, published in 1956 by Stanley High, editor of *Reader's Digest*, observed that Graham's associates divided his career into two parts: before and after Los Angeles. "Prologue" was how they presciently labeled the years before that fateful campaign.[88]

Outsiders held similar notions. Journalists often employed what might be called pivot or benchmark imagery. *Time* magazine observed that in the Los Angeles campaign contributions averaged twenty-five cents per person, compared with the usual seven cents per person.[89] Both during and after the meetings, the press compared Graham favorably to Aimee Semple McPherson[90] and, more often, to Billy Sunday. For one reporter, Graham ranked as "America's mid-century Billy Sunday." For another, he was the "outstanding young evangelist of this generation."[91] The same issue of *Time* magazine judged that Graham "[wielded] the revival sickle as no one since Billy Sunday."[92] Pivot imagery emerged in additional ways. "That old time religion has gone modern as an atomic bomb in the thunderous revival meetings that Rev Billy Graham conducts nightly."[93] There it was in a sentence. With Graham, the revival tradition had entered the atomic age.

86. Charles D. Fuller, "Introduction," in *Revival in Our Time*, 6.

87. Larson, "Tasting Revival," 11.

88. High, *Billy Graham*, 134.

89. "Sickle for the Harvest," *Time*, November 14, 1949.

90. See, for example, Wild, "Brother, Can You Spare a Prayer?," page number not shown.

91. Both lines quoted in an ad, accompanying a news article, in the *Los Angeles Mirror*, September 24, 1949, 11. The Committee likely supplied the ad itself, but the words were carefully quoted, including an ellipsis, suggesting that they came from elsewhere. "Media 2," http://www2.wheaton.edu/bgc/archives/exhibits/LA49/06media02.html.

92. "Sickle for the Harvest."

93. Richard Reynolds, "That Old Time Religion Goes Modern," *Los Angeles Daily News*, September 30, 1949, 3, shown in "Media 4," http://www2.wheaton.edu/bgc/archives/exhibits/LA49/06media04.html.

CHAPTER 12

Lausanne '74 and American Evangelicalism's Latin Turn

Darren Dochuk

It is hardly novel to label the International Congress on World Evangelization held July 1974 in Lausanne, Switzerland, a "turning point" in the history of modern American evangelicalism. A legion of pundits has already identified it as the start of something new.

Take, for instance, the prominent church leaders who cite this event as "seismic" in their vocational development and the movement they help to guide. Widely acclaimed pastor John Piper recalls sitting in awe as speakers such as congress organizer Ralph Winter upended his worldview. A Cal Tech–trained engineer and Fuller Seminary professor, Winter delivered a paper challenging conventional assumptions that Christianity had already penetrated "every political country." With charts and pointer in hand, the technocrat implored delegates to recognize that 2.5 billion people remained cut off from the gospel, and the way to reach them was to identify them as "people groups" possessing unique cultural characteristics, whose embrace of God's word would come only through sophisticated outreach methods. "At the Lausanne Congress," Piper muses, "Winter reached up and pulled the unseen rope called 'unreached peoples' that rang a bell that reverberates to this day. It gripped me." It gripped well-known Reverend Rick Warren too: "Ralph Winter engineered a revolution and it changed all of us," he reflects. "No one would ever look at the world again the same after that. It influenced an entire generation." Warren, Piper, and their generation would indeed take the inspiration and lessons of Lausanne '74 and translate them into decades-long ministries of international breadth. Appropriately enough, in the early 2000s several publications (including *Time* magazine) compiled rankings of the "most influential evangelicals" in America, on which they included these two pastors and their mentor. In no small way, these "who's who" lists testified to the enduring force of the religious awakening that Winter helped to initiate in Switzerland during the 1970s and Piper and Warren helped carry into the new millennium.[1]

Several religious historians concur with Piper and Warren that Lausanne '74 should be singled out in the chronicles of modern American evangelicalism as the moment everything changed. Students of missiology stand at the fore when it comes to highlighting Lausanne's significance. As Al Tizon declares,

> By its sheer attendance and worldwide representation, by its ambitious scope yet clear evangelistic focus, and by its accomplishments in both theological reflection and strategic mobilization, the July 1974 International Congress on World Evangelization held in Lausanne, Switzerland stands alone in the annals of evangelical mission history.

A "watershed event" in missions, Lausanne also marked a breakthrough in evangelicalism's structuring. Grant Wacker notes that this congress facilitated the coming together of "a worldwide community of fellow travellers" who shared principal convener Billy Graham's desire to "meet personally" for the first time, frame a culturally sensitive vision of evangelism, and construct an ecumenism that could rival the World Council of Churches in terms of impact. Lausanne, in this way—and as historian David King agrees—"proved that evangelicalism had circled the globe." Lausanne also revealed evangelicalism's turn toward a different sensibility. "Lausanne marked the internationalization of evangelicalism," Fred Beuttler writes, affirming David King and Grant

---

1. Steve Shadrach, "The Legacy of Lausanne 1974: 40 Years Later and a Personal Look at the Man behind the Revolution," Center for Mission Mobilization, http://www .mobilization.org/blog/the-legacy-of-lausanne-1974/; "Ralph Winter: Looking for the Hidden Peoples," *Christianity Today*, September 7, 1981; http://www.missionfrontiers. org/issue/article/remembering-a-life-well-lived-tributes-from-around-the-world. See "The 25 Most Influential Evangelicals in America," *Time*, February 7, 2005. Piper was not included on this list, but was cited in other related and subsequent (and equally impressionistic) lists as one of America's most important evangelical leaders. Piper and Warren proved their indebtedness to Winter and the Lausanne movement by supporting subsequent Lausanne Congresses in Manila, Philippines (1989), and Cape Town, South Africa (2010).

Wacker, but in a way that for the first time shattered "the division between missionary-sending and missionary-receiving nations" and shifted evangelical confidences and mandates from Western-centrism to a new "Great Commission" dictated by the sensitivities of the "two-thirds" developing world.[2]

No historian has done more to highlight the importance of the Lausanne Congress than Mark Noll, a man who found himself alongside Winter, Warren, and Piper on evangelicalism's "who's who" lists mentioned above. In *Turning Points: Decisive Moments in the History of Christianity*, Noll underscores the importance of Lausanne '74 by pairing it with another event of serious consequence: the Second Vatican Council. "No single event has occupied the same place for the evangelical-Pentecostal-independent cohort" as Vatican II, he acknowledges, nor was Lausanne an "exact parallel." Still, in both cases, "the meetings shone a spotlight on new directions and, in some measure, contributed themselves to shaping the moves in those new directions." Noll cites several of Lausanne '74's key outcomes: it drew a multitude of the world's evangelical Christians together in one conclave, defined common theological grounds on which they could act, voiced a wish for reconciliation and spiritual regeneration on local and international scales, mapped out these ideals in one document (the "Lausanne Covenant"), and established institutional mechanisms that would allow the "Lausanne Movement" to continue for years to come. Both events, Noll summarizes, represented shifts "to broader conceptions of faith—Vatican II by expanding attention to the laity and coming out clearly for universal religious freedom, Lausanne by drawing explicitly on Majority World insights and coming out clearly for the necessity of social action to accompany evangelism." He concludes by hedging his bets. "Whether or not responsible students at the end of the twenty-first century will identify the Second Vatican Council and the Lausanne Congress on World Evangelization as *the* key turning points of the late twentieth century," Noll writes, "both events will probably still

2. Al Tizon, *Transformation after Lausanne: Radical Evangelical Mission in Global-Local Perspective* (Eugene, OR: Wipf & Stock, 2008), 37; Grant Wacker, *America's Pastor: Billy Graham and the Shaping of a Nation* (Cambridge, MA: Harvard University Press, 2014), 18; David P. King, "Seeking a Global Vision: The Evolution of World Vision and American Evangelicalism" (PhD diss., Emory University, 2012), 173; Fred W. Beuttler, "Evangelical Missions in Modern America," in *The Great Commission: Evangelicals and the History of World Missions*, ed. Martin I. Klauber and Scott M. Manetsch (Nashville: B&H Publishing Group, 2008), 126–27.

demand attention as significant signposts in the ongoing history of the Christian faith."[3]

Signposts indeed, and, more likely than not, "*the* key turning points of the late twentieth century." Though it may still be too early to make the pronouncement Noll artfully dodges in his parting words, this declaration is a surer bet than the dean of religious history lets on, certainly with regard to Vatican II, but also with respect to its Protestant counterpart. Testimonials from those whose attendance reshaped their futures, careful study by leading scholars, and sheer numbers of participants all suggest that Lausanne '74 did change evangelicalism radically, and forever. As an event that drew together 2,700 evangelicals from one hundred fifty different countries and seven continents, Lausanne '74's public promise "to take the whole gospel to the whole world" was legitimate. *Time* magazine described it as "possibly the widest ranging meeting of Christians ever held," and it was indeed that. By all measures, in other words, Lausanne '74 was spectacularly reorienting in the way it thrust evangelicalism—US evangelicalism in particular—out of its insularities into the chronic give-and-take of a boundless and dynamically plural new world order.[4]

When surveying Lausanne '74 at a slightly lower altitude, one can identify yet another reason why this congress proved to be so reorienting. The purview required here is hemispheric rather than global, and calibrated to a south-north axis of exchange. As much as this global gathering in Switzerland turned American evangelicalism's gaze toward distant shores across the Pacific and Atlantic Oceans and onto African, Asian, and European soil, in dramatic fashion Lausanne also revealed evolving forces of change that were committing American evangelicalism to a Latin turn. Through their outsized importance at the conference several evangelical spokesmen from Latin America challenged evangelicals to take seriously a gospel of revolution that had been nurtured in their societies for a generation. Counterestablishment in their theology and politics, these men also spoke from the soul about social, ecclesiastical, and cultural dynamics that had touched them at home amid rapidly shifting local circumstances, and made them anxious to inform American evangelicals about the tides of change that would soon redefine their

3. Mark A. Noll, *Turning Points: Decisive Moments in the History of Christianity*, 3rd ed. (Grand Rapids: Baker Academic, 2012), 289, 304.
4. "A Challenge from Evangelicals," *Time*, August 5, 1974, 48–50.

existence as well. A brief glimpse at the lives and careers of two particularly important spokesmen illustrates the way in which Lausanne '74 helped to accentuate and accelerate three processes of "Latinization" in American evangelicalism. Encompassing theology and worship, along with demographics, politics, and flows of human and material resources, these three dynamic transitions also hint at the vitality of an emerging scholarship, which itself is laying out next directions for the study of modern evangelicalism by navigating a Latin turn.

When the thousands of delegates and dozens of speakers settled in for a week of fellowship in Switzerland during the summer of 1974, they bore witness to American evangelicalism's boomerang effect along a north-south axis. Two outspoken prophets from South America highlighted this dynamic, simply by being there and by bringing with them a critical self-awareness that would lend Lausanne its dominant spirit. As pronounced in the Lausanne Covenant, this mode was one of "humility," stemming from an attitude of "evangelical penitence" rather than "evangelical triumphalism." "'Triumphalism' is an attitude of self-confidence and self-congratulation," the Covenant's authors acknowledged, "which is never appropriate in God's children." Products of a Cold War–context shaped partly by US intervention in their home region, but also by cultural conditions indigenous to their societies and a spirit of reciprocity crafted out of the movement of people and ideas, Samuel Escobar and René Padilla, South American evangelicalism's apostles, not only embodied humility and penitence but also approached Lausanne set on proselytizing it as necessary for world Christianity's next steps.[5]

Escobar and Padilla's biographies surely testify to the way in which US evangelicalism realized its own ricochet in the 1970s. Both men were profoundly shaped by North American missionary efforts, which targeted Latin America with particular intensity in the aftermath of World War II. As war with Japan and Germany subsided and epic struggle with the Soviet Union and global Communism began, several key fronts emerged for evangelical missionaries, ranging from South Korea to Sudan, the South Pacific to the West Indies. By 1962 evangelicals were (in the words

---

5. John Stott, "Introduction to the Covenant," in *Making Christ Known: Historic Mission Documents from the Lausanne Movement, 1974–1989,* ed. John Stott (Grand Rapids: Eerdmans, 1997), 8.

of a missionary to Brazil) "carrying forth God's truth to those in spiritual darkness" and penetrating the globe's thickest jungles, remotest deserts, and densest cities to do so. Moreover, they were infiltrating all of these territories at a rate that outpaced their liberal peers. In 1950 evangelical and mainline Protestant missionary organizations operated as fifty-fifty partners in the exportation of America's gospel, but within a matter of a few decades the evangelical proportion of US Protestant outreach would be 91 percent, with 38,000 of 42,000 missionaries laboring under its label. Also disproportionately large in this equation was the South American continent as a destination of rising import. By 1972 more US Protestant missionaries (of all theological persuasions) were at work in Latin America than in any other geographical region, outpacing even Africa and Asia by notable margins.[6]

The Latin American mission field garnered special attention from postwar US evangelicals because of its unique promise and vulnerability. Proximate to California and the nation's southern rim—sites of booming populations, military industrial economies, and evangelical ministries—South America seemed like a logical target, and a land whose future was tied most directly to postwar America's dreams of development. What the southern US had once been to the northern US, a frontier with untapped growth potential, South America was now to the Sunbelt South: the next "blank slate" for progress. Of course that blank slate was also populated by feared rivals—Catholics, Communist sympathizers, and revolutionaries—and caught up in the violent transitions precipitated by nationalist uprisings, economic and demographic upheaval, and the hardening of ideological fault lines between the Cold War's two super-powered combatants. Cuba's revolution and subsequent friendship with the Soviet Union provided concrete proof of this region's menacing aura. So while they looked with both raised enthusiasm and alarm at other missionary fronts across the globe, American evangelicals' gaze on postwar South America produced an apocalyptic sense of urgency and

6. Robert S. Rapp, "Motivation for Biblical Missions," *Biblical Missions* 28, no. 8 (October 1962): 12. On the shifting proportion of "evangelical" and "liberal Protestant mainline" missionary efforts in post–World War II America, see Joel Carpenter, "Evangelical Missionary Force," in *Mission Handbook 2001-2003*, 18th ed., ed. John A. Siewert and Dotsey Wellner (Wheaton, IL: EMIS, 2001), 41. Statistical comparison of Protestant missionaries in Africa, Asia, Europe, the Soviet Union, Oceania, and Latin America gleaned from Mark A. Noll, *The New Shape of World Christianity: How American Experience Reflects Global Faith* (Downers Grove, IL: IVP Academic, 2009), 81.

a concomitant conviction that God's work needed to be exercised there out of "prophetic necessity."[7]

Few countries figured more prominently in this awareness than Peru and Ecuador. Much of this had to do with the extraordinary efforts of William Cameron Townsend and the independent missionary organizations that he founded and associated with during the Cold War era. As a young man, committed to the teachings of an American fundamentalist movement centered at Moody Tabernacle and Bible Institute in Chicago and its sister establishment (and his home base) on the West Coast, Church of the Open Door and the Bible Institute of Los Angeles (BIOLA), Townsend yearned to transport his gospel to Central and South America. After dropping out of Occidental College in Los Angeles, he started selling Spanish Bibles in Guatemala, then, two years later in 1919, joined the Central American Mission. Sensing a need for evangelicals to reach indigenous populations by offering them truth in their vernacular languages, Townsend founded Wycliffe Bible Translators and then its subsidiary, the Summer Institute of Linguistics, an anthropological outfit focused on the science of translation rather than proselytization. Together the two agencies, along with a third partner, the Jungle Aviation and Radio Service, supplied Townsend leverage with friendly governments, who appreciated his help in reaching and "modernizing" native populations, and the wherewithal to expand his ministry's interests across the entire South American continent.[8]

These agencies were the strongest in Mexico in the 1930s; by the 1950s the Wycliffe reach had extended farther south into places such as Ecuador and Peru. In the latter, Townsend leaned on his longstanding alliance with Texas evangelical engineer and businessman R. G. LeTourneau to carve out a deal with Peru's president: in exchange for the two Americans' help with supplying aviation and engineering expertise and materials that could facilitate development of the nation's remote eastern sections, US missionaries were granted access to the inhabitants of those isolated terrains. It proved to be a win-win arrangement, at least for the two main parties doing the arranging. While federal officials in Lima

---

7. Angela M. Lahr, *Millennial Dreams and Apocalyptic Nightmares: The Cold War Origins of Political Evangelicalism* (New York: Oxford University Press, 2007), 105.

8. For insight into Townsend's life and career see William Lawrence Svelmoe, *A New Vision for Missions: William Cameron Townsend, the Wycliffe Bible Translators, and the Culture of Early Evangelical Faith Missions, 1917-1945* (Tuscaloosa: University of Alabama Press, 2008).

gained an advantage over neighboring nations (Ecuador especially) in the race for control of the Amazon's resources, Townsend, LeTourneau, and their network of technicians and missionaries infiltrated secluded native populations and began drawing them in to a transnational Christian democratic and capitalist orb.[9]

Townsend worked with other evangelical initiatives, meanwhile, to penetrate Ecuador's eastern jungle. Sponsored by Wycliffe, Mission Aviation Fellowship, and local Brethren churches in the US, several missionaries worked expeditiously in the 1950s to gain a foothold in this remote zone. The flashpoint for their endeavors, of course, came in 1956 when five especially eager young sojourners—Jim Elliot, Nate Saint, Roger Youderian, Pete Fleming, and Ed McCully—attempted to reach the Huaorani tribe, which lived beyond contact along the Curaray River, a tributary of the Amazon River. The Huaorani's spearing of this quintet rocked the Protestant realm, made the men martyrs for the gospel, and intensified the imagination of American evangelicals. Aided by *Life* magazine's photo-documentation of the tragedy and the subsequent testimonies of those who lived through the experience, the narrative of the "Auca martyrs" "became a lodestar of ideal piety" and "a beacon reaffirming the missionary imperative." More than that, it reaffirmed Americans' special interests in Latin America as a way to test their own nation's mettle. As Kathryn Long writes, "Earnest young men and women taking the gospel to the jungles of South America symbolized the goodness and innate decency of ordinary Americans as the nation's true ambassadors. Missionaries epitomized the strength of American families and the ultimate triumph of those who sacrificed for others and who followed the dictates of their own conscience." Under the thick tree canopy of Amazonia, along the sandbanks of the Curarary where these men died, America could and did identify its best self.[10]

---

9. On Townsend, LeTourneau, and partnered advances into Mexico and Peru, see, for instance, William L. Svelmoe, "The General and the Gringo: W. Cameron Townsend as Lázaro Cárdenas's 'Man in America,'" in *The Foreign Missionary Enterprise at Home: Explorations in North American Cultural History*, ed. Daniel H. Bays and Grant Wacker (Tuscaloosa: University of Alabama Press, 2003), 169–86; and Darren Dochuk, "Moving Mountains: The Business of Evangelicalism and Extraction in a Liberal Age," in *What's Good for Business: Business and American Politics since World War II*, ed. Kim Phillips-Fein and Julian E. Zelizer (New York: Oxford University Press, 2012), 72–90.

10. Kathryn T. Long, "In the World, but Not of It: The 'Auca Martyrs,' Evangelicalism, and Postwar American Culture," in *The Foreign Missionary Enterprise at Home*,

Even as American evangelicals were enraptured by their young cru-saders' courage in Ecuador and Peru, young Ecuadorian and Peruvian Christians were carving out different narratives about their church and their country, and the contested futures both faced. Granted, they too were inspired by the work of American missionaries, particularly those af-filiated with the independent, nondenominational agencies represented by Townsend, Wycliffe, and the martyred five. "Independent faith mis-sions," Samuel Escobar would later acknowledge, "played an important role" in awakening the evangelical desires of many young South Ameri-cans by "representing a new generation that threw itself with great vigour into the task of planting churches, translating Scripture and reaching the restless masses." Among young Peruvian and Ecuadorian Christians, who in the 1950s and 1960s sought to upset political dominances that seemed to constrict them, unbendingly idealistic warriors such as Elliot, Saint, and their peers stood apart as radicals fighting heroically for good against evil in an unjust world.[11]

Still, conditions peculiar to his own local life played an even more sig-nificant role in awakening Escobar's evangelical faith. Escobar grew up in Arequipa, Peru (the "Rome of Peru"), during the mid-century period of political upheaval that saw nationalists, Communists, and Catholics clash over future plans for the country. Born in 1934 to evangelical par-ents who associated with Iglesia Evangelica Peruana, a collective created out of late-nineteenth- and early-twentieth-century missionary agencies that included the Brethren Assemblies and Christian and Missionary Al-liance, Escobar knew from a young age what it meant to be a religious minority struggling for religious liberty. Always afraid of succumbing to "martyrdom by fire and stones," he spent his youth not only struggling for hope in troubled times but also searching for an ideology that could carry him and his church through the tumult. Through close readings of Peruvian radicals who critiqued Catholic powerbrokers and demanded justice for the country's underclasses—especially Indians, workers, and

---

225; Kathryn T. Long, "Missionary Realities and the New Evangelicalism in Post–World War II America," in *American Evangelicalism: George Marsden and the State of American Religious History*, ed. Darren Dochuk, Thomas S. Kidd, and Kurt W. Peterson (Notre Dame: University of Notre Dame Press, 2014), 435.

11. Samuel Escobar, "Missionary Dynamism in Search of Missiological Discern-ment," *Evangelical Review of Theology* 23, no. 1 (1999): 70; Sharon E. Heaney, *Contextual Theology for Latin America: Liberation Themes in Evangelical Perspective* (Eugene, OR: Wipf & Stock, 2008), 55.

farmers trapped in the uneven economic conditions of the Amazon interior—exposure to Marxist writings, and immersion in Latin American liberation theology, Escobar began to forge a hybrid doctrine of salvation and reform. "My fledgling Protestantism," he would later write, perceived "the possibility of a different, more authentic, Christianity that was both deeply biblical and Latin American."[12]

Escobar cultivated this theology of dissent as a college student. In 1951 he began attending San Marcos University in Lima, where he enlisted in the participatory politics of fellow students, many of whom fashioned themselves as Marxists, existentialists, anti-government activists, and members of a global revolt. Soon after attending his first classes, Escobar experienced a conversion out of these ideological commitments and back into the evangelical ones he had been exposed to at home. Inspired by the writings of theologian Carl Henry and the support of young evangelical brethren, he committed his life to Christ, then started acting out his convictions by working in a church and in a street ministry and joining the International Fellowship of Evangelical Students (IFES), affiliated with the global InterVarsity ministry. His enrollment in this British-founded college ministry gave Escobar entry to an expansive interdenominational movement whose basic tenor and structures promoted transnational cooperation and exchange. As Brian Stanley describes it, InterVarsity "disseminated a non-polemical and essentially rather British, even Anglican, style of conservative evangelicalism that transcended continental and imperial boundaries." By the late 1950s and 1960s, even as British imperial ambition waned, InterVarsity "continued to nourish the growth of international conservative evangelicalism into the post-colonial age." Escobar had found an outlet for his hybrid doctrine, at the ideal time.[13]

And he recognized it. In 1959, after earning an undergraduate degree at San Marcos (he eventually earned a PhD in Spain), Escobar joined the IFES staff. On campuses around South America he saw firsthand the spirit of change that was animating young evangelicals, and he gained added exposure to leading lights of a transcontinental evangelicalism, such as F. F. Bruce, James Packer, and John Stott. He supplemented this labor by working with the Latin American Mission (LAM), "a vast network of

12. Escobar's biographical information and self-reflection are drawn from David R. Swartz, *Moral Minority: The Evangelical Left in an Age of Conservatism* (Philadelphia: University of Pennsylvania Press, 2008), 114-15.

13. Brian Stanley, *The Global Diffusion of Evangelicalism: The Age of Billy Graham and John Stott* (Downers Grove, IL: InterVarsity, 2013), 60.

evangelical educational, media, and medical outlets," which at that time was being "latinized" by a new crop of South American leaders. Escobar stepped up his ministerial efforts during the 1960s by participating in several evangelical conferences, the most important of which was the 1969 Congreso Latinoamericano de Evangelizacion (CLADE), held in Bogata, Colombia. Sponsored by LAM, the Billy Graham Evangelistic Association, and the National Association of Evangelicals, CLADE was highlighted by the appearance of C. Peter Wagner, a missionary in Bolivia whose new book *Latin American Theology: Radical or Evangelical?* was singled out as a definitive and much-needed text. Escobar grimaced at CLADE's many displays of American narrow-mindedness, yet welcomed the chance to speak to the Latin American audience and strengthen relationships with his North American allies. It is in part through these connections that he negotiated his next bold move, this one in 1972, to Hamilton, Ontario, to assume leadership of the InterVarsity Christian Fellowship Canada.[14]

René Padilla was also on the move at this time. Born in Quito, Ecuador, a major center of American evangelical missions during the 1940s and 1950s, Padilla grew up in a strict Protestant home governed by parents who had been converted to Christianity by American missionaries, and a father whose subsequent devotion was intense and unwavering, so much so that he preached anti-Catholicism (a daring venture at the time) and worked full-time as a chaplain at the Voice of the Andes Hospital and for the affiliated evangelical radio station HJCB. The Padillas' direct ties to this media outlet meant that they had direct ties to the information hub, not just of South American evangelicalism, but also of a worldwide Christian missionary endeavor. "The Voice of the Andes," HJCB was in fact the first Christian missionary radio station in the world, and by the 1960s—three decades after its founding in 1931—it commanded the air waves with multilingual programming that reached far beyond the South American continent. In the 1950s, however, HJCB's mainstay remained hemispheric. Established by Clarence Wesley Jones, a graduate of Moody Bible Institute, and Reuben Larson, a Christian and Missionary Alliance missionary, HJCB always saw Latin America as its primary calling. Throughout the early Cold War years, it served the Andean peoples, centered in Ecuador, Bolivia, and Peru, with a sense of special duty; it also served the Western Protestant missionaries who worked in these ar-

14. For full description and analysis of Escobar's vocational trajectories and involvement with CLADE, see Swartz, *Moral Minority*, 116-17.

eas. While broadcasting evangelical messages to this listenership, HJCB also helped transmit news from South America back north to supporters in the US. It was HJCB that first alerted a wide audience in 1956 to the plight of the five missing Americans in Huaorani territory.[15]

Through his father's work, René Padilla thus gained access to American evangelicalism's most powerful communications network and, by extension, the powerful American evangelical people and institutions that supported it. This included Wheaton College in Illinois, where he moved in the early 1950s for undergraduate training. While there, he joined InterVarsity and committed to several outreach programs, including work among Mexican migrant workers. His effective service caught the notice of InterVarsity administrators, and in the late 1950s he was hired to found chapters of the movement throughout Latin America. Even while carrying out this task, Padilla pursued doctoral studies at the University of Manchester under the mentorship of renowned theologian F. F. Bruce. By the early 1970s, just as Escobar was traveling north to Canada, Padilla was crisscrossing two continents—North America and South America—speaking and writing on behalf of IFES and testifying on behalf of the grassroots ministry he had become involved with in Buenos Aires, Argentina. There, American evangelicals learned, he was implementing his fusion of liberation theology and social action and welcoming into the Christian family the metropolis's most forsaken and forgotten people.[16]

Navigating intersecting paths from early Cold War American missionary work and familial Christian commitments through the vibrant transnational networks of student-inspired, Latin-led university fellowship and exchange, Padilla and Escobar were destined to shake the evangelical world together, as allies in thought and purpose. This destiny unfolded as they made their way to Lausanne. There they hoped to facilitate another evangelical ricochet, this one in sentiment. Joining a delegation of Latin American evangelical leaders, Padilla and Escobar approached Switzerland in 1974 determined to tell American evangelicals that their way of conducting the work of the church needed to change. The evangelical triumphalism and American self-assurance embodied in the missionaries who inspired them in their youth may have triggered a healthy revolt in

15. René Padilla interview, February 22, 2001, audiotape in Carlos René Padilla Collection, Billy Graham Center Archives (BGCA), Wheaton, Illinois; Elisabeth Elliot, *Through Gates of Splendor* (New York: Harper & Brothers, 1957), 197.
16. Padilla interview, BGCA.

Latin America, but Padilla and Escobar believed the day had arrived for a humbler disposition. Mindful of their experience as workers in South America's streets, ministers on militant university campuses, citizens of countries in revolt, and sojourners spreading inspiration across continents, both men deemed Lausanne a God-given opportunity to nudge their peers into a gentler, inclusive, self-reflective, and service-focused faith. "The Gospel of Jesus Christ is a personal message," Padilla was prepared to say, but "it is also a cosmic message . . . [given] to the individual as a member of the old humanity in Adam, marked by sin and death, whom God calls to be integrated into the new humanity in Christ, marked by righteousness and eternal life." In order to carve out evangelicalism's future, evangelicals needed to shed the jingoisms of their Cold War moment and realize a new dispensation of collective compassion and grace, and a recognition of a broken humanity in need of healing and hope.[17]

Escobar's and Padilla's contributions to Lausanne meant more than the culmination of American evangelicalism's Cold War boomerang and the beginning of its shift in outlook from imperialist myopias to third-world emphases on the connectedness of humanity. They also represented a revolution in ethics that was altering evangelical conceptions of social action. Historian David Swartz asserts that Padilla and Escobar were two "prophetic voices" from outside US borders that helped instigate a "global reflex" in American evangelicalism. In their ministerial travels throughout North America and their frequent, public recounting of their life experiences and reflections on hardship in Latin America, the two men compelled a new generation of evangelicals to reconsider the full implications of faith. Exposed to this "aid and inspiration" from afar, and the unabashed radicalization of their parents' doctrine, these young people turned left in their persuasions and went to war against the injustices of their own society.[18]

Thanks to the rigorous networking of Latin American evangelicals in the 1960s and early 1970s, the logics of revolution that Padilla and Esco-

---

17. René Padilla, "Evangelism and the World," in *Let the Earth Hear His Voice: International Congress on World Evangelization, Lausanne, Switzerland*, ed. J. D. Douglas (Minneapolis: World Wide Publications, 1975), 116.

18. Swartz, *Moral Minority*, 114, 134. David Swartz's current scholarship is opening up wider perspectives on the globalization of Western evangelicalism in the post–World War II period. Some of the critical claims and analysis offered in his stellar work—on which I heavily rely in this chapter—can be accessed in David R. Swartz, "Embodying the Global Soul: Internationalism and the American Evangelical Left," *Religions* 3 (2012): 887-901.

bar brought to Lausanne and sold to evangelical youth were already well formulated and well tested. CLADE, the 1969 conference held in Bogata that frustrated yet inspired Escobar, proved critical in this regard. Heavily geared toward North American evangelical fascinations with Latin America, the gathering hinged on a fundamental question made clear by its sponsors and the writings of C. Peter Wagner. As announced on the cover of Wagner's book, *Latin American Theology: Radical or Evangelical?*, American evangelicals identified a battle in the Latin American church between liberal Protestantism, with its ecumenical and radicalized priorities of societal restructuring, and conservative evangelicalism, with its traditional emphasis on personal conversion as the key to solving individual *and* societal sin. Would Latin American theology end up "radical" or "evangelical"? Though invested in this query, Latin Americans in attendance rejected Wagner's simple two-pronged characterization of their society's theological tendencies and the heavy imposition of North American–based categories on their unique situation. Their desire for a "truly Latin American approach to evangelical theology—one that embraced a clear call to socio-political engagement in response to the stark human needs evident in Latin America"—intensified, and this led to a follow-up conference the next year and ultimately to the creation of the Fraternidad Teológica Latinoamericana (FTL), or Latin American Theological Fraternity. In Escobar's words, Latin American theologians were "tired of the evangelical power centers in North America telling us how to think, who to read, and what it meant to be evangelical"; "we decided it was time to start reflecting the faith as grownups and on our own."[19]

Over the next few years, Escobar, Padilla, and the FTL firmed up and sold their liberation theology to the Western world. Borrowing from Marxist analyses, they accepted class struggle as real, and they highlighted the exploitative capacities of capitalism in a world governed by the rich. Poverty was the result of this structural failing, as well as of the sin of greed born out of rabidly free market economics. Rather than dwell on the problems, however, Padilla, Escobar, and their Latin American liberation front emphasized solutions: that God was on the side of the poor, and that the New Testament's "good news" was that "God works in

19. On the Latin American approach and Escobar quote see Michael Clawson, "*Misión Integral* and Progressive Evangelicalism: The Latin American Influence on the North American Emerging Church," *Religions* 3 (2012): 791; see also Daniel Salinas, *Latin American Evangelical Theology in the 1970s: The Golden Decade* (Leiden and Boston: Brill, 2009), 11.

history to overcome and to eradicate *all* forms of sin and injustice." This was Christianity's great hope; its commission: to vigorously challenge all forms of inequality. Indeed, because sin was both personal and structural in nature, salvation itself was something to be pursued through "spiritual redemption and physical, political liberation." The global church, in their estimation, had to "join God's work by identifying with the poor and working for their holistic salvation" through complete reforms of extant social, economic, and political systems.[20]

Loaded with far-reaching implications, this social gospel established a footing across national borders during this period of proliferating political disruption. To be sure, the particular brand of liberation theology that FTL offered was but one interpretative mode in a constellation of radicalized thought. Even as Escobar and Padilla were formulating their doctrine of "integral mission" as a way to combat injustices against the mind, body, and soul, other Latino activists were framing theirs more specifically as strategies for civil, landholders', and workers' rights. From Texas to New Mexico, and along the Central Valley of California, Mexican, Mexican American, and Latino laborers in the 1960s and early 1970s coalesced around interfaith and interdenominational forms of lay spirituality; hybrid practices of Catholic-Protestant, Baptist-Pentecostal-Mennonite devotion; and politically charged social-justice thinking that empowered them in the fight for "La Causa." With their pliable theologies in hand, imbued with moralistic fervor, they marched arm-in-arm as if on "religious pilgrimage" and "penitential procession," not simply a path of political defiance. As several recent histories have shown, at the head of this cavalcade of social action stood towering, charismatic figures such as Cesar Chavez and Reies Lopez Tijerina, whose appeals to other-worldly "symbols and motifs . . . ideals of justice and equality" as justification of this-world revolt were explicitly calibrated to the liberation theologies that flowed between Latin America and their own locales of struggle.[21]

20. Brantley W. Gasaway, *Progressive Evangelicals and the Pursuit of Social Justice* (Chapel Hill: University of North Carolina Press, 2014), 204.

21. Alan J. Watt, *Farm Workers and the Churches: The Movement in California and Texas* (College Station: Texas A&M University Press, 2010), 3–4; Rudiger V. Buston, "'In the Outer Boundaries': Pentecostalism, Politics, and Reies Lopez Tijerina's Civic Activism," in *Latino Religions and Civic Activism in the United States*, ed. Gaston Espinosa, Virgilio Elizondo, and Jesse Miranda (New York: Oxford University Press, 2005), 4, 73. See also Felipe Hinojosa, *Latino Mennonites: Civil Rights, Faith, and Evangelical Culture*

Within the mainstream of American evangelicalism at this time, FTL's vision of liberation caused the greatest stir. During the early 1970s, Escobar and Padilla gained large and lively hearings with young evangelical students at Wheaton College, at Trinity Divinity School, on Christian and public campuses around the country, and at the triannual Urbana Missions conference held at the University of Illinois. At the 1970 conference, which was dubbed the "largest student missions convention ever held," Escobar delivered a provocative talk titled "Social Concern and World Evangelism." Twelve thousand attendees heard him rail against the "white, middle-class God represented by American culture." "Christianity has become synonymous with gay, unconcerned and irrelevant selfishness," he bellowed, "Communism synonymous with a committed, disciplined, sacrificial way of living." The task facing young evangelicals was to internalize some of the latter and to "show by word and deed that we are being liberated from those sins of social injustice, social prejudice, abuse and selfish individualism." Escobar's words, echoed in other speeches he, Padilla, and their brethren delivered at subsequent Urbana gatherings and in similar venues around South America and North America, hit the mark with a young public and garnered the attention of a curious press.[22]

The same was true when Padilla and Escobar gained their largest and liveliest hearing at the Lausanne Congress of 1974. Both accepted their invitations to speak with seriousness, and both delivered their messages with an equal dose of solemnity. But neither shied away from attacking common assumptions. In his simply titled paper "Evangelism and the World," Padilla decried the commercialization of evangelicalism and stressed the need for brethren to assume a "radical discipleship" that resisted capitalism's comforts. He raised this plea in the context of history and what he saw evidenced in nineteenth-century British missionary enterprises and those promoted by the twentieth-century US, which too readily blended the requisites of evangelism and empire building. Especially in Latin America, he charged, American evangelicalism had

---

(Baltimore: Johns Hopkins University Press, 2014), and Luis D. León, *The Political Spirituality of Cesar Chavez: Crossing Religious Borders* (Berkeley: University of California Press, 2014).

22. Samuel Escobar, "Social Concern and World Evangelism," in *Christ the Liberator*, ed. John Stott (Downers Grove, IL: InterVarsity, 1971), 104, 108; Richard Hauser, "Missionary Convention Bids for New Concept: Student Group Attempts to Redefine Evangelism Need in Revolutionary Age," *Los Angeles Times*, January 2, 1971, 23.

been too eager to contribute to a Cold War quest for economic and ideological hegemony, and too willing to fold the message of the gospel into propagation of the "American way of life." Going forward, evangelism in his home region and around the world needed to detach itself from US dependence; be sensitive to local, organic needs; and be "oriented toward breaking man's slavery in the world."[23]

Escobar opined in even stronger, condemnatory terms. It was time, he declared, for the world's evangelicals to see rebirth in social and structural terms, not just personal ones, and for believers to follow a new political path.

> Christians, evangelicals in particular oppose the violence of revolution but not the violence of war; they condemn the totalitarianism of the left but not that of the right; they speak openly in favor of Israel, but very seldom speak or do anything about the Palestinian refugees; they condemn all the sins that well-behaved middle class people condemn but say nothing about exploitation, intrigue, and dirty political maneuvering done by great multinational corporations around the world.

In Escobar's estimation, evangelicals had to shed the apolitical apathies, cynicisms, and conservative assumptions of Richard Nixon's era and accept their "discipleship in the daily social, economic, and political aspects of life . . . as a sign of the kingdom and anticipation of the new creation." Ever the radical, always the optimist, Escobar managed to level his condemnations with a glint and promise that however bad, the world could get better, with patient and dedicated labor by Christ's followers, far in advance of his millennial reign.[24]

With these declarations, Latin America's two apostles turned their community upside down. Both men received praise for their speeches. One journalist called Padilla's address "the best theological presentation of the congress," while *Time* said it was definitely "one of the meeting's most provocative speeches." Escobar's utterances received similar approval. Together, the heartfelt sermons were singled out by other participants as a "major breakthrough," a "coming of age for evangelicals," and the spark that "really set the Congress alight" and demarcated a

23. Padilla, "Evangelism and the World," 121, 125–26.
24. Escobar, "Evangelism and Man's Search for Freedom, Justice, and Fulfillment," in *Let the Earth Hear His Voice,* 303–4, 317.

"significant shift in Christian thinking." A usually restrained Billy Graham noted that "if one thing has come through loud and clear it is that we evangelicals should have social concern." "Radical discipleship," he averred, "has caught fire."[25]

Some conferees, however, had slightly less sanguine opinions of Padilla's and Escobar's offerings. Ralph Winter spoke in unison with the two on most matters but differed where practicalities were involved: yes, evangelism had to be led by "local Christians" attuned to indigenous concerns, but in some cases, where such workers were absent, Western evangelicals needed to proceed on their own, even if it meant risking charges of "cultural imperialism." Sharing the same outlook as Winter, his colleague at Fuller Theological Seminary, Professor Donald McGavran stated that American evangelicals still needed to take a lead in worldwide evangelism in the postcolonial era, and that evangelism itself needed to be socially and politically responsive but overwhelmingly focused on winning the souls of individuals. This endeavor to win people to Christ had to maximize cooperation between believers from South America and North America, Asia and Africa. Without "reborn men" attacking the world's spiritual crisis together as one, he asserted, no hope existed that the just world Padilla and Escobar sought could be imagined, let alone realized.[26]

In the short term, Escobar's and Padilla's sentiments won the day, though in the long term Winter's and McGavran's gained some steam. Following the Lausanne Congress, a group of delegates led by Padilla and Escobar drafted a document urging the committee in charge of formulating the Lausanne Covenant, the convention's concluding statement of purpose, to include a heavy emphasis on social justice as an evangelical priority. Their voices were heard. Assembled by Escobar, John Stott, and a handful of their colleagues, the Covenant bore the marks of the Latin Americans' priorities, if in a somewhat muted form that placed personal regeneration ahead of societal reform. "Although reconciliation with

25. As quoted in Clawson, "*Misión Integral* and Progressive Evangelicalism," 795–96; Gerald Davis, "A Coming of Age for Evangelicals," *Church Scene*, August 1, 1974; John A. Coleman, "Aftermath of Lausanne! Evangelism in a Changing World," *New Life*, August 28, 1974; Billy Graham, "Our Mandate from Lausanne '74: An Address to the Lausanne Continuation Committee," *Christianity Today*, July 4, 1975, 3–6.

26. Ralph Winter, "The Highest Priority: Cross-Cultural Evangelism," in *Let the Earth Hear His Voice*, 220; Donald McGavran, "The Dimensions of World Evangelization," in *Let the Earth Hear His Voice*, 106, 111, 109.

man is not reconciliation with God, nor is social action evangelism, nor is political liberation salvation," Article 5 of the Covenant read, "nevertheless we affirm that evangelism and socio-political involvement are both part of our Christian duty." But there was no mistaking the effort by the Covenant's drafters to stress social action as part-and-parcel of the true gospel, and the need for indigenous, local leaders to take charge of their society's encounters with Christ.[27]

This imperative weakened slightly over the course of the next decade as the Lausanne movement continued to mature into a sustainable worldwide enterprise. In 1975 the forty-eight members of the Lausanne Continuation Committee (eventually called the Lausanne Committee for World Evangelization) met in Mexico City to iron out evangelical ecumenism's next steps. Still smoldering from the debates that surfaced in Switzerland between those who championed the social and political imperatives of the Latin American liberationists and those who cautioned against their overemphasis, the Mexico convention resulted in a tempering of the radical social-justice orientation that Padilla and Escobar had successfully lobbied for in the Lausanne Covenant. Subsequent meetings in Atlanta (1976) and in Pattaya, Thailand (1980), also whittled away at the social-action imperative outlined in the Lausanne Covenant, even as they affirmed the Covenant's mandate for evangelicals "in every major region of the world unitedly to form regional networks" and ultimately work as a well-coordinated and collective whole. Dimmed by these challenges, Padilla's and Escobar's vision nevertheless continued to hold significant sway, and in 1983, at a conference labeled the Consultation on the Church in Response to Human Need, hosted by Wheaton College, it received another powerful endorsement. "Wheaton '83" produced a "landmark document" in support of the Latin American agenda that exploded "the perennial dichotomy" between evangelism and social action and articulated the two imperatives as one. Padilla himself later designated this "the strongest evangelical affirmation of commitment to integral mission in the last quarter of the twentieth century."[28]

27. "The Lausanne Covenant," in *Making Christ Known*, 24.

28. Lausanne Continuation Committee, "Minutes of the Lausanne Continuation Committee," January 21, 1975, 2-4, BGCA, http://www2.wheaton.edu/bgc/archives/docs/Lausanne/704/min02.htm; Lausanne Committee for World Evangelization, "News," January 27, 1975, Records of the World Evangelical Fellowship, Collection 338, Box 4, Folder 3, ICOWE Relations, 1972-1975, N.D., BGCA. On Wheaton '83 see Vinay Samuel and Christ Sugden, eds., *The Church in Response to Human Need* (Grand Rapids:

Whatever internal discourse persisted between competing emphases in the Lausanne movement, the Latinization of American evangelicalism was more broadly and profoundly—if subtly—felt beyond its organizational boundaries. Indeed, as David Swartz, Brantley Gasaway, and Michael Clawson have demonstrated, Lausanne's liberation front most affected US religious and political culture by helping to inspire a wider agenda of reform embraced by a broader constituency of progressive evangelicals. Solidified in 1973 by the drafting of the Chicago Declaration of Evangelical Social Concern and related efforts to create an organization (Evangelicals for Social Action and Sojourners), popular magazines (*Post-American* and *The Other Side*), and a network of activists headed by Jim Wallis, Sharon Gallagher, Ron Sider, and others, the evangelical left internalized the teachings of the Latin American theologians and applied them in outreach methods that were conducive to their national circumstances.[29]

They did so with an appreciative yet critical eye. As Gasaway recounts, during the entire 1970s, but with greater intensity after the Lausanne Congress of 1974, the American evangelical left zealously processed FTL doctrines in print, in classrooms and seminars, and through the formal and informal structures of information gathering and dissemination that enlivened their grassroots activities. In all of these venues, FTL philosophies were embraced almost—not entirely—as a whole. Such was the case with money matters. Liberation theologians, evangelical progressives asserted, "rightly challenged North Americans to assess how capitalist presumptions and economic self-interests distorted their theology to the point that many evangelicals perversely justified 'the privilege of the powerful and poverty of the poor.'" Yet left-wing evangelicals also cautioned against liberation theology's Marxist tendencies to privilege the existentialism of oppression over biblical revelation as the "primary authority" when passing judgment on economic injustice, and they "rejected any reduction of the meaning of liberation (or salvation) to political and economic emancipation." They also discarded liberation theology's allowances for violent revolt. True reform, they believed,

Eerdmans, 1987); David Bosch, *Transforming Mission: Paradigm Shifts in Theology of Mission* (Maryknoll, NY: Orbis, 1991); C. René Padilla, "Integral Mission and Its Historical Development," in *Justice, Mercy and Humility: Integral Mission and the Poor*, ed. Tim Chester (Waynesboro, GA: Paternoster, 2002), 42–58.

29. Gasaway, *Progressive Evangelicals*, 47–48; Clawson, "*Misión Integral* and Progressive Evangelicalism," 797.

needed to come peacefully, through regeneration within, and through quieter labor on streets, in schools and courts, by policy implementation, and across all spectrums of civil society. None of this, however, dampened their enthusiasm for liberationists' core conviction: that the gospel's "good news for the poor" impelled all Christians to undermine all forms of economy that produced inequality.[30]

The fruits of Escobar, Padilla, and their American friends' revolution in ethics were abundantly evidenced by the late 1970s. With a sophisticated communications apparatus in hand, left-wing evangelicals lobbied hard for a "post-American" reality in which nationalist, sectarian, and hyper-individualistic conceptions of the gospel and the believer's duties gave way to a boldly cooperative program for structural change. In this mode they championed women's rights and racial reconciliation, crusaded for anti-poverty legislation and a culture of economic modesty, and even weighed in on issues of foreign policy. On this latter front they advocated the type of peace initiatives President Jimmy Carter undertook to broker accord between Israel and Egypt, and they spoke out (as Carter did) against continued US control of the Panama Canal. They did so loudly during the public debates that revolved around the signing of a new Panama Canal treaty. Convinced that America's involvement in Panama was corrupt from the very beginning, post-American evangelicals condemned their nation's imperialist ambitions in the region, and charged that the "'American Way of Life' [fed] in no small proportion on the blood which gushes 'from the open veins of Latin America.'" "We exhort you as brothers and sisters in Christ to write your senators," they urged, "indicating your support for the new treaty as a step toward justice for Panama and better relations with all Latin America." Carter signed the treaty in 1977, guaranteeing Panama's possession of the canal in 1999, and progressive evangelicalism won the day—in a manner, and with a discourse, that surely made Escobar and Padilla proud.[31]

The rising conservative movement that opposed the Panama treaty did, of course, produce a win of its own in 1980 with the defeat of Carter and election of Ronald Reagan, one that more than offset this victory by the evangelical left. Due to internal fracturing and struggles with divi-

---

30. Gasaway, *Progressive Evangelicals*, 204.

31. Quotes taken from "An Open Letter to North American Christians," *Vanguard*, January-February 1977, 4–5. For further context, and for insight into this and other related statements by progressive evangelicals, see Swartz, *Moral Minority*, 128–29.

sive issues such as abortion, progressive evangelicals spent the next two decades in a perpetual recovery mode made more difficult by the dominant discourse of the Religious Right, which championed free-market economics, limited government, nationalism, and conservative social values, as the way to rebuild a country hurt by the 1970s "liberal secular" drifts. During the Reagan years and the heyday of the Religious Right in Bill Clinton's 1990s, it appeared that the Latin turn in US evangelicalism had been stalled, the effects of Lausanne and its Peruvian and Ecuadorian influences curtailed.

Yet that was not entirely the case; the Latin turn in fact continued during this time. It was on broader religious and cultural planes, not in politics, where the lingering effects of Lausanne '74 and liberation thought were most notable. The continuing expansion of the Lausanne movement itself, and its sequence of high-profile international gatherings, was the clearest indication that the transformation sparked by Latin America's apostles in 1974 was still regenerating global evangelicalism. Yet other byproducts were just as striking. Although Escobar, Padilla, and the FTL did not necessarily associate or entirely agree with them, their work was instrumental in creating these byproducts. Out of their calls for revolution evolved subtler commands for renewal that still embodied Lausanne's mantra of "a whole gospel for the whole world." These nudges produced new emphases in late-twentieth-century evangelical doctrine, community, and politics.

As René Padilla articulated it in his speech to the Lausanne Congress in 1974, for evangelicals to impact the modern world they had to recognize the modern individual's need for a holistic gospel. The "only true evangelism," he stated, "is that which is oriented toward . . . 'the restoration of all things' in Christ Jesus." "Salvation is wholeness"; "salvation is total humanization"; "salvation is eternal life . . . that begins here and now . . . and touches all aspects of man's being." Continuing with more teachings from the book of Acts, he implored: "Today, more than ever, the Christian hope in its fullest dimensions must be proclaimed with such conviction and with such force that the falseness of every other hope should not need to be demonstrated." Not only did evangelicals need to proclaim a fully restorative creed; they also needed to embrace one that allowed for the signs and wonders of the unseen realm.

The universe is not a closed universe, in which everything can be explained by an appeal to natural causes. It is, rather, the arena in which

268

God—a God who acts in history—is engaged in a battle with the spiritual powers that enslave men and hinder their perception of the truth revealed in Jesus Christ.

Although taken with Marxist readings of unjust material systems, Padilla was far from a materialist when it came to measuring the cosmic causes, contexts, and outcomes in which injustice played out. In his preaching about the mysteries and fullness of Christian life, and the demands of an evangelistic mission attuned to them, Padilla spoke in Pentecostal tones.[32]

Though Padilla did not fully embrace Pentecostalism, his holistic gospel in fact gained legitimacy through this phenomenon's outsized importance in the 1980s and 1990s. By this time, Padilla was active again in street-level outreach as a Baptist pastor in Buenos Aires. There, Padilla put into practice his social gospel: while committing church resources to the rescue of the city's drug addicts, he also expended energy solving housing crises and ongoing escalations of crime, violence, and ghettoization. "You have to become concerned about the totality of life of the person, the person who is destroyed," he explained to inquiring evangelicals. The only other evangelicals to join him in the slums, he acknowledged, were Pentecostals. Although their aim was primarily "to get people converted" and promote church growth, and while they had "very little concept of service," these brethren were tackling social dislocation in a manner that made him understand why their brand of evangelism was so appealing to Latin America's lost. What Padilla saw evidenced in Argentina, pundits across the Americas were seeing with equally clear eyes: the next Latin progression in evangelicalism was coming via the Charismatic church.[33]

Charismatic renewal was indeed *the* catalyst that helped to remake American evangelicalism in a Latin American image. To be sure, the Pentecostal (including Neo-Pentecostal) movement that swept the US after the 1970s was not solely because of happenings in the Southern Hemisphere. Pentecostalism was a parochial movement first generated in California and the American Southwest before it garnered attention as a transnational sensation. Nevertheless, as several historians have shown, by the late twentieth century Pentecostalism's momentum came by way of a new southern revolution. In Latin America itself, Pentecos-

32. Padilla, "Evangelism and the World," 117–18, 130.
33. Padilla interview, BGCA.

talism came to dominate the Protestant orb. As Philip Jenkins reports, after 1950 Pentecostals accounted "for 80 or 90 percent of Protestant ... growth across Latin America." In Chile, Pentecostalism grew into the largest body of Protestant believers; in Brazil it enjoyed "massive gains" that thrust it into mainstream cultural—not just religious—standing. By the end of the century, there were "more followers of the Assemblies of God in the greater São Paulo region alone than in the entire United States," and Pentecostal influence was felt well beyond the pew in local economics and civil life and in mass politics at the national level.[34]

Why the popularity, and with what consequences for the US? In the late twentieth century, Latin America's profound sociological disruptions left significant populations alienated from established institutions (such as the Catholic Church) and vulnerable to the unsettledness of the modern age. Sociologist David Martin observes, "what moves people on the move and turns their atomized being into a corporate movement is a repertoire of religious images corresponding to their circumstances." In Pentecostalism, so attuned to the rapturous features of life and lived faith amid extreme change, Latin Americans found release "from ascribed categories and indelible markers"; amid society's "bewildering open-endedness" they located meaning and agency "by a discipline that offers a destination." Sensitive to the needs of people caught up in the machinery of advanced society, respectful of the miraculous elements of a New Testament faith—despite the preponderance of science and technology—Pentecostalism simply made sense. So too for those trying to navigate the late century's "neo-liberal" turn to free markets. Recently, social scientists have reassessed secularization theories first advanced by thinkers such as Max Weber, which held that modernity would make the planet "more rationally comprehensible and manageable," demystify human understandings of the systems (especially economics) in which they existed, and lead to the "disenchantment of the world" and a secular outlook. They have done these reassessments because global shocks of the late century incited very different responses to modernity, particularly in regions such as Latin America, where reverberations of economic change were most jarring. There, instead of fomenting secularization, emerging market dynamics produced a reenchantment and mystification of economic systems, and a different "spirit of capitalism," one legitimiz-

34. Philip Jenkins, *The Next Christendom: The Coming of Global Christianity* (New York: Oxford University Press, 2011), 80–81, 195.

ing speculation, profit motives, and the accumulation of wealth. Latin American Pentecostalism played no small part in ensuring that the new age of global capitalism would re-center God, and in particular a God who prospers people who have abundant faith.[35]

It is no wonder that, fostered in an environment of disruption, a transported Latin American Pentecostalism, melded with homegrown versions of this faith, had such a profound effect in the US during its own tumultuous late-century decades. Against the backdrop of increased immigration and dramatic economic and demographic changes, Latino Christians helped to accelerate the growth of charismatic renewal groups and gave a boost to the fortunes of the Vineyard Movement and Neo-Pentecostal megachurch networks. A Chicago report conducted in the early 2000s revealed what this one city had seen happen as a result of these trends. It found that 50 percent of all Latino Protestant congregations in the city defined themselves as Pentecostal; impressive on its own, this statistic nevertheless ignored the critical roles Latino Pentecostals were playing in other independent evangelical institutions, as well as within the Catholic Church, which (according to one priest) was "roaring" with Latino-led charismatic renewal. Chicago was merely one epicenter of this ecclesiastical transformation. As Kate Bowler shows, along the southern rim of the nation especially, global flows of Latino people, resources, and thought galvanized Pentecostal growth in multiple metropolises, especially one particularly potent strand of it: the prosperity gospel. Much like their brethren in Chile and Brazil, US Latinos spent the 1980s and 1990s proliferating a doctrine of health and wealth that addressed the universal dreams, anxieties, and aspirations of humanity in the late modern age. By doing so they made prosperity theology a lingua franca for a multitude of America's born-again believers.[36]

35. David Martin, *Pentecostalism: The World Their Parish* (Malden, MA: Blackwell, 2002), 168, 170; Peter Berger, "The Desecularization of the World: A Global Overview," in *The Desecularization of the World: Resurgent Religion and World Politics*, ed. Peter Berger (Washington, DC: Ethics and Public Policy Center, 1999), 2–3; Max Weber, "The Protestant Ethic and the Spirit of Capitalism," in *A Reader in the Anthropology of Religion*, ed. Michael Lambek (Malden, MA: Wiley-Blackwell, 2002), 51; Elsie Lewison, "Pentecostal Power and the Holy Spirit of Capitalism: Re-Imagining Modernity in the Charismatic Cosmology," *Symposia* 3, no. 1 (2001): 31–32. See also Allan Anderson, *An Introduction to Pentecostalism: Global Charismatic Christianity* (Cambridge: Cambridge University Press, 2004), and David Martin, *Tongues of Fire: The Explosion of Pentecostalism in Latin America* (Cambridge, MA: Blackwell, 1990).

36. Andrea Althoff, "Religious Identities of Latin American Immigrants in Chi-

If effective in leveling class divisions by generating dreams of em-powerment, and in reshaping American evangelicalism theologically, Latin American–inflected Pentecostalism also contributed to a second process of renewal, this one sociological. During the 1980s and 1990s, Escobar's and Padilla's vision of greater inclusiveness and multicultural awareness was implemented by a new wave of evangelical activists. In pursuing these aims, American evangelicalism itself assumed different social properties as a "salad bowl" of alternatives rather than a melting pot of consensus witnessed (and encouraged) in the Cold War epoch.

Escobar and Padilla certainly remained crucial to evangelicalism's shift in these directions. Even as the "culture wars" overwhelmed the American church, squelching some of its progressive impulses, the Latin American liberation front remained alive and well. The formation of the International Fellowship of Evangelical Mission Theologians (INFEMIT) in 1987 supplied it with a fresh shot of energy. The precipitating factor for INFEMIT's creation actually transpired in 1980 when FTL-associated theologians voiced frustration with the Lausanne-sponsored meeting in Pattaya, Thailand, which resulted in the movement's backpedaling slightly in its social-justice stand. As INFEMIT's own official history explains,

> Feeling the dire need to grow in the integration of evangelism and social justice, as well as to give voice to churches in the non-Western world, an international group of evangelical theologians resolved to organize together in order to advance holistic, contextual mission the-ology not only for the worldwide evangelical community, but for the whole church.

With Padilla and other veteran liberationists on board, INFEMIT for-mally came to fruition in 1987, and thereafter took the lead in planning

---

cago: Preliminary Findings from Field Research," paper presented at the Martin Marty Center, Chicago, and published on the Religion and Culture Web Forum (June 2006), 4–5; Wes Granberg-Michaelson, "Think Christianity Is Dying? No, Christianity Is Shifting Dramatically," *Washington Post*, May 20, 2015, www.washingtonpost.com/news/acts-of-faith/wp/2015/05/20/think-christianity-is-dying-no-christianity-is-shifting-dramatically/. On Latin Americans and the prosperity gospel, see, for instance, Jairo Namnún, "Stirrings of Revival in Latin America," www.thegospelcoalition.org/article/stirrings-of-revival-in-latin-america. And for broader, scholarly coverage, see Kate Bowler, *Blessed: A History of the American Prosperity Gospel* (New York: Oxford University Press, 2013).

several large, international conferences where plenary themes as diverse as "The Holy Spirit" and "Freedom and Justice in Church-State Relationships" were discussed in global contexts of pluralism, diversification, and multicultural engagement. During the 1990s, INFEMIT continued to facilitate regional networks of "two-thirds-world" Christian leaders, with increased attention to local activism, but also extended fellowship to "one-third-world" partners in North America and Europe. Under Padilla's watch as INFEMIT board chairperson, the association established the Oxford Centre for Mission Studies in Britain; started a journal, *Transformation*; founded a publishing company, Regnum Books, and created partnerships with others, such as Kairos Press, which helped produce books by the likes of Samuel Escobar; supported research centers such as the Kairos Centre in Argentina and branches in the US; and all the while maintained institutional "bridges" with the Lausanne movement.[37]

Meanwhile, other evangelical activists tweaked Padilla's and Escobar's outlook to suit the unique landscapes they faced in the US. During the 1980s and 1990s, a network of social-justice evangelicals, whose education in activism came during the heyday of liberation theology in the 1960s and 1970s, continued to wield theological tools passed on to them by their mentors. Much like Padilla in Buenos Aires, they attacked with special intensity the city streets of America, which suffered from drugs, crime, and deindustrialization. Their priorities included reforming urban neighborhoods through community-development programs and cooperatives promoted by leading black evangelical advocates John Perkins and Tom Skinner. In 1989 they created the Christian Community Development Association (CDA). Led by Perkins and Wayne Gordon, comprised of forty member organizations, with a base on Chicago's West Side, the CDA quickly emerged as a key advocate for local reforms. By 1995 its membership counted three hundred organizations in thirty-five states and one hundred American cities. Meanwhile, progressives associated with the CDA supported higher-profile campaigns as well by throwing their support behind progressive presidential candidates (John Anderson and Jesse Jackson), starting a People's Party, and populating national public housing organizations such as Housing Now![38]

37. A brief history appears on the INFEMIT webpage, http://infemit.org/sample-page/history/; Tizon, *Transformation after Lausanne*, 73–79.

38. John Perkins, ed., *Restoring At-Risk Communities: Doing It Together and Doing It Right* (Grand Rapids: Baker, 1995), 239; Swartz, *Moral Minority*, 252. This network of urban outreach is documented fully by Stephanie Wolfe in her dissertation, "Urban

Another urban landscape witnessed its own demonstration of a Latin American–inspired, wear-it-on-the-sleeve faith. This one came in yet another guise, one that clashed with a few of FTL's and INFEM-IT's priorities. Informed by his own life experience in Bolivia, C. Peter Wagner, now a Fuller theologian, spent the 1980s promoting a holistic gospel that shared most—though not all—of the requisites of the original Lausanne Covenant. At this juncture he remained firm in his opposition to liberationists' tendency to privilege social restructuring over traditional evangelism; yet his endorsement of a "signs and wonders" theology and ambitions to restructure evangelicalism itself in accordance with the multiethnic dynamics of his day placed him within Escobar's and Padilla's theological purview. Because of the rising influence of the global South, and its reach north through immigration, the US's "melting pot" had become a "stew pot" of cultural and theological possibilities; in Wagner's mind, this necessitated a restrategizing of the Great Commission. Wagner's work toward this end transpired through mentorship of international seminarians such as Enrique Torres, a Chilean-American who studied at Fuller and planted Hispanic churches in Los Angeles, and network-building enterprises that drew Korean, Japanese, and especially Hispanic ministers into a collective mandate for cross-cultural evangelism. Regarding their new neighbors, Wagner reminded Anglo evangelicals, "God cares for their bodies, their souls, their minds, their spirits, and their social relationships. And he calls us as Christians, no matter what our racial or national background, to be his instruments for reaching them with the message of the kingdom of God." "What an enormous vision."[39]

This vision inspired a major undertaking in 1985, the first National Convocation on Evangelizing Ethnic America, held in Houston. Co-sponsored by the Billy Graham Evangelistic Association and the North American Lausanne Committee, and co-led by area Hispanic and African American pastors (including John Perkins), the congress gathered seven hundred pastors, missionaries, lay leaders, and academics to "acknowledge the depth of the population shifts and to design strategy for turning 'unevangelized' ethnic families into Christians." The takeaway

Renewal: The Evangelical Encounter with Race, Poverty and Inequality in Chicago, 1968-Present" (PhD diss., Northwestern University, 2015).

39. C. Peter Wagner, "A Vision for Evangelizing the Real America," *International Bulletin of Missionary Research* 10, no. 2 (April 1986): 59, 62.

for those who attended the event was one of renewal—and a sense that American evangelicalism was crossing a threshold of the world's making. Wagner's keynote address, later distributed through the national press, proclaimed that an ethnic revolution was offering the church a fresh chance to dismantle prejudices, stress unity over difference, and move forward into an epoch of unprecedented cooperation and growth. Even in this multicultural milieu, social injustice would not disappear easily, Wagner assured his audience: "We must work at it." But witnessed in this gathering, he continued, were signs that intercultural contact was enriching and was the necessity of the age, for Christians and for the country. "Today's America is a multi-ethnic society on a scale that boggles the imagination. The teeming multitudes of all colors, languages, smells, and cultures are not just a quaint sideline in our nation; they are America."[40]

In order to help a new generation of American evangelicals to come to terms with the disorienting transformations of their day, leaders in Wagner's, Perkins's, and Padilla's expanding circles endeavored in a final realm of renewal: international humanitarianism. This enterprise operated on multiple altitudes of interest, with widening breadth as the century drew to a close.

At the lowest altitude, evangelical pastors, members of their parishes, and educational institutions facilitated cross-cultural encounter through exchange programs. As Michael Clawson writes, during the 1980s and 1990s progressive evangelicals affiliated with the Latin American liberationists "kept a toe-hold in certain key locations within the evangelical world, most importantly in its seminaries and liberal arts colleges as well as prominent youth and campus ministries." A case in point was Escobar himself, who spent these years teaching spring semesters at the Baptist Seminary of Madrid (Spain), the fall semesters at the Eastern Baptist Theological Seminary and Eastern University in Pennsylvania, and much of his free time speaking to college-aged young people, including at the Urbana convention of 1990. In these intellectual hubs, the ideas of "integral mission" gained another life; besides absorbing Escobar's pedagogical offerings, many students from colleges such as Eastern spent

40. "Immigrants Called 'Ripe for Harvest Field' for Churches," *Los Angeles Times*, April 20, 1985, 1; Wesley D. Balda, ed., *Heirs of the Same Promise: Using Acts as a Study Guide for Evangelizing Ethnic America* (Arcadia, CA: National Convocation on Evangelizing Ethnic America, 1984), 1, 61, 65; Wagner, "A Vision for Evangelizing the Real America," 59.

their summer months undertaking short-term missions that espoused social-justice teachings. Local churches supported this effort by sponsoring their young parishioners' trips to the "two-thirds-world" settings of Central America and South America for their inculcation in the dynamics of a plural world. Helping on all fronts were agencies such as The Micah Network, which INFEMIT established in the 1990s to provide "leadership development for mission groups," facilitate collaboration, connect "global evangelical agencies engaged in integral mission," and even "coordinate evangelical support for the United Nations Millennium Development Goals."[41]

While the goals stayed the same, this engagement unfolded on a more impressive scale when guided by some of America's most influential and recognizable church movements and pastors. Each embraced international humanitarianism as a second facet of the Great Commission. For pastor Rick Warren, the mandate was clear. In the late twentieth century and as the millennium turned, Warren brought to fruition years of deep interest in world affairs—and built on the example of his mentor, Ralph Winter—by making his megachurch in Southern California a marshaling zone for collaboration in the global South. Prison outreach, recovery programs, AIDS programs: these and a host of other social initiatives drove Warren to write about a New Testament gospel with sweeping social implications and to build direct ties to Latin America by way of church planting and philanthropy. In return, Latin American Christians readily digested his published teachings on the *Purpose Driven Life* and *Purpose Driven Church*. The latter proved especially popular in Latin America and spurred church-growth conferences in Mexico, Costa Rica, Colombia, Argentina, and Venezuela; by the early 2000s it was adopted by more than five hundred congregations in Brazil as a model to follow.[42]

Warren's was not the only churchly venture into cross-cultural association. During the last years of the twentieth century, the "emerging church" movement within American evangelicalism consciously adopted the progressive ethics of the Latin American liberationists and folded them into a postmodern theological quest to "contextualize" the gospel for young people. With increasing intent, "emergent" evangelicals de-

41. Clawson, "*Misión Integral* and Progressive Evangelicalism," 798-99.
42. On Rick Warren's international program and popularity in Latin America, see www.christianpost.com/news/rick-warrens-popularity-and-influ ence-in-latin-america-50624/; and http://www.pewforum.org/2009/11/13/ the-future-of-evangelicals-a-conversation-with-pastor-rick-warren/.

fined their view in the familiar terms of "integral mission" and reimagined "the church as existing to serve the world in a more holistic way." Helped along by popular veteran left-wing evangelical authors such as Jim Wallis and Tom Sine, "emergent" evangelicals "turned toward an explicit emphasis on social justice as integral to the meaning of the gospel and the mission of the church." Leading them was pastor Brian McLaren, who personified the theological evolution. Besides overseeing a collective intellectual conversion to ideas of integral mission, he also furthered it through his own personal encounters with Latin America. With the Padilla family's assistance, he spent several months in Latin America, getting to know local pastors and absorbing their evangelistic style, then returned to the US where he endorsed integral mission theology through his writings, most notably his 2005 text *Everything Must Change: Jesus, Global Crises, and a Revolution of Hope*.[43]

While McLaren journeyed through South America and penned his reflections for the benefit of American evangelicals, more ambitious schemes for evangelical cross-border collaboration played out in the hands of nonprofit and developmental agencies. For many evangelicals in the private sector, business was seen as the best way of transmitting the New Testament message to globalizing societies. "Great Commission Companies," proponents claimed, could avoid some of the anti-missionary hostilities present in "two-thirds" nations and deliver the "Good News" to under-developed, under-evangelized populations by way of intentionally Christian corporate mobilization. While borrowing some of the same logic that said the Christian message should be packaged and delivered with economic development in mind, several other evangelical agencies nevertheless tweaked the agenda so that nonprofit labors received the heaviest emphasis. Al Tizon, a member of INFEMIT's council, recalled the amount of energy that American evangelicals poured into humanitarian efforts during the 1970s, especially helping to rebuild disaster zones (such as the one created by the Nicaragua earthquake in 1972), and the manner in which this impulse "began to broaden from primarily relief work to development work." "Indeed," he writes, "by the mid-1970s, thanks to the social affirmation at Lausanne I, devel-

43. Clawson, "*Misión Integral* and Progressive Evangelicalism," 800–801; Brian McLaren, "Introduction: A Conversation about Justice," in *The Justice Project*, ed. Brian McLaren, Elisa Padilla, and Ashley Bunting Seeber (Grand Rapids: Baker, 2009), 13–20. See also Bryant L. Myers, *Walking with the Poor: Principles and Practices of Transformational Development*, rev. ed. (Maryknoll, NY: Orbis, 2011), 48–49.

opment became a major missiological activity. Many evangelical relief agencies became agencies of relief *and* development."[44]

The most impressive institutional conduit for this objective was World Vision. During the 1970s this agency, created to help rebuild post–World War II Korea, extended its international, bureaucratic, and theological reach as an integrated and multifaceted international non-governmental organization (INGO). As the Reagan and Clinton eras unfolded, and with them heated culture wars in domestic politics, World Vision led other religious INGOs into a shared imperative "to promote human transformation, seek justice and bear witness to the good news of the Kingdom of God" and turn evangelical eyes away from home to crucial systemic needs abroad. With Latin America figuring prominently in their expansion—and as a source of inspiration—World Vision carved out impressive influence across the global South. By the early twenty-first century, it staffed 40,000 employees and maintained an annual budget of $2.6 billion for the sake of providing "emergency relief, community development, and advocacy alongside the world's poor and oppressed."[45]

Because of their wide-ranging agendas, World Vision and its peer evangelical INGOs were forced to enter politics as well. On US soil they found it prudent to forge friendships with Washington politicians and operate as lobbies in order to structure faith-government alliances large enough to combat the largest of world humanitarian crises. On foreign fronts, meanwhile, these organizations assumed the added burdens and conundrums that arose when trying to deal with authoritarian regimes that operated according to their own rules, with little compunction where social and economic justice, democracy, and religious freedom were concerned. The awkwardness of this stand, evidenced most acutely in Latin America, put evangelicals in perpetually vulnerable spots. While in one case, for instance, they felt forced by expediency to side with the socialist-friendly Sandinista government in Nicaragua, in another they had to frame an alliance with the Guatemalan military dictatorship of José Ríos Montt.[46]

44. On the corporate side of Christian outreach see, for instance, Steve Rundle and Tom Steffen, *Great Commission Companies: The Emerging Role of Business in Mission* (Downers Grove, IL: InterVarsity, 2003); Tizon, *Transformation after Lausanne*, 33-34, 36.

45. David King, "The New Internationalists: World Vision and the Revival of American Evangelical Humanitarianism, 1950-2010," *Religions* 3 (2012): 924.

46. Karl-Wilhelm Westmeier, *Protestant Pentecostalism in Latin America: A Study in the Dynamics of Missions* (Cranbury, NJ: Associated University Presses, 1999), 77-79.

Evangelical interventions in these regions not only affected US foreign policy but also brought to the forefront yet another core concern: religious liberty. Not unlike Samuel Escobar and René Padilla, who as young men felt firsthand the fear of being persecuted for their religious commitments and who took it upon themselves to fight on behalf of their own religious minorities, late-twentieth-century evangelical INGOs committed themselves to protecting freedom of conscience as a fundamental human right. This drive received forceful articulation in the National Association of Evangelicals' "Peace, Freedom and Human Rights" resolution of 1987 and "Statement of Conscience Concerning Worldwide Religious Persecution" of 1997, which demanded government action against all repression of religious (especially evangelical Protestant) freedoms throughout the world. Although unsettled by the compromises that their evangelical brethren often entertained and yet encouraged as a result of this purview, Padilla, Escobar, and their allies understood the discourse around which earnest believers now rallied.[47]

They also appreciated the broader context in which this discourse gained traction. As historians such as David King, David Swartz, Andrew Preston, and Lauren Turek have documented, by the end of the century American evangelicals' most impressive political commitments were not necessarily those that fueled the culture wars of the Religious Right, but rather those that framed an "evangelical internationalism" whose outward focus on global human rights, economic development, and social justice signified the legacy of Latin American liberationists and their longstanding quest to push back against Western assumptions and insularities and compel Western Christians to accept their new age of reliance on the rest of the world.[48]

It remains to be seen just how accepting American evangelicals will be of this reality as the new millennium unfolds. But it is safe to

---

47. On the rise of religious liberty and human rights in the late twentieth century, see Allen D. Hertzke, *Freeing God's Children: The Unlikely Alliance for Global Human Rights* (New York: Rowman & Littlefield, 2004).

48. See King, "The New Internationalists"; Swartz, "Embodying the Global Soul"; as well as Lauren Turek, "To Bring the Good News to All Nations: Evangelicals, Human Rights, and U.S. Foreign Policy, 1969-1994" (PhD diss., University of Virginia, 2015), and Andrew Preston, "Evangelical Internationalism: A Conservative Worldview for the Age of Globalization," in *The Right Side of the Sixties: Reexamining Conservatism's Decade of Transformation*, ed. Laura Jane Gifford and Daniel K. Williams (New York: Palgrave Macmillan, 2012), 221-41.

say (as Swartz indeed says) that these "emerging structural and global sensibilities are likely a mere shadow of the future." Whether American evangelicals are ready and accepting or not, "international voices will most certainly swell to a chorus in the next century." Among them will be heard—likely overwhelming the others—the Spanish intonations of Christianity spoken in Latin American dialects.[49]

Recent indications from around the world certainly do suggest that the Latin turn in American evangelicalism sparked by Cold War ricochets of people and ideas and the revolutions and renewals of purpose that followed Lausanne '74 will only accelerate in the coming years. The Lausanne movement itself continues to enlist its members in the integral mission of its founders and extend the aims of the alliance through "implementation of diaspora missiology," which seeks to enhance "understanding and [participation] in God's redemptive mission among people living outside their place of origin." One mission field that has been labeled especially needy in this regard is North America, a place that leaders of the ascendant "Third Church" of the global and Latin American South have targeted with particular fervor. South-north paths once traveled in relative isolation by Samuel Escobar and René Padilla are now virtual highways, with missionaries, pastors, and laypeople streaming north to save a society they fear is being lost to secularism. Meanwhile, thanks in part to Escobar and the Padilla family (now led by Ruth Padilla DeBorst), the work of InterVarsity, INFEMIT, the International Fellowship of Evangelical Students, and their peer ministries to young evangelicals continues to bear fruit, evidenced in part by the thousands that regularly attend "International Urbana" congresses and related conferences in South America's largest centers.

This vigorous give-and-take between the global North and South is a spirit that is also lighting up Protestant-Catholic relations. Every bit as striking a Latin American reflex is seen in the challenging conditions that now face a Latin American Catholic pope who embodies the counter-establishment spirit of liberation theology and the reforming mindset of Vatican II. A bridge-builder who is seeking better relations with other faiths, including evangelical Protestantism, Pope Francis is also fully aware that the evangelical movement that has swept his South American continent in the past generation, and seemingly made Pentecostalism the church of the future and Catholicism the church of the past, must

49. Swartz, "Embodying the Global South," 898.

be offset if his church is to survive. Signs suggest that he also recognizes that the way to do it will be through implementation of a dynamic, holistic gospel of radical renewal—not too different from the homegrown gospel Padilla, Escobar, and their friends first brought to America and enunciated in Switzerland long ago. So it is that the two "major turning points" Mark Noll suggested as parallels in his assessment of late-twentieth-century Christianity have essentially become one.[50]

50. Chandler H. Im and Amos Yong, eds., *Global Diasporas and Mission* (Eugene, OR: Wipf & Stock, 2014), 214-15; Samuel Escobar, *The New Global Mission: The Gospel from Everywhere to Everyone* (Downers Grove, IL: InterVarsity, 2003), 16. On the pope, Catholicism, and evangelicalism in South America, see, for instance, Virginia Garrard-Burnett, "Catholicism Can Win Back Evangelicals in Latin America," *New York Times*, March 15, 2013.

Afterword

Martin E. Marty

Once a revolution has occurred, it is difficult for those who live on and look on after it to recall what life was like before it was experienced. Some survivors "freeze" their image of life as it was "back then" and want to preserve it as they remember its days. Paul Tillich, for one example, contended that most of the conservative Daughters of the American Revolution organization had no comprehension of what a revolution is or how to interpret "their" American Revolution. Others picture a revolution as a total break with the past and fail to see the continuities between "before" and "after."

Happily, readers of this book did not have to contend with a revolution in the career of American evangelicalism, since the editors and authors made no more drastic claims than that "turning points" had occurred. Each writer disciplined his or her approach by assessing, at chapter length, one major "point" among them. Also, happily, the authors did not turn the book into a set of expansive philosophical discourses about the value of the term "turning points" when they were dealing with one of them within the flow of time and history. A few contributors, expressing themselves as historians and not as philosophers, did admit to some reservations about the adequacy and accuracy of the "turning point" trope. Then, as we have seen, each quickly concentrated on his or her assigned business of isolating what happened as American evangelicalism was being transformed in its course within national life. Like the honored dedicatee of the book, Mark Noll, they knew that some big and decisive things *had* occurred and they were called to be responsible in telling their part of the story of what historian Noll, with caution and finesse, had treated as "turning points."

As one who has published historical writings on American religion through the whole period covered in this book, I can testify that "big and decisive" and even "transformative" events and conceptual changes forced themselves into the agendas and understandings of both publics and historians. These did alter the understanding of what evangelicalism was and is and how it and the surrounding host culture have changed the larger story of American life. As citizens and as historians, many of us experienced the jolts of change, some from the centers of action and others from nearer the margins.

As a participant in many scholarly conferences on evangelicalism through the decades, I was used to getting introduced as "this year's non-evangelical participant" until I reminded the evangelical hosts and majority present that I was the only person in the symposium who was a member of a church body whose very name included the word "evangelical." I have used my ambiguous stance as a way to enjoy and appraise these chapters, just as I am sure that readers with "secular," "other-religious," and "evangelical" presuppositions alike found themselves doing.

Here are two samples of change: one, treatments of women, their roles and their stories, implicit in the chapters; and the other, formal accounts here of newcomers within evangelicalism called fundamentalism and Pentecostalism.

Women, first. When I started teaching and writing, I think there were only two or three women members of the American Society of Church History. (The American Catholic Historical Society, with its numbers of members from orders of religious women, had all the rest of us beat!) It is hard to picture a more impressive "turning point" for our profession than the arrival of women and, with them, feminist perspectives and women-centered narratives. So drastic have been many of the alterations in language, choices of topics, scholarly approaches, and, of course, perspectives, which the editors in this book could almost take for granted, that they did not find it necessary to assign a generic chapter on "women." Women show up as subjects of historians' inquiries everywhere, whether assigned as a subject or not.

Thus, for one sample, Catherine Brekus, without stopping to write a theoretical or programmatic essay on "feminism," found it valid to tell a fresh story of the Enlightenment as it was interwoven with evangelicalism, not by turning to "Enlightened" Harvard or Yale or other settings where scholars are committed to hermeneutical ventures on topics like these. Instead, she found it revelatory to exegete the homely reflections of an apparently otherwise overlookable Sarah Osborn to throw light on a subject that historians had often tended to bypass. Similarly, Marguerite Van Die could not likely have found a ready readership on a story of "domesticity," had not the academic and much in the encompassing culture been quickened to be curious about the extraordinary thinking of ordinary people, who so often "happened" to be women.

Second, *fundamentalism and Pentecostalism*. "Overt" evangelical scholars increasingly came to find places as students, on faculties, and as published scholars in what came to be called "mainstream" or "mainline" institutions within the half-generation after Mark Noll & Company came to prominence. Before this vocational "turning point," researchers and writers in what we might call "standard brand" scholarly circles tended to neglect or disdain the millions of Americans who were distant from them, "overlookable," and not the subject of curiosity or fair treatment. However, just before the times of turning that Noll chronicled in his books, a new version of evangelicalism called fundamentalism had emerged (ca. 1925) to further distance evangelicals from the zones most historians inhabited.

Some of the inherited distance resulted from the attacks, polemics, and sneers of once-born-and-bred fundamentalists themselves who had been turning-pointers, as they moved emphatically outside their traditional camp. They thus became "apostates," and enjoyed their new status. Philosopher Max Scheler observed that apostates tend to spend their entire subsequent career taking revenge on their own spiritual pasts. Earlier, who would have noticed the fundamentalists, except to sneer at them? Who would have shown curiosity, done research among long-neglected resources, and fairly told the story of fundamentalism or the even more outlandish Pentecostalism?

In those "pre-turning point" years, study of these topics had had to be almost covert. I recall one time visiting the study of Donald Dayton, a then-emerging scholar of Pentecostalism, in an hour when we were assessing his in-house library. I'd been at my business for several decades, but I found his collection of books to be unfamiliar, even alienating. I noticed and confessed that almost none of his books would be found in my "typical" library. Dayton bade me carefully to notice his collection of titles. Hundreds of his sources, until then virtually unknown to me, he happily pointed out, had outsold the books most colleagues and I considered to be "standard brand." These writings spoke about and to crowds of citizens who were making their kind of impacts on the larger culture and society. But who cared? Who cared until the "turning point" periods discussed in chapters here by George Marsden and Edith Blumhofer? Then came transformations.

What brought about the historiographical changes? Part of the answer, well-noticed and well-chronicled in this book, were scholars such as Mark Noll and other authors of chapters in this book who had quietly, within one generation, invaded the precincts of the long-established cultural standard bearers. They focused on these long-overlooked variants within evangelicalism and treated them with (albeit critical) respect. These scholars were themselves being discovered, and they have been making their way onto elite faculties and into the rosters of writers of influential journals and academic book markets. They no longer have to hide, apologize for their existence, take refuge, or disguise themselves and appear under false banners. Without being ostentatious about it, they have been winning academic prizes, garnering influential reviews, and educating generations of successors who share their interests.

Authors of forewords have one basic assignment: to help readers of a text anticipate its contents, which may mean to tantalize, inspire curiosity, or make preliminary judgments concerning the relative value of different elements in the content of what is to follow. Authors of afterwords, however, address readers who, presumably, have already used their own intelligence to make judgments about what they have just read. In the present case, they have been introduced into a discussion of "turning points" and then had twelve content-rich chapters to help them locate themselves in the flow and flux of history as they go about their own scholarly pursuits, their quest for intellectual satisfaction, and—it sounds banal to say—their daily lives.

In my view, one of the best guides for future pursuit of turning points, transformations, or quasi-revolutionary changes is the Spanish philosopher José Ortega y Gasset. I would like to use him as a kind of witness to the need by citizens and especially historians to locate themselves in the midst of change. "Decisive historical changes," he wrote, "do not come from great wars, terrible cataclysms, or ingenious inventions. It is enough that the heart of man incline its sensitive crown to one side or the other of the horizon." He went on to mention an inclination "toward optimism or toward pessimism, toward heroism or toward utility, toward combat or toward peace." Here we might point to the animating forces described in the chapters in this book.

It is not difficult to chronicle "decisive events," such as the Civil

War, but most of what concerns historians about it now is not merely the counts of victims or the number of cannon, but the chronicles of pain, suffering, loneliness, and moral debate, which, taken together, involve the inclinations of the sensitive crown of hearts to the stirrings that in different times added up to "Pentecostalism," events named, for example, "The Great Awakening," or adjustments such as those toward "domesticity." A commentator on Ortega, my colleague and mentor in this realm, Karl J. Weintraub, reflected on Ortega's observations thus:

> Man [pardon the overuse of "man"] is characteristically a fabricator of "worlds." In response to the problems posed by his circumstances, he shapes an interpretation of his reality and develops instruments and techniques for acting within this reality. The interpretations of his reality, and his actions in and upon it, *are* his world. The human drama consists then of the following sequence: man finds himself amid circumstances—he builds his world out of these and out of his own activity—he thereby creates new circumstances—these again demand a response, a new creation, and so forth. "Each transformation of the world and its horizon brings a change in the structure of life's drama."

This kind of "transformation"—or in the terms of this book, "turning point"—serves thus. Survivors of the Civil War, as they compared notes and told their stories, located themselves in their world, and thus in ours. In evangelicalism, one person may be "converted" or "awakened," but when she is seen as part of a company of the "born again," we observe a transformation that will be widely regarded as and used as a "turning point."

The authors in this book have not merely entertained or transmitted packaged facts as they set out to detail elements in the rise of modern American evangelicalism. They have paid attention to the "sensitive crown" of the human heart and, responsive to the signals around them, "fabricated" worlds for themselves, for us readers, and more. The company of fabricators in this book, I have no doubt, would be ready to speak, in English versions, of the ascription T. S. Eliot used for the dedicatee of his great poem "The Waste Land:" "For Ezra Pound *il miglior fabbro*," "the greater craftsman." In the craft of historical writing about American evangelicalism and its world, they and many other scholars would be ready to pay their respects by calling dedicatee Mark Noll *il miglior fabbro*, the greater craftsman indeed.

Contributors

Edith L. Blumhofer is professor of history at Wheaton College. Her published works include *Aimee Semple McPherson: Everybody's Sister* (Eerdmans, 1993) and *Restoring the Faith: The Assemblies of God, Pentecostalism*, and *American Culture* (University of Illinois Press, 1993).

Catherine A. Brekus is Charles Warren Professor of the History of Religion in America at Harvard Divinity School and in the Department of American Studies at Harvard University. She is the author of *Sarah Osborn's World: The Rise of Evangelical Christianity in Early America* (Yale University Press, 2013).

Jon Butler is Howard R. Lamar Professor Emeritus of American Studies, History, and Religious Studies at Yale University and adjunct research professor of history at the University of Minnesota, Twin Cities. He is the author of *Awash in a Sea of Faith: Christianizing the American People* (Harvard University Press, 1992) and *Becoming America: The Revolution before 1776* (Harvard University Press, 2001).

Heath W. Carter is an assistant professor of history at Valparaiso University. He is the author of *Union Made: Working People and the Rise of Social Christianity in Chicago* (Oxford University Press) and coeditor of *The Pew and the Picket Line: Christianity and the American Working Class* (University of Illinois Press).

Richard Carwardine served as Rhodes Professor of American History and as president of Corpus Christi College at Oxford University. He is the author of *Lincoln: A Life of Purpose and Power* (Vintage, 2007) and *Evangelicals and Politics in Antebellum America* (University of Tennessee Press, 1997). He has a particular interest in the religion and politics of the Civil War era.

Dennis C. Dickerson is James M. Lawson Jr. Professor of History at Vanderbilt University. He is the author of *Out of the Crucible: Black Steelworkers in Western Pennsylvania, 1875-1980* (State University of New York Press, 1986), *Militant Mediator: Whitney M. Young Jr.* (University Press of Kentucky, 1998), and *African American Preachers and Politics: The Careys of Chicago* (University Press of Mississippi, 2010).

Darren Dochuk is associate professor of history at the University of Notre Dame. He is author of *From Bible Belt to Sunbelt: Plain-Folk Religion, Grassroots Politics, and the Rise of Evangelical Conservatism* (Norton, 2012) and, most recently, coeditor of *Faith in the New Millennium: The Future of Religion and Politics* (Oxford University Press, 2016).

Luke E. Harlow is associate professor of history at the University of Tennessee, Knoxville. He is the author of *Religion, Race, and the Making of Confederate Kentucky, 1830-1880* (Cambridge University Press, 2014), and coeditor, with Mark A. Noll, of *Religion and American Politics: From the Colonial Period to the Present* (Oxford University Press, 2007).

Nathan O. Hatch is president of Wake Forest University and author of *The Democratization of American Christianity* (Yale University Press, 1989).

Mark Hutchinson is dean of education and arts and professor of history and society at Alphacrucis College, Sydney, Australia. He is an intellectual historian who has written widely on the history of evangelical Christianity and on the history of Australian higher education.

George M. Marsden has held teaching positions at Calvin College, Duke Divinity School, and the University of Notre Dame. His books include *Fundamentalism and American Culture* (Oxford University Press, 1980), *Jonathan Edwards: A Life* (Yale University Press, 2003), and *C. S. Lewis's* Mere Christianity: *A Biography* (Princeton University Press, 2016).

Martin E. Marty is the Fairfax M. Cone Distinguished Service Professor Emeritus at the University of Chicago and author or editor of dozens of books. More recently he coedited a revised edition of *The Unrelieved Paradox: Studies in the Theology of Franz Bibfeldt* (Eerdmans, 2012).

Laura Rominger Porter is an independent scholar based in Des Moines, Iowa. Her current research examines evangelicals and moral politics in the nineteenth-century South.

Harry S. Stout is the Jonathan Edwards Professor of American Religious History at Yale and general editor of The Works of Jonathan Edwards. He has authored numerous books and articles in the field of American history. His forthcoming book is entitled *The Andersons of Kentucky: Land, Anxiety, and the Making of America.*

Marguerite Van Die is professor emerita of history and religion at Queen's University in Kingston, Ontario, Canada. Her research and publications focus on lived religion, family, and gender in the nineteenth century.

Grant Wacker is Gilbert T. Rowe Professor Emeritus of Christian History at Duke Divinity School. He is the author of *Heaven Below: Early Pentecostals and American Culture* (Harvard University Press, 2003) and *America's Pastor: Billy Graham and the Shaping of a Nation* (Harvard University Press, 2014).

Index

Abington School District v. Schempp, 58

Abolitionism, 16–17, 71–74, 79–80, 109, 116, 119–22. *See also* Emancipation; Slavery

Abraham, 5

Abuse, clerical sex, 51

Action. *See* Social action

Acts, book of, 37, 114, 268

Adams, Hannah, 47

Adger, John, 74

Aesthetics, 13–14

Affections, 14–15

African Americans, 40, 70; and the Civil War, 110, 113, 117–19, 125–27, 130; and the Great Migration, 181–85, 189–90, 193–96; and music, 198–201; women, 197–98. *See also* Blacks

African Methodist Episcopal Church (AME), 117; and the Great Migration, 180–85, 189–90, 195–96

Ali, Noble Drew, 193. *See also* Drew, Timothy

Alito, Samuel, 62–63

Allen, Richard, 116–17

Amendments to the US Constitution: Eighteenth, 143; Fifteenth, 124; First, 47–51, 63; Fourteenth, 124; Nineteenth, 143; Thirteenth, 107, 124

American Anti-Slavery Society (AASS), 71, 73, 79, 119

American Colonization Society (ACS), 72, 73, 117

Amos (the prophet), 29

Andrew, James, 76

Apostolic Faith, 163–64, 168

Appadurai, Arjun, 204–5

Arensbach, C. N., 166

Arlington School District v. Schempp, 50

Atoms, enlightenment notions of, 11–13

Awakenings. *See* Great Awakening, the; Second Great Awakening, the

Azusa Street, 163, 191–92

Bangs, Nathan, 77

Baptists: Southern, 74–77, 126; Swedish, 160–62, 168–69

Bebbington, David, 24, 105, 209

Becker, Carl, 18

Beecher, Catharine, 92–93

Beecher, Henry Ward, 95

Beecher, Lyman, 68, 72–73, 119

Bendroth, Margaret, 95

Benevolence, 16, 36, 66, 68–69

Berg, Daniel, 168–69

Best, Wallace, 197

Beuttler, Fred, 248–49

Bibb, Henry, 113

Bible, the, 20, 111
Biblicism, 112, 114–15, 130, 132, 135, 140, 145
Bie, Mary Ellen, 164
Birney, James, 79, 119, 120
Blacks: and the Civil War, 113, 117, 118; and the Enlightenment, 37, 38, 40; and the Great Migration, 180–94, 197–201; and Pentecostalism, 177, 178. *See also* African Americans
Blain, James G., 55
Blain Amendment, 55
Blair, Samuel, 26
Blumhofer, Edith, 136
Bowron, Fletcher, 232
Bradby, Robert, 186–87
Brainerd, David, 46
Brazil, 167, 169, 270
Brekus, Catherine, 15–16
Brennan, William, 58, 60
Brinkman, George, 176
Brinkman, Klazien Balkema, 176
Brookes, Iveson, 74
Brown, Bob, 209
Brown, Candy Gunther, 86
Bryan, William Jennings, 133–35, 148
Burger, Warren, 60–61
Burning Bush, the (holiness group), 163
Burwash, Nathanael, 96
Burwell v. Hobby Lobby, 45, 62–63
Bushnell, Horace, 96, 122
Business, 59–63
Butler, Jon, xvi, 1

Calvinism, 8, 10–11, 67
Campbell, David, 52
Carlson, Martin, 168
Carter, Jimmy, 267
Case, Shirley Jackson, 142
Catholics, 51, 55–58, 62, 69–70, 280
Cemeteries, rural, 99–100
Chauncy, Charles, 30
Chiang Kai-shek, 217, 220
Chicago Alliance, the, 158–59, 170, 173–75

Child, Harriet, 84–85
Children: and domestic religion, 85–87, 90, 92, 94–97; Enlightenment notions of, 28
China, 208–11, 216–20, 229–30
Christian and Missionary Alliance, 156, 165, 173. *See also* Chicago Alliance
Christian Businessmen's Committee of Los Angeles, 230–34, 239, 240, 242–43, 245
Christian Catholic Church, the, 156
Christian Community Development Association (CDA), 273
Church and state, separation of, 35, 50, 55, 67, 78, 100, 105
Churches, black, 113, 114, 125, 178; and the Great Migration, 180–201
Church growth, and the Great Migration, 184
Church of God in Christ (COGIC), 192–93, 198
Civil rights, 132
Civil War: and antebellum reform, 83; and conservative evangelicalism, 107, 109–11, 115, 123, 125–28; and domesticity, 98
Clark, Theodore, 65–66
Clark, Thomas, 58
Clawson, Michael, 275
Coker, Daniel, 116–17
Colby, Charles, 84–85
Collier, John, 55–56
Colonization, 72–73, 117–18
Colored Union Church, the, 40
Communism, 211, 229–30, 262
Confederates, 109, 122
Congreso Latinoamericano de Evangelizacion (CLADE), 257, 260
Constitution, the Federal, 44, 47, 58
Contraceptives, 62–63
Conversion, 33, 67, 95–97, 137, 142, 172
Corinthians, First Letter to the, 114
Court, the Supreme, 57–58, 60–63

Daniel, Everard, 186–87
Darby, John Nelson, 138

Darwinism, 147-48
Davies, Samuel, 19-20, 25, 28-31, 33, 35-36; conversion of, 26; *Miscellaneous Poems, Chiefly on Divine Subjects*, 26; and slavery, 37
Davis, Jefferson, 83
Death, 97-99
DeMille, Cecil B., 61
Democrats, 81, 127
Discipleship, radical, 262-64
Dispensationalism, 138-40, 145, 149-51
Dixon, Calvin, 198-99
Domesticity, cult of, 85, 92
Dorsey, Thomas, 200-201
Douglass, Frederick, 70-71, 121-22
Dowie, John Alexander, 156, 157, 160, 174
Dred Scott, 55
Drew, Timothy (became Noble Drew Ali), 193
Duckrey, James Henry, 186
Durham, William Howard, 164-67, 169-78
Dwight, Sereno, 40
Dwight, Timothy, 95

Eckert, Craig, 208
Ecuador, 253-55
Edwards, Jonathan, 1, 7-18, 87; "A Divine and Supernatural Light," 13; heirs of, 16; *Notes on the Mind*, 11; "On Being," 11; *Treatise on the Religious Affections*, 14-15; *Treatise on True Virtue*, 16
Edwards, Jonathan, Jr., 16-17
Eisenhower, Dwight D., 59-60
Elliot, Jim, 254-55
Emancipation, 72, 110, 117, 130
Engel v. Vitale, 50, 58-60
Enlightenment, the: and evangelicalism, 21-25, 27-31, 33-35, 42-43; and the Great Awakening, 8, 10, 13-17
Ericson, Brenda, 218
Escobar, Samuel, 251, 257-59, 263-65, 267-68, 272, 274-75, 279-81; early life and conversion of, 255-56; and Frater-

nidad Teológica Latinoamericana (FTL), 260-62; and Lausanne, 259
Evangelicalism, radical, 165
Evans, Mary G., 194-97
Evolution, 141, 144, 147-48
Exodus, book of, 111
Exodus, African American, 126, 181-84, 186, 190, 194
Experience, individual, 7-9, 15, 18, 21-22, 24, 31-33. *See also* Sensation

Falwell, Jerry, 152
Family, 84-87, 90-101, 103-6
Faust, Drew Gilpin, 97
Federal Council of Churches, the, 134
Fiering, Norman, 21
Finney, Charles Grandison, 65, 67, 78, 116, 119
Flanders, Ralph, 58
Folke-Vennen, 168
Ford Motor Company, 186-87
Fosdick, Harry Emerson, 145
Foster, Charles, 68
Francescon, Luigi, 161, 167
Francis (Pope), 280-81
Fraternidad Teológica Latinoamericana (FTL), 260-62, 266
Free African Union Society, the, 40
Freedom, religious, 35-36, 39, 45, 47, 50-52
Freud, Sigmund, 14
Fuller, Charles, 246
Fuller, Richard, 112
Fundamentalism, 131, 135, 139, 141, 144-51, 153, 284; and politics, 152
Fundamentalists, definition of, 135, 153

Galatians, letter to the, 114
Gallup, George, Jr., xiv
Gardner, Newport (original African name Occramar Marycoo), 20, 37-43
Garr, A. G., 163
Garr, Lillian, 163
Garrison, William Lloyd, 71, 119-22
Garver, Edward, 244
Gasaway, Brantley, 266

Index

Gay, Peter, 22
Gender, 85, 91, 194
Gentry, William, 173
Gillis, John, 105
Ginsburg, Ruth Bader, 62–63
Glossolalia, 191, 196
Gospel, social. *See* Social gospel
Grace, supernatural, 12–15
Gradualism, 69, 72, 117–19
Graham, Billy, 60, 151, 210, 211, 226–35,
    239–46, 264; appearance of, 236;
    sermons of, 237–38
Graham, Franklin, 215, 220–21
Grant, Ulysses S., 55–56
Great Awakening, the, 1–3; and George
    Whitefield, 5–9; and Jonathan
    Edwards, 11, 13, 15, 17. *See also* New
    Birth, the
Great Commission, the, 249, 276
Great Migration, the, 181; and church
    growth, 184; and housing, 185. *See
    also* Church growth; Housing; Labor;
    Social gospel; Women
Guyes, John, 26

Hamblen, Stuart, 240–41
Hamburger, Philip, 50–51
Hanley, Charles, 159–60
Hanley, Minnie (née George), 159–60,
    162
Hatch, Nathan, 17
Haynes, Lemuel, 17
Haywood, Garfield T., 191, 193
Healing, by faith, 51, 156, 164
Hearst, William Randolph, 241–43
Heaven, 97–99
Heimert, Alan, 2
Heiskell, Sue, 84–85
Hell, 30
Hempton, David, 24
Hendley, George, 97
Henry, Carl, 256
Henry, Patrick, 26, 48
Heyrman, Christine, 89
Hibbard, F. G., 96
Hillenbrand, Laura, 240

Hilton, Conrad, 60
Hindmarsh, Bruce, 21, 25
HJCB (radio station), 257–58
Hjerstrom, J. W., 161
Hobby Lobby, 45, 62–63. *See also Burwell
    v. Hobby Lobby*
Hoelkeboer, Tena, 208–9
Holiness, 104, 136, 142, 165, 191–92
Home, the, and the domestic ideal, 85,
    88, 92–95, 98–102
Hoover, Herbert, 207
Hope, and the evangelical movement,
    43
Hopkins, Samuel, 37–38
Hopson, Cora, 199
Hose, Sam, 129
Housing, and the Great Migration,
    185–86
Howe, Daniel Walker, 17
Humanitarianism, 36, 275–76
Hutcheson, Francis, 23, 33
Hutchinson, Anne, 7

Immediatism, 119
Immigration, 53, 56–57
Individualism, 34–35
Industrialization, 90–91
International Fellowship of Evangelical
    Mission Theologians (INFEMIT),
    272–73, 276
International Fellowship of Evangelical
    Students (IFES), 256
International nongovernmental organi-
    zation (INGO), 278
InterVarsity, 256, 258
Isaac, 5
Itinerancy, 1–3

Jackson, Andrew, 78–79
Jackson, Robert, 57–58
Jefferson, Thomas, 46–47, 50
Jehovah's Witnesses, 57–58
Jenkins, Craig, 208
Jenkins, Philip, 270
Jeremiah, book of, 41
Jesus, 42, 141–42

Jewish Naturalization Act, the, 45
Jim Crow, 128, 182
John, Gospel of, 26, 237
Jones, Absalom, 116–17
Jones, Charles, 113
Jones, Sam, 129
Junkui, Han, 216
Justice. *See* Social justice

Kagan, Elena, 61–62
Kelly, Otha, 191
Kennedy, Aimee. *See* McPherson, Aimee
    Semple
Kennedy, Anthony, 61, 63
Kent, James, 55
Keys, Martha Jayne, 194–95, 197
King, David, 215, 248–49
Kruse, Kevin, 59

Labor, and the Great Migration, 186–89
Lane Theological Seminary, 72–73
Language, 8–10
Larson, Mel, 246
Latin American Mission (LAM), 256,
    257
Lausanne Covenant, 249, 251, 264–65,
    274
Laws, Curtis Lee, 144–45
Left, evangelical, 214, 259, 266–67, 277
LeTourneau, R. G., 253–54
Liberalism, 28, 110, 122, 130, 140,
    145–46, 151–52
Liberation theology, 256, 260–61, 266
Liberator, the, 119
Liberty Party, the, 79–80
Lincoln, Abraham, 44, 82, 107–9, 126
Link, Frederick, 176
Literalism, biblical, 130, 132, 136
Locke, John, 7–11, 13–15, 23–24; *Essay
    concerning Human Understanding*,
    10, 22
Long, Kathryn, 254
Love, Edwardian definition of, 16
Luce, Henry R., 217
Lynching, 128–29, 182
Lynch v. Donnelly, 60–61

MacArthur, William, 158, 173, 174
MacCleod, Ann Scott, 94
Machen, J. Gresham, 131, 145
Manly, Basil, 83
Mark, Gospel of, 42
Marriage, 85, 88
Marsden, George, 13
Martin, David, 270
Martin, Lerone, 198–99
Marxism, 255–56, 260, 266, 269
Marycoo, Occramar. *See* Gardner,
    Newport
Mason, Charles Harrison, 191, 193
Mather, Increase, 3
Matthew, Gospel of, 42, 108, 118
May, Henry, 23
McCampbell, William, 84–85
McClintock, John, 80
McConnell, Michael, 50
McCreary County v. ACLU of Kentucky,
    61
McGavran, Donald, 264
McGee, F. W., 199
McLaren, Brian, 277
McPherson, Aimee Semple, 147,
    169–70, 201, 227, 246
Meredith, Thomas, 77
Methodist Episcopal Church, South
    (MECS), 125
Methodists, 25, 53, 70, 76–77, 88, 117,
    123, 136
Micah, book of, 126
Micah Network, the, 276
Militancy, 135, 140, 143, 145–46, 148–53
Millennialists, 17, 66–67, 72–74, 81–83
Miller, Perry, 2–3, 9, 12, 14
Miller, Steven P., xiv
Minersville School District v. Gobitis, 57
Mission, integral, 261, 265–66, 275–77,
    280
Missionaries, 56, 160, 163, 165, 251–55,
    257
Missions: and antebellum reform, 67,
    73, 75, 76; and the Civil War, 123; and
    disestablishment, 55; and domestic
    religion, 102; and fundamentalism,

138, 145; and globalization, 217; Latin American, 248-49, 256, 258, 262, 276-78, 280; and Pentecostalism, 156, 158, 164, 166-75, 177-78
Moody, Dwight, 103, 131, 137-39, 227
Moody Bible Institute, 138
Moore, Joseph S., 44
Mossel, Sadie Tanner, 189
Motherhood, 84, 90, 92, 94-96, 101
Music, 198-201, 232
Myland, David Wesley, 175

Native Americans, 55-56
Nelson, Grover, 186
New Birth, the, 4-5, 7-8, 12, 14-15, 18
New Testament, the, 155, 163
Newton, Isaac, 10-12
Noll, Mark A., xvi, 24-25, 45, 86, 203, 225; *American God*, 52-54; and Lausanne, 249-50
Nongovernmental organizations (NGOs), 206-8, 216, 222
Nubia, Salmar, 30
Nurture, Christian, 95-96

Olin, Robert, 96
Olson, Adolf, 168
Onesimus, 111
Osborn, Sarah, 15-16, 19-20, 25-26, 28-31, 34, 36, 38-39; conversion of, 32; faith of, 32-33; *Nature, Certainty and Evidence of True Christianity*, 35; and slavery, 37
Ottolini, Pietro, 167

Padilla, René, 251, 277, 279-81; early life of, 257-58; and International Fellowship of Evangelical Mission Theologians (INFEMIT), 272-75; and Lausanne, 259-68; and Pentecostalism, 269
Palmer, Benjamin M., 109
Palmer, Phoebe, 104
Palmer, Walter, 104
Panama, 267
Parachurches, 6-7

Parents, 87, 95-97
Parham, Charles, 163
Paul (the apostle), 92, 111
Payne, Thomas, 21-23, 54
Peace Policy, the (1869), 55
Pentecostals, 136-37, 154-56, 171-72, 175-77, 179; black, 178; Italian, 161, 167; Latin American, 269-72; Persian, 170-71; Swedish, 161-62, 168-70
Perfectionism, 66
Perkins, John, 273-74
Peru, 253, 255
Phelps, Elizabeth Stuart, 97
Philemon, letter to, 111
Physics, theological relevance of, 11-12
Pierce, Bob, 208-16, 218-20
Piper, John, 247-48
Piper, Lydia Markley, 174-77
Piper, William Hamner, 174-77, 179
Pledge of Allegiance, the, 57, 59
Plessy v. Ferguson, 128
Plumer, William, 77
Polk, James, 80
Porter, Roy, 22
Postmillennialism, 67, 103, 140, 217, 218-19
Powell, Adam Clayton, Sr., 184-85
Prayer, school, 58, 63
Premillennialism, 142-45
Presbyterians, 217, 136; black, 190-91; northern, 145-46; southern, 73, 77, 109, 124
Prior, Margaret Barrett Allen, 100
Progressives, evangelical, 266-67
Prohibition, 50, 134, 143
Protestantism, 134; and the Enlightenment, 24; liberal, 110, 122, 130, 140, 142, 260
Protestants, 45, 56, 133; Italian, 160-61; white, 134-35
Psalms, book of, 30, 40, 108
Puritans, 32
Putnam, Robert, 52

Qiriazi, Gjerazim, 203, 206
Quanrud, John, 203, 206

Race riots, 128, 189-90
Racism, 114, 128-29, 192
Radicals, 71-72; Peruvian, 255
Randolph, Florence Spearing, 196
Ransom, Emma, 180, 189
Ransom, Reverdy, 180, 189, 196
Reason, 21-22
Reconciliation, 128-31
Reconstruction, 123-24, 127
Redemption, 109, 126-27
Reform, 100; and disestablishment, 56; and fundamentalism, 133; and Lausanne, 266, 273
Reform, antebellum, 66, 70, 72, 78, 83
Rehnquist, William, 58
Religion, black, 181
Religion, domestic, 97, 99, 102, 105-6
Religious Freedom Restoration Act (RFRA), 62-63
Religious Right, the, 268, 279
Republican Party, 81-82
Resistance, 9, 11-13
Revivalism, 4, 79, 88, 94-95, 116, 137, 140
Revivals, 3-4, 6-8, 95, 102-3; and Billy Graham, 228-33, 235-36, 239-40, 243-46. See also Great Awakening, the; Second Great Awakening, the
Rhetoric, 1-2, 4, 6-7, 14
Rights, civil, 132
Riley, William B., 144-45
Robinson, Ida, 197
Romans, letter to the, 114
Romanticism, 14, 92
Ross, Leora, 199
Ryan, Mary, 90

Sacriscapes, 205-6
Saillant, John, 17
Saint, Nate, 254-55
Samaritan's Purse International (SPI), 215, 220-21
Sanctification, 172
Schneider, A. Gregory, 88
Scofield, C. I., 139
Scofield Reference Bible, 139, 149

Scopes, John, 134-35
Scopes Trial, 134, 148
Secession, 82-83, 107
Second Great Awakening, the, 66
Segregation, 128
Sehat, David, 49, 51, 54; Myth of Religious Freedom, 50
Semple, Aimee. See McPherson, Aimee Semple
Sensation, 2, 4, 6-9, 13-15, 33. See also Experience, individual
Shaftesbury, Anthony Ashley Cooper, the third earl of, 27-28, 33
Simpson, Albert B., 158
Sin, 12, 28, 237-38
Sinclair, John, 164, 170, 173
Sinclair, Mary, 164
Slavery, 16, 36-37, 71-83, 109-32; and Scripture, 111-15. See also Abolitionism; Emancipation
Smith, Benjamin, 76
Smith, Joseph, 49, 53-54
Smith, Lucy, 176, 197
Snowden, Samuel, 119
Social action, 261, 264-65
Social gospel, 133, 140-41, 222, 261, 269; and the Great Migration, 180-81, 185, 187, 189
Social justice, 261-66, 272-73, 276
Social order, 3-4, 141, 189
Societies, benevolent, 68, 70
South, the American, 73-77, 79, 82
Southey, Robert, 21, 54
Soviet Union, the, 229-30, 252
Stanley, Brian, 256
Statute for Religious Freedom, Virginia's, 47, 49
Statute on Religious Freedom, Jefferson's, 48
Stephan, Scott, 97
Stevens, John Paul, 61
Stewart, Lyman, 140
Stirling, E. W., 154-55
Stone Church, 174-78
Stott, John, 213-14, 264
Stowe, Harriet Beecher, 93, 99

Straton, John Roach, 146
Stringfellow, Thornton, 112
Strong, Josiah, 56
Stuart, Moses, 114, 115, 122
Stutzman, Linford, 205
Sullivan, Winnifred, 50-51
Sunday, Billy, 143, 227
Supreme Court, the, 57-58, 60-63
Swartz, David, 259, 279-80

Tappan, Arthur, 119, 120
Tate, Mary Magdalena Lewis, 196-97
Taylor, Nathaniel, 95
Taylor, Nora, 195-96
Taylor, Zachary, 81
Temperance, 101
Ten Commandments, the, 61
Theology, liberation. *See* Liberation
   theology
Thorngate, Steve, 62
Tindley, Charles Albert, 200
Tizon, Al, 248, 277
Toleration, Act of, 45
Toleration, religious, 45-46
Tongues, speaking in, 154, 155, 161,
   164-65, 171, 174, 192
Town of Greece v. Galloway, 61-62
Townsend, William Cameron, 253-55
Triumphalism, 211, 251, 258
Trusty, Charles, 190
Turner, Henry, 199-200
Turner, Nat, 119

Unionists, 109, 122
Urshan, Andrew, 170-71, 178-79

Van Orden v. Perry, 61
Vatican II, 249
Vesey, Denmark, 118
Vingren, Gunnar, 168-69
Virtue, 16, 102

Wacker, Grant, 216-17, 248-50
Wagner, C. Peter, 257, 260, 274-75
Walker, David, 118, 119, 122
Wannamaker, John, 103

Warfield, Benjamin, 131
Warren, Rick, 247-48, 276
Washington, George, 48
Waters, Malcolm, 205
Watts, Isaac, xviii
Wayland, Francis, 96, 112
Weaver, George, 92-93
Webster, Samuel, 28
Weld, Theodore Dwight, 65-66, 71-73,
   119-20, 122
Welles, Gideon, 44
Wesley, Charles H., 183, 185
Wesley, John, 25, 87
*West Virginia State Board of Education v.
   Barnette*, 50
Whigs, 78-81
Whitefield, George, 1-8, 11-12, 15-18. *See
   also* Itinerancy; Revivals; Rhetoric
White supremacy, 114, 117, 119, 126-27,
   129
Whithall, D. E., 164
Whitmore, Bessie Mae, 165
Will, the, Jonathan Edwards's concep-
   tion of, 14-15
Willard, Samuel, 3
Wilson, Woodrow, 133, 134
Winter, Ralph, 247-48, 264
Women, 16, 53, 71; and domestic reli-
   gion, 89-90, 92-94, 98-100; and the
   Great Migration, 194, 196; ordination
   of, 195; and temperance, 101
Women, African American, 197-98
World's Faith Missionary Association
   (WFMA), 159-60, 162, 165
World Vision International (WVI),
   206-8, 210-16, 219-25, 278
World War I, 133, 135
Wright, Richard R., Jr., 180
Wycliffe Bible Translators, 253-55

Youth for Christ (YFC), 210-11, 242-43
Yushan, Xu, 216

Zamberini, Louis, 240
Zion Tabernacle, 156, 157, 158, 163, 164,
   174